ABSTRACTS
of
SALES *of* CONFISCATED
LOYALIST'S
LAND *and* PROPERTY
in
NORTH CAROLINA

Compiled by:
Dr. A.B. Pruitt

Southern Historical Press, Inc.
Greenville, South Carolina

Please direct all correspondence and book orders to:
www.southernhistoricalpress.com
or
SOUTHERN HISTORICAL PRESS, Inc.
1071 Park West Blvd.
Greenville, SC   29611

southernhistoricalpress@gmail.com

Table of Contents

A. B. Pruitt

INTRODUCTION

This book contains abstracts of material about sales of land and property of loyalists (tories) confiscated in North Carolina. Most of this material is in a series of boxes among the Treasurer and Comptroller's Papers in the North Carolina Archives. The boxes are numbered 2 through 6 and titled "Lands, Estates, Boundaries, and Surveys". Also included is material from some court minutes. The abstracts have been arranged so the counties are in alphabetical order. Within each county, the abstracts are in the same order (usually chronological order) as they appear in the Treasurer and Comptroller's Papers. These papers are loose sheets, so it will be helpful to future researchers if this order is maintained. For the purposes of the index, a number has been assigned to each abstract.

The bulk of the material in each county is (a) a few receipts for amounts paid county surveyors for surveying tracts (a a rate of £2 per survey) sold and (b) surveys for lands sold. In addition, there are (a) some petitions to the Legislature (usually handled by the Committee on Propositions and Grievances), (b) lists of property confiscated (including livestock and debts owed to merchants), (c) bonds for commissioners, & (d) reports by clerks indicating what had happened to the confiscated property in a county. As will be seen, the amount of material varied from county to county.

The following list gives the source of the material in this book.

Treasurer & Comptroller Papers Box 2 contains folders for: Anson, Beaufort, Bertie, Bladen, Brunswick, Camden, Carteret, Chatham, Chowan, & Craven Counties.

Treasurer & Comptroller Papers Box 3 contains folders for: Currituck, Dobbs, Duplin, Edgecombe, Granville, Guilford, Halifax, Hertford, Hyde, Lenoir, Lincoln, Martin, Mecklenburg, & Montgomery Counties.

Treasurer & Comptroller Papers Box 4 contains folders for: Moore, Nash, New Hanover, Northampton, Orange, Pasquotank, Pitt, Randolph, Richmond, & Rowan Counties.

Treasurer & Comptroller Papers Box 5 contains folders for: Sampson, Surry, Tyrrell, & Wake Counties, "no or more than one" county, and the first McCulloch folder.

Treasurer & Comptroller Papers Box 6 contains folders for: Henry E McCulloch.

The above for Lincoln County is supplemented by information recorded in the Pleas and Quarter Sessions Court minutes.

The material on Rutherford County is in the Pleas and Quarter Sessions Court minutes and Morgan District Court papers. A number was assigned to each Court session with "A, B, etc" following the number for each paragraph. This material is mostly about various people accused and/or tried as loyalists. Much of this material mentions attempts by the wives of loyalists to retain their dower share of the estate if the court confiscated it. The trials in county court should have been held in district court; and the district court did void the results of the county court trials in Apr. 1783 (see No. 586B). At the end of this book are abstracts of material from Salisbury District Court loose papers and Equity Court minutes primarily related to H E McCulloch's land sold by the Trustees of UNC.

When selling land, the Commissioners of Confiscated Property usually hired the local county surveyor to survey the land. The Commissioner or surveyor decided how to divide large plots into smaller tracts prior to the sale. Many times, the surveyor prepared a plot and description of the metes and bounds (certificate). The land was then sold. The buyer's name and sale price were then inserted near the beginning of the certificate and the Commissioner signed the plat. Thus, the certificate, with a little additional information, became a deed from the Commissioner to the buyer. Some of these "deeds" are recorded in county deed books. In some cases, the State regranted the land using the same description found in the certificate signed by the Commissioner.

The folders on H E McCulloch contain plats for tracts in various counties. Some of these are duplicates of plats found in the county folders. This duplication happened because the surveyor would make a plat and sign it. Then the Commissioner of Confiscated Property would make a copy of the surveyor's plat, sign it, indicate the amount paid and the buyer, and use this duplicate as a deed. During Archives rearrangement, one copy was placed in the county folder, and the other was in H E McCulloch's folder.

Henry E McCulloch and Trustees of UNC property

Henry E McCulloch departed North Carolina without selling all the land he owned or for which he was an agent (a list of some of this land is found in McCulloch's application to Parliament for a pension; this material is in the British records on microfilm at the NC Archives). For some of the land McCulloch had taken mortgages from settlers who would receive a deed when the mortgage was paid. McCulloch's land was confiscated, and most of the settlers with mortgages stopped paying installments during the Revolution. To endow the new University of North Carolina, the Legislature gave McCulloch's former land to the University. In disposing of their land holdings, the Trustees of the University divided the state into areas with one or two trustees in charge of each area. The Trustees proceeded to foreclose on the unpaid mortgages many of which were in Mecklenburg County. Some of these cases were handled in Mecklenburg County Pleas and Quarter Sessions Court. Others were heard in Salisbury District Superior Court. The Trustees were required to advertise each case in a newspaper in the state where the mortgagee, or his heirs, were thought to live. The mortgagee, if found, had to pay the balance due on the mortgage to the Trustees. If no heir was found, the Trustees sold the land. After these cases were settled, George McCulloch, Henry E McCulloch's illegitimate son, claimed the land as Henry's "agent and heir" in North Carolina due to a power of attorney dated Apr. 28, 1796 (roll Z 5.146N p. 441 in the Archives; additional correspondence between George and Henry E McCulloch form the British records is on this roll). George brought suit in at least two cases--one in Wilmington District against Robert Ray and one in Salisbury District. The former case was appealed to the North Carolina Supreme Court (see No. 804 on p. 177 of this book). That Court held that George did have a valid claim to the tracts Henry had mortgaged to various persons, and the Legislature had no right to give the land to the University. To settle these claims, the Legislature passed an act by which mortgagees received the amounts they had paid for their land provided they had receipts to prove how much they paid H E McCulloch or the Trustees. The mortgagees were allowed interest on their payments, except that no interest was counted during the Revolution. Mortgagees had to apply to the North Carolina Treasurer for this money. The money was then to be paid to George McCulloch, agreeable with the the Supreme Court's opinion. Many mortgagees chose to forego the round-trip to Raleigh and signed a power of attorney to George McCulloch. So, many of the payments were made to George McCulloch, but the powers of attorney indicate the owner of each tract.

If all the paper work for a case survives in the Treasurer & Comptroller's Papers, there are (a) a sheet indicating how much was paid to George McCulloch, (b) receipts indicating the number of payments and amounts of each, (c) a copy of the court execution indicating how much was paid to the Trustees, (d) and a statement by the mortgagee or heir about the mortgage to H E McCulloch. Very few of the cases have all this information. In his payment to George McCulloch, the Treasurer usually indicated the amount of payments made, the interest allowed on the payments, and the date of each payment. In the abstracts, one number is assigned to each case. The sheets, after the first sheet, have a number and letter assigned to them.

The British records cited above (on microfilm in the Archives) contain many of the loyalist applications for pensions to Parliament. Some of these applications include detailed lists of debts owed which indicate who owed the money, the amount, and (sometimes) where the debtor lived (or if he had died). So these records can be a valuable source for locating loyalists (in Great Britain) as well as people (in the U S) who were in debt to the loyalists.

Legislation about Confiscated Property

Legislation against the loyalists in North Carolina began as early as Dec. 1774 when the Halifax Committee of Safety passed a resolve against Andrew Miller. In Apr. 1776 the Provincial Congress (or Legislature) passed a resolve to move loyalist prisoners while allowing them to dispose of their property. In May 1776 the same body passed a resolve to confiscate the property of people who were convicted of taking up arms against the United States. In Apr. 1777, the Legislature passed a law defining treason (Capt. 6). This law also included an oath of allegiance to the State to be taken by persons who had "traded directly" with Great Britain during the previous 10 years. By an act passed in Dec. 1777 the oath was required of every male over 16 years old.

Because many citizens failed to take the oath, the law was revised in 1778. The Commissioners of Confiscated Property in each county were allowed to summon the loyalists and make a list of their property. The property could be rented in tracts of 640 acres or less. The Commissioners or the county court could sell the remaining property (including slaves); however, a dower share was reserved for the widow and children if they remained in the state. The Commissioners could also settle any outstanding debts owed to the loyalists. The Commissioners were allowed   percentage of the sale.

But protests to the Legislature were made against this act including one in Oct. 1779 by Mecklenburg County residents. The complainants felt the land should be sold, rather than rented, and that the heirs should only have claims to the estate for a fixed period.

In Nov. 1779, the confiscation law was made more stringent by naming prominent loyalists and allowing confiscation of the property of people who had left the state. This law mentions the following people:

William Tryon esq
Josiah Martin esq
Sir Nathaniel Duckinfield
Henry Eustace McCulloch
Henry McCulloch
Samuel Cornell
Edmund Fanning
Thomas Macknight
   "late" of Currituck Co
James Parker
William McCormack
John Dunlap
Neal Snodgrass
John Lancaster
   "late" of Pasquotank Co
James Green mariner
John Alexander
   "late" of Craven Co
Thomas Oldham
   "late" of Chowan Co
Thomas Christie of England
Frederick Gregg
   "late" of New Hanover Co
Andrew Miller
Alexander Telfair
Hugh Telfair
John Thompson
John Hamilton
Archibald Hamilton
   "late" of Halifax Co
George Alston
   "late" of Granville Co
Michael Wallace
John Wallace
   "late" merchants of Virginia
William Field
John Field jr
Robert Turner
   "late" of Guiford Co
John Moore "late" of Tryon Co
James Roberts
   "late" of Surry Co
George Miller
   "late" of Dobbs Co
James Cotten

Walter Cunningham
Samuel Williams
   "late" of Anson Co
Samuel Bryan
William Spergen
Mathias Sappinfield
   "late" of Rowan Co
William McClellan
   "late" of Edgecombe Co
Messrs. Dinwiddie,
   Crawford, & Company
   "late" of Bute Co
Robert Palmer
   "late" of Beaufort Co
Edward Brice Dobbs
Ralph McNair
John McNair
Joseph Field
James McMell
Archibald McCoy
Alexander McCay
Niel McArthur
John Leggett
John McCloud
Colin Shaw
William Campbell
James Gamble and Company
Thomas Rutherford
William Rose
Alexander McCoy
Messrs. Waller and Bridgen
   merchants of London
Alexander McAuflen
   "late" of New Bern
Alexander Campbell
Robert Bell
Duncan Campbell
   "late" of Granville Co
Francis Williamson
   "late" of Currituck Co
Chancey Thownsend
Doctor Tucker
   "late" of Wilmington
Buchanan, Hastle, & Company

By 1780 many people had been arrested, but the state was in danger of invasion by the British. So in Sept. 1780 an act allowed the prisoners to be tried by county magistrates. If guilty, the prisoner could be executed and his property confiscated by the sheriff. To aid prosecutions, the Governor was allowed (in 1781) to call special sessions of court and name special judges. Confiscation of property became very profitable. So it was regulated by law. The Commissioners of Confiscated Property or sheriffs were the only ones allowed to confiscate property (partly because some innocent people had their property taken). Only minor changes were made to the confiscation laws in 1781 and 1782 partly due to the British presence in the state. Some loyalists tried to sell their property and avoid confiscation. But these sales were declared void by the Legislature.

In the 1782 legislative papers (Box 2--bill to try persons for treason) are two separate, probably incomplete, lists of loyalists.   These people are:

Samuel Marshall	Stephen Newman
Thomas Graham	John Downie
Maturin Calvill	John Ringrose
John Slingsby	Arthur Bining
David Godden	Davis Ross
Faithful Graham	John Smith
Duncan Morrison	Samuel Iveson
William Maultsby	Peter Brown
Duncan Taylor	Thomas Stead
Daniel McPherson	Isaac Duboise
William White	[blank] Howell
[blank] Ellison *	John White Taylor
Peter Mallett	Alexander McLean
James Monroe	Daniel Sutherland
Henry Hightower	George Parker
Stephen Holloway	John Cruder
Stephen Hightower	John Rutherford
Joseph McLillen	John McDonaald
William McLillen	James Walker
Richard Edwards	Lewis DeRosset
Peter Brewer	Joseph Murray
Jerman Baater	William Campbell
Thomas Horn	William Evans
Stephen Scarlet	George Logan
Thomas Dohorty	Joseph Bland
James Scarlet	John Wilkins
"late" of Orange Co	Thomas Brown
William Colston	George Meek
"late" of Montgomery Co	Andrew Thompson
Simon Davis	[blank] Carmical
Durham Lee	John Nutt
Samuel Alleston sr	Doctor John Ferguson
Richard Stephens	James Fergus
Middleton Mobley	Jacob Fryout
William Roberts	Henry Gurmillion
Felix Kinan	Charles Jewkes
"late" of Duplin Co	Henry Toomer
John Burgwin	Robert Benermon
John London	Archibald Ronaldson
Thomas Colham	William Hill
Samuel Campbell	Walter Gibson
George Hooper	James Bradley
Thomas Hooper	James Duboise
Joseph Tilley	John Kirkwood
John Gordan	Martin Leonard
Francis Bruce	Thomas Henderson
Barner Stead	John Martin
George Smith	"Littleton"
Jonathan Dubibin	Daniel Ferguson
Bergin Hoof	Savage Littleton
Arthur Harper	Daniel McCorm_?_
Doctor James Gukie	Martin Martin
Alexander Hoster	"late" of Richmond Co
William Lawd	Nicholas Worlich
Henry Rookes	Philip Worlich
James Moran	Thomas Black

James Mansfield
Williat Natt
David Flowers
John Jarrett
John Root
Francis Clayton
  "late" of New Hanover Co
Jacob Agnor
George Agnor
Peter Johnston
Abraham Cooke
  "late" a captain
  of Mecklenburg Co
William Scarbrough
  of Campden Co
James Keer
John Keer
Henry Giffard
James Keer jr
Benjamin Boothe Boote
  "late" of Rowan Co
Visey Husbands
Thomas Whitson
Luke Lee
Jeremiah Clarke
Alexander Clarke
John Deale
William Murray
Reubin Simpson
  "late" of Burke Co
John Coleston
Isaac Faulkingbury
John Coleston jr
Nathaniel Ashley
Lewis Lowrey
James Childs
Henry Childs
Peter Lewis, lieut.
  of Anson Co
Henry Williams
Duncan Ray
William McQueen
John Martin
  "late" a major
Thomas Murphy
Rd Carleton
Solomon Cormack
William Russell
Rd Fare
James Taylor
John Taylor
Besley Taylor
Abraham Taylor
John Taylor jr
  "late" of Craven Co
John Poils sr
  "late" of Chatham Co

Moses Moor
Samuel Buckerstaff
Abel Beatty
Alexander Reynolds
Solomn Beason
John Acre
Nicholas Welch
Adam Duke
Frederick Hager
  "late" of Lincoln Co
John Honeycutt
  "late" of Sullivan Co
Gideon Wright
Hezekiah Wright
Richard Murphy
  "late" of Surry Co
John Cameron
Dushe Shaw
James Muse
Donner Dowed
Archibald McCoy
Malcom McCoy
Duncan McNabb
Robert Gillis
  "late" of Cumberland Co
James Hunter
Joseph Dobson
Henry Strawther
Capt. [blank] Campbell
[blank] Campbell
[blank] Campbell, Deep R
Daniel Evans
David Tate
James Green
John Philips Clap
Jno Boon
Samuel McDonald
Aaron Short
[blank]
  "late" of Guilford Co
Thomas Torrens
  "late" of Dobbs Co
John Cox
Thomas Prevatt
James Cook
Gideon Rooker
Benja Adams
Wm Battle
Aaron Bickerstaff
Benja Bickerstaff
Stephen Longford
Ambrose Milles
Wm Hall
John Hudson
Joseph McDonald
John Maurcie
Mark Powell

Trustom Norsworthy
Benjamin Vickers
Stephen Vickers
John Vickers sr
  "late" of Edgecombe Co
Reubin Hines
Kedar Hines
Jonathan Keathley
  "late" of Wayne Co
Demsey Jones
George Harrison
  "late" of Onslow Co
John Rains
Ebenezer Willison
Michael Lawley
Adam Rainbolt
Nicholas Lawley
Michael Robins
John Richardson
Hanson Collett
  "late" of Randolph Co
Joseph Lawrence
Benja Moor

Saml Richardson
John Richardson
John Ashworth
John Thomson
William Thompson
Jonas Bedford
James Capsher
Esum Capsher
Elias Brook
Jilies Reynold
Shadra McAlley
Wm Going
Thomas Welch
George Thomson
Thomas Reynold
James Chitwood
Isaac Cooper
John Morgan
John Luck
Pheneas Creighton
  "late" of Rutherford Co
Thomas Tier
  "late" of Craven Co

* [blank] Ellison is described as "whose estate is in possession of Mrs. Sarah Bowen of Bladen Co".
Also in the same folder is a shorter list which omits some of the above names.   But neither of these lists are mentioned in a law; the bill was referred to the next session of the Assembly and was evidently forgotten.

    A big push to depose of confiscated property culminated in passage of a law for that purpose in Apr. 1782 and in 1784.   Sales were to be held in each district of superior court.   But the sales were to be on different days, which allowed some people to appear as buyers at several sales.

    The Treaty of Paris forbade confiscation.   But under the Articles of Confederation, this treaty wasn't automatically binding on North Carolina.   So the sales in 1784 proceeded.   Following the war, the Legislature passes an act of "pardon and oblivion" which aided loyalists who returned to the state in a year (except Peter Mallett, David Fanning, Samuel Andrews, & others convicted of various crimes.   Also in 1784 and 1785 there were some acts passed to aid former loyalists.   In 1786 an act pardoned all loyalists returning to counties in Tennessee (or western North Carolina).   After North Carolina accepted the Constitution, an act was also passed to accept the Treaty of Paris which ended confiscation.

    There are also several cases related to confiscation which reached the North Carolina Supreme Court (or Court of Conference).   Among these is one in North Carolina Reports vol. 1 p. 514-515 concerning land of Young, Miller, & Company.   In this case the members of the company are: John Alston, James Young, James Morton, Alexander Grindley, Andrew Miller, William Littlejohn, & George Alston.   Also in the same volume (pages 537-619) is the decision by the U S Court of Appeals (N C District) in the case of Archibald and John Hamilton (merchants of Great Britain) vs John Eaton (surviving obligator of Gabriel Long decd of Halifax Co) at June term 1796.   This case concerned a bond for £800 dated Aug. 11, 1777 for payment of £400.   In its decision, the Court of Appeals also found the part of the confiscation acts which conflicted with the Treaty of Paris were unconstitutional, because the Legislature had accepted the Treaty in 1787 as cited above.   The court also found that debts owed to British subjects, which had been paid to the State Treasurer, could be recovered by the loyalists; this part agreed with the finding of the N C Supreme Court in G McCulloch vs R Ray cited above.

    It should be noted that inflation was rampant during the Revolution.   So amounts paid at sales near the end of the war were large due to the small value of the currency.   For example a blanket might sell for £100.   Inflation also aided those who owed the loyalists merchants.   These debts were often paid without allowance for the deflated value of the money used to pay the debts.

    The most through book of loyalists in North Carolina is Loyalist in North Carolina During the Revolution by Robert O DeMond.   The actions in North Carolina's General Assembly are printed in North Carolina Colonial and State Records by Clark and Sanders.   A general description of North Carolina records of genealogical interest is in North Carolina Research Genealogy and Local History by H. F. M. Leary and

M. R. Stirewalt. An appendix to this book contains a short glossary of legal terms.

INDEX

The index which accompanies this book is divided into two parts. The first part mentions people. The second part mentions geographical locations such as creeks, rivers, counties, and towns. The numbers in the index refer to the numbers assigned to each abstract in this book.

The map which accompanies this book is an enlarged copy of one of the series of maps drawn by L Polk Denmark. This map is included so the reader can locate the counties mentioned in this book. Copies of the complete series of Mr. Denmark's maps can be obtained from the Archives or in the book North Carolina Research mentioned above. Also available from the Archives is a set of North Carolina maps including maps in 1775, 1808, and 1833. More detailed maps showing smaller creeks are available from the Water Resources Department and Highway Department.

ACKNOWLEDGMENTS

The author wishes to thank the North Carolina Archives for preserving and caring for the records abstracted in this book. Also thanks to the staff for the courteous retrieval of the records and encouragement with this publication. The author also wishes to thank the people who brought forth affordable computers, software, and printers without which the preparation of this book would have been much more arduous.

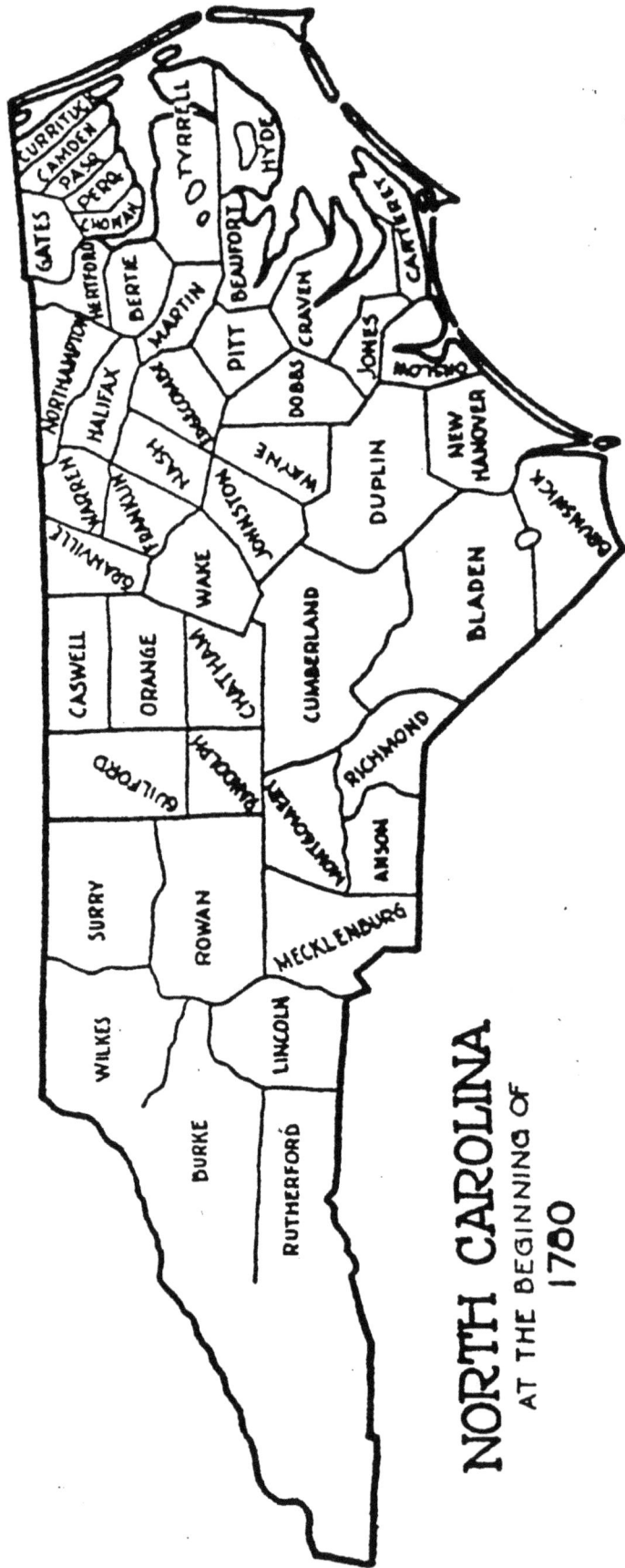

NORTH CAROLINA
AT THE BEGINNING OF
1780

CURRITUCK
CAMDEN
PASQ
PERQ
CHOWAN
GATES
TYRRELL
HYDE
HERTFORD
BERTIE
BEAUFORT
MARTIN
PITT
CRAVEN
CARTERET
NORTHAMPTON
HALIFAX
DOBBS
JONES
ONSLOW
EDGECOMBE
WAYNE
NASH
FRANKLIN
JOHNSTON
DUPLIN
NEW HANOVER
WARREN
GRANVILLE
WAKE
BRUNSWICK
CASWELL
ORANGE
CHATHAM
CUMBERLAND
BLADEN
GUILFORD
RANDOLPH
MONTGOMERY
RICHMOND
SURRY
ROWAN
ANSON
MECKLENBURG
WILKES
BURKE
LINCOLN
RUTHERFORD

Sales of Confiscated Land

ANSON COUNTY

1. A petition by William Morris (of Anson Co) to the Legislative Committee of Propositions & Grievances. Morris bought a fourth of 640 ac sold as the property of Moses Saunders by Charles Bruce. The land wasn't Moses Saunders' but belonged to James Cotten and wasn't liable to confiscation. James Cotten has a deed in 1775. Morris can't get the land and has had a judgment against him due to the bond he gave the State when he bought the land. The committee proposes the following resolution: proceedings against Morris and his securities to be stopped. [signed] John Moore, chairman. Read & concur in House Dec. 3, 1800, in Senate Dec. 3, 1800. No. 225 £90 certificates, the papers delivered Dec. 15, 1800 to Daniel Ross.

2. A petition by Patrick Boggan to the Legislative Committee of Propositions & Grievances. In 1785 or 1786, Richard Farr bought 300 ac in Anson Co from Charles Bruce, supposed to be the property of Robert Raney. A £250 bond was given. In 1791, David Love claimed the land and had a judgement in an ejectment to recover the land at July Anson Co Court. The State also brought an action against Farr and Boggan in April Hillsborough Superior Court 1799 and obtained a judgment of £400. Farr became "insolvaent" and left the State. The committee proposes the following resolution: Boggan, as security of Farr, is to get the amount of the judgment at Hillsborough Superior Court 1799 from the State Treasurer. [signed] J Moore, chairman. Read & concur in House Dec. 15, 1800, in Senate Dec. 15, 1800 and second & third readings. No. 219 £250 [sic] Richard Farr & Patrick Boggan.

3. Receipt No. 545 Oct. 4, 1787 to Morgan Brown, Anson Co surveyor, £44 for 22 surveys.

4. Receipt No. 568 Apr. 26, 1790 to Stephen Hide £503 for land sold as confiscated land as per resolve of the Assembly; [on back] "Anson Co son-in-law John Colson"; £503 + £188.12.9 (interest) = £691.12.9 (total); [on a second line:] £503 = £125.14.11 (interest) = £628.14.11 (total).

5. Jun. 8, 1786 sold 150 ac to Sampson Lanier for £30; No. 6; on both sides of Lawyers Road and on Cowpen Br of Cedar Cr; formerly Thomas Bailey jr's property; [signed] Charles Bruce; chain carriers James King Huchason & Thomas Bailey.

6. Sept. 22, 1786 sold 400 ac to William Wood for £303; No. 10; on both sides of Brown Cr; formerly John Coulson's property; border: Ben Smith's first line, Denson, & John Cheek; [signed] Charles Bruce.

7. Sept. 22, 1786 sold 200 ac on Anthony Sharpe for £213; No. 13; on both sides of Goulds Fork; formerly Robert Boyd's property; border: John Leverit and William Philips; [signed] Charles Bruce; sworn chain carriers Dennis McClendon & Frederick McClendon.

8. Jun. 8, 1786 sold 100 ac to Thomas Clark for £20; No. 3; on both sides of Richardsons Cr; formerly Henry E McCulloch's property; [signed] Charles Bruce; sworn chain carriers Jesse Gilbert & Gideon Green.

9. Jun. 8, 1786 sold 81 ac to Thomas Clark for £52; No. 4; on both sides of Richardsons Cr; formerly Henry E McCulloch's property; border: Hudson; [signed] Charles Bruce.

10. Jun. 8, 1786 sold 54 ac to Thomas Clark for £83; No. 5; on E side of Richardsons Cr; formerly Henry E McCulloch's property; border: "a little" above tract No. 4; [signed] Charles Bruce.

11. Jun. 8, 1786 sold 30 ac to Thomas Clark £28; No. 7; on S side of Rocky R; formerly Henry E McCulloch's property; border: an oak near a fish dam in said river; includes Thomas Pool's improvement; [signed] Charles Bruce.

12. Jun. 8, 1786 sold 64 ac to Thomas Clark £35; No. 2; on E side of Richardsons Cr; formerly Henry E McCulloch's property; border: top of a hill on E side of the creek; includes McDonald's improvement; [signed] Charles Bruce; sworn chain carriers Jesse Gilbert & Robert Broudaway.
13. Jun. 8, 1786 sold 30 ac to Thomas Clark for £12.10; No. 8; on S side of Rocky R; formerly Henry E McCulloch's property; [signed] Charles Bruce.

Sales of Confiscated Land

14. Sept. 22, 1787 sold 200 ac to Thomas Clark for £380; No. 14; on Jones' Cr; formerly Robert Palmer's property; border: George Gould's beginning corner hickory on N side of Jones' Cr and crosses N fork of said creek; [signed] Charles Bruce.

15. Sept. 22, 1787 sold 300 ac to Patrick Boggan for £100; No. 9; on both sides of Goulds Fork; formerly Robert Boyd's property; [signed] Charles Bruce; sworn chain carriers Frans Faulkner & John Faulkner.

16. Sept. 22, 1787 sold 300 ac to Sampson Lanier for £120 who transferred to James Boggan; No. 17; on both sides of Goulds fork; formerly Robert Rainey's property; border: the fourth corner of Gould's upper survey; [signed] Charles Bruce.

17. Sept. 21, 1787 sold to John Wright jr for £80; No. 14; on waters of Jones Cr; formerly Robert Palmer's property; border: Capt. Thomas Clark's corner and Gould's corner; [signed] Charles Bruce; sworn chain carriers Benjamin Philips and John Philips.

18. a summary by Jonathan Jackson, late Anson Co sheriff, to State of North Carolina:

Dec. 15, 1782   credit:
a) amount of sales for 8 tracts of confiscated land sold at Salisbury District Court House   £498.10
b) to balance for 1 Negro boy sold by execution, formerly James Langford's property   £33.7.8
[total]   £531.17.8 + "to balance" £0.1.7 = £531.19.3

Dec. 15, 1782   deficit:
a) by settlement with district commissioner as per receipt   £498.10
b) by commissions on £498.10   £29.17.3
c) by commissions on £33.7.8   £ 2.0
d) by hiring an express to go to Charlote after confiscated patents   £1.12
[total]   £531.19.3   [written over £562.2.3]
[the following lined out:] "balance due the state £29.15.5"

April Court 1784   the above amount sworn in Court and allowed. [signed] Mich Auld, Clk ct.
[on back]   recd. Apr. 22, 1784

19. a bond Apr. 17, 1782 by William Thredgill, Patrick Boggan sr, & Jesse Gilbert (Anson Co) to the governor; for £10,000 for William Threadgill [sic] to be Anson Co Commissioner.   Signed Wm Threadgill, Patk Boggan, & Jesse Gilbert. Witness Thomas Wade jr, clk.

20. "Account of land sold by Griffith Rutherford Dec. 1782"
20A. numbers 1 through 55 formerly Henry E McCulloch's property:
1. 119 ac sold to John Lewis Bard for £213.1
2. 316 ac sold to Robert Mackie for £346
3. 216 ac sold to Andrew Bostan for £282
4. 124 ac sold to Andrew Bostan for £133
5. 192 ac sold to Abraham Womack for £201
6. 159 ac sold to Spruce Macay for £160
7. 167 ac sold to David Smith for £167.10
8. 152 ac sold to Elijah Merrel for £170
9. 237 ac sold to Humphery Brooks for £392
10. 237 ac sold to Humphrey Brooks for £267.5
11. 220 ac sold to Andrew Bostan for £107
12. 202 ac sold to Andrew Bostan for £101

Sales of Confiscated Land

13. 218 ac sold to Andrew Bostan for £204.10
14. 208 ac sold to Andrew Bostan for £417
15. 193 ac sold to Mathew Lock for £258
16. 238 ac sold to George H Barger for £238
17. 274 ac sold to Ludwick Winkler for £76
18. 373 ac sold to Ludwick Winkler for £130
19. 310 ac sold to Joseph Cunninghan for £207
20. 416 ac sold to Samuel Cummon for £503
21. 180 ac sold to Wm Millsaps for £45
22. "not sold"
23. 287 ac sold to John Willson for £348
24. 155 ac sold to Beachion Helton for £115
25. 175 ac sold to Antony Newnan for £277
26. 200 ac sold to Antony Newnan for £227
27. 305 ac sold to Zebulon Bard for £392
28. 400 ac sold to Jos Cunningham for £351
29. 154 ac sold to Jno Ford for £200
30. 244 ac sold to Richmon Peoson for £346
31. "not sold"
32. 343 ac sold to Benjm Abbot for £43.9
33. 405 ac sold to Wm Brandon for £301
34. 425 ac sold to Mathew Lock for £204
35. 343 ac sold to Jacob Wiseman for £100
36. 375 ac sold to Jno L Bard for £200
37. 375 ac sold to Jno L Bard for £301
38. 375 ac sold to David Crage for £150.10
39. 375 ac sold to F Brandon for £101
40. 267 ac sold to Thomas Larson for £100
41. 275 ac sold to John Clover for £100.1
42. 266 ac sold to John Billing for £120.1
43. 193 ac sold to Andrew Baird for £71.1
44. "is wanting"
45. 201 ac sold to Benjm Roansebel [or Rounsebel] for £203
46. 231 ac sold to Benjm Roansebel for £151
47. 366 ac sold to Maxvel Chambers for £428
48. 147 ac sold to Abraham Lewis for £100
49. 113 ac "not sold"
50. 189 ac sold to Maxvel Chambers for £236
51. 190 ac "not sold"
52. 126 ac sold to Spruse Macay for £301
53. 278 ac sold to Spruse Macay for £301
54. "not sold"
55. 265 ac sold to Jas Scrivner for £202

20B. numbers 1 through 25 formerly Henry E McCulloch's property:
1. 640 ac "sold by vartue an execution for £3,000 on the suit of Frohock vs
   H E McCalloch
2. 336 ac sold to Volintine Beard for £826
3. 270 ac sold to James Crage for £226 [385--lined out]
4. 308 ac sold to James Crage for £385
5. 253 ac sold to Henery Horon for £310
6. 200 ac sold to Robert Martan for £230

Sales of Confiscated Land

7. 178 ac sold to Henery Sewel for £163
8. 115 ac ac sold Peter Foust for £117
9. 200 ac sold to Francis Lock for £200.1
10. 340 ac sold to Radford Elles for £341.1
11. 268 ac sold to David Wootson for £420
12. 482 ac sold to Jo L Beard for £200
13. 282 ac sold to David Craig for £291
14. 299 ac sold to Jon Steel for £300
15. 146 ac sold to David Wootson for £150
16. 213 ac sold to David Wootson for £300
17. 355 ac sold to David Crage for £256
18. 365 ac sold to Francis Lock for £266
19. 314 ac sold to Jos McConoughey for £352
20. 110 ac sold to David Craig for £67.0.4
21. 99 ac sold to David Craig for £52.8.1
22. 247 ac sold to Francis Lock for £200
23. 282 [or 202] ac sold to William Brandon for £203
24. 200 ac sold to Franis. Lock for £306
25. 109 ac sold to William Brandon for £100   [total] £16,355.3.5

20C. Account of land sold in Anson and "Surrey" County
1. 500 ac sold to Wm Teral Lewis for £903 formerly Jas Roberts' property
Anson, all formerly James Cotton property:
1. 200 ac sold to Sprus Macay for £80
2. 300 ac sold to Sprus Macay for £100.10
3. 100 ac sold to Samuel Young for £51
4. 100 ac sold to [see No. 5]
5. 640 ac sold to Thomas Gillaspie for £105.10
6. 200 ac sold to Benjm Robinson for £61
7. 164 ac sold to Wm Boman for £30.10
8. 58 ac sold to Wm Boman for £20   [total] £1,378.10

20D. Account of the Negroes, formerly Saml Bryant's property sold for certificates:
a Negro woman Temer sold to Maj. Joel Lewis for £135
a Negro Dick sold to James Cathey for £1,150
a Negro Ben sold to Maj. Lewis for £710   [total] £1,995

[grand total for sale] £20,228.13.5
"errors excepted" Oct. 15, 1791 [sic] Griffith Rutherford

BEAUFORT COUNTY
21. Feb. 15, 1786 surveyed 168 ac for Richard Blackledge of Washington; formerly Andrew Sprowl's property; on N side of Pamplico R; border: the town of Washington, mouth of a creek that parts said land from James Bonner,& runs on the river up to said town; [signed] John Smaro [or Smaw], surveyor; chain bearers Thomas Worsley & Mery S Bonner; sold Dec. 13, 1785 for £6,100; certified [no date] at Bath by James Armstrong, commissioner for Newbern Dist.

22. Aug. 10, 1785 surveyed 128 ac on N side of Pamplico R and E side of Goose Cr; formerly Robert Palmer's property; border: John Boyd's corner and Mallard Creek Swamp; [signed] John Smaro, surveyor; sold Dec. 19, 1785 to Col. Joseph Leech for £65; [signed] James Armstrong, commissioner

BERTIE COUNTY

Sales of Confiscated Land

23. Receipt No. 302 Oct. 12, 1786 to Humphrey Hardy, Bertie Co surveyor, for £8 for 4 surveys; [on back] Apr. 23, 1787 recd of Humphrey Nichols the within [signed] Theophilus Reddit.

24. Receipt No. 152 Dec. 29, 1785 to Humphrey Hardy £44 for 19 surveys; [on back] Apr. 5, 1786 recd. of Humphry Nicholls £16.17.4 of within order, balance due £27.2.8; [signed] Constantine Redditt; J Jacocks tax £21.12 + money paid £3.15.8 + Geo Capehart £1.5 = £27.2.8 + £16.7.4 = £44.0

25. Dec. 15, 1785 surveyed 374 ac due to order of Col. Hardy Murfree, Edenton Dist. Commissioner; lettered "B"; part of land formerly Sr. Nathl Duckenfield's property; on N side of Black Walnut Swamp; border: a corner of tract "C", a tree near Tombstone Landing, & runs down Salmon Cr.   [signed] Humpry Hardy, surveyor; [on back] No. 17 Geo Ryon.

26. Dec. 15, 1785 surveyed 213 ac due to order of Col. Hardy Murfree, Edenton Dist. Commissioner; part of land formerly Sr. Nathaniel Duckenfield property; border: John Bevens' line at Morgan Swamp, Burn's line, Walnut Swamp Run, & the mouth of Catterpillar Br; [signed] Humpry Hardy, surveyor; chain carriers John Burn & Wm Ashburn; [on back] No. 12 Catterpillar tract   Wm Asburn.

27. Dec. 14, 1785 surveyed 193 ac due to order of Col. Hardy Murfree, Edenton Dist. Commissioner; part of land formerly Sir Nathaniel Duckenfield property; on N side of Black Walnut Swamp; border: the run of said swamp, Capt. Thos Baker, Capt. Christopher Clark, a branch near "his" fence, & runs down the branch; [signed] Humphry Hardy, surveyor; [on back] Chris Clark.

28. Dec. 15, 1785 surveyed 400 ac due to order of Col. Hardy Murfree, Edenton Dist. Commissioner; "piney" land formerly Sir Nathaniel Duckinfield's property; border: "the" Meadows of Cyprus and George Capehart; [signed] Herbert Pritchard, D S; [on back] Humphrey Hardy.

29. Dec. 15, 1785 suveyed 280 ac due to order of Col. Hardy Murfree, Edenton Dist. Commissioner; "piney" land formerly Sir Nathaniel Duckinfield's property; border: "the" Meadows of Cyprus and Humphry Hardy; [signed] Herbert Pritchard, D Surv; [on back] Humphry Hardy No. 2   Hardys Boxes [sic].

30. Dec. 15, 1785 surveyed 235 ac due to order of Col. Hardy Murfree, Edenton Dist. Commissioner; part of land formerly Sir Nathl. Duckinfield's property; on N side of Black Walnut Swamp; border: the run of said swamp, runs up a branch to where it forks near Capt. Clark's line, along the right hand fork & said Clark's line to the head of said branch, along Capt. Clark's line to a road, along the road to the head of a bottom near Dwyer's fence, & runs down another branch; [signed] Humphrey Hardy, surveyor; [on back] No. 15 Jona Jacocks.

31. Dec. 15, 1785 surveyed 475 ac due to order of Col. Hardy Murfree, Edenton Dist. Commissioner; part of land formerly Sr. Nathl Duckenfield's property; border: the mouth of Morgan Swamp, runs along the sound to John Burn's line, & along Burn's line; [signed] Humphrey Hardy, surveyor; chain carriers John Burn & Wm Ashburn; plat shows Albermarle Sound; [on back] No. 13 [Morgan tract--lined out] Wm Asburn.

32. Dec. 9, 1785 surveyed 462 ac due to order of Col. Hardy Murfree, Edenton Dist. Commissioner; "piney" land formerly Sir Nathaniel Duckinfield's property; border: George Capehart, Asburn, Ducking Run, Hooten, & a road; [signed] Humphrey Hardy, surveyor; plat says Jacocks Boxes; [on back] Jonathan Jacocks.

33. Dec. 6, 1785 surveyed 225 ac due to order of Col. Hardy Murfree, Edenton Dist. Commissioner; "piney" land formerly Sir Nathaniel Duckinfield's property; on Ducking Run; border: William Ashburn; [signed] Humphrey Hardy, surveyor; [on back] Wm Ashburn.

34. Dec. 9, 1785 surveyed 425 ac due to order of Col. Hardy Murfree, Edenton Dist. Commissioner; "piney" land formerly Sir Nathnaiel Duckinfield's property; border: hear of Green Br, Mr. [or Ms] Rason, Cophel, Dicks Br, & Mrs. Dauson; [signed] Humphrey Hardy, surveyor; [on back] John Capehart.

Sales of Confiscated Land

35. Jan. 10, 1786 surveyed 1 ac with a warehouse thereon due to order of Col. Hardy Murfree, Edenton Dist. Commissioner; formerly Wm Lowther's property; on Cashoke Cr at a place called the Ship yard; border: on the creek where a point of high land runs down & makes to a causway into the pocoson, runs up the creek, across the point of high land, & along the pocoson; [signed] Humphrey Hardy, surveyor; [on back] George Ryon.

36. Dec. 9, 1785 [in pencil] surveyed 225 ac due to order of Col. Hardy Murfree, Edenton Dist. Commissioner; "piney" land formerly Sir Nathaniel Duckinfield's property; border: the back line of said Duckinfield and Hardy; [signed] Humphrey Hardy, surveyor; [on back] Thos W Pugh.

37. Dec. 15, 1795 surveyed 550 ac lettered "A" due to order of Col. Hardy Murfree, Edenton Dist. Commissioner; part of land formerly Sir Nathaniel Duckinfield's property; includes the mansion house and improvements with two dwelling houses, kitchen, barn, stables, & a garden on N side of Black Walnut Swamp; border: tract "B", the mouth of "the" creek, runs along "the" river to the landing, & the mouth of Black Walnut Swamp at the river; [signed] Humphrey Hardy, surveyor; [on back] Geo Ryan.

38. Dec. 15, 1785 surveyed 425 ac lettered "C" due to order of Col. Hardy Murfree, Edenton Dist. Commissioner; part of land formerly Sir Nathaniel Duckinfield's property; on N side of Black Walnut Swamp; border: the runs of said swamp, tract "D", edge of a hill near the head of a branch, a tree near the head of Dwyer's fence, runs down a branch, down Salmon Cr, near Tombstone Landing, & the run of Walnut Swamp; [signed] Humphrey Hardy, surveyor; [on back] No. 16 Geo Ryon [John Capehart--lined out].

39. Dec. 15, 1785 surveyed 333 ac due to order of Col. Hardy Murfree, Edenton Dist. Commissioner; part of land formerly Sir Nathaniel Duckinfield's property; border: the mouth of Morgan Swamp, runs along the sound to Mrs. Lockhart's corner, Evans, & runs up Walnut Swamp to the mouth of Catterpillar Br; [signed] Humphrey Hardy, surveyor; plat shows Albermarle Sound; [on back] Simon Totevine.

40. Dec. 15, 1785 suveyed 518 ac due to order of Col. Hardy Murfree, Edenton Dist. Commissioner; "piney" land formerly Sir Nathaniel Duckinfield's property; border: Ducking Run at the mouth of Miery Br and Hooten; [signed] Humphrey Hardy, surveyor; plat has rectangle for "Charles Hootens"; [on back] Elisha Ashburn.

41. Dec. 9, 1785 surveyed 290 ac due to order of Col. Hardy Murfree, Edenton Dist. Commissioner; "piney" land formerly Sir Nathaniel Duckinfield's property; border: Hooten's line at a road, runs along the road, George Capehart, & "the" ack line; [signed] Humphrey Hardy, surveyor; plat shows Cyprus Meadows; [on back] "NW side of Hootens Road" No. 4 John Hagen.

42. Dec. 16, 1785 surveyed 579 ac due to order of Col. Hardy Murfree, Edenton Dist. Commissioner; "piney" land formerly Sir Nathaniel Duckinfield's property; border: Ducking Run Bridge, runs along Cricket's Road, & Mr. Rasor; [signed] Humphrey Hardy, surveyor; plat shows St. Thomas' Church and Miery Br and calls the survey "Boxed Pines"; [on back] "Chappell" No. 8 Jere. Fleetwood.

43. Nov. 30, 1785 surveyed 640 ac due to order of Col. Hardy Murfree, Edenton Dist. Commissioner; part of land formerly Sir Nathaniel Duckinfield's property; border: the mouth of Salmon Cr, mouth of Green Br, runs up the branch, runs along Cricket's Road to a bridge on Duckin Run, & mouth of said run; [signed] Humphrey Hardy, surveyor; plat shows Ryan's mill on Duckin Run and Hickory Run and calls survey "boxed pines"; [on back] Hickory Neck No. 10 Geo Ryan.

44. Jan. 25, 1786 surveyed 203 ac due to order of Col. Hardy Murfree, Edenton Dist. Commissioner; formerly property of William Buchanan's "or" Walace & Company; on N side of White Swamp; [signed] Humphrey Hardy, surveyor; plat shows rectangle called "White's"; [on back] Geo West.

Sales of Confiscated Land

45. Jan. 18, 1786 surveyed 506 ac due to order of Col. Hardy Murfree, Edenton Dist. Commissioner; part of land formerly Henry Ustace McCulloch's property; known as Green pond land; in the Indian Woods; border: the back line of Indian land at a dividing corner of Wm Williams, Thos Pugh, & Willie Jones; [signed] Humphrey Hardy, surveyor; [on back] No. 2 John Johnston.

46. Jan. 18, 1786 surveyed 506 ac due to order of Col. Hardy Murfree, Edenton Dist. Commissioner; part of land formerly Henry Ustae McCulloch's property; known as Green pond land; border: a corner on John Johnston's land, the back Indian line, & McCulloch's line near a road; [signed] Humphrey Hardy, surveyor; [on back] John Johnston.

47. Dec. 16, 1785 surveyed 166 ac due to order of Col. Hardy Murfree, Edenton Dist. Commissioner; formerly property of Wallace & Company; border: Charles Sowel and William Virgin; [signed] Humphrey Hardy, surveyor; [on back] John Pons.

48. Dec. 15, 1785 surveyed 0.5 ac lot No. 78 in town of Windsor due to order of Col. Hardy Murfree, Edenton Dist. Commissioner; formerly McKitrick's property; "well improved" with a dwelling house, store room in "the" end of the house, a kitchen, garden, & stable; 105 ft on "the" street by 210 ft back; [signed] Humphrey Hardy, surveyor; [on back] John Pons.

49. An account of Confiscated Property sold in Bertie Co:
a) 225 ac in piney woods, unimproved; formerly Sir Nathl Duckenfield's property; bought by Thomas Whitmill Pugh for £75 certificates
b) 280 ac in piney woods, unimproved; formerly Sir Nathl Duckenfield's property; bought by Humphrey Hardy; £101.10 certificates
c) 400 ac in piney woods, unimproved; formerly Sir Nathl Duckenfield's property; bought by Humphrey Hardy for £329 certificates
d) 290 ac in piney woods, unimproved; formerly Sir Nathl Duckenfield's property; bought by John Hagen for £103 certificates
e) 462 ac in piney woods, unimproved; formerly Sir Nathl Duckenfield's property; bought by Jonathan Jacocks for £332 certificates
f) 225 ac in piney woods, unimproved; formerly Sir Nathl Duckenfield's property; bought by William Ashburn for £104.5 certificates
g) 425 ac in piney woods, unimproved; formerly Sir Nathl Duckenfield's property; bought by John Capehart for £310 certificates
h) 579 ac in piney woods, unimproved; formerly Sir Nathl Duckenfield's property; bought by Jeremiah Fleetwood for £462.10 certificates
i) 518 ac in piney woods, unimproved; formerly Sir Nathl Duckenfield's property; bought by Elisha Ashburn for £553.15 certificates
j) 640 ac in piney woods, unimproved; formerly Sir Nathl Duckenfield's property; bought by George Ryon for £766 certificates
k) 333 ac called Morgan's tract on Black Walnut Swamp; formerly Sir Nathl Duckenfield's property; bought by Simon Totevine for £3,335 certificates
l) 213 ac in piney woods, unimproved; formerly Sir Nathl Duckenfield's property; bought by William Ashburn for £515.15 certificates
m) 475 ac in Black Walnut Swamp; formerly Sir Nathl Duckenfield's property; bought by William Ashburn for £1,805.5 certificates
n) 193 ac on Salmon Cr; formerly Sir Nathl Duckenfield's property; bought by Christopher Clarke; £1,120 certificates
o) 235 ac on Salmon Cr; formerly Sir Nathl Duckenfield's property; bought by Jonathan Jacocks for £1,620 certificates
p) 425 ac called Shipyard on Salmon Cr; formerly Sir Nathl Duckenfield's property; bought by George Ryon for £5,800 certificates
q) 374 ac Tomb Stone on Salmon Cr; formerly Sir Nathl Duckenfield's property; bought by George Ryon for £4,955 certificates

r) 550 ac on Sound side with improvements; formerly Sir Nathl Duckenfield's property; bought by George Ryon for £9,191 certificates

s) 166 ac pines woods near Windsor; formerly property of Michl & John Wallace; bought by John Pons for £260 certificates

t) lot No. 78 in Windsor improved; formerly McKitrick's property; bought by John Pons for £225 certificates.

u) lot No. 79 in Windsor unimproved; formerly McKitrick's property; bought by Benjamin Bryer for £362.10 certificates

v) lot No. 81 in Windsor unimproved; formerly McKitrick's property; bought by Benjamin Bryer for £530.10 certificates

[total] £32,859 [signed] H Murfree, Comr.

BLADEN COUNTY

50. Jul. 7, 1786 surveyed 100 ac; No. 70; formerly Hector McNeill's property; on NE side of Beverdam Swamp; includes the "plantation" where he formerly lives; [signed] J Rhodes, D. surveyor; chain carriers John Ferguson & Malcom Shaw; [on back] James Spiller £22.3.

51. Nov. 2, 1785 surveyed 50 ac; No. 41; formerly Neal McFall's property; on both sides of McFall's mill Swamp a branch of Raft Swamp; [signed] J Rhodes, D. surveyor; chain carriers Neal McNiell & Danl McFall; [on back] Jacob Rhodes £76.

52. Nov. 2, 1785 surveyed 100 ac; No. 42; formerly Neal McFall's property; on NE side of McFall's mill Swamp a branch of Raft Swamp; border: said McFall's field; [signed] J Rhodes, D. surveyor; chain carriers Neal McNiell & Danl McFall; [on back] Jacob Rhodes £56.

53. Oct. 17, 1785 surveyed 0.5 ac lot No. 78 in town of Elizabeth; formerly John McDonald's property; border: 104' 5" on Poplar St and 208' 9" back; [signed] J Rhodes, D. surveyor; [on back] purchased May 22 by William Kirk Patrick [sic] £20.

54. Oct. 17, 1785 surveyed 0.5 ac lot No. 14 in town of Elizabeth; formerly John McDonald's property; border: 104' 5" on Bens St and 208' 9" back; [signed] J Rhodes, D. surveyor; [on back] purchased May 22 Jessue Lassiter £9.15.

55. Nov. 17, 1785 surveyed 124 ac; No. 51; formerly Joseph Mercer's property; on NE side of Drowning Cr "a little" below Raft Swamp; border: a pine on the creek about 20 chains above Mercer's Ferry; [signed] J Rhodes, D. surveyor; chain carriers Francis Colvell & John Copeland jr; [on back] Jessee Lassiter £83.10.

56. Oct. 17, 1785 surveyed 0.5 ac lot No. 83 in town of Elizabeth; formerly Thomas Christy's property; border: 208' 9" on lot 80, 104' 5" on lot 82, 208' 9" on lot 84, & 104' 9" on Broad St; [signed] J Rhodes, D. surveyor; [on back] Henry E Lutterloh.

57. Oct. 31, 1785 surveyed 120 ac; No. 40; on NE side of Little Marsh; formerly Danl Southerland's property; border: an oak on W side of Boggy Br about 25 chains N of said Southerland's "plantation"; [signed] J Rhodes, D. surveyor; chain carriers John McCollum & Angus Paterson; [on back] Jarred Ervin [or Jarrett Erwin] £101.1.

58. Oct. 17, 1785 surveyed 0.5 ac lot 34 in town of Elizabeth; formerly Thomas Chaistie's property; border: 104' 5" on No. 35 on Ritch St, 208' 9" on No. 36, 104' 5" on Poplar St, & 208' 9" on Ritch St; [signed] J Rhodes, D. surveyor; [on back] Jarrett Erwin.

59. Oct. 17, 1785 surveyed 0.5 ac lot No. 12 in town of Elizabeth; formerly Thomas Christie's property; border: 208' 9" on No. 13, 104' 9" on No. 16, 208' 9" on Queen St, & 104' 5" on Ben St; [signed] J Rhodes, D. surveyor; [on back] Jarrett Erwin.

Sales of Confiscated Land

60. Oct. 17, 1785 surveyed 0.5 ac lot No. 60 in town of Elizabeth; formerly Thomas Christy's property; border: 104' 5" on No. 58, 208' 9" on No. 59, 104' 5" on Bens St, & 208' 9" on Queens St; [signed] J Rhodes, D. surveyor; [on back] W Watson.

61. Oct. 17, 1785 surveyed 0.5 ac lot No. 33 in town of Elizabeth; formerly William Campbell's property; border: 208' 9" on No. 32, 104' 5" on No. 31, 208' 9" on Bens St, & 104' 5" on Ritch St; [signed] J Rhodes, D. surveyor; [on back] Jarrett Erwin.

62. Oct. 17, 1785 surveyed 0.5 ac lot No. 80 in town of Elizabeth; formerly John McDonald's property; border: 104' 5" on front "the back" of Broad St by 208' 9" back; [signed] J Rhodes, D. surveyor; [on back] purchased May 22 by Curtis Ivey & G J McRee £100.

63. Oct. 17, 1785 surveyed 0.5 ac lot 100 in town of Elizabeth; formerly Thomas Christy's property; border: 208' 9" on No. 99, 104' 5" on No. 98, 208' 9" on Pine St, & 104' 5" on Broad St; [signed] J Rhodes, D. surveyor; [on back] Henry E Lutterloh.

64. Oct. 11, 1785 surveyed 640 ac; No. 10; formerly Faithful Grayham's property; on SW side of NW [Cape Fear] R; being upper part of a grant to John Porter of Virginia; border: Saml Ashe's lower corner about 1.5 chains below Davis's Landing; [signed] J Rhodes, D. surveyor; chain carriers Thomas Brown & Richard Brown; [on back] G J McRee £2,505.

65. Oct. 17, 1785 surveyed 0.5 ac lot 40 in town of Elizabeth; formerly Thomas Christie's property; border: 208' 9" on No. 41, 104' 5" on No. 44, 208' 9" on No. 39, & 104' 5" on Lower [or Sower] St; [signed] J Rhodes, D. surveyor; [on back] Danl Shaw.

66. Aug. 8, 1786 surveyed 208 ac; No. 77; formerly Mark Robeson's property; on both sides of Fryer Swamp; being upper part of Robeson's lower survey; border: a dividing corner of said survey about 20 chains E of Saml Casman's "plantation"; [signed] J Rhodes, D. surveyor; chain carriers Isaac Powel & Jeremiah Bigford; [on back] Jarred Ervin [or Jarrett Erwin] £102.4.

67. Jul. 26, 1786 surveyed 320 ac; No. 76; formerly Mark Robeson's property; on both sides of Fryers Swamp; border: on E side of said swamp "a little" below Jeremiah Bigford and a dividing line of said tract; [signed] J Rhodes, D. surveyor; chain carriers Isaac Powel & Jeremiah Bigford; [on back] Jarred Erwin [or Jarrett Erwin] £111.3.

68. Jul. 25, 1786 surveyed 320 ac; No. 75; formerly property of William Palmer, surveyor general; on E side of White Marsh Swamp; border: a pine "a little" below John Demory's "plantation"; [signed] J Rhodes, D. surveyor; "present" [chain carriers] John Dimory & Simon Dimory; [on back] Jarred Ervin [or Jarrett Erwin] £120.3.

69. Jul. 24, 1786 surveyed 195 ac; No. 74; formerly George Parker's property; on E side of White Marsh; "supposed to be" the lower part of 640 ac granted to Lyons; border: a gum on E side of the marsh near Thos Mims's upper corner; [signed] J Rhodes, D. surveyor; chain carriers Elijah Renolds & John Cohoon; [on back] William Bryant £753.1.

70. Jul. 7, 1786 surveyed 100 ac; No. 71; formerly Peter McFarland's property; S of Rockfish Cr and on both sides of Pedlers Br; [signed] J Rhodes, D. surveyor; chain carriers Angus Molloy & John McLain; [on back] William Watson £95.

71. May 20, 1786 surveyed 87 ac; No. 67; formerly David Godwin's property; on W side of Porters Swamp and both sides of Uncles Br; border: Joshua Peavey; [signed] John Yates, surveyor; [on back] G J McRee and Curtis Ivey £57.

72. Nov. 18, 1785 surveyed 100 ac; No. 54; formerly Archibald McEacharn's property; on E side of Ashpole Swamp; border: a hill about 8 poles below Benjn Odam's old Ford and about 2 miles below McKisick's Mill; [signed] J Rhodes, D. surveyor; chain carriers Henry Thomson & George Thomson; [on back] Elias Barns £25.5.

Sales of Confiscated Land

73. Nov. 17, 1785 surveyed 150 ac; No. 53; formerly Jacob Kersey's property; W of Drowning Cr, W of Back Swamp, & on both sides of Jacobs Swamp; border: a pine and oak on "the" side of "the" main road being the lower corner of "another" survey and Thompson's lower line; [signed] J Rhodes, D. surveyor; chain carriers William Thompson & James Roland; [on back] Elias Barns £87.

74. No. 14, 1785 surveyed 290 ac; No. 48; formerly Jacob Kersey's property; about 1.5 miles N of Drowning Cr on Bear Swamp; border: Lewis Thomas' upper corner pine on N side of said swamp "just above" Oldfield Br at the lower corner of said Kersey's old field; [signed] J Rhodes, D. surveyor; chain carriers Wm Townsend & James Adkins; [on back] Curtis Ivey & G J McRee £220.10.

75. Nov. 14, 1785 surveyed 180 ac; No. 49; formerly Jacob Kersey's property; on Bear Swamp; between said Kersey's old field and John Moore's land; border: a gum on N side of said swamp "just below" said Moore's "plantation" and a corner of another survey; [signed] J Rhodes, D. surveyor; chain carriers William Townsend & James Atkins; [on back] Curtis Ivey & G J McRee £106.5.

76. Nov. 14, 1785 surveyed 100 ac; No. 47; formerly Jacob Kersey's property; on W side of Raft Swamp; border: a pine on "the" side of the swamp "just below" Fed's Br about 20 chains above travers's Mills; [signed] J Rhodes, D. surveyor; chain carriers Wm Townsend & Jas Adkins; [on back] Curtis Ivey & G J McRee £40.10.

77. Oct. 31, 1785 surveyed 243 ac; No. 38; formerly David Leggitt's property; on N side of Big Marsh and SW side of Little Marsh; border: a black gum dividing corner on the run of said Little Marsh about 0.75 miles above where Jas Ard lives; [signed] J Rhodes, D. surveyor; chain carriers Wm Blyther & John McKinsey; [on back] Curtis Ivey & G J McRee £40.

78. Oct. 31, 1785 surveyed 100 ac; No. 62; formerly David Legatt's property; on NE side of Little Marsh; border: a large red oak on "the" side of the marsh "a little" below Dutch ford and about 1.5 miles above Jas Ard; [signed] J Rhodes, D. surveyor; chain carriers Wm Blyther & John McKinsey; [on back] Matthew Roan White £15.

79. Oct. 22, 1785 surveyed 344 ac; No. 27; formerly John Colvill's property; between waters of NW [Cape Fear] R and Drowning Cr opposite Col. Owen; border: John Owen's back corner in Thos Owen's upper line; [signed] J Rhodes, D. surveyor; chain carriers William Chesser [or Chisser] & John Bryan; [on back] G J McRee & Curtis Ivey £16.

80. Oct. 31, 1785 surveyed 100 ac; No. 63; formerly David Leggitt's property; NE of Little Marsh and on SE side of "the" Big Pecoson; border: near the path from Jas Ard's to McCollum's; [signed] J Rhodes, D. surveyor; chain carriers Wm Blyther & John McKinsey; [on back] Thomas White £20.

81. Oct. 31, 1785 surveyed 177 ac; No. 39; formerly David Leggitt's property; on N side of Big Marsh and SW side of Little Marsh; border: a black gum dividing corner in the run of Little Marsh about 0.75 miles above where Jas Ard lives; [signed] J Rhodes, D. surveyor; chain carriers Wm Blyther & John McKinsey; [on back] David Flours £12.

82. Oct. 7, 1785 surveyed 51 ac; No. 8; formerly David Godwin's property; on S side of Porters Swamp; border: about 0.75 miles above widow Godwin and a cypress on the edge of said swamp the upper corner of "another" survey about 12 chains above said Godwin's upper field; [signed] J Rhodes, D. surveyor; chain carriers William Lewis & Swift Brookshear; [on back] Curtis Ivey & G J McRee £10.10.

83. Oct. 7, 1785 surveyed 130 ac; No. 7; formerly David Godwin's property; on Porters Swamp; border: upper line of "another" survey and on S side of said swamp about 30 chains above where widow Godwin lives; [signed] J Rhodes, D. surveyor; chain carriers Wm Lewis & Swift Brookshear; [on back] Curtis Ivey & G J McRee £72.

84. Oct. 6, 1785 surveyed 577 ac; No. 4; formerly David Godwin's property; on both sides of Porters Swamp; border: a pine about 5 chains W of where "the" main road crosses said swamp, an old field, & said Yates' corner; plat also

shows the mouth of Uncles Br at Porters Swamp; [signed] J Rhodes, D. surveyor; chain carriers Wm Lewis & Swift Brookshear; [on back] John Yates £221.

85. Oct. 6, 1785 surveyed 50 ac; No. 5; formerly David Godwin's property; on E side of Porters Swamp; border: two pines on "the" side of said swamp "a little" below a small improvement made by Pearce Godwin; [signed] J Rhodes, D. surveyor; chain carriers William Lewis & Swift Brookshear; [on back] Richard Brown £12.10.

86. Oct. 5, 1785 surveyed 118 ac; No. 3; formerly David Godwin's property; on Porters Swamp; border: a poplar on "the" edge of said swamp about 15 chains below the mouth of Cypress Br; plat shows land is on both sides of Porters Swamp and shows mouth of Cypress Br; [signed] J Rhodes, D. surveyor; chain carriers Wm Lewis & Swift Brookshear; [on back] Alexander Godden £50.

87. Oct. 4, 1785 surveyed 100 ac; No. 59; formerly David Godwin's property; on NE side of Drowning Cr; border: the upper edge of an island between said creek and John Brown's land; [signed] J Rhodes, D. surveyor;; chain carriers Alexander Campbell & Joseph Nobles; [on back] Matthew Roan White £14.

88. Sept. 29, 1785 surveyed 50 ac; No. 2; formerly David Godwin's property; on NE side of Drowning Cr about a mile W of said Godwin's Quarter; border: side of said creek swamp about 10 chains below an old field and Griffin; [signed] J Rhodes, D. surveyor; chain carriers Frederick Taylor & Alexander Godwin; [on back] Alexander Godden [sic] £50.

89. Nov. 14, 1785 surveyed 148 ac; No. 46; formerly Noah Mercer's property; on NE side of Drowning Cr above Raft Swamp; border: Wm Townsend's lower line about 15 chains from said creek swamp; [signed] J Rhodes, D. surveyor; chain carriers Wm Townsend & Jas Adkins; [on back] William Moore £105.5.

90. Oct. 31, 1785 surveyed 143 ac; No. 37; formerly David Leggitt's property; on NE side of Little Marsh; border: upper corner of "the other" part in the run of said marsh about 0.75 miles above where Jas Ard lives and a dividing line; [signed] J Rhodes, D. surveyor; chain carriers Wm Lewis & Swift Brookshear; [on back] Peter Smith £14.10.

91. Oct. 17, 1785 surveyed 0.5 ac lot No. 97 in town of Elizabeth; formerly John McDonald's property; border: 104' 5" on Pine St, 208' 9" on King St, & 104' 5" back from King St; [signed] J Rhodes, D. surveyor; Robert Scott £9.10.

92. Oct. 31, 1786 surveyed 150 ac; No. 60; formerly David Leggitt's property; on both sides of Great Marsh at the mouth of Beverdam Swamp; border: an oak & sassafras on W side of the marsh "a little" above Beverdam Swamp; [signed] J Rhodes, D. surveyor; chain carriers William Lewis & Swift Brookshear; [on back] Jacob Rhodes £22.

93. Oct. 30, 1786 surveyed 200 ac; No. 81; formerly Randal McDugal's property; on NE side of NW Cape Fear R; border: David Lock decd's upper corner on the river; [signed] J Rhodes, D. surveyor; chain carriers David Lock & Thomas Lock; [on back] Daniel Shaw £20.

94. Oct. 31, 1785 surveyed 77 ac; No. 36; formerly David Leggitt's property; on NE side of Little Marsh; border: a black gum in the run of said marsh about 0.75 miles above where Jas Ard lives; improved with a log house and about 3 acres cleared; [signed] J Rhodes, D. surveyor; chain carriers Wm Lewis & Swift Brookshear; [on back] Robert Raiford £20.

95. Oct. 22, 1785 surveyed 344 ac; No. 28; formerly John Colvill's property; on waters of NW [Cape Fear] R and Drowning Cr opposite Col. Thos Owens; border: a pine near the head of Pine log Bay, Thos Owens, & "another" survey; [signed] J Rhodes, D. surveyor; chain carriers William Chesser & John Bryan; [on back] Robert Raiford £20.

96. Oct. 31, 1785 surveyed 100 ac; No. 61; formerly David Leggitt's property; on both sides of Great Marsh Swamp; border: a white oak & sassafras on W side of the swamp "a little" above Beaverdam Swamp; [signed] J Rhodes, D. surveyor; chain carriers William Lewis & Swift Brookshear; [on back] Jacob Rhodes £10.5.

Sales of Confiscated Land

97. Oct. 17, 1785 surveyed 0.5 ac lot No. 2 in town of Elizabeth; formerly John McDonald's property; border: 104' 5" on Poplar St, 208' 9" on Harverford St, & 104' 5" back of Harverford St; [signed] J Rhodes, D. surveyor; purchased May 22 by Robert Raiford £6.10.

98. Sept. 29, 1785 surveyed 88 ac; No. 56; formerly David Godwin's property; in the fork of Porters Swamp and Cow Br; border: said Godwin's lower line of a tract known as Cow Branch "plantation" on E side of Cow Br; [signed] J Rhodes, D. surveyor; chain carriers Alex Godwin & Fredrick Tayler; [on back] Jacob Rhodes £121.

99. Sept. 29, 1785 surveyed 100 ac; No. 58; formerly David Godwin's property; on W side of Drowning Cr; border: a cypress on lower end of "the" Great Lake; [signed] J Rhodes, D. surveyor; chain carriers James Rising & Theophilus Griffin; [on back] Jacob Rhodes £12.13.

100. Sept. 29, 1785 surveyed 239 ac; No. 1; formerly David Godwin's property; on NE side of Drowning Cr and on Cow Br; border: a red oak on E side of said branch about 20 chains above the mouth and about 10 [chains] below said Godwin's orchard field; [signed] J Rhodes, D. surveyor; chain carriers Frederick Tayler & Alexander Godwin; [on back] Joseph Rhodes £315.

101. Jul. 15, 1786 surveyed 50 ac; No. 72; formerly Thomas Stewart's property; on E side of Shoeheel Cr; between Hugh McLain & John Stewart and on the creek swamp; [signed] J Rhodes, D. surveyor; chain carriers Hugh McLain & Malichiah Dees; [on back] Jacob Rhodes £28.3.

102. Jul. 24, 1786 surveyed 300 ac; No. 73; formerly George Parker's property; in White Marsh; border: near Thos Mims's upper corner on E side of said marsh; [signed] J Rhodes, D. surveyor; chain carriers Elijah Renold & John Cohoon; [on back] John Reess jr £54.

103. Nov. 22, 1785 surveyed 100 ac; No. 55; formerly Archibald McEacharn's property; SW of Raft Swamp and E of McFall's Mill; border: the head of Mirey Br about 20 chains S of Raft Swamp Bridge; [signed] J Rhodes, D. surveyor; chain carriers Jacob Rhodes & Danl McFall; [on back] Major Robt Raiford £30.

104. Jul. 26, 1786 surveyed 280 ac; No. 79; formerly Mark Robeson's property; on both sides of Fryer's Swamp; being the upper part of Robeson's upper survey; border: a dividing corner of said swamp; [signed] J Rhodes, D. surveyor; chain carriers Isaac Powel and Jeremiah Powell; [on back] Robert Raiford £60.

105. Jul. 26, 1786 surveyed 304 ac; No. 78; formerly Mark Robeson's property; on both sides of Fryer's Swamp; being the lower part of Robeson's upper survey; border: the lower corner of said survey about 30 chains E of the swamp and a dividing corner; [signed] J Rhodes, D. surveyor; chain carriers Isaac Powel & Jeremiah Powell; [on back] Robert Raiford £60.

106. Account of sales of confiscated property in Bladen Co 1786:
106A. May 22
1) Robert Raiford--lot 2 in Elizabeth town for £6.10; formerly John McDonnell's property
2) Jessee Lassiter--lot No. 14 in Elizabeth town for £9.15; formerly John McDonnell's property
3) William Kirkpatrick--lot No. 78 in Elizabeth town for £20.0; formerly John McDonnell's property
4) Robert Scott--lot No. 97 in Elizabeth town for £9.10; formerly John McDonnell's property
5) G J McRee & Curtis Ivy--lot No. 80 in Elizabeth town for £100.10; formerly John McDonnell's property
6) Griffith John McRee--640 ac for £2,505.0; formerly Faithfull Graham's property; [subtotal 1 through 6 = £2,651.5]
7) Alexander Godden--50 ac No. 2 for £50.0; formerly David Gooden's property
8) Alexander Godden--118 ac No. 3 for £50.0; formerly David Gooden's property
9) John Yates--577 ac No. 4 for £221.0; formerly David Gooden's property
10) Richard Brown--50 ac No. 5 for £12.10; formerly David Gooden's property
11) Joseph T Rhodes--239 ac No. 1 for £315.0; formerly David Gooden's property
12) Curtis Ivy & G J McRee--130 ac No. 7 for £72.0; formerly David Gooden's property; [subtotal 7 through 12 =

Sales of Confiscated Land

£720.10]

13) Curtis Ivy & G J McRee--50 ac No. 8 for £10.10; formerly David Gooden's property

14) Jacob Rhodes--50 ac No. 41 for £76.0; formerly Niel McFall's property

15) Jacob Rhodes--100 ac No. 42 for £56.0; formerly Niel McFall's property

16) Curtis Ivy & G J McRee--100 ac No. 47 for £40.10; formerly Jacob Kersey's   property

17) Curits Ivy & G J McRee--290 ac No. 48 for £220.10; formerly Jacob Kersey's   property

18) Curtis Ivy & G J McRee--180 ac No. 49 for £106.5; formerly Jacob Kersey's   property

19) Elias Barns--150 ac No. 53 for £87.0; formerly Jacob Kersey's   property

20) Elias Barns--100 ac No. 54 for £25.5; formerly Archd McEachern's property; [subtotal 13 through 20 = £622.0]

21) Robert Raiford--100 ac No. 55 for £30.0; formerly Archd McEachern's property

22) Robt Raiford--77 ac No. 36 for £20.0; formerly David Legat's [sic] property

23) Peter Smith--143 ac No. 37 for £14.10; formerly David Legatt's property

24) Curtis Ivy & G J McRee--243 ac No. 38 for £40.0; formerly David Legatt's property

25) David Flours--177 ac No. 39 for £12.0; formerly David Legatt's property

26) G J McRee & Curtis Ivy--344 ac No. 27 for £16.0; formerly John Colvill's property; [subtotal 21 through 26 = £132.6]

27) Robt Raiford--344 ac No. 28 for £20.0; formerly John Colvill's property

28) William Moore--148 ac No. 46 for £105.5; formerly Noah Nercer's property

29) Jessee Lassiter--124 ac No. 51 for £83.10; formerly Joseph Mercur's property

30) John McKinny--Negro fellow Humor for £500.0; formerly David Gooden's property

31) Jacob Leonard--Negro wench Amy & 3 children for £1,630.0; formerly David Gooden's property; [subtotal 27 through 31 = £2,338.15]

32) John McKinny--Negro boy Casar for £555.0; formerly David Gooden's property

33) Jacob Leonard--Negro girl Jinny for £500.0; formerly David Gooden's property

34) Jacob Leonard--Negro fellow Jack for £585.0; formerly David Gooden's property

35) Joseph Rhodes--a set of blacksmith's tools for £56.0; formerly David Gooden's property

36) Duncan Stewart--3 steel traps for £6.15; formerly D Gooden's property

37) G John McRee--50 hogs for £31.0; formerly D Gooden's property

38) Robt Raiford--2 horses for £200.0; formerly D Gooden's property; [subtotal 32 through 38 = £1,933.15]

39) John Brown--10 sheep for £17.10; formerly D Gooden's property

40) Dan Schaw, Robt Raiford, Richd Plumnur, & Jos Stewart--40 cattle for £150.0; formerly D Goodin's property; [subtotal 39 through 40 = £167.10]

106B. Nov. 6

41) Jacob Rhodes--100 ac No. 58 for £12.13; formerly David Gooden's property

42) Matthew Roan White--100 ac No. 59 for £14.0; formerly David Gooden's property

43) John McMillan--100 ac No. 57 for £6.1; formerly David Gooden's property

44) Jacob Rhodes--88 ac No. 56 for £121.0; formerly David Gooden's property

45) Jacob Rhodes--150 ac No. 60 for £22.0; formerly David Legatt's property

46) Jacob Rhodes--100 ac No. 61 for £10.5; formerly David Legatt's property

47) Matthew Roan White--100 ac No. 62 for £15.0; formerly David Legatt's property

48) Thomas White--100 ac No. 63 for £15.0; formerly David Legatt's property; [total 41 through 48 = £215.19]

49) Jarred Ervin--120 ac No. 40 for £101.1; formerly Daniel Southerland's property

50) G J McRee & Curtis Ivy--87 ac No. 67 for £57.0; formerly David Godden's property

51) James Spiller--100 ac No. 70 for £22.3; formerly Hector McNiell's property

52) Jacob Rhodes--50 ac No. 72 for £28.3; formerly Kenner Stewart's property

53) John Ress--300 ac No. 73 for £54.0; formerly George Parker's property

54) William Bryant--195 ac No. 74 for £753.0; formerly George Parker's property; [subtotal 49 through 54 = £1,015.7]

55) Jarred Ervin--920 ac Nos. 75, 76, & 77 for £333.10; formerly Mark Robeson's property

55) Robert Raiford--304 ac No. 78 for £60.0; formerly Mark Robeson's property

57) Robert Raiford--200 ac No. 79 for £60.0; formerly Mark Robeson's property

58) [blank] McDugall--350 ac No. 80 for £110.0; formerly Randal McDugall's property

13

Sales of Confiscated Land

59) Daniel Schaw--200 ac No. 81 for £201.0; formerly Randal McDugall's property
60) William Watson--100 ac No. 71 for £95.0; formerly Peter McFarlin's property; [total 55 through 60 = £559.10]
    [grand total] £10,357.1.   "errors excepted" G J McRee

107. Receipt No. 294 Sept. 13, 1786 to John Yates £24 for 12 surveys; [on back] No. 510.

108. Receipt No. 286 Jul. 14, 1786 to John Yates £24 for 12 surveys; [on back] No. 632.

109. Receipt No. 242 May 15, 1786 to John Yates £40 for surveying confiscated land [no number of surveys]; [on back] No. 391.

110. Receipt No. 243 May 15, 1786 to John Yates £100 for surveying confiscated land [no number of surveys]; [on back] No. 230.

111. Receipt No. 562 Dec. 15, 1787 to John Yates £4 for surveying confiscated land [no number of surveys]; [on back] No. 248.

112. Sept. 6, 1783 Report of Commissioners to the Comptroller General: on Aug. 16 the Comptroller asked for an accounting of Confiscated property. The answer is: James Council, John King, & John Yates were appointed commissioners "whether legally or not I am not prepared to say". They started to act, but were stopped by "supersedias" from Superior Court and "I don't know" if they did anything.   The Comptroller asked for a list of sheriffs for 1780-1783: for 1780 William McRee jr was sheriff; for 1781 the county was overrun and had no sheriff; for 1782 James Moorhead was sheriff and collected [taxes] for 1781; for 1783 William McRee jr was sheriff.
    Assessor's [account] is inaccurate so exact assessments can't be sent; they "generally" mention those who haven't given [tax] in and those who haven't taken the State oath; no sums are "extended" to the names and the lists don't distinguish married from unmarried men; however here is the total:
        for 1780   £2,537,553.5.11
        for 1781   £1,584,983.16.8
        for 1782   £ 208,500.2.0;   current years total aren't completed yet.
[signed] John White, cc.
[postscript:] "I almost forgot" William Kirkpatrick esq was County Commissioner of Specific Tax in 1780 and 1781; Peter Robeson for 1782.
recd. Sept. 15, 1783   "R C"

BRUNSWICK CO
113. Mar. 29, 1797 a bond in Wake Co by Griffith John McRee to Gov. Samuel Ashe for £1,217.3.8; on Sept. 18,1787, McRee bought "sundry" confiscated land in Brunswick Co, and his bill of £608.11.10 certificates is due with interest from Sept. 18, 1788; this bond void if McRee pays the bill.   Signed G J McRee. Witness John Haywood.

114. Sept. 18, 1787 a list of land sold:
a) 500 ac John White's land on Fishing Cr; bought for £75 by James Conyers
b) 240 ac James White's land on a branch of Lockwoods folly R; bought for £8 by Alexis Mardamas Foster
c) 100 ac Hope & Buck Willit's land on Lockwoods folly R; bought for £6 by John Hankins.
[signed] G J McRee, commissioner

115. Receipt No. 270 Jul. 5, 1786 to William Goodman £28 for 14 surveys; [on back] No. "(10) 497".

116. Receipt No. 325 Nov. 20, 1786 to Alisius Mador. Foster £22 for 11 surveys; [on back] No. 615.

117. Sept. 18, 1787 Account of sales of confiscated property in Brunswick Co:
Sept. 18, 1787
a) to 3,630 ac; formerly Thomas Hooper's property; bought by John McKenzie for £5,117

Sales of Confiscated Land

b) to 494 ac on Cape Fear [R] and Allens Cr; formerly William Tryon esq's property; called Lelliput; bought by G J McRee for £2,510

c) to 500 ac on Fishing Cr & W side of Cape Fear [R]; formerly James White's property; bought by James Conyers for £75

d) to 240 ac on Rattlesnake Br of Lockwoods Folly [R]; formerly James White's property; bought by Alexis M Foster for £8

e) to 100 ac on Lockwoods Folly [R]; formerly property of Hope & Buck Willit's; bought by John Hankins for £6 [total] £7,716 The above land of Hooper's & Tryon's were formerly sold to Gen. Howe, but he failed to comply with the condition of the sale [and] it ws again advertised and resold as above. [signed] G J McRee.

118. Account of sale Sept. 18, 1786:
a) William Gauss--0.5 ac lot B for £13.0; formerly Hepburn & Reynolds' property
b) Benjamin Mills--0.5 ac lot B for £10.0; formerly Hepburn & Reynolds' property
c) Howell Tatum--lot in Brunswick for £45.6; formerly William Tryon's property
d) Nathaniel Wooten--lot in Brunswick for £6.10; formerly James White's property
e) Jacob Leonard--lot in Brunswick for £20.10; formerly John McDowell's property
f) James Chairs--2,223 ac Nos. 1, 2, 3, & 5 for £2,875; formerly Christr Cains' property; [subtotal a through f £2,970.5]
g) Lewis Dupré--160 ac No. 4 for £100; formerly Christr Cains' property
h) Robert Howe--492 ac for £3,080; formerly William Tryon's property
i) Howell Tatum--640 ac for £3,000; formerly Thomas Hooper's property
j) Robert Howe--3,630 ac for £6,250; formerly Thomas Hooper's property
k) Howell Tatum--500 ac for £4,000; formerly Thomas Cobham's property
l) Robert Bell--50 ac for £14.5; formerly Joseph Buck & Hope Willit's property [subtotal g through l = £16,444.5]
[grand total] £19,414.10 "errors excepted" [signed] G J McRee.

119. Oct. 28, 1785 surveyed 492 ac known as Liliput; formerly Wm Tryon esq's property; plat shows an old road to Brunswick town, Cape Fear R, Perdreau's or Allen's Cr, & a marsh; [signed] Alexr M Foster, c. surveyor; sold to Robert Howe for £3,080.

120. Oct. 27, 1785 surveyed 0.5 ac in Brunswick town; formerly Messrs. Heburn & Reynolds' property; border: John McIlhenny, 266' on a street, 88.5' on McIlhenny's lot, 266' on a lot of estate of Richard Quince esq, & 82.5' on another street; [signed] Alexr M Foster, c. surveyor; sold to Benj Mills for £10.

121. Oct. 27, 1785 surveyed [omitted] ac a lot in Brunswick town; formerly William Tryon esq's property; border: runs 180' on a lot of estate or Parker Quince esq to Cape Fear R, 82.5' on a street, 170' on a lot of estate of Richd Quince esq to the river, & has an old warf 140' into the river on "upper part" beside Peter Quince's lot; [signed] Alexr M Foster, c. surveyor; sold to Howell Tatum for £45.5.

122. Oct. 27, 1785 surveyed [omitted] ac a lot in Brunswick town; formerly Messrs Heburn & Reynolds' property; border: 170' on a street to Cape Fear R, 82.5' on another street, & 128' on a lot of estate of Richard Quince esq to the river; [signed] Alexr M Foster, c. surveyor; William Gauss [or Gaass] for £13.

123. Oct. 26, 1785 surveyed [omitted] ac a lot in Brunswick town; formerly John McDowell's property; border: 44' on a street, 82.5' on the back, on E by part of a lot of estate of Col. Wm Dry, on W by part of Angelo Stone's lot, & "the" street on S; [signed] Alexr M Foster, c. surveyor; Jacob Leonard for £20.10.

124. Oct. 27, 1785 surveyed 0.5 ac a lot in Brunswick town; formerly James White's property; border: 82.5' on a street, 266' on Thos Kimbo's lot, 82.5', & 266' to the beginning; [note added] on the lot is a house 26' by 24' with two brick chimneys, a pailed [sic] yard, & a water well; [signed] Alexr M Foster, c. surveyor; sold to Nathl Wooten for £6.10.

Sales of Confiscated Land

125. Oct. 25,1785 surveyed 160 ac; formerly Christopher Cain's property; on both sides of Mulberry Br of Shallote R; plat shows border: A M Foster and Thomas Staneland; [signed] Alexr M Foster, c. surveyor; chain carriers Thos Staneland & Saml Staneland; sold to Lewis Dupre for £100.

126. Oct. 17, 1785 surveyed 640 ac; formerly Christopher Cain's property; border: on E by Shallote R, SW by land late Christopher Cain's, Saucepan Cr, & "the" marsh; plat also shows border: Wm Gause esq & Goose Cr; [signed] Alexr M Foster, c. surveyor; sold to James Chairs for £1,605.

127. Oct. 18, 1785 surveyed 523 ac; formerly Christopher Cain's property; border: on SE by Shallote R, NE partly by land lately Christopher Cain's, & "other" parts by Wm Gause esq; plat also shows land is on both sides of Sausepan Cr and shows a lower dam, a middle dam, & a mill dam on the creek, a marsh and "little beech" at Shallote R, & mouth of Landing Cr at Shallote R; [signed] Alexr M Foster, c. surveyor; sold to James Chairs for £1,065.

128. Oct. 22,1785 surveyed 550 ac; formerly Christopher Cain's property; on the Sea Beach; border: on SE by the Atlantic Ocean, NW by creeks [sic] landing from Bacons Inlet to Shallote R, NE by Bacons Inlet, & NW by land lately Cain's; [signed] Alexr M Foster, c. surveyor; sold to James Chairs for £100.

129. Oct. 22, 1785 surveyed 350 ac; formerly Christopher Cain's property; on the Sea Beach; border: SE by the Atlantic Ocean, NW by Shallote R, SW by Shallote Inlet, & NE by a creek and land lately said Cain's; plat shows land is opposite the mouth of Saucepan Cr on Shallote R; [signed] Alexr M Foster, c. surveyor; sold to James Chairs for £105.

130. Sept. 26, 1786 surveyed 480 ac; No. 16; formerly Doc. Thomas [John--lined out] Cobham's property; on SW side of NW [Cape Fear] R, at the mouth of a small branch, & runs up said branch; [signed] Wm Goodman, c surveyor; sold to Howell Tatum for John B Ashe for £4,000.

131. Sept. 27, 1786 surveyed 640 ac; No. 17; on W side of NW Cape Fear R; border: N & W by Mr. Henry & Joseph Watters and S by land of estate of Robert Schaw esq; [signed] Wm Goodman, c surveyor; sold to Howell Tatum for J B Ashe for £3,000.

132. Nov. 6, 1786 G J McRee, commissioner, certifys William Godman, Brunswick Co surveyor, furnished 4 surveys; [on back] No. 364, warrant issued Jan. 6, 1787 £8 No. 364.

133. Receipt No. 364 Jan. 6, 1787 to William Goodman £8 for 4 surveys; [on back] No. 329; Oct. 5, 1787 William Goodman received the money from John Cains, Brunswick Co sheriff.

134. May 6, 1786 surveyed 391 ac; No. 8; formerly Thomas Hooper's property; on lower side of Allens Cr about the old mill; border: upper line of 268 ac tract; [signed] Wm Goodman, c. surveyor; chain carriers Benjamin Williams & Job Goodman; sold to Jno Mackinzie [Robert Howe--lined out] for £500.

135. May 4, 1786 surveyed 268 ac; No. 7; formerly Thomas Hooper's property; on lower side of Allens Cr; plat also shows "a" large bay; [signed] Wm Goodman, c. surveyor; chain carriers Benjamin Williams & Job Goodman; sold to John Mackinzie [Robert Howe--lined out] £390.

136. May 4, 1786 surveyed 591 ac; No. 9; formerly Thomas Hooper's property; on lower side of Allens Cr; plat also shows "Fountain" Spring and a small branch both running into Allens Cr; [signed] Wm Goodman, c. surveyor; sold to John Mackinzie [Robert Howe--lined out] for £848.10.

137. May 3, 1786 surveyed 429.25 ac; No. 3; formerly Thomas Hooper's property; border: the "given" line, the "first" line, & near Nut's line; [signed] Wm Goodman, c. surveyor; sold to John Mackenzie [Robert Howe--lined out] for £500.

Sales of Confiscated Land

138. May 2, 1786 surveyed 448.25 ac; No. 2; formerly Thomas Hooper's property; on lower side of Allens Cr; border: an old mill pond on Allens Cr and includes an old field; [signed] Wm Goodman, c. surveyor; sold to John Mackinzie [Robert Howe--lined out] for £500.

139. May 3, 1786 surveyed 300 ac; No. 1; formerly Thomas Hooper's property; on upper side of Allens Cr; border: upper corner of Lilliput land and below the mill dam; [signed] Wm Goodman, c. surveyor; sold to G J McRee [Robert Howe--lined out] for £426.

140. May 3, 1786 surveyed 625 ac; No. 5; formerly Thomas Hooper's property; on upper side of Allens Cr; border: upper corner of 353 ac tract and a swamp; [signed] Wm Goodman, c. surveyor; chain carriers Benjamin Williams & Job Goodman; sold to John Mackinzie [Robert Howe--lined out] for £570.
141. May 3, 1786 surveyed 353 ac; No. 4; formerly Thomas Hooper's property; on lower side of Allens Cr; border: "the" side of the old mill pond "just below" the mouth of Stup Br; [signed] Wm Goodman, c. surveyor; chain carriers Benjamin Williams & Job Goodman; sol to Robert Howe £[blank]; [on back] John Mackinzie £570.

142. May 5, 1786 surveyed 225 ac; formerly Thomas Hooper's property; on lower side of Allens Cr; border: Kindal and a bluff below a marsh; [signed] Wm Goodman, c. surveyor; sold to John Mackinzie [Robert Howe--lined out] for £848.10.

143. May 24, 1788 surveyed 500 ac; formerly James White's property; on W side of Cape Fear R and in the fork of Fishing Cr; border: runs up NW branch of the creek, near the Fort Road, & on White Spring Br; [signed] Wm Goodman, c. surveyor; sold to [buyer omitted].

144. May 21, 1788 surveyed 100 ac; formerly Hope Willet & Buck Willet's property; on W side of Lockwoods folly R and below Doe Cr; border: Moore's lower line; [signed] Wm Goodman, c. surveyor; sold to John Hankins for £[omitted] [James Conyers £75--lined out].

145. May 24, 1788 surveyed 240 ac; formerly James White's property; on N side of NE branch of Lockwood's folly R; border: upper corner of Robert Daniel on the swamp and Nathaniel Bell; plat also shows the mouth of Rattlesnake Cr on Lockwoods folly R, Bell's land, patented land, & R Daniel's land; [signed] Wm Goodman, c. surveyor; sold to Alexr M Foster for £[omitted].

CAMDEN COUNTY
146. Receipt No. 504 Oct. 12, 1786 to Benjamin Jones, Camden Co surveyor, £0.40 for one survey.

147. [no date] surveyed 310 ac; formerly Mr. Andrew Sprowle's property; on Pasquotank R and Aranure Cr; known as Plummers Point; plat also shows Sawyer's & Ferrell's line, Litten's line, & a run; [signed] B Jones, surveyor; [on back] Hardy Murfree.

148. Oct. 1, 1783 a letter to Gov. Richard Caswell:
On 21st ul., we received your "commands" of Aug. 15. Since our appointment as Commissioners of Confiscated Property, no land has been sold. We hired some Negroes the first year, the money for which we haven't been paid. All confiscated property in this county, except a tract of Andrew Sprowle's of Virginia, now under litigation in Superior Court, has been taken in execution. The former commissioners made some sales; a report of which we suppose has been made. When any property of that sort comes to our care, we shall make a report. [signed] Peter Dauge, Thomas Nichols, & Nathan Snowden; [on back] Dempsey Burges, clk of Camden Co Ct; amot of assessr. sher. etc 1780 to 1784; recd Apr. 19, 1784.

CARTERET COUNTY
149. Dec. 19, 1782 surveyed 27 ac for Eli West; formerly George Harison's property; on Holstons Cr; border: Job Medor and James Beary's corner of his new survey; [signed] Wm Ws Taylor, surveyor; chain bearers James Beary & Job Medor jr; surveyed due to Act of Assembly & order of Newbern Dist. "Superintendant Commissioner".

Sales of Confiscated Land

150. Oct. 28, 1782 surveyed 136 ac for Eli West; formerly Samuel Cornell's property; on N side of White Oak R; border: Wm Ramsy on E side of Houstons Cr; [signed] Wm Ws Taylor, surveyor; chain bearers James Beary & Eli West; surveyed due to Act of Assembly & order of Newbern "Superintendant Commissioner".

151. Receipt May 17, 1783 to William Wilkins Taylor, Carteret Co surveyor, £10 for 5 surveys.

152. Jul. 7, 1787 surveyed 0.25 ac or the East half of lot No. 20 in the "old" town of Beaufort; formerly William Brimage's property; border: on front or Water St, 33' wide, & 20 poles deep; includes "the front" thereunto belonging as far as the channel; [signed] Saml Leffers, tn Clk & county surveyor; sold on same day; [on back] recd £70 for the within lot from William Dennis [signed] James Armstrong, coms.

153. Sept. 17, 1783 a letter to Comptroller at Kingston:
clerk's office Beaufort. Received yours of Aug. 16 requesting an account of Confiscated Estates. Not any sold in this county; what have been confiscated "was" sold at Newbern; enclosed are the gross assessments for 1780, 1781, & 1782; I can't "gett at the 1783" as yet. Will sent it as soon as "convenienecy" will permit; have also enclosed the list of sheriff's names; Malachi Bell, commissioner, has certificates of delinquents and insolvents and what money to be subtracted from the gross that paid no "provition" tax. [signed] Rob. Read, clk; [on back] recd. Oct. 2, 1783.

CHATHAM COUNTY
154. August session 1783 Chatham Co:
Return of John Ramsey, John Montgomery, & Zacha Harmon, Comm. of said County of confiscated property taken by them & how disposed:
a) Mar. 12, 1782 hired the following Negroes & recd. payment for 5 months "in proportion to" 6 months: Peg, George, Africa, Sandy, Julius, Bristow, & Peter--£68.2.7
b) "August" sold 5 of said Negroes under inspection of Col. William Moore, Supr. Comr. for specie certificates--£4,437.0
c) "August" sold 2 Negroes for Continental officers certificates--£4,505.2.7
d) to certificates & bonds in full of the sales paid to Col. Moore including commissions--£486 £4,437 [sic]
e) ballance due the public--£68.2.7
f) returned to Col. Moore 4 tracts of land in this county supposed to be property of Ralph McNair [signed] Geo Glascock, D C C; [on back] returned Chatham Co 1783

155. Report of John Ramsey, Zachariah Harman, & John Montgomery:
a) to certificates paid Col. William Moore--£4,173 specie
   to commissions on £4,173 at 2%--£268
   to John Ramsey's public acct for balance--£64.2.7 [total] £4,505.2.7
   to Continental officer's certificates paid Col. Moore with bond in full
      per receipt--£486.0
b) by amount of sales of 5 Negroes for certificates "rendered" Col. William
      Moore, Supt. Commissioner--£4,437.0
   by amount [for] hire 7 Negroes for 5 months preceeding day of sale
   --£68.2.7 [total] £4,505.2.7
   by 2 Negroes sold for Continental officer's certificates--£486
Apr. 1784 [signed] J Ramsey and Zachr Harman before Jos Brantly.

156. Jan. 24, 1783 Wm Moore received of John Ramsey, John Montgomery, & Zacha Harman, commissioners (a) £4,437 currency & specie certificates for 5 Negroes sold and (b) £486 in Continental officers certificates, including a bond given by Nicholas Long sr, for 2 Negroes sold. [signed] Wm Moore.

157. top half of a letter to Comptroller in Kingston from Geo Glascock, Chatham Co clerk, dated oct. 14, 1783:

Sales of Confiscated Land

Enclosed is a return of Commissioners of Confiscated Property, statement "with" the Court, books, vouchers & papers, & names of sheriffs & commissioners.

158. Receipt No. 337 Dec. 8, 1786 William Finley esq, Chatham Co surveyor, £8 for 4 surveys.

159. Account of sales Feb. 1788 in Chatham Co:
a) 100 ac on Rocky R, formerly H E McCulloch's property; bought by John Ramsey for £60
b) 200 ac on Rocky R, formerly H E McCulloch's property; bought by Lewis Horniday for £200.1
c) 150 ac on Rocky R, formerly H E McCulloch's property; bought by Mathew Ramsey for £41
d) 144 ac on Rocky R, formerly H E McCulloch's property; bought by John Ramsey for £26
[total] £327.1; [on back] A Lytle, comms Hillsborough Dist.

160. May 18, 1786 surveyed 200 ac; formerly Henry Eustace McCullock's property; on middle fork of Rocky R; border: widow Pugh; [signed] W Finley, c surveyor; chain bearers Robert Stinson & Thos Pugh; sold Feb. 1788 for £200.1 to Lewis Horniday by Arch Lytle, comms.

161. May 18, 1786 surveyed 144 ac; formerly Henry Eustace McCullock's property; on middle fork of Rockey R; border: county line at Levi Branson's corner and Pigot; [signed] W Finley, c surveyor; chain bearers Levi Branson & Robert Stinson; sold Feb. 1788 for £26 to John Ramsey by Arch Lytle, comr.

162. May 13, 1786 surveyed 100 ac; formerly Henry Eustace McCullock's property; on both sides of middle prong of Rocky R; border: Pigot an James Vestal; [signed] W Finley, c surveyor; chain bearers William Vestal & Isaac Cox; sold for £60 to Jas Ramsey by A Lytle, comr.

163. May 19, 1786 surveyed 150 ac; formerly Henry Eustace McCullock's property; on S side of middle fork of Rocky R; border: Vestal, a corner of lot [blank], McCullock's "original" line, & Isaac Cox; [signed] W Finley, c surveyor; chain bearers William Vestal & Isaac Cox; [on back] Feb. 1788 sold for £26 to Jno Ramsey by Archd Lytle, comr.

CHOWAN COUNTY
164. Henry bond received £0.36 for cryer's fee in 1786 from Hardy Murfree, Comr. of Confiscated Property for Edenton Dist; [on back] No. 5.

165. Receipt No. 306 Oct. 12, 1786 to John Norcam, Chowan Co surveyor, £0.40 for one survey; [on back] Jul. 20, 1787 recd payment in full of Edmund Blount, Chowan Co sheriff, for the within. [signed] Jno Norcom.

166. Receipt No. 151 Dec. 29, 1785 to John Norcom £26 for surveying 12 town lots and one tract.

167. Receipt No. 36 May 24, 1788 to John Norcom, Chowan Co sheriff, £4 for 2 surveys.

168. An account of comfiscated property sold in Chowan Co:
a) lot No. 1 in Edenton improved, formerly Mrs. Clarke's property; bought by Selby Harney for £3,100 certificates
b) lot No. 50 in Edenton unimproved, formerly Honey's property; bought by John Pons for £380
c) lot No. 51 in Edenton unimproved, formerly Honey's property; bought by John Pons for £460
d) lots 97 & 98 in Edenton unimproved, formerly Weir & Clarke's property; bought by Michael Payne for £0.10
e) lot No. 119 in Edenton unimproved, formerly Thomas Wright's property; bought by John Mare for £150
f) lot No. 120 in Edenton unimproved, formerly Thomas Wright's property; bought by John Mare for £100
g) lot No. 121 in Edenton unimproved, formerly Thomas Wright's property; bought by Edmund Blount for £97
h) lot No. 201 in Edenton, formerly John Hendley's property; bought by Federick Ramkey for £245
i) lot No. 202 in Edenton, formerly John Hendley's property; bought by Federick Ramkey for £425
j) lot No. 203 in Edenton, formerly John Hendley's property; bought by William Boratz for £342
k) lot No. 204 in Edenton, formerly John Hendley's property; bought by William Littlejohn for £353
l) 216 ac with improvements, formerly Thomas Coffield's property; bought by Nathan Lassiter for £2,510

Sales of Confiscated Land

[total] £8,162.10 [signed] "E E" H Murfree, comr.

169. No. 18, 1785 surveyed lot No 1 in the "old" plan in Edenton; formerly Mrs. Clark's property and now possessed by Joseph Whedbee; border: 320' along Broad St on W, Water St on S, & lot 2 on E; lot has on it an old house 24' by 30', one "Do" 30' by 15', a small "Do", & several other small houses the property of said Whedbee; [signed] Jno Norcom, surveyor C C; South end of lot is sold to Selby Harney.

170. Apr. 15, 1787 surveyed lot 16 in the "old" plan in Edenton; formerly Dr. Benjamin Elleson's property and "for debt" was leased for one year to Dr. Robt Lenox and presently in possession of William Bennet esq; lot has "ellegant" dwelling house 2 story and very "roomly" and "part of" a very good garden; border: King St on S, lot 17 on W, Eden Alley on N, & lot 15 on E; [signed] Jno Norcom, surveyor C C; [on back] Capt. Wm Bennett £180.

171. Apr. 15, 1787 surveyed nearly 0.5 ac lot 17 in the "old" plan in Edenton; formerly Dr. Benjamin Elleson's property and "for debt" was leased "for years" to Dr. Robt Lenox and is presently in possession of William Bennet esq; lot has on it a kitchen, "smoak" house, & little house; border: King St on S, lot 18 on W, Eden Alley on N, & lot 16 on E; [signed] Jno Norcom, surveyor C C; [on back] £181.

172. Nov. 18, 1785 surveyed 0.5 ac lot 50 in the "old" plan in Edenton; formerly Mr. Honey's property; border: Queen St on N, lot 49 on W, lot 51 on E, & lot 28 on S; lot has no improvements; [signed] Jno Norcom, surveyor C C; [on back] John Pons.

173. Nov. 18, 1785 surveyed 0.5 ac lot 51 in the "old" plan in Edenton; formerly Mr. Honey's property; border: Oakum St on E, Queen St on N, lot 50 on W, & lot 29 on S; lot has no improvements; [signed] Jno Norcom, surveyor C C; [on back] John Pons.

174. Nov. 18, 1785 surveyed 0.5 ac lot 97 in the "new" plan in Edenton; formerly Clark & Weir's property; border: Queen St on S, Church St on N, lot 98 on W, & Granville St on E; lot has no improvements; [signed] Jno Norcom, surveyor C C; [on back] Michl Payne.

175. Nov. 18, 1785 surveyed 0.5 ac lot 98 in the "new" plan in Edenton; formerly Clark & Weir's property; border: Queen St on S, Church St on N, lot 99 on W, & lot 97 on E; [signed] Jno Norcom, surveyor C C; [on back] Michl Payne.

176. Nov. 18, 1785 surveyed 0.5 ac lot 119 in the "old" plan in Edenton; formerly Thomas Wright's property now in possession of William Summers; lot has a log house on it 20' by 15'; border: Gale St on S, Albermarl St on N, lot 118 on W, & lot 120 on E; plat shows lot is 320' deep; [signed] Jno Norcom, surveyor C C; [on back] John Mare.

177. Nov. 18, 1785 surveyed 0.5 ac lot 120 in the "old" plan in Edenton; formerly Thomas Wright's property; border: Gale St on S, Albemarl St on N, lot 119 on W, & lot 121 on E; lot has no improvements; plat shows lot is 66' by 320'; [signed] Jno Norcom, surveyor C C; [on back] John Mare.

178. Nov. 18, 1785 surveyed 0.5 ac lot 121 in the "old" plan in Edenton; formerly Thomas Wright's property; border: Gale St on S, Albermarl St on N, lot 120 on W, & lot 122 on E; lot has no improvements; plat shows lot is 320' deep; [signed] Jno Norcom, surveyor C C; [on back] Edmd Blount.

179. Nov. 18, 1785 surveyed nearly 0.5 ac in the "new" plan in Edenton; formerly Mr. John Henley's property; border: Eden Alley on S, Queen St on N, lot 200 on E, & lot 202 on W; lot has no improvements; plat shows lot is 305' deep; [signed] Jno Norcom, surveyor C C; [on back] Fredk Ramkey.

180. Nov. 18, 1785 surveyed near 0.5 ac in the "new" plan in Edenton; formerly Mr. John Henley's property; border: Eden Alley on S, Queen St on N, lot 201 on E, & lot 203 on W; lot has no improvements; plat shows lot is 305' deep; [signed] Jno Norcom, surveyor C C; [on back] Fredk Rankey [sic].

Sales of Confiscated Land

181. Nov. 18, 1785 surveyed near 0.5 ac in the "new" plant in Edenton; formerly Mr. John Henley's property; border: Eden Alley on S, Queen St on N, lot 202 on E, & lot 204 on W; lot has no improvements; plat shows lot is 305' deep; [signed] Jno Norcom, surveyor C C; [on back] Wm Boretz.

182. Nov. 18, 1785 surveyed near 0.5 ac in the "new" plat in Edenton; formerly Mr. John Henley's property; border: Eden Alley on S, Queen St on N, lot 203 on E, & lot 205 on W; lot has no improvements; plat shows lot is 305' deep; [signed] Jno Norcom, surveyor C C; [on back] William Littlejohn.

183. Sept. 20, 1786 surveyed 118 ac near Edenton; known [sic] as Henley's; includes "the" swamp; border: Mr. Wm Roberts' corner on edge of Matchacomack Creek Swamp, Mr. Joseph Blount, Wm Roberts' land known as Hall's, & runs up Matchacomack Cr; land has no improvements; [signed] Jno Norcom, surveyor C C; [on back] Wm Roberts.

184. Nov. 24, 1785 surveyed 216 ac on E side of Chowan R; formerly Thomas Coffield's property willed to him by his father Thomas Hoskins [sic] and now in possession of John Coffield jr; border: Job Parker's corner on the river, Deep Br, Michael Bonds, & Wm Jackson; land has about 50 ac of cleared land, an old house about 25' by 16' a square roof and some old log houses on it; in a "very good" place for fishing "the land very valuable"; [signed] Issacher Branch, D S C C; [on back] Nathan Lassiter.

CRAVEN COUNTY

185. [a deed] Mar. 15, 1780 John Daly, William Pasteur, & John Sitgreaves to Thomas & Titus Oglen, merchants (New Bern); for £6,950 sold 40' by 40' on Front St or SE part of lot 15 in New Bern; formerly Samuel Cornell's property; Craven Co Court appointed John Daly, William Pasteur, & John Sitgreaves, Commissioners of Confiscated Property due to Act of Assembly passed at New Bern in 1777 and Act passed at Halifax in 1779; the commissioners now "possess" the land which was sold Mar. 15 "instant". Signed John Daly, Will Pastaer, & Jno Sitgreaves. Witness Rd Cogdell jr & William Hannis jr. Wit. oath Jan. 1784 by William Hannis jr. Rec. Jul. 5, 1784 in Book 2N p. 224.

186. to Dr. William McClure:
a) storage of confiscated property, formerly belonging to Gov. Josiah Martin, from Mar. 1, 1786 to Jul. 1, 1787 or 16 months @ 40/ per month--£32.0
b) hire of hands and a boat for 3 days to remove the above property from the country to New Bern--£2.14
   [total] £34.14
sworn before John Davis, JP Dec. 12,1787
allowed £16 "only the Comt. of claims J D"; [on back] No. 15 Doc. Wm McClure £16.0; in the House Nov. 14, 1789, in the Senate Nov. 20, 1789, alld. £16

187. State of North Carolina in account with John Daly, William Pasteur, & John Sitgreaves, Craven Co Commissioners for selling Confiscated Property:
a) Jun. 26, 1786 to cash paid treasurer of Newbern Dist and per his rect filed this day--£35,000
b) Jul. 26 to "ditto" paid "ditto" as "ditto"--£20,200
c) [blank] to "ditto" paid "ditto" as "ditto"--£80,863.11.0 3/4
d) to each Commissioner's & sheriff's commission @ 2%--£11,831.12
   [total] £147,895.3. 3/4
e) Mar. 15, 1780 acct of sales of sundry pieced of land, lots, & hosues this day at public sale--£144.960
f) ballance of James Coores acct with Saml Cornell--£218.10
g) cash recd of Thos Ogden for oats formerly property of Samuel Cornell--£160
h) ballance of Spyers Singleton's acct with Saml Cornell--£2,556.13. 3/4
   [total] £147,895.3. 3/4

Dec. Court 1780 Craven Co. Account was settled, examined, & allowed in open Court. [signed] Chrisr. Neale, cc; "a true copy" from the original in Clerk's Office [signed] Chrisr Neale, cc.

Sales of Confiscated Land

188. State of North Carolina in account with Andrew Blanchard, John Daley, & William Pasteur, Craven Co Commissioners of Confiscated Property:

a) Oct. 11, 1779 cash paid Richard Cogdell, treasurer of Newbern Dist--£13,000

b) Nov. 23, 1779 cash paid "ditto ditto"--£20,335

c) Feb. 23, 1780 cash paid "ditto ditto"--£30,025.4

d) Mar. 9, 1780 cash paid "ditto ditto"--£20,000

above sums paid, see treasurer's receipts with the commissioners

e) Commissioner's commissions on amount of money credited--£6,810.18

f) sheriff's commissions for selling "etc"--£2,270.6   [total] £101,441.8

g) Mar. 1780 amount of sales and hire of confiscated property as per acct returned in Court this day--£113,516.5.11

-£101,441.8

balance due the State   £ 12,074.17.11.

[signed] Will Pasteur & John Daly. March Court 1780 settled in open court, [signed] Chrisr Neale, cc

h) John Daley, William Pasteur, & Andrew Blanchard, Commissioners to State of North Carolina:

Mar. 1780 balance of your acct settled to this Court--£12,074.17.11

Jun. 14, 1780 cash paid treasurer of Newbern Dist by receipt this day--£12,074.17.11

June Court 1780 settled in open Court; [signed] Chrisr Neale, cc; "true copy" of the original in the clerk's office [signed] Chrisr Neale, cc.

189. John Sitgreaves, Commissioner of Confiscated Property for Craven Co:

a) Aug. 20, 1780 cash received of Messrs. Richard Blackledge & Spyers Singleton for their bond & inerest due to Honl Saml Cornell--£5,750.5

b) cash received of Jacob Blount esq for his bond & interest due Saml Cornell--£629.16

c) cash received of William Blount esq for his bond & interest due Saml Cornell--£626.8

d) cash received of Benjamin Sheppard esq for his note & interest due Saml Cornell--£177.18.8

e) cash received of William Faircloth for his obligation & interest due Saml Cornell--£67

f) case received of James Glasgow for his obligation & interest due Saml Cornell--£85

g) cash received of James Wood for his note & interest due Saml Cornell--£63

[total] £7,399.7.8

h) amount brought over £7,399.7.8 "note" this sum received in Aug. 1780 is equal at 100 to 1 in specie to £73.19.10½

i) Mar. 20, 1783 cash paid into the treasury--$181.25 specie   £72.10.3

j)   commissions at 2% on £73.19.10½--£1.9.7½   [total] £73.19.10½

k) by amount of credits within--£73.19.10½

"errors excepted" [signed] Jno Sitgreaves; Apr. 2, 1783 the above amount was proved before Wm Speight, JP

190. State of North Carolina account with Jno C Bryan, Craven Co sheriff:

a) amount of debt due to Craven Co suit John Taylor & wife & "ots" vs Saml Cornell, June term 1783--£680.4.3

Court cost on the same--£2.12.3

sheriff's fees serving the same--£0.5.4

commissions--£17.1.4   [total] £700.3.2

b) amount of debt due to Craven Co Court suit Sarah Smith vs Saml Cornell, Dec. term 1782--£135

Court cost--£2.7.3

sheriff's service--£0.5.4

commissions--£3.8.4   [total] £141.0.11

c) [total of both suits] £ 841.4.11

balance due the state £ 348.15.11

£1,190.

d) amt of sales due to suit executed on land in town of Newbern lot No. 11 on Front St sold to Stanly & Green for £1,190 "debt paid plaintiff"--£1,190

Sales of Confiscated Land

by balance per contra--£348.15.11

191. Reciept No. 174 Jan. 27, 1786 to Messrs. Stanly & Green £50 towards £1,190 "granted" them by the General Assembly for amount they paid for a house & lot sold by John Council Bryan, Craven Co sheriff, to satisfy an execution against estate of Samuel Cornell.

192. Receipt No. 176 Jan. 27, 1786 to Messrs. Stanly & Green £50 towards £1,190 "granted" them by the General Assembly for amount they paid for a house & lot sold by John Council Bryan, Craven Co sheriff, to satisfy an execution against estate of Samuel Cornell.

193. Receipt [no number] Jun. 18, 1782 to Craven Co Commissioner of Confiscated Property to pay [Honorable--hole in page] Abner Nash esq, delegate of this State in Continental Congress, £400 specie from sale of houses, lots, & estate of late Samuel Cornel esq of Newbern.

194. Receipt. No. 108 Dec. 16, 1785 to James Gatlin £42 for one survey.

195. Dec. 10, 1785 surveyed 22 ac on S side of Nuce R & E side of Mosleys Cr; border: Blackledge's corner near Griffin's corn field and Loftin's old line; [signed] Jas Gatlin, surveyor; [on back] sold Dec. 15, 1785 to John Davis esq for £26 by James Armstrong, Newbern Dist. commr.

196. Dec. 10, 1785 surveyed 100 ac "by a warrant of" Richard Teers; on S side of Nuce R and E side of Mosleys Cr; border: Jno West's second corner, Grifin, Blackledge, & near an old tar kill bed; [signed] Jas Gatlin, surveyor; [on back] sold Dec. 15, 1785 to Wm Griffin for £51 by James Armstrong, Newbern Dist. comr.

197. Dec. 10, 1785 surveyed 22 ac for John Davis esq; formerly Richard Teer's property; on S side of Nuce R & E side of Mosleys Cr; border: Blackledge's corner near Griffin's corn field and Loftin's old line; [signed] Jas Gatlin, surveyor; [on back] sold [no date] to John Davis esq for £65 by James Armstrong, Newbern Dist. comr. [note: This plat and description same as No. 195 above].

198. May 28, 1787 surveyed 65 ac; formerly Robert Palmer's property; on N side of Nuce R & Contentnea Cr and on the path to Parry's ferry on great Contentnea Cr; border: Hardin's survey, on E side of Grindle Creek Bridge, Bexleys Swamp, Wm Bexley, & Joseph Harden; [signed] Jas Gatlin, surveyor; [on back] sold [no date] to John Coart esq for £25.5 by James Armstrong, comr.

199. May 28, 1787 surveyed 520 ac; formerly Ewd Brice Dobbs' property; for Robert Hunt on S side of Nuce R & on Jumping Run a branch of Batcheldrs [sic] Cr; border: the edge of "the" great pond and Dobbs' 15th corner; [signed] Jas Gatlin, surveyor; [on back] sold [no date] to Robert Hunt for £512 by James Armstrong, comr.

200. May 28, 1787 surveyed 100 ac; for Wm McClure on S side of Neuse R; includes part of the low grounds opposite Hollingsworth; border: Lewis Bryan, "the" side of a great swamp, & Sellenton's old field; [signed] Jas Gatlin, surveyor; [on back] sold [no date] to William McClure for £80 by James Armstrong, comr.

201. Dec. 12, 1785 surveyed 200 ac; formerly Thomas Brown's property; on N side of Nuce R & W side of Swift Cr; border: on N side of Popplar Br and Williams' patent; [signed] Jas Gatlin, surveyor; [on back] sold Dec. 15, 1785 to John Davis esq for £135 by James Armstrong, Newbern Dist. comr.

202. [no date] surveyed 0.5 ac lot No. 119 in New Bern on Front St & Queen St; formerly Samuel Cornell's property; plat shows lot is 107' 3" on Front St and 214' 6" on Queen St and at the corner of the two streets; sold [no date] to William Slade for £710 by James Armstrong, comr; [on back] "G M O" Jan. 1790

Sales of Confiscated Land

203. Mar. 20, 1783 surveyed 640 ac; formerly William Brimage's property; for Wright Stanley on S side of Neuse Cr and in the fork of Brice Cr; border: William Brimage's corner of land patented by Bazel Smith near William Shepard Foster's line, Great Br, & the lower end of "the" little pocoson; [signed] Jas Gatlin, surveyor. [no sale mentioned]

204. May 27, 1787 surveyed 640 ac; formerly Josiah Henrey Martin's property; for John W Standly on SW side of long lake "called the No Wt"; border: No Wt Lake at the Surveyrs' Camp and David Barran's fourth corner; [signed] Jas Gatlin, surveyor; [on back] sold [no date] to John Wright Stanley for £641 by James Armstrong, comr.

205. Oct. 21, 1790 surveyed 336 ac; formerly Francis Christancy Dobbs' property; for Wright Stanley; being 3 islands in Neuse R: (1) between Mr. Fonveille's survey on N side of the river & Mr. Dayley's on S side of the river and (2) & (3) between a former survey of "her" own on N and survey formerly Hennis' and Mr. Fomveille's [sic] "plantation"; [signed] Jas Gatlin, surveyor; plat also shows Greens Thirrefare and Kemps thirrefare; sold [no date] to W Stanley for £75 by "the commissioner".

206. Jun. 26, 1787 surveyed 640 ac formerly Francs. Christina Dobbs' property; for John W Stanley esq; on N side of Nuse R; border: the upper corner of said Dobbs' survey on said river, a road, Therrifare R, & the mouth of Pinetree Cr; [signed] Jas Gatlin, surveyor; chain bearers Charles Taylor & Jesse Taylor; [on back] sold [no date] to John W Stanly esq for £881 by James Armstrong, comr.

207. Jul. 27, 1787 surveyed 225 ac; part of 875 ac formerly Frances Christina Dobbs' property; for John W Stanly esq; on N side of Nuse R; border: Therrifare R, the mouth of Pinetree Cr, his "last" corner of his 640 ac "grant", & a road; [signed] Jas Gatlin, surveyor; [on back] chain bearers Chars Taylor & Jesse Taylor; sold [no date] to John W Stanly for £300.1 by James Armstrong, comr.

208. Aug. 15, 1787 surveyed 0.5 ac lot No. 16 in Newbern on Front St; formerly Patrick Cleary's property; surveyed by order of James Armstrong, commissioner; lot is 6.5 poles by 13 poles back; [signed] Jas Gatlin, surveyor; [on back] sold [no date] to John Craddock for £3,975.

209. [no date] surveyed N half of "Front" lot No. 7 in New Bern on E side of Front St; formerly Saml Cornell's property; border: James Davis on S, John Fonveille on N, Front St on W, & chanell of Neuse R on E; includes a brick still house thereon; plat says "James Davis' half of lot 7"; [signed] Jas Gatlin, surveyor; sold [no date] to William Slade for £580.

210. Nov. 20, 1793 surveyed 75 ac; formerly Thos Tarrans' property; for Jacob Rhem on S side of Neuse R; border: on S side of Juniper Swamp "on the Snow Hills" and Beeton; [signed] George Lane, surveyor; sold [no date] Jacob Rhem for £50.

211. May 27, 1787 surveyed 640 ac; for John Benners on S side of Nuse R & at the head of Clubfoots Cr; border: the mouth of the smallest gut on E side of the creek "against" Indian Landing and the head of the small gut; [signed] Jas Gatlin, surveyor; [on back] sold [no date] to John Brenners esq for £1,471 by James Armstrong, comr.

212. Jun. 13, 1786 surveyed lot 256 which fronts on Broad St and lot 259 which fronts on New St; adjoining lots in Newborne [sic]; formerly Martain [sic] Howard's property; for Mrs. Elizabeth Cook on Broad St, Hancock St, & New St; border: corner of Broad & Hancock Streets at Mrs. Cook's corner, runs 26 poles on Hancock St to New St, 6.5 poles 4 links on New St, 26 poles on Broad St, & to the beginning; [signed] Jas Gatlin, surveyor; [on back] sold [no date] to Elizabeth Cook for £1,100 "mortgage right" of late Martin Howard & improvements by James Armstrong, Newbern Dist. comr.

213. May 28, 1787 surveyed 640 ac; formerly Edwd Brice Dobbs' property; for James Mccaferty [sic] on N side of Neuse R and W side of Swifts Cr; border: Josiah Rigway's corner at the creek and John Fonville; [signed] Jas Gatlin, surveyor; [on back] sold [no date] to James McCafferty for £404 by James Armstrong, comr.

Sales of Confiscated Land

CURRITUCK COUNTY

214. Report of Currituck Co Commissioners: William Ferebee, James Ryan, & John Humphries:

a) Mar. 25, 1780 took possession of Negro fellow late property of James Richardson of Virginia "who attached himself with the enemy & went with them";

b) Apr. 22 took possession of remainder of the estate of Thomas MacKnight & Co consisting of books & other publishable article; and £250 debt due "one" Owens, absentee, from Mr. James Ryan;

c) Apr. 29 took possession of Francis Williamson's estate, late of this county, but said Williamson leaving the estate under the "Indulgence of the Law", had conveyed his whole estate to Thomas King and Jonathan Hearing;

d) "May" took possession of lands, tenements, etc of late Thos MacKnight & Co in this county; surveyed, plotted, & divided them in "several convient" lots;

e) June Court--the above mentioned property being advertised "agreeable to law" and intended for sale, the Court forbid the sale due to claim of Mr. Alexr Diake, in behalf of widow of William Aytchesson decd, for a third of the estate of Thos McKnight by "articles of coparienary", except a Negro man sold for £3,000 and claim of Thomas King & Jonathan Hearing, for all the estate of Francis Williamson "as appeared by deeds & other" conveyances;

f) Having Court's advice about letting out land of Thomas MacKnight & Co, it was thought "most" for the public's benefit to rent them for coin due to the rapid depreciation of currency and "great call for provisions in several camps", so we rented them:

Jan. 5, 1781 for year 1781 for 70 barrels of corn

Jan. 1, 1782 for year 1782 for 78 barrels of corn

"Sept." All the estate of Thomas MacKnight & Co was taken out of our hands due to "sundry" executions from superior & inferior courts; see attached list of sale. Obligations for above mentioned corn weren't met, so suits have been filed in county court and are yet undetermined; "the notes" are filed in the "office thereof". And received from the trustees of said estate £2,120 from vendues, rents of land, etc;

g) Geo Powers, sheriff in account with estate of Thos MacKnight:

debit Oct. 17, 1782 to sundry books etc £244.6.8

	a tract of land	£450
	a tract of land	£611
	a tract of land	£500
	a tract of land	£500
Nov. 27	a tract of land	£ 80
	a tract of land	£152
	a tract of land	£ 87
	a tract of land	£ 75.5
	"sundries"	£ 10.8
Jan. 17, 1783	a tract of land	£140 [total] £2,899.19 [sic]

credit:

by Jno Humphries Ec on	£113.3.7	by J Iredell's Ec	£466.3
by J Gregory's Ec	£322.0.3	by M Cumming's Ec	£ 33.19.8
by Warner's Admr Ec	£638.11	by H Williams Ec	£ 18.19.6
by M Wilson's Ec	£258.19.11	by F Blount's admr Ec	£ 20.15.3
by H Abbott's Ec	£ 17.6.3	by M Ferebee's Ec	£ 46.10,11
by D Burges's Ec	£16.2.9	by A Lindsey's Ec	£161.2
by Nash's Ecetr Ec	£ 15.13.3	by A McGowen's Ec	£261.5.4
by Scavill's Ec	£ 45.6.3	by Dauge's Ecetr Ec	£ 30.8.11
Thos Humphries Ec	£206.19.10	shff's comm.	£ 75.1.7
		[total]	£2,747.5.3
		J Gregory Ec	£132.19.3
		shff's comm.	£ 3.16.10
		[total]	£2,884.1.4
		J Perkins' Ec	£ 15.8.6
		[total]	£2,899.19.0

[signed] George Powers, sheriff;

h) [no date] took possession of a Negro girl, a small piece of poor land, 3 cattle--late property of John Bennet, who "attached himself to the enemy"; said estate being judged by the Court barely able to support Bennet's wife & family "which was appropriated acordingly";

i) This being "a full state" of all such estates that came under our care and the manner of disposing thereof:

The State of North Carolina to Currituck Co Commissioners:

debit 1780 cash paid to Treasurer	£798.6.8	
Commission on sale of Negro	£180.0	
"bale" in certificates	£2,095.16	
1782 cash paid to Treasurer	£2,120.0	[total] £5,194.2.8

credit amount of sales of a Negro fellow	£3,000.0	
cash received from Justices	£2,120.0	[total] £5,120.0
cash recd from Jas Ryan	£ 50.0	[total] £5,170.0
balance due	£ 24.2.8	[total] £5,194.2.8

[signed] James Ryan & John Humphries "surviving" Commissioners
Sept. term 1783--report made in court [signed] Wm Ferebee, c c.

215. State of North Carolina to Currituck Co Commissioners:
1780   25 days each in "discharge of our duty" @ 16/ per day   £60.0
          expence for finding 2 surveyors & 2 chain bearers 6 days @ 6/ each per day   £12.12
          cash paid for advertising land   £8.0
          cash paid surveyors for surveying & dividing land in 9 lots @ 32/ each   £14.8
          cash paid chain bearers for 6 days @ 8/ each per day   £4.16   [total] £99.16
[signed] Jas Ryan & Jno Humphries, "surviving" Commissioners; "a true copy" [signed] Wm Ferebee, c c.

216. Feb. 21, 1782 Wm Skinner, Edenton Dist Treasurer, received £2,120 from William Ferebee esq, Currituck Co Commissioner for Disposing Confiscated Property.

217. Apr. 3, 1782 W Skinner, Treasurer, recieved £960 from James Ryan esq, Currituck Co Commissioner for Disposing Confiscated Property.

218. Oct. 25, 1781 W Skinner, Edenton Dist Treasurer, received £2,035.4 from James Ryan esq, Currituck Co Commissioner for Disposing of Confiscated Property; [on back] "charged of £798.6.8 calculated by scale".

219. Receipt No. 305 Oct. 12, 1785 to Josiah Nichols, Currituck Co surveyor, £0.40 for one survey.

220. Aug. 26, 1786 surveyed 129.75 ac; formerly John Bennett's property; in Moyock Dist of Currituck Co; border: Nancy Dauge, James Ferebee, Goodman, & Bright; [signed] Josiah Nicholson, C surveyor; chain bearers George Powers & John Northern; [on back] Griffith Douge.

DOBBS COUNTY
221. Dobbs Co Commissioners of Confiscated Property: Charles Markland, John Herritage, & Richard Caswell the younger, to State of North Carolina:

Apr. 1783   "so much" due, condemned by County Court, from Wm Blount esq, adm
          of Gilbert Kerr decd   £314.14.1½
          "do do" from Jesse Cobb as debtor to Commins, Warwick & Co   £200
                              John Alexander   £392.0.4½
                              [total]   £592.0.4½
          "do do" from Thomas Williams as "do" to Hamilton & Co   £129
                              10 yrs interest   £ 77.7.6
                              to Saml Cornell   £168.0
                              with 9.5 years interest   £ 90.4.3

Sales of Confiscated Land

[total]   £465.1.9

"do do" from Benja Exum as "do"

to John Hamilton & Co	£ 60.0 by bond on interest
John Wallis & Co	£530.0 by bond on interest
James Gibson & Co	£1,000. part of which by bond with interest
George Miller	£ 72.15.8 with 6 years interest £26.4
Saml Cornell	£ <u>7.10</u>
[total]	£1,696.9.8

"do do" from Benjamin Shepperd as debtor to Hamilton & Co   £650

"do do" from John Sheppard   £120 "and to"

Saml Cornell	£129 [total] £249.0
with 8 years interest	£119.10 [total] £368.10

"do do" from John Herritage as a debtor to Geo Miller   £140.0

with 6 years interest	£ 50.8 [total] £190.8

"do" from Wm Faircloth as "do" to Geo Miller   £16.0

with 6 years interest	£5.15 [total] £21.15

[grand total] £3,713.18.11

222. [no date] "A few days" since Dobbs Co Commissioners presented accounts of debts due from sundry individuals to persons prescribed in the confiscation law "and presented certificates for payment"; but due to a resolve passed "last Assembly implying no suits against others who also owed", I refused to take the certificates; but if I'm wrong, I will be glad for your instructions on the matter; "I am your Excellencies obd" [not signed]; [random numbers on the back of the sheet].

223. Receipt No. 319 Nov. 9, 1786 to Charles Markland, Dobbs Co surveyor, £32 for 16 surveys.

224. Receipt No. 29 Dec. 22, 1791 to John Holliday, Dobbs Co surveyor, £6 for 3 surveys.

225. [no date] surveyed 150 ac in Dobbs formerly Johnston Co; part of 193 ac granted Nov. 26, 1757 to Thomas Dick and confiscated as his property; the remainder of the grant is in the bounds of earlier grants; on N side of Neuse R and E side of Atkin Br; border: John Linton, Richard Caswell, Mr. Herritage, Job Ives' grant now in possession of Isaac Ingram, Dick, & William Williams' land now Joshua Croom; [signed] C Markland, surveyor; chain bearers Samuel Caswell & John Caswell; sold to Richard Caswell; [on back] 1787

226. [no date] surveyed 400 ac for Richard Caswell; in Dobbs formerly Craven Co; granted Nov. 17, 1738 to James Mackilwean who sold it to late Gov. Dobbs & by heirs of Gov. Dobbs "forfieted and confiscated"; on N side of Neuse R; border: Doctor Stringer; [signed] C Markland, surveyor; chain bearers Saml Caswell & J S Mackilwean.

227. Jul. 23, 1790 surveyed 200 ac for Moses Standley; formerly Thomas Torrans' property; on both sides of Trent R; includes the place called Wm Gray's folly; [signed] Jno Holliday, surveyor; chain bearers John Erwin & John Gray.

228. Oct. 20, 1790 surveyed 200 ac for Jesse Cobb; formerly Thomas Torrans' property; on S side of "the South West" and S side of Neuse R; border: Samuel Thomas & Richard Caswell; [signed] Jno Holliday, surveyor; chain bearers Francis McIlwean & Wm Goodman; [on back] 4 [Nos. 225 through 228] confiscated plans for Dobbs G M O Nov. 1790 at Fayetteville.

229. Jul. 23, 1790 surveyed 200 ac for Jesse Cobb; formerly Thomas Torrans' property; on N side of Trent R above Browns Br; border: "the" side of the river marsh at David George's lower corner; [signed] Jno Holliday, surveyor; chain bearers Edward Erwin & Joseph Gray.

230. Jul. 24, 1790 surveyed 197 ac for Jesse Cob; formerly Thomas Torrans' property; on S side of a prong of Great Br; [signed] Jno Holliday, surveyor; chain bearers Windal Davis & John Smith.

Sales of Confiscated Land

DUPLIN COUNTY

231. a bond Sept. 23, 1779 James Kinan, James Gillaspe, Charles Ward, Andrew McIntire, [Joseph Dickson--lined out] John Molten, William Dickson, & James James (all of Duplin Co) to Gov. Richard Caswell for £250,000; bond is for James Kinan, James Gillaspie, & Charles Ward serving as Commissioner of Confiscated Property. [signed] Jas Kinan, Jams Gellespie, Charles Ward, Andw McIntire, John Molten, Wm Dickson, & James James. Witness Joseph Dickson & David Smyth.

232. Receipt No. 244 May 16, 1786 to Joseph Dickson, Duplin Co surveyor, £24 for 9 surveys in Duplin Co and 3 surveys in New Hanover Co; [on back] Jun. 3, 1786 recd the contents in full from Wm Wells, collector, [signed] Jo Dickson.

233. Apr. 5, 1785 surveyed 400 ac; formerly property of Frederick Grigg esq, merchant of Wilmington; on E side of NE Cape Fear R; border: Grigg's & Wilson's corner pine on Butcher's Bluff, an old patent, a pine 20 poles E of a road, & Jesper Cox's corner now Suffield's; [signed] Jo Dickson, surveyor; [on back] No. 6 Jos T Rhodes.

234. May 24, 1785 surveyed 640 ac; formerly William Tryon esq's property; being the lower or SE part of 1,000 ac granted to Wm McRee esq; border: a corner of the old patent and Jesse George; [signed] Jo Dickson, surveyor; [on back] No. 1 Wm Jones.

235. May 24, 1785 surveyed 585 ac; formerly William Tryon esq's property; on N side of Rockfish Cr; border: a cypress about 50 yards below the mouth of Cummins Cr and a pocoson; [signed] Jo Dickson, surveyor; [on back] No. 2 Curtis Ivey & G J McRee.

236. May 24, 1785 surveyed 555 ac; formerly William Tryon esq's property; on N side of Rockfish Cr; border: the lower corner of another survey that "lies above" and a pocoson; [signed] Jo Dickson, surveyor; [on back] No. 3 Curtis Ivey & G J McRee.

237. May 24, 1785 [signed] Jo Dickson, surveyor; 540 ac; formerly William Tryon esq's property; being the upper or NW part of 1,000 ac granted to Wm McRee esq; border: a corner of the old patent "a little" E of a road, a pine "a little" W of the road, & an old field; [signed] Jo Dickson, surveyor; [on back] No. 4 Wm Jones.

238. May 25, 1785 surveyed 60 ac; formerly William Tryon esq's property; on both sides of the public road by Rockfish Bridge; border: Sampson's old corner on N side of Rockfish Cr, a corner of "the" Hickory Hill land, between two ponds near the bridge, & a cypress on the creek about 50 yards below the mouth of Rockfish Cr; [signed] Jo Dickson, surveyor; [on back] No. 7 David Jones.

239. May 25, 1785 surveyed 640 ac; formerly William Tryon esq's property; in the fork of NE Cape Fear R and Rockfish Cr; border: the lower corner of another survey on Rockfish Cr about a mile above the mouth of the creek and runs on NE Cape Fear R; [signed] Jo Dickson, surveyor; [on back] No. 5 Curtis Ivey & Griffith J McRee.

EDGECOMBE COUNTY

240. a petition by Richard Blackledge to the Legislative Committee of Claims: on Sept. 26, 1785, [hole in page, "he" ?] purchased from Col. Nicholas Long, Halifax Dist. Commissioner of Confiscated Property, lot 80 in town of Tarborough for £1,160 certificates at 12 months; formerly William McClennan's property. The sum was paid--see Nicholas Long's statement to the Treasurer. Blackledge sold the lot to Barbara Hill (of Tarborough) for which she gave a bond of $750. A suit was started by John Simpson on the bond. There's been a judgment and an injunction to Barbara Hill on the judgment. Barbara says the lot belongs to her children--see deed Jun. 28, 1777 by William McClennan to her deceased husband James Hill, and the title she held from Blackldge is no good; "which" was answered by Blackledge and Simpson. The last decree was that the injunction should be perpetual and Blackledge & Simpson to pay the cost, heirs of James Hill should "reconvey" to Blackledge all their right from Barbara Hill which they have done, & Blackledge now has only a title from the State.

Sales of Confiscated Land

The committee decides the State had no title, Blackledge is to be refunded the purchase money agreeable to an act in 1791 which says for the certificates to be paid at the rate of £0.4 per pound with interest from payment date "which appears" to have been Sept. 26, 1786 [sic], & Blackledge is allowed cost of the suits at a future date since he doesn't have the vouchers at this time; the following resolution proposed: Public Treasurer is to pay Richard Blackledge £401.7 principal and interest on said certificate agreeable to an act in 1791. [signed] James Marshall, chairman; in the Senate Dec. 20, 1798 concur; in House of Commons Dec. 22, 1798 concur.

241. Receipt No. 116 Dec. 17, 1785 to Benjamin Dicken, Edgecombe Co surveyor, £48 for surveying 7 tracts and 17 town lots.

242. Receipt No. 327 No. 23, 1786 to Benjamin Dicken, Edgecombe Co surveyor, £4 for 2 surveys.

243. two lists both dated Sept. 26, 1785: Account of sale of property "suggested" to be confiscated in Edgecomb Co:
a) 460 ac on a branch of Hendrick's Mill Cr, sold by Acquilla Sugg to Anthony Bacon; bought by Edward Hall for £784 in bond;
b) 100 ac on N side of Tar R, sold by Acquilla Sugg to Anthony Bacon; bought by Solomon Sessums for £212 in bond;
c) 150 ac on Town Cr; bought by Amos Johnston for £411 in certificates;
d) 320 ac on Town Cr, sold by J Vickers to Jos Ruffin; bought by Charles Jerrard for £752 in certifictes;
e) 100 ac on N side of Town Cr, sold by J Vickers to Joseph Ruffin; bought by Noah Sugg for £201 in certificates;
f) lot 1 in Tarborough, "drawn" by Timothy Nicholson; bought by Abner Roberston for £70 [this lot mentioned on only one list];
g) lot 117 in Tarborough, "drawn" by Timothy Nicholson; bought by Richard Blackledge for £76 in bonds;
h) lot 16 in Tarborough, "drawn" by Robert McKey; bought by John Ingles for £252 in certificates;
i) lot 16 in Tarborough, "drawn" by Andrew Little, claimed by his orphans "at" Edenton and sold for them "by" Richard Blackledge; bought by Richard Blackledge for £7 in bonds;
j) lot 44 in Tarborough, "drawn" by Andrew Little, claimed by his orphans "at" Edenton and sold for them "by" Richard Blackledge; bought by Richard Blackledge for £5 in bonds;
k) lot 101 in Tarborough, "drawn" by William Lowther; bought by John Gray Blount for £580 in certificates;
l) lot 100 in Tarborough, "drawn" by William Lowther, late property of William McLellan; bought by John Gray Blount for £302 in certificates;
m) lot 48 in Tarborough, "drawn" by James Moire; bought by William Tutom for £406 in certificates;
n) lot 73 in Tarborough, "drawn" by James Moire; bought by James Armstrong for £210 in bonds;
o) lot 8 in Tarborough, "drawn" by John Agan [or Ager]; bought by Edward Hall for £40 in bonds;
p) 100 ac on N side of Tar R, sold by William McLellan to James Hill; bought by Barbary Hill for £705 in bonds;
q) 50 ac on N side of Tar R, sold by William McLellan to James Hill; bought by Edward Hall for £760.10 in bonds;
r) lot 78 in Tarborough, sold by William McLellan to Jas Hill; bought by Jonathan Loomiss [or Loomass] for £130 in bonds;
s) lot 79 in Tarborough; bought by Jonathan Loomiss [or Loomass] for £325 in bonds;
t) lot 80 in Tarborough; bought by Richard Blackledge for £1,160 in bonds;
u) lot 91 in Tarborough; bought by Edward Hall for £600 in bonds;
v) lot 3 [in Tarborough ?], "drawn" by Joseph Turton; bought by Archd Thompson for £53 in bonds;
w) lot 107 [in Tarborough ?], "drawn" by Joseph Turton; bought by Richard Blackledge for £33.
[total] £2,904 in certificates and £5,110.10 [or £5,180.10] in bonds for [grand total] £8,004.10 [or £8,074.10]. [difference in total is item (f) being on one list & not the other list]

244. [no date] surveyed 460 ac; sold by Aquilla Sugg to Anthony Bacon of Great Britain; border: William Davis's corner on a branch of Hendrick's Cr, William Sugg, & Robert Humphries; [signed] Benjamin Dicken, C surveyor; [on back] Edwd Hall.

Sales of Confiscated Land

245. Jun. 26, 1785 surveyed 123 ac; sold by Aquilla Sugg to Anthony Bacon of Great Britain "for" 150 ac; on N side of Town Cr; border: John Hurod's corner on the creek, Tanton's line, & Tanton's Br; [signed] Benjamin Dicken, C surveyor; chain bearers John Nettle & Wm George; [on back] Amos Johnston.

246. Jun. 28, 1785 surveyed 114.5 ac; sold by Benjamin Vickers to John Vickers who sold to Joseph Pender "for" 100 ac; on S side of Town Cr; border: mouth of Farmer's Br at Town Cr; [signed] Benjamin Dicken, C surveyor; chain bearers Joseph Ruffin & Arthur Lee; [on back] Noah Sugg.

247. Jun. 28, 1785 surveyed 400 ac; sold by Benjmain Vickers to John Vickers who sold to Joseph Ruffin "for" 320 ac on S side of Town Cr; border: runs up Fort Br and along "the" back line; [signed] Benjamin Dicken, C surveyor; [on back] Chas Garret.

248. Jul. 7, 1785 surveyed 78 ac; sold by Aquilla Sugg to Anthony Bacon of Great Britain "for" 100 ac; on N side of Tar R; border: Richard Sessum's corner near Chuks [or Checks] Mill Cr, the head of Bearskin Swash, Indian Cr, & Thomas Spell; [signed] Benjamin Dicken, C surveyor; chain bearers Grisham Coffield & John Lackey; [on back] Solo Sessums.

249. Sept. 13, 1785 surveyed 135 ac; sold by Wm McClellan to James Hill decd; on N side of Tar R; border: the mouth of Great Br at the river, Mill Br, & Edward Hall; [signed] Benjamin Dicken, C surveyor; [on back] Edwd Hall.

250. Sept. 21, 1785 surveyed 246 ac; sold by Wm McClellan to James Hill decd "for" 100 ac; on N side of Tar R; border: Thomas H Hall's corner in William Usher's line, runs down Mill Br, Thomas Newsom, & up Indian Cr; [signed] Benjamin Dicken, C surveyor; chain bearers William George & James Dicken; [on back] Barbary Hill £705.

251. Apr. 27, 1786 surveyed 225 ac; sold by Alexander Godwin to John Deloach; on N side of Homney Swamp; [signed] Benjamin Dicken, C surveyor; [on back] Andrew Greer.

252. Jun. 23, 1786 surveyed lot 1 in Tarborough on St. John St; drawn by Timothy Nicholson "a subject of Great Britain"; sold by Halifax Dist. Commissioner of Confiscated Property to Abner Robinson; 152.5' by 152.5'; [signed] Benjamin Dicken, C surveyor; [on back] "17 grants for Confiscated Town Lotts in Tarborough".

253. Jun. 23, 1786 surveyed lot 3 in Tarborough; the corner lot where St. James St crosses Trade St; drawn by Joseph Turton "a subject of Great Britain"; sold by Halifax Dist. Commissioner of Confiscated Property to Archibald Thompson; 152.5' by 152.5'; [signed] Benjamin Dicken, C surveyor.

254. Jun. 23, 1786 surveyed lot 16 in Tarborough; the corner lot where St. James St crosses St Georges St; drawn by Robert Mackie "a subject of Great Britain"; sold by Halifax Dist. Commissioner of Confiscated Property to John Ingles; [signed] Benjamin Dicken, C surveyor.

255. Jun. 23, 1786 surveyed lot 42 in Tarborough; on the "lower" side of Church St where it crosses St. Patricks St; drawn by Andrew Little "a subject of Great Britain"; sold by Halifax Dist. Commissioner of Confiscated Property to Andw Little decd; 152.5 by 152.5'; [signed] Benjamin Dicken, C surveyor; plat shows the streets.

256. Jun. 23, 1786 surveyed lot 44 in Tarborough; on the "lower" side of Church St where it crosses St. David's St; drawn by Andrew Little "a subject of Great Britain"; sold by Halifax Dist. Commissioner of Confiscated Property to orphans of Andw Little; 152.5' by 152.5'; [signed] Benjamin Dicken, C surveyor; plat shows the streets.

257. Jun. 23, 1786 surveyed lot 48 in Tarborough; on the "upper" side of St. James St where it crosses St. George St; drawn by James Moire; sold by Halifax Dist. Commissioner of Confiscated Property to William Tuton; 152.5' by 152.5'; [signed] Benjamin Dicken, C surveyor; plat shows the streets.

Sales of Confiscated Land

258. Jun. 23, 1786 surveyed lot 73 in Tarborough; on the "upper" side of Pitt St where it crosses Andrews St; drawn by James Moire; sold by Halifax Dist. Commissioner of Confiscated Property to James Armstrong; 152.5' by 152.5'; [signed] Benjamin Dicken, C surveyor; plat shows the streets.

259. Jun. 23, 1786 surveyed lot 78 in Tarborough; on the "lower" side of Pitt St; sold by William McClellan to James Hill; border: Back St next to Holleys Cr; sold by Halifax Dist. Commissioner of Confiscated Property to Jonathan Loomiss; 152.5' by 152.5'; [signed] Benjamin Dicken, C surveyor; plat shows the two streets; [on back] Jonathan Loomass [sic].

260. Jun. 23, 1786 surveyed lot 79 in Tarborough; the corner lot on the "lower" side of Pitt St where Pitt St crosses Trade St; sold by William McClellan to James Hill; sold by Halifax Dist. Commissioner of Confiscated Property to Jonathan Loomiss; 152.5' by 152.5'; [signed] Benjamin Dicken, C surveyor; plat shows the streets; [on back] Jonathan Loomass [sic].

261. Jun. 23, 1786 surveyed lot 80 in Tarborough; on the "lower" side of Pitt St where it crosses Trade St; sold by William McClellan to James Hill; sold by Halifax Dist. Commissioner of Confiscated Property to Richard Blackledge; 152.5' by 152.5'; [signed] Benjamin Dicken, C surveyor; plat shows the streets.

262. Jun. 23, 1786 surveyed lot 91 in Tarborough; on the "upper" side of Granvil St where it crosses Trade St; sold by William McClellan to James Hill; sold by Halifax Dist. Commissioner of Confiscated Property to Edward Hall; 152.5' by 152.5'; [signed] Benjamin Dicken, C surveyor; plat shows the streets.

263. Jun. 23, 1786 surveyed lot 100 in Tarborough; on the "lower" side of Granvil St; lot was "left by" William McClellan "a subject of Great Britain"; border: Back St next to Holleys Cr; sold by Halifax Dist. Commissioner of Confiscated Property to Jno Gray Blount; 152.5' by 152.5'; [signed] Benjamin Dicken, C surveyor; plat shows the two streets.

264. Jun. 23, 1786 surveyed lot 101 in Tarborough; on the "lower" side of Granvil St where it crosses Trade St; drawn by William Lowther "a subject of Great Britain"; sold by Halifax Dist. Commissioner of Confiscated Property to Jno Gray Blount; 152.5' by 152.5'; [signed] Benjamin Dicken, C surveyor; plat shows the streets.

265. Jun. 23, 1786 surveyed lot 107 in Tarborough; on the "lower" side of Granvil St where it crosses St. Patricks St; drawn by Joseph Turton "a subject of Great Britain"; sold by Halifax Dist. Commissioner of Confiscated Property to Richard Blackledge; 152.5' by 152.5'; [signed] Benjamin Dicken, C surveyor; plat shows the streets.

266. Jun. 23, 1786 surveyed lot 117 in Tarborough; on St. Andrews St; drawn by Timothy Nicholson "a subject of Great Britain"; sold by Halifax Dist. Commissioner of Confiscated Property to Richard Blackledge; 152.5' by 152.5'; [signed] Benjamin Dicken, C surveyor; plat shows the street.

GRANVILLE COUNTY
267. a petition by Jeremiah Bullock to Legislative Committee of Propo. & Grievances: the peitioner paid £95 for 154.25 ac, tract No. 41, sold by Commissioner of Confiscated Property; he never obtained a title. So the committee recommends the Granville Co surveyor make a plat of said land and send the plat to Secretary of State who shall issue a grant for it to the petitioner. [signed] Is Guion, chairman; in House of Commons Dec. 21, 1793 concur; in Senate Dec. 21, 1793 concur.

268. Receipt No. 299 Sept. 28, 1786 to Micajah Bullock, Granville Co surveyor, £90 for 45 surveys.

269. Mar. 1788 Accounts of sales of Granville Co Confiscated Property:
a) no. 1--270 ac on Picture Br; formerly H E McCulloch's land; bought by James Forsyth for £140;
b) no. 34--246 ac on Ledge of Rocks Cr; formerly H E McCulloch's land; bought by Howell Lewis for £290;
c) no. 35--321 ac on B Dam Cr; formerly H E McCulloch's land; bought by Howell Lewis for £353;

Sales of Confiscated Land

d) no. 28--236 ac on Smith Cr; formerly H E McCulloch's land; bought by B McCulloch for £323;

e) no. 26--129 ac on Smith Cr; formerly H E McCulloch's land; bought by Jeremiah Baily for £141;

f) no. 30--241 ac on Beavr Dam Cr; formerly H E McCulloch's land; bought by B McCulloch for £270;

g) no. 10--283 ac; formerly H E McCulloch's land; bought by Phil Hawkins for £55;

h) no. 43--217 ac on Ledge of Rock [sic] Cr; formerly H E McCulloch's land; bought by Charles Turner for £70;

i) no. 38--97 ac on Br Dam Cr; formerly H E McCulloch's land; bought by George Taylor for £76.6;

j) no. 12--255 ac on Ceder Cr; formerly H E McCulloch's land; bought by Elijah Parker for £305.10;

k) no. 11--320 ac; formerly H E McCulloch's land; bought by Phil Hawkins for £253.10;

l) no. 8--310 ac; formerly H E McCulloch's land; bought by Phil Hawkins for £200.

m) no. 5--307 ac on Ceder Cr; formerly H E McCulloch's land; bought by Reuben Tully for £301;

n) no. 45--175 ac; formerly H E McCulloch's land; bought by Israel Eastwood for £131;

o) No. 9--225 ac on Ceder Cr; formerly H E McCulloch's land; bought by George Parker for £251;

p) no. 33--127 ac; formerly H E McCulloch's land; bought by Phil Hawkins for £201;

q) no. 36--180 ac; formerly H E McCulloch's land; bought by Howell Lewis for £180;

r) no. 37--214 ac; formerly H E McCulloch's land; bought by Howell Lewis for £255.10;

s) no. 32--75 ac on Smith Cr; formerly H E McCulloch's land; bought by John Hooker for £135;

t) no. 39--126 ac; formerly H E McCulloch's land; bought by Howell Lewis for £120;

u) no. 4--300 ac on Ledge of Rocks Cr; formerly H E McCulloch's land; bought by John Brown for £260;

v) no. 6--365 ac; formerly H E McCulloch's land; bought by Phil Hawkins for £111;

w) no. 25--345 ac on Swift Cr; formerly H E McCulloch's land; bought by Jeremiah Baley for £221;   [total for a through w = £4,643.16]

x) no. 44--240 ac; formerly H E McCulloch's land; bought by Joseph Ellis for £160;

[total] a through x = £4,803.16 + £1,068.6.9 + £327.1 = £6,199.3.9

[on back] lands sold by A Lytle Hillsboough Dist Commissioner

270. May 27, 1786 surveyed 270 ac; formerly Henry Eustace McCulloch's property; on the drains of Picture Br & on both sides of "the" main road; border: Townsend & Job Green; [signed] Micajah Bullock, surveyor; sworn chain carriers John Williams & Edmun Cernes; sold Mar. 1788 to Saml Parker for £140 by Archd Lytle, Com; [on back] No. 1.

271. Jun. 1, 1786 surveyed 307 ac; formerly Henry Eustace McCulloch's property; on the drains of Ceder Cr; border: Joseph Cash, a large meadow, & Bullock; [signed] Micajah Bullock, surveyor; sworn chain carriers John Williams & Edmun Cernes; [on back] sold Mar. 1788 to Reuben Tally [or Taylor] for £301 by Archd Lytle, Com; No. 5.

272. Jun. 1, 1786 surveyed 225 ac; formerly Henry Eustace McCulloch's property; on E side of Cedar Cr; border: Thomas Clement an Grant; [signed] Micajah Bullock, surveyor; sworn chain carriers John Williams & Edmund Carns; sold Mar. 1788 to Samuel Parker for £251 by Archd Lytle, Com; [on back] No. 9.

273. Jun. 1, 1786 surveyed 255 ac; formerly Henry Eustace McCulloch's property; on both sides of Cedar Cr; border: Clement and West corner; [signed] Micajah Bullock, surveyor; sworn chain carriers John Williams & Edmund Carns; [on back] Mar. 1788 sold to Samuel Parker for £305.10 by Archd Lytle, Comr; No. 12.

274. Jun. 3, 1786 surveyed 126 ac; formerly Henry Eustace McCulloch's property; on S side of Middle fork of Beaverdam Cr; border: David Bradford; [signed] Micajah Bullock, surveyor; sworn chain carriers Phil Bradford jr & Booker Bradford; [no date] sold to Howell Lewis for £120 by Archd Lytle, Comr; [on back] No. 39.

275. Jul. 2, 1786 surveyed 236; formerly Henry Eustace McCulloch's property; on both sides of Smiths Cr; includes a small part of Benja McCulloch's "plantation"; border: an oak 24 poles S of tract known as Smith's old field, John Hooker jr's fence, & runs through Hooker's field; [signed] M Bullock, surveyor; sworn chain carriers Harwood Nace & Philip Bullock; [on back] Mar. 1788 sold to Benjamin McCulloch for £323 by Archd Lytle, Comr; No. 28.

Sales of Confiscated Land

276. Jul. 2, 1786 surveyed 241 ac; formerly Henry Eustace McCulloch's property; on both sides of Middle fork of Beaverdam Cr; includes "the greater" part of Benja McCulloch's "plantation", all of Patterson's field, & the improvements in each place; border: a fence and Cowpen fork of Beaverdam Cr; [signed] Micajah Bullock, surveyor; sworn chain carriers Harwood Nance & Philip Bullock; [on back] Mar. 1788 sold to Benjamin McCulloch for £271 by Archd Lytle, Comr; No. 30.

277. Jul. 3, 1786 surveyed 246 ac; formerly Henry Eustace McCulloch's property; on both sides of Middle fork of Beaverdam Cr; border: Booker Bradford, Joseph Fuller, & John Champion; [signed] Micajah Bullock, surveyor; sworn chain carriers Phil Bradford jr & Booker Bradford; [no date] sold to Howell Lewis for £290 by Archd Lytle, Comr; [on back] No. 34.

278. Jul. 3, 1786 surveyed 321 ac; formerly Henry Eustace McCulloch's property; on both sides of Middle fork of Beaverdam Cr; border: Joseph Fuller, John Champion, & crosses Fullers Cr; [signed] Micajah Bullock, surveyor; sworn chain carriers Phil Bradford jr & Booker Bradford; [no date] sold to Howell Lewis for £353 by Archd Lytle, Comr; [on back] No. 35.

279. Jul. 3, 1786 surveyed 180 ac; formerly Henry Eustace McCulloch's property; on N side of Middle fork of Beaverdam Cr; border: the head of a drain of Indian Br, crosses Indian Br, Fuller, & George Taylor; [signed] Micajah Bullock, surveyor; sworn chain carriers Phil Bradford jr & Booker Bradford; [no date] sold to Howell Lewis for £180 by Archd Lytle, Comr; [on back] No. 36.

280. Jul. 3, 1786 surveyed 214 ac; formerly Henry Eustace McCulloch's property; on S side of Middle fork of Beaverdam Cr; border: David Bradford and tract 35; [signed] Micajah Bullock, surveyor; sworn chain carriers Phil Bradford jr & Booker Bradford; [no date] sold to Howell Lewis for £255.10 by Archd Lytle, Comr; [on back] No. 37.

281. Jul. 3, 1786 surveyed 97 ac; formerly Henry Eustace McCulloch's property; on N side of Middle fork of Beaverdam Cr; includes the improvement of John Hooker sr and part of "plantation" & houses where George Taylor lives; border: George Taylor and tract 36; [signed] Micajah Bullock, surveyor; sworn chain carriers Phil Bradford jr & Booker Bradford; [on back] Mar. 1788 sold to George Taylor for £76.6 by Archd Lytle, Comr; No. 38.

282. Jul. 5, 1786 surveyed 217 ac; formerly Henry Eustace McCulloch's property; on W side of Ledge of Rock Cr; border: Ann Wheelar's meadow field; includes "plantation" & houses where Charles Taylor lives; [signed] M Bullock, surveyor; sworn chain carriers Ephraim Emery & Harmond Bagley; [on back] Mar. 1788 sold to Charles Turner for £10 [sic] by Archd Lytle, Comr; No. 43.

283. [no date] surveyed 254.75 ac; tract 2; formerly H E McCulloch's property; on both sides of Nuce Road; border: Townsend, Thomas Bottom, & Joseph Cash; [signed] Micajah Bullock, surveyor; sworn chain carriers John Williams & Joseph Carner; [on back] sold Aug. 2, 1803 at Granville Co Court house to John Lyon for $221 by H Shepperd, Hillsborough Commissioner of Confiscated Property; No. 550 "date" Aug. 23, 1805.

284. [no date] surveyed 330.75 ac; tract 3; on both sides of Middle fork & Cowpen fork of Beaverdam Cr; formerly H E McCulloch's property; border: Abraham Laurrence; [signed] Micajah Bullock, surveyor; sworn chain carriers Philip Bullock & Harwood Nance; [on back] sold Aug. 2, 1803 at Granville Co Court house to William Shepperd for $220 by Henry Shepperd, Hillsborough Commissioner of Confiscated Property; No. 536 "date" Aug. 6, 1804.

285. [no date] surveyed 226 ac; tract 5; formerly H E McCulloch's property; border: "said" Hooker's fence & McCulloch's "quarter" fence; [signed] Micajah Bullock, surveyor; sworn chain carriers Philip Bullock & Harwood Nance; [on back] sold Aug. 2, 1803 at Granville Co Court house to William Shepperd for $176 by Henry Shepperd, Hillsborough Commissioner of Confiscated Property; No. 538 Aug. 6, 1804.

286. [no date] surveyed 241.75 ac; tract 6; formerly H E McCulloch's property; on both sides of Middle fork of Beaverdam Cr; includes the "greatest" part of McCullok's [sic] "plantation", "that" field at Patterson's place, &

Sales of Confiscated Land

improvements at both places; border: Patterson's fence and Cowpen fork; [signed] Micajah Bullock, surveyor; sworn chain carriers Philip Bullock & Harwood Nance; [on back] Aug. 2, 1803 sold at Granville Co Court house to William Shepperd for $328 by Henry Shepperd, Hillsborough Commissioner of Confiscated Property; No. 537.

GUILFORD COUNTY

287. "Part" of a copy of a vendue list of Confiscated Property sold by Col. John Paisley, Col. John Gillaspy, & James Miller, Commissioners for Guilford Co sold on Feb. 23, 1780:

a) Daniel Gillaspy 6 sheep £127
b) Daniel Gillaspy 6 sheep £127
c) Willm Stublefield 6 sheep £69
   [or William Stubblefield]
d) Hardie Perkins 6 sheep £51
   [or Hardin]
e) Hardie Perkins 7 sheep £46
f) Capt. John Gallaspy 1 sheep £4
g) Thos Henderson 1 cow £70
h) David Peoples 1 cow & 1 sheep £80
i) James Lanier 1 cow £72
      [or Lenier]
j) Robert Peoples 1 cow £86
k) Ann Gillaspie 1 cow £88.10
l) John Hamilton 1 cow £52

m) John Hamilton 1 cow £51.5
n) James Lanier 1 cow & calf £80
   [or Lenier]
o) John Hamilton 1 cow £52
p) Thomas Black 1 cow £80
q) Isaac Wright 1 cow £55.10
r) Thos Henderson 4 steers £410
s) Isaac Wright 4 steers
t) Daniel Gilaspie 4 yearlings £72
u) Isaac Wright 4 steers £240
v) Thos Henderson 1 steer &
      1 heifer £50.5
w) Thos Henderson 7 young cattle
      £141
[total] £2,298.10

May 28, 1780 Ja Martin certifys the above is a true copy of the sales list of cattle & sheep but he has "no account of who they belong to Col. Paisley & Col Gilaspie can tell"; [signed] Ja Martin;

[on back] also the following sold on same day:
x) Col. James Martin bought 198 ac for £250; formerly Joseph Fields' property;
y) Col. John Paisly bought "one tract of land" for £200 [written over 157];
z) Col. John Paisly bought a Negro fellow Dick for £3050; formerly Wm Fields' property;
aa) Robert Martin bought a Negro fellow Toney for £2,667; [formerly] property of Wm Fields;
[signed] Ja Martin.

288. A second copy of the same sale as in 287 above; "a" through "w" are the property of William & Joseph Fields; "y" is 157 ac; "aa" is omitted; & the following are added:
a) Thomas Henderson bought a tract where Guilford Court House stands for £8,001; formerly Young, Miller & Co property;
b) Capt. John Gellaspie bought 420 ac for £1,555; [formerly] property of Fethergill "or Bearbuk";
c) James Martin bought 400 ac adjoining the above tract for £2,025; [formerly] property of the same persons;
d) Robert Martin bought 400 ac adjoining the above tract for £1,005; "same property";
[grand total] £18,384.10 + £2,667 = £21,051.10
   certified the above is a true copy, [signed] Ja Martin & John Peasley, commissioners.

288E. [a small sheet that belongs with #288 above] A list of Confiscated Property sold Feb. 23, 1780 by Guilford Co Commissioners--Col. John Peaslay, Col. John Martin, & Capt. John Gillaspie with 6 months credit given.

289. Aug. session 1786 Guilford Co Hance Hamilton, sheriff, is allowed £5 for commissions on confiscated land sold by Salisbury Commissioner June last. Aug. 2[hole in page], 1786 [signed] Tho Searcy; [on back] "in cash & warrants £470.7"; 1784 Law passed in Oct. obliges the Treasurer to take this ticket" Jno Hamilton, clk; No. 403 "Jno Hunter for James Hunter".

Sales of Confiscated Land

290. Receipt No. 289 Aug. 8, 1786 to Charles Bruce esq £50 for 25 surveys in Guilford Co; [on back] received thw within Aug. 12, 1786 Jas Malloy.

291. a list of land sales in Guilford, Anson, Rowan, & Montgomery Counties by Charles Bruce, Salisbury Dist. Commissioner of Confiscated Property:
291A. the following in Guilford Co "sold Jun. 20, 1786":
#1--350 ac; formerly Henry E McCulloch's property; bought by John Willis for £850;
#2--332 ac; formerly Henry E McCulloch's property; bought by John Willis for £615;
#3--262 ac; formerly Henry E McCulloch's property; bought by John Willis for £700;
#4--374 ac; formerly Henry E McCulloch's property; bought by John Willis for £1,065;
#5--394 ac; formerly Henry E McCulloch's property; bought by John Willis for £1,400;
#6--276 ac; formerly Henry E McCulloch's property; bought by John Willis for £725;
#7--200 ac; formerly Henry E McCulloch's property; bought by Daniel McKindley for £201;
#8--200 ac; formerly Henry E McCulloch's property; bought by Daniel McKindley for £250.7;
#9--268 ac; formerly Henry E McCulloch's property; bought by James Hamilton for £801;
#10--372 ac; formerly Henry E McCulloch's property; bought by James Williams for £741;
#11--330 ac; formerly Henry E McCulloch's property; bought by James Williams for £708;
#12--328 ac; formerly Henry E McCulloch's property; bought by John Willis for £920;
#13--223 ac; formerly Henry E McCulloch's property; bought by Robert Shaw for £600;
#14--234 ac; formerly Henry E McCulloch's property; bought by John Willis for £450;
#15--416 ac; formerly Henry E McCulloch's property; bought by Samuel McDill for £417.1;
#16--324 ac; formerly Henry E McCulloch's property; bought by John Willis for £631;
#17--261 ac; formerly Henry E McCulloch's property; bought by John Willis for £667;
#18--256 ac; formerly Henry E McCulloch's property; bought by John Willis for £687;
#19--270 ac; formerly Henry E McCulloch's property; bought by James Lyne for £457;
#20--150 ac; formerly Henry E McCulloch's property; bought by James Lyne for £326;
#21--130 ac; formerly Henry E McCulloch's property; bought by James Lyne for £206;
#22--240 ac; formerly Henry E McCulloch's property; bought by James Bell for £560;
#23--204 ac; formerly Henry E McCulloch's property; bought by Roddy Hanna for £550;
#24--156 ac; formerly Henry E McCulloch's property; bought by William Dick for £513;
#27--147 ac; formerly Henry E McCulloch's property; bought by James Lyne for £356;
#28--141 ac; formerly Henry E McCulloch's property; bought by John Alcorn for £283.1;   [subtotal] £15,679.9

291B. the following in Anson Co:
#6--150 ac; formerly Thomas Bailey jr's property; bought by Sampson Lancer for £30;
#2--64 ac; formerly Henry E McCulloch's property; bought by Thomas Clark for £35;
#3--100 ac; formerly Henry E McCulloch's property; bought by Thomas Clark for £20;
#4--81 ac; formerly Henry E McCulloch's property; bought by Thomas Clark for £52;
#5--54 ac; formerly Henry E McCulloch's property; bought by Thomas Clark for £83;
#7--30 ac; formerly Henry E McCulloch's property; bought by Thomas Clark for £28;
#8--30 ac; formerly Henry E McCulloch's property; bought by Thomas Clark for £12.10;
#9--300 ac; formerly Robert Boyd's property; bought by Patrick Boggan for £100;
#10--400 ac; formerly John Coulson's property; bought by William Wood for £330;
#11--150 ac; formerly John Coulson's property; bought by William Wood for £112;
#12--100 ac; formerly John Coulson's property; bought by William Wood for £61;   [subtotal] £963.10

291C. the following in Rowan Co:
[blank]--220 ac; formerly Matthias Sapperfield's property; bought by Edward Yarbrough for £420;
[blank]--60 ac; formerly Matthias Sapperfield's property; bought by Edward Yarborough for £375;
#4--124.75 ac; formerly Henry E McCulloch's property; bought by Henry Ghiles for £1,000;
#13--218 ac; formerly Henry E McCulloch's property; bought by John Armstrong for £1,015 [written over 1,000];
#3--216 ac; formerly Henry E McCulloch's property; bought by Henry Ghiles for £1,050;

Sales of Confiscated Land

#14--208 ac; formerly Henry E McCulloch's property; bought by John Armstrong for £1,460;
#11--220 ac; formerly Henry E McCulloch's property; bought by James Mulloy for £515;
#12--202 ac; formerly Henry E McCulloch's property; bought by James Mulloy for £522;
[blank]--200 ac; formerly Edward Turner's property; bought by John Armstrong for £1,025;
[blank]--320 a; formerly George Spraker's property; bought by James Houston for £2,000;
21 lots in Salisbury; formerly James Kerr's property; bought by James Houston for £410;
#39 a lot in Salisbury; formerly James Kerr's property; bought by Peter Faust for £10;
#40 a lot in Salisbury; formerly James Kerr's property; bought by Joseph Robinson for £31;
#52 a lot in Salisbury; formerly James Kerr's property; bought by Peter Brown for £14.5;
#55 a lot in Salisbury; formerly James Kerr's property; bought by Alexr Nelson for £11.10;
#58 a lot in Salisbury; formerly James Kerr's property; bought by Robert Martin for £35.5;
#59 a lot in Salisbury; formerly James Kerr's property; bought by Lewis Beard for £10;
#60 a lot in Salisbury; formerly James Kerr's property; bought by Lewis Beard for £14.5;
[blank]--229 ac "adj do" [Salisbury]; formerly James Kerr's property; bought by Henry Ghiles for £1,010;
#9 half a lot in Salisbury; formerly James Kerr's property; bought by Henry Ghiles for £1,175; [subtotal] £11,603.5;
"NB there are 5 lots sold for which bonds were not executed on thea bove town & are not inserted"

291D. in Montgomery Co:
[blank]--70 ac; formerly Henry E McCulloch's property; bought by Mark Allen for £71;
#1--160 ac; formerly Josiah Martin's property; bought by Alexander Frazier for £31.15;
#2--160 ac; formerly Josiah Martin's property; bought by William Sanders for £17.10;
#3--160 ac; formerly Josiah Martin's property; bought by William Sanders for £20;
#4--160 ac; formerly Josiah Martin's property; bought by William Saunders for £10;
[blank]--120 ac; formerly Henry E McCulloch's property; bought by William Sanders for £40;
[blank]--54 ac; formerly Henry E McCulloch's property; bought by William Sanders for £29;
[blank]--35 ac; formerly Henry E McCulloch's property; bought by William Sanders for £17;
[blank]--360 ac "more or less"; formerly Henry E McCulloch's property; bought by William Sanders for £1,202;
[blank]--174 ac; formerly Henry E McCulloch's property; bought by Thomas Clark for £62;
[blank]--222 ac; formerly Henry E McCulloch's property; bought by Jesse McClendon for £500.10;
[blank]--320 ac "more or less"; formerly Henry E McCulloch's property; bought by Richard Tindal for £2,632;
[blank]--300 ac; formerly Josiah Martin's property; bought by John Hopkins for £121; [total] £4,753.15
"NB there were two tracts of land sold in the above county for which bonds were not executed & therefore not listed"

292. Jan. 23, 1787 Charles Bruce certifys Mr. William Dick paid in certificates for 156 ac lot No. 24 he purchased June 20 "last".

293. Jan. 23, 1787 Charles Bruce certifys Mr. Robert Shaw paid in certificates for 223 ac lot No. 13 he bought June 20 "last".

294. Dec. 6, 1785 surveyed 270 ac for James Lyne; No. 19; formerly Henry Eustace McCulloch's property; on waters of Alimance Cr; [signed] A Philips; sworn chain carriers William Cunningham & Sampson Lanier; [on back] No. 128 £457.

295. Dec. 13, 1785 surveyed 150 ac for James Lyne; No. 20; formerly Henry Eustace McCulloch's property; on both sides of Little Alimance Cr; border: Peter Julin and "the" dividing line; [signed] A Philips; sworn chain carriers William Cunningham & Sampson Lanier; [on back] No. 126 £326.

296. Dec. 13, 1785 surveyed 130 ac for James Lyne; No. 21; formerly Henry Eustace McCulloch's property; on a fork of Little Alimance Cr; border: No. 20 and Peter Julian; [signed] A Philips; sworn chain carriers William Cunningham & Sampson Lanier; [on back] No. 129 £206.

Sales of Confiscated Land

297. Dec. 19, 1785 surveyed 147 ac for James Lyne; No. 27; formerly Henry Eustace McCulloch's property; on waters of Great Alamance Cr; border: George Clap and crosses two branches; [signed] A Philips; sworn chain carriers William Cunningham & Sampson Lanier; [on back] [on back] No. 127 £356.

298. Jun. 20, 1786 sold 200 ac to Daniel McKindley for £201; No. 7; formerly Henry Eustace McCulloch's property; on waters of Travis's Cr; border: Jacob Troak, Lodowic Isley, & No. 8; [signed] Charles Bruce, CSCPSD; sworn chain carriers Jesse McCallister & John McCallister.

299. Jun. 20, 1786 sold 200 ac to David McKindley for £250; No. 8; formerly Henry Eustace McCulloch's property; on waters of Travis's Cr; border: Orange Co line, Jacob Troak, Peter Sullinger; [signed] Charles Bruce, CSCPSD; sworn chain carriers Jesse McAlister & John McAlister.

300. Jun. 20, 1786 sold 223 ac to Robert Shaw for £600; formerly Henry Eustace McCulloch's property; on both sides of Little Alamance Cr; border: George Ingles and Jno Philip Clap; [signed] Charles Bruce, CSCPSD; sworn chain carriers Wm Cunningham & Sampson Lanier; [on back] "13".

301. Jun. 20, 1786 sold 416 ac to Samuel McDill for £417.1; No. 15; formerly Henry Eustace McCulloch's property; on S side of Alamance Cr; border: No. 13, George Ingles, Peter Low, crosses Jacobs Br, & No. 14; [signed] Charles Bruce, CSCPSD; sworn chain carriers William Cunningham & Sampson Lanier.

302. Jun. 20, 1786 sold 270 ac to James Lyne for £457; No. 19; formerly Henry Eustace McCulloch's property; border: No. 14; [signed] Charles Bruce, CSCPSD; sworn chain carriers William Cunningham & Sampson Lanier.

303. Jun. 20, 1786 sold 150 ac to James Lyne for £326; No. 20; formerly Henry Eustace McCulloch's property; on both sides of Little Alamance Cr; border: Peter Julian & No. 21; [signed] Charles Bruce, CSCPSD; sworn chain carriers William Cunningham & Sampson Lanier.

304. Jun. 20, 1786 sold 130 ac to James Lyne for £206; No. 21; formerly Henry Eustace McCulloch's property; on a fork of Little Alamance Cr; border: No. 20 and Peter Julian; includes Robert Adams' improvement; [signed] Charles Bruce, CSCPSD; sworn chain carriers William Cunningham & Sampson Lanier.

305. Jun. 20, 1786 sold 147 ac to James Lyne for £356; No. 27; formerly Henry Eustace McCulloch's property; on waters of Great Alamance Cr; border: George Clapp and crosses a branch; [signed] Charles Bruce, CSCPSD.

HALIFAX COUNTY

306. List of people who "rendered on oath" to Halifax Commissioners the amounts of debts owed Messrs Archbald Hamilton & Co, merchants which were confiscated & paid to the Commissioners:

306A. [people who have paid their debts:]

Isaac Aaron £6.4	Thomas Thrower £13	Richard Pemberton £10
William Muir £85	Thomas Pace £25.14.4	William Jones £1.7
Joseph Cock £0.15	Joseph Ward £10.5.3	Sarah Tucker £11.10
Maryan Aaron £15.10	Richard Heath £2.5	[subtotal] £1,529.2.6
James Fawceit £16.8.6	David Marshall £19.18	Nicholas Gurley £25.5
John Eaton £460	Jesse Williams £17.5	Adam Hamil £43.8
George Kerkley £3.0	John Williams	Thomas Hawkins £46.7.6
William & Lewis	Bradley "slaughter" £40	Gabriel Long £466
as exrs of Philip	John Wallace £3.9.4	Jacob Harper £13.18
Bradley decd £36.0	John Long £22.10	William Flewellin £4
Andrew Gootie £503.13	John Croxon £1.10	Jonathan Garland £3
Pinkethman Eaton £80	Christopher Pritchet £0.12.3	

Sales of Confiscated Land

Luke Nichols £1.15
Jesse Butt £9
Thomas Lant Hall £6.4
Abraham Heath £49.12
Christopher Bustian £6.3
Stephen Sampson £5.15

William Pullen £25.19
Samuel Williams "H" £4
William Richardson £2.8
William Harvey £0.12
John Barrott £2.12
John Coats £3.10

Nathaniel Bradford £1.15
Oroondates Davis for
  Joseph Long's
  estate £380
Henry Montfort £3,500
[total] £5,987.11

306B. [same as above, but people haven't paid the Commissioners:]

Robert Hall £261
Mary Rodgers £8.0.6
James Pasteur £575
Joseph Borden £6.16.4
Willie Jones £1,145.10.3
William Barksdale £31.6
Coupland Whitfield £13.3
Caleb Moncrief £2.9.4
Drury Harrington £367.10
Joseph Edwards £75.12.8
John Long £273.12
William Moran £40.12
John Scoals £5.2
Elizabeth Hath £28

William Wright £20
Richard Hill £23.10
Eli Williams £25.16.8
Isaac Dean £25.16.9
Aaron Clark £14.7
Thomas Matthis £79.1
[subtotal] £3,022.14.6
John Powers £38.1.2
Prisley Cox £20.13
John Stevens £11.7.4
Joel Hurt £200
Philip Kearney £815
Thomas Ring £142.12
William Hurt £19.15.2

Benjamin Nevil £2.10
James Fawceit £5.11.8
John Powers £28.1.3
William Burt £46.11.5
William Crabb £0.2.0
John Saxon £92.13
James Hogg £8.12.8
Isaac Jackson £10.13.4
Charles Blanton £17.3
Willis Alston £9
Richard Stevens £4.8
[page torn]
Pemberton [blank]

307. List of people who own confiscated property, whose property it was formerly, & the Commissioner who received the money:

307A [page 2]:
Isaac Aaron; property of Archibald Hamilton & Co; paid £6.4 to Wm Wooten
William Muir; property of Robert McKittrick; paid £8 to Wm Wooten
William Muir; property of Archibald Hamilton & Co; paid £85 to Wm Wooten
Joseph Cock; property of Archibald Hamilton & Co; paid £0.15 to Wm Wooten
Maryan Aron; property of Archibald Hamilton & Co; paid £15.10 to Wm Wooten
James Fawceit; property of Archibald Hamilton & Co; paid £16.8.6 to William Wooten
George Williamson; property of Archd Cunnison; paid £26.15 to Saml Welden
George Williamson; propertyof Jno Thompson; paid £1.15 to Saml Welden
Wm Weldon esq; property of Miller & Co; paid £46 to Saml Welden
Wm Weldon esq, for Littleberry Mason; property of Miller & Co; paid £4.10 to Saml Welden

307B [page 3]:
Elijah Pitman; property of David Telfair & Co; paid £5.15 to Wm Wooten
Elijah Pitman; property of Andw Miller & Co; paid £0.8 to Wm Wooten
Benjamin Rowell; property of David Telfair; paid £19.16.6 to Wm Wooten
James Ward; property of David Telfair; paid £1.10 to Wm Wooten
James Churchill; property of Andw Miller & Co; paid £9.18.4 to Wm Wooten
John Whitaker esq; property of David Telfair & Co; paid £12.6.8 to Wm Wooten
John Whitaker esq; property to Jno Thompson; paid £2 to Wm Wooten
James Gains; property of John Gruion [or Greeour], Bertie Co; paid £0.13 to Wm Wooten
John McDaniell; property of David Telfair & Co; paid £14.1.5 to Wm Wooten
Richard Whitaker; property of David Telfair & Co; paid £24.15.5 to Wm Wooten
Richard Whitaker; property of Andw Miller & Co; paid £2.16 to Wm Wooten
Richard Whitaker; property of Jno Thompson; paid £5.10 to Wm Wooten
David Ward; property of David Telfair & Co; paid £9 to Wm Wooten

Sales of Confiscated Land

Samuel Pitman; property of David Telfair & Co; paid £1.6.8 to Wm Wooten
Samuel Pitman; property of Andw Miller & Co; paid £48.10.5 to Wm Wooten
James Wyatt sr; property of David Telfair & Co; paid £1.1.8 to Wm Wooten
John Eaton; property of Alexanr Telfair & Co; paid £29.11.6 to Wm Wooten
John Eaton; property of John Thompson; paid £5.4 to Wm Wooten
John Eaton; property of Andw Miller & Co; paid £66.6.3 to Wm Wooten
John Eaton; property of Archd [Hamilton--page torn]; paid £460 to Wm Wooten
   [subtotal] £79 to Saml Welden;   £852.8.6 to Wm Wooten

307C. [page 4]:
William Martin; property of John Thompson; paid £287.10 to Wm Wooten
William Martin; property of Buchanan Scoal [? page torn]; paid £19.10.10 to Wm Wooten
William Martin; property of Martin Howard; paid £139.16 to Wm Wooten
George Kerkley; property of Andw Miller & Co; paid £6 to Wm Wooten
George Kerkley; property of Andrew [Hamilton] & Co; paid £3 to Wm Wooten
Thomas Moye; property of David Telfair; paid £4 to Wm Wooten
Joseph Carter; property of Alexr Horsbrought [? page torn], Va; paid £20.10 to Wm Wooten
Joseph Carter; property of David Russel, Va; paid £44 to Wm Wooten
Joseph Carter; property of John Green, Va; paid £3.17.4 to Wm Wooten
Lewis Whitehead; property of David Telfair; paid £0.12 to Wm Wooten
Micajah Fort; property of John Thompson; paid £2.2 to Wm Wooten
Wm Rawles; property of James Gibson & Co, Va; paid £1.12 to Wm Wooten
Joseph Whitehead; property of David Telfair & Co; paid £5.1 to Wm Wooten
Solomon Turner "(DC)"; property to Hugh Telfair; paid £5.0 to Wm Wooten
David Alsobrook; property of Hugh Telfair; paid £4.0 to Wm Wooten
James Hodges; property of Hugh Telfair; paid £[page torn] to Wm Wooten

307D. [page 5]:
Lemuel Hobgood; property of Hugh Telfair; paid £14.5.10 to Wm Wooten
Thomas Dew; property of Hugh Telfair; paid £6 to Wm Wooten
James Cain; property of Hugh Telfair; paid £2 to Wm Wooten
Jacob ODonniell; property of Hugh Telfair; paid £6.9.2 to Wm Wooten
Jessie Haynie; property of David Telfair; paid £1.10 to Wm Wooten
Jessie Haynie; property of Jno Thompson; paid £3.5 to Wm Wooten
William Cotton; property of David Telfair; paid £18.12 to Wm Wooten
Phillip Rawles; property of David Telfair; paid £17 to Wm Wooten
Phillip Rawles; property of Andw Miller & Co; paid £7 to Wm Wooten
Edwd Emmery; property of Hugh Telfair; paid £0.8 to Wm Wooten
William & Lewis Bradley, as executors of Phillip Bradley decd; property of Andrew Hamilton & Co; paid £36
 to Wm Wooten
William & Lewis Bradley, as executors of Phillip Bradley decd; property of Michael & Jno Wallace; paid £21.1.6
 to Wm Wooten
Benjamin Vick; property of John Thompson; paid £2.10 to Wm Wooten
Absalom Merrit; property of David Telfair & Co; paid £1.11.2 to Wm Wooten
Jeremiah Nelms; property of David Telfair; paid £2.7 to Wm Wooten
Benjamin Blackburn; property of Mathew McCummery; paid £0.11 to Wm Wooten
   [subtotal] £79 to Saml Welden;   £1,544.0.10 to Wm Wooten

307E. [page 6]:
John Hull; property of Richd Ginis; paid £2.8 to Wm Wooten
Arthur Smith; property of Gibson & Granbury, Virginia; paid £18.13.4 to Wm Wooten
Randolph Robertson; property of David Telfair; paid £20 to Wm Wooten

Sales of Confiscated Land

Nathan Brown; property of Gibson & Donaldson, Virginia; paid £17.6.8 to Wm Wooten

Jesse Wrenn; property of Andw Miller & Co; paid £6.4 to Wm Wooten

Thomas Merrit; property of Cunnison & Co; paid £19.0.7½ to Wm Wooten

Thomas Merrit; property of McClellan, Wallace & Co; paid £4.16.5 to Wm Wooten

Thomas Merrit; property of John Thompson; paid £7.15.10 to Wm Wooten

James Pulley; property of Andw Miller & Co; paid £6.12 to Wm Wooten

Thomas Davis; property of Andw Miller & Co; paid £4.0 to Wm Wooten

Theophelus Cotton; property of David Telfair; paid £0.10 to Wm Wooten

Peter Morgan; property of Andw Miller & Co; paid £8.16.4 to Wm Wooten

John Young; property of Alexr Graham, Elizabeth City, Va; paid £7.6.8 to Wm Wooten

Lemuel Wattson; property of Andw Miller & Co; paid £6 to Wm Wooten

307F. [page 7]:

John Ricks; property of Andw Miller & Co; paid £91 to Wm Wooten

John Ricks; property of Cunnisons & Co; paid £41 to Wm Wooten

John Ricks; property of John Thompson; paid £12 to Wm Wooten

John Ricks; property of Alexr Telfair & Co; paid £3.3 to Wm Wooten

Samuel Coapland; property of Andw Miller & Co; paid £2.0 to Wm Wooten

Isaac Ricks; property of David Telfair; paid £4.10 to Wm Wooten

Isaac Ricks; property of Cunnison & Co; paid £20 to Wm Wooten

Wm Pearce; property of Cunnison & Co; paid £62.16.6 to Wm Wooten

Wm Pearce; property of Alexr Telfair; paid £27.3 to Wm Wooten

Saml Walden; property of Andw Miller & Co; paid £9.1 to Wm Montfort

Henry Joyner; property of Alexr Telfair & Co; paid £45 to Wm Wooten

Henry Joyner; property of Jno Thompson; paid £23.8 to Wm Wooten

Henry Joyner; property of Andw Miller & Co; paid £70.10 to Wm Wooten

James Brantley; property of [blank]; paid £5.1 to Wm Wooten

Andw Gootie; property of Alexr Telfair & Co; paid £9.0 to Wm Wooten

Andw Gootie; property of Jno Thompson; paid £21.0.6 Wm Wooten

Andw Gootie; property of Andw Miller & Co; paid £29.13 to Wm Wooten

Andw Gootie; property of Archd Hamilton & Co; paid £[hole in page].13 to Wm Wooten

Thos Hodges; property of Andw Miller & Co; paid £8.16.6 to Wm Wooten

  [subtotal] £79 to Saml Welden; £9.1 to Wm Montfort; £2,714.19.10½ to Wm Wooten

307G. [page 8]:

Joseph Pearce; property of David Telfair & Co; paid £[hole in page] to Wm Wooten

Joseph Pearce; property of Alexr Telfair & Co; paid £12 to Wm Wooten

Joseph Pearce; property of Andw Miller & Co; paid £45 to Wm Wooten

Robert Hulmn; property of Alexr Telfair & Co; paid £0.18 to Wm Wooten

John Bradley; property of David Telfair & Co; paid £5.3.6 to Wm Wooten

John Bradley; property of Andw Miller & Co; paid £5.11.4 to Wm Wooten

John Moore; property of Alston Young & Co; paid £7.8.8 to Wm Wooten

Pinkethman Eaton; property of Alexr Telfair & Co; paid £40 to Wm Wooten

Pinkethman Eaton; property of Alexr Hamilton & Co; paid £80 to Wm Wooten

Cullen Edwards; property of Buchanan Hostia & Co; paid £232.11.10 to Wm Montfort

Cullen Edwards; property of James Gibson & Co, Virginia; paid £124.0 to Wm Montfort

Cullen Edwards; property of Andw Miller & Co; paid £115.4.0 to Wm Montfort

Cullen Edwards, in half of what he & Thos Hunter owe them; property of Buchanan Hostia [or Hostiee] & Co; paid £460.8.4¼ to Wm Montfort

Shadrach Rutland; property of Gibson, Donaldson, & Hamilton; paid £354.17.6½ Wm Montfort

Shadrach Rutland, as exr. or Lewis Powell decd; property of Gibson, Donaldson, & Hamilton; paid £354.17.6½ to Wm Montfort

Sales of Confiscated Land

307H. [page 9]:
James Baker; property of Andw Miller & Co; paid £9.0 to Wm Wooten
Richd Suit; property of David Telfair & Co; paid £0.5 to Wm Wooten
Thomas Lorton; property of David Telfair & Co; paid £5.0 to Wm Wooten
Wm Parker; property of David Telfair & Co; paid £0.16 to Wm Wooten
John Marshall; property of James McNeil; paid £1.10 to Wm Wooten
Daniell "(Ambrose)"; property of James McNeil; paid £5.0 to Wm Wooten
Israel West; property of David Telfair; paid £26.1.6 to Wm Wooten
Luke Nichols; property of Alexr Hamilton & Co; paid £1.15 to Wm Wooten
Luke Nichols; property of David Telfair; paid £0.10.8 to Wm Wooten
Jeremiah Turner; property of David Telfair & Co; paid £1.6.8 to Wm Wooten
Jesse Butt; property of Alexr Hamilton & Co; paid £9 to Wm Wooten
Nathan Council; property of David Telfair & Co; paid £1.10 to Wm Wooten
Nathan Council; property of James McNeil paid £0.0.8 to Wm Wooten
Thos Lant. Hall; property of Alexr Hamilton & Co; paid £6.4 to Wm Wooten
Jesse Christie; property of Alston Young & Co; paid £1.16.7 to Wm Wooten
James Bradfield; property of Andw Miller & Co; paid £1.12 to Wm Wooten
Abraham Heath; property of Alexr Hamilton & Co; paid £49.12 to Wm Wooten
James Neil; property of David Telfair & Co; paid £9 to Wm Wooten
   [subtotal] £79 to Saml Welden; £1,651.3¼ to Wm Montfort; £3.051.1.5½ to Wm Wooten

307I. [page 10]:
Christopher Bustion; property of Alexr Hamilton & Co; paid £6.13 to Wm Wooten
Stephen Sampson; property of Alexr Hamilton & Co; paid £5.15 to Wm Wooten
John Heath; property of James McNeil paid £10 to Wm Wooten
Thomas Thrower; property of James McNeil; paid £22.1.8 to Wm Wooten
Thomas Thrower; property of Alexr Hamilton & Co; paid £13 to Wm Wooten
Wm West sr; property of James McNeil; paid £77.17.6 to Wm Wooten
Thomas Pace; property of Andw Miller & Co; paid £41.6 to Wm Wooten
Thomas Pace; property of David Telfair & Co; paid £7.4 to Wm Wooten
Thomas Pace; property of Alexr & Hugh Telfair & Co; paid £20 to Wm Wooten
Thomas Pace; property of Alexr Hamilton & Co; paid £25.14.4 to Wm Wooten
Joseph Ward; property of Alexr Hamilton & Co; paid £10.5.3 to Wm Wooten
Richard Heath; property of Alexr Hamilton & Co; paid £2.5 to Wm Wooten
Willis Powell; property of James McNeil; paid £0.2.6 to Wm Wooten
Robert Etherage; property of James McNeil; paid £3.15 to Wm Wooten
Joshua Butt; property of David Telfair; paid £25.7.3 to Wm Wooten
Arthur Davis; property of Young, Miller & Co; paid £15 to Wm Wooten

307J. [page A]:
Wm Etherage; property of James McNeil paid £29.4.1 to Wm Wooten
Caleb Etherage; property of David Telfair; paid £1.6.8 to Wm Wooten
David Marshall; property of Archd Hamilton & Co; paid £19.18 to Wm Wooten
Isaac Mathis; property of Andw Miller & Co; paid £0.9 to Wm Wooten
Aaron Etherage sr; property of James McNeil; paid £1.13.5 to Wm Wooten
Wm Walker; property of David Telfair & Co; paid £11.10 to Wm Wooten
Robert Pasmore; property of James McNeil; paid £1.16.8 to Wm Wooten
Jesse Williams; property of James McNeil; paid £116.10 to Wm Wooten
Jesse Williams; property of Archd Hamilton Co; paid £17.5 to Wm Wooten
John Williams "(Slaughter)"; property of Gibson, Donaldson, & Hamilton, Virginia; paid £160.0 to Wm Wooten
John Williams "(Slaughter)"; property of Andw Miller & Co; paid £24 to Wm Wooten

Sales of Confiscated Land

John Williams "(Slaughter)"; property of Archd Hamilton & Co; paid £40 to Wm Wooten
Reps Mathis; property of Jams McNeil; paid £21.1.4 to Wm Wooten
Reps Mathis; property of David Telfair Co; paid £22.4 to Wm Wooten
Caleb Etherage; property of James McNeil; paid £32.3.4 to Wm Wooten
   [subtotal] £79 to Saml Welden; £1,651.0.3½ to Wm Montfort; £3,836.15.5½ to
   Wm Wooten

307K. [page B]:
John Cone; property of Andw Miller & Co; paid £3.0 to Wm Wooten
John Wallace; property of Archd Hamilton & Co; paid £3.9.4 to Wm Wooten
John Long; property of Archd Hamilton & Co; paid £22.10 to Wm Wooten
James Conner; property of Andw Miller & Co; paid £0.5 to Wm Wooten
Burrill Broom; property of Andw Miller & Co; paid £0.18.4 to Wm Wooten
Elijah Humphries; property of Alston Young & Co; paid £10.13.4 to Wm Wooten
Solomon Butt; property of Andw Miller; paid £0.1 to Wm Wooten
Lovick Worldly; property of James McNeil; paid £4.10 to Wm Wooten
John Croxon; property of Archd Hamilton & Co; paid £1.10 to Wm Wooten
Christopher Pritchet; property of Archd Hamilton & Co; paid £0.12.3 to Wm Wooten
Wm Pullen; property of Archd Hamilton & Co; paid £25.19 to Wm Wooten
Samuel Williams "H"; property of Archd Hamilton & Co; paid £4 to Wm Wooten
Wm Richardson; property of Archd Hamilton & Co; paid £2.8 to Wm Wooten
David Pulley; property of David Telfair & Co; paid £1.18.10 to Wm Wooten
David Pulley; property of James McNeil; paid £1.3.4 to Wm Wooten

307L. [page C]:
William Harvey; property of Archd Hamilton & Co; paid £0.12 to Wm Wooten
William Harvey; property of Andw Miller & Co; paid £13.8.3 to Wm Wooten
John Barrott; property of Archd Hamilton & Co; paid £2.12 to Wm Wooten
Wm Palmer; property of Andw Miller & Co; paid £0.10.6 to Saml Welden
Wm Coats; property of [blank]; paid £0.19 to Saml Welden
Wm Brown; property of Archd Telfair & Co; paid £3.11 to Saml Welden
Wm Brown; property of Andw Miller & Co; paid £1.15 to Saml Welden
John Coats; property of Alexr Hamilton & Co; paid £3.10 to Saml Welden
John Coats; property of Alexr Telfair & Co; paid £1.0 to Saml Welden
Thos Jackson; property of Andw Miller & Co; paid £13.18 to Saml Welden
Thos Jackson; property of Andw McCoy; paid £8.0 to Saml Welden
Benjamin Coats; property of Andw Miller & Co; property of 4.0.6 to Saml Welden
John Brown; property of Anw Miller & Co; paid £2.0 to Saml Welden
Wm Morris jr; property of Alexr Telfair & Co; paid £0.15 to Saml Welden
Joseph Helton; property of Anthy Warwick & Co; paid £5 to Saml Welden
John Corlew; property of Jno Thompson; paid £5.2.6 to Saml Welden
John Corlew; property of Andw Miller & Co; paid £10.6.10½ to Saml Welden
   [subtotal] £139.8.4 to Saml Welden; £1,651.0.3½ to Wm Montfort; £3,936.6.2 to Wm Wooten

307M. [page D]:
Wm Carter; property of Andw Miller & Co; paid £2.19 to Saml Welden
Joseph Carter; property of Anthoy. Warwick & Co; paid £1.10 to Saml Welden
James Jinkins; property of Alston Young & Co; paid £11.16.11 to Saml Welden
Richard Pemberton; property of Andw Miller & Co; paid £27.3.8 to Saml Welden
Richard Pemberton; property of Jno Thompson; paid £3.8.10 to Saml Welden
Richard Pemberton; property of Archd Hamilton & Co; paid £10 to Saml Welden
Richard Pemberton; property of Anthy Warwick & Co; paid £7.4 to Saml Welden

Sales of Confiscated Land

Augustin Willis; property of Dinwiddie Crawford & Co; paid £317.6.8 to Wm Montfort
Jonathan Carpenter; property of Anthy Warwick & Co; paid £16 to Saml Welden
Elizabeth Ballard; property of Andw Miller & Co; paid £53.5 to Saml Welden
Ann Coley; property of Anthy Warwick & Co; paid £2.6.8 to Saml Welden
Benjamin Bradley; property of Andw Miller & Co; paid £7.10 to Saml Welden
John Story; property of Alston Young & Co; paid £9.7.7 to Saml Welden
John Story; property of Anthy Warwick & Co; paid £0.10 to Saml Welden
Robert Coley; property of McGeorge & Co; paid £1.1.4 to Saml Welden
Wm Jones; property of Archd Hamilton & Co; paid £1.7 to Saml Welden

307N. [page E]:
Wm Smith; property of Andw Miller & Co; paid £0.10.4 to Saml Welden
Henry Haws Tucker; property of Anthy Warwick & Co; paid £6.0 to Saml Welden
Wm Jinkins; property of Andw Miller & Co; paid £4.0 to Saml Welden
Sarah Tucker; property of Alexr Hamilton & Co; paid £11.10 to Wm Montfort
Sarah Tucker; property of Jno Thompson; paid £1.9 to Wm Montfort
Sarah Tucker; property of Anthy Warwick & Co; paid £16.0 to Wm Montfort
William Morris sr; property of Anthy Warwick & Co; paid £2.13.4 to Saml Walden
James Hockaday; property of Jno Thompson; paid £1.6.8 to Saml Welden
James Hockaday; property of Alexr Telfair & Co; paid £2.11.8 to Saml Welden
Nicholas Gurley; property of Archd Hamilton & Co; paid £25.5.10 to Wm Montfort
Reuben Harper; property of Andw Miller & Co; paid £6.5.5 to Saml Welden
Reuben Harper; property of Alexr Telfair & Co; paid £0.8.4 to Saml Welden
Addam Hamil; property of Archd Hamilton & Co; paid £43.8 to Saml Welden
William Carpenter; property of Anthy Warwick & Co; paid £4 to Saml Welden
   [subtotal] £366.2.1 to Saml Welden; £2,022.11.8½ to Wm Montfort; £3,936.6.2
   to Wm Wooten

307O. [page F]:
James Moore; property of Jno Thompson; paid £9.8 to Saml Welden
James Moore; property of Alexr Telfair & Co; paid £14.13 to Saml Welden
Wm Powell jr; property of Alexr Telfair & Co; paid £10.18 to Saml Welden
James Spann; property of Alexr Telfair & Co; paid £10.18 to Saml Welden
John Norwood; property of Jhn Thompson; paid £16.1.2 to Saml Welden
John Norwood; property of Anthy Warwick & Co; paid £10.13.4 to Saml Welden
Hannah Green; property of Andw Miller & Co; paid £8 to Saml Welden
Elizabeth Irby; property of Andw Miller & Co; paid £5 to Saml Welden
George Yarborough; property of Andw Miller & Co; paid £1.0 to Saml Welden
Jarriot Wallace; property of Alexr Telfair & Co; paid £6.17.9 to Saml Welden
James Easley; property of Anthony Warwick & Co; paid £5 to Saml Welden
Joshua Jones; property of Jno Thompson; paid £3.12.9½ to Saml Welden
Wm Corlew; property of Thompson & Co; paid £0.18.8 to Saml Welden

307P. [page 11]:
Thomas Hawkins; property of Archd Hamilton & Co; paid £46.7.6 to Wm Wooten
Jonathan Hale; property of Andw Miller & Co; paid £0.16 to Wm Wooten
Williamson Hale; property of Andw Miller & Co; paid £0.16 to Wm Wooten
Thomas Vinson; property of Andw Miller & Co; paid £12.0.10 to Wm Wooten
Joseph Hawkins; property of Jno Thompson; paid £4.0 to Wm Wooten
William Whitfield; property of John Thompson; paid £3.0 to Wm Wooten
William Whitfield; property of Alexr Telfair & Co; paid £3.10 to Wm Wooten
Gabriel Long; property of Archd Hamilton; paid £466 to Wm Wooten

Sales of Confiscated Land

John Jones, in part of Jas McNeil, Hamilton & Co; property of David Telfair; paid £498.9 [written over £625.9.5] to Saml Welden

Wm Rose; property of Jno Thompson; paid £8 to Saml Welden

Wm Rose; property of Miller & Co; paid £1.15 to Saml Welden

Jacob Harper; property of Hamilton & Co; paid £13.18 to Saml Welden

Wm Branch esq; property of Andw Miller & Co; paid £14.9 to Wm Wooten

   [subtotal] £1,126.19.2 to Saml Welden; £2,022.11.8½ to Wm Montfort; £4,487.5.5½ to Wm Wooten

307Q. [page 12]:

Samuel Pitman, or the estate of Thos Burgess decd; property of Andw Miller & Co; paid £80 to Wm Wooten

Lazarus Gunter; property of David Telfair & Co; paid £2.13 to Wm Wooten

John Gunter; property of Andw Miller & Co; paid £6 to Wm Wooten

William Flewellin; property of Archd Hamilton & Co; paid £4 to Wm Wooten

William Phillips; property of David Telfair & Co; paid £10 to Wm Wooten

William Phillips; property of John Thompson; paid £2.19.6 to Wm Wooten

Samuel Rawlings; property of David Telfair & Co; paid £4.14 to Wm Wooten

Thos Merritt; property of David Telfair & Co; paid £3.2 to Wm Wooten

Frederick Merritt; property of David Telfair & Co; paid £3.15 to Wm Wooten

Jonathan Garland; property of Andw Miller & Co; paid £9.17.4 to Wm Wooten

Jonathan Garland; property of Archd Hamilton & Co; paid £3 to Wm Wooten

Isham Phillips; property of David Telfair & Co; paid £10.10 to Wm Wooten

Wm Duncan; property of Andw Miller & Co; paid £7 to Wm Wooten

John Turner; property of John Thompson; paid £2.18 to Wm Wooten

307R. [page 13]:

Margaret Warren; property of Jno Thompson; paid £0.15 to Wm Wooten

Margaret Warren; property of Andw Miller & Co; paid £1.10 to Wm Wooten

Wm West; property of James McNeil; paid £4.4 to Wm Wooten

Thomas Ingram; property of Jno Thompson; paid £0.5 to Wm Wooten

Nicholas Dilliard; property of Young, Alston & Co; paid £14.0.8 to Wm Wooten

Francis Partridge; property of David Telfair & Co; paid £4.10 to Wm Wooten

Nathl Bradford; property of David Telfair & Co; paid £31 to Wm Wooten

Nathl Bradford; property of Alexr Telfair & Co; paid £4.14.4 to Wm Wooten

Nathl Bradford; property of Archd Hamilton & Co; paid £1.15 to Wm Wooten

Elisha Pitman; property of David Telfair & Co; paid £12.5.6 to Wm Wooten

Elisha Pitman; property of Alexr & Hugh Telfair; paid £1.6 to Wm Wooten

Elisha Pitman; property of Andw Miller & Co; paid £3.15 to Wm Wooten

Daniel Pointer; property of Archd Cunninson & Co; paid £6.10 to Wm Wooten

Daniel Pointer; property of Alexr Telfair & Co; paid £39.17.4 to Wm Wooten

Daniel Pointer; property of Andw Miller & Co; paid £114.17.3 to Wm Wooten

   [subtotal] £1,126.19.2 to Saml Welden; £2,022.11.8 to Wm Montfort; £4,878.19.4 to Wm Wooten

307S. [page 14]:

Bridgman Joyner; property of Andw Miller & Co; paid £74.8 to Wm Montfort

Bridgman Joyner; property of Archd Cunnerson & Co; paid £16.10 to Wm Montfort

Bridgman Joyner; property of John Thompson; paid £8 to Wm Montfort

Josiah Leek; property of Andw Miller & Co; paid £84.4 to Wm Montfort

Josiah Leek; property of John Thompson; paid £11.14.4 to Wm Montfort

George Young; property of Andw Miller & Co; paid £5.11.7 to Wm Montfort

Lamaster Barnes; property of Andw Miller & Co; paid £20 to Wm Montfort

Lamaster Barnes; property of Alexr Telfair & Co; paid £6 to Wm Montfort

Sales of Confiscated Land

Zachariah Langford; property of Alston Young & Co; paid £1.15 to Wm Montfort
Turner Mason; property of Andw Miller & Co; paid £6.5.9 to Saml Welden
Oroondates Davis; property of Young, Miller & Co; paid £17 to Saml Welden
Oroondates Davis; property of Alexr Telfair & Co; paid £103 to Saml Welden
Oroondates Davis, for Joseph Long's estate; property of Young, Miller & Co;
    paid £170 to Saml Welden

307T. [page 17]:
Oroondates Davis, for Joseph Long's estate; property of Alexr Telfair & Co;   paid £72 to Saml Welden
Oroondates Davis, for Joseph Long's estate; property of Archd Hamilton & Co; paid £380 to Saml Welden
Oroondates Davis, for Joseph Long's estate; property of Archd Cunnerson & Co; paid £120 to Saml Welden
Oroondates Davis, for Joseph Long's estate; property of James McNeil; paid £38 to Saml Welden
Henry Montfort; property of Archd Hamilton & Co; paid £3,500 to Wm Montfort
    [totals] £2,033.4.11 to Saml Welden; £5,746.14.7 to Wm Montfort; £4,878.19.4 to Wm Wooten
Wm Wooten, "C Ct", certifys the foregoing is a true copy of the books kept by Halifax Co Commissioner of
Confiscated Property.

307U. [page 18]:
List of persons who haven't paid for confiscated property to Saml Welden, Wm Montfort, & Wm Wooten, Halifax Co
Commissioners of Confiscated Property, whose property it was formerly, & amount due:
William Gridstead; property of Andw Miller & Co; amount due £27.18
James Hinton; property of Andw Miller & Co; amount due £39.12
William Lowe; property of John Thompson; amount due £12.18
William Lowe; property of Andw Miller & Co; amount due £7.10
William Lowe; property of Alexr Telfair & Co; amount due £20
Robert Hall; property of Archd Hamilton; amount due £261
James Leslie; property of Andw Miller & Co--Postleworth's Dictionary; amount due £[blank]
Mary Rodgers; property of Archd Hamilton & Co; amount due £8.0.6
Mary Rodgers; property of Alexr Telfair & Co; amount due £2
Major Smith; property of Alexr Telfair & Co; amount due £1.8.6

307V. [page 15]:
Christopher Dudley; property of John Thompson; amount due £46.12
James Pasteur; property of Archd Hamilton & Co; amount due £575
Christopher Haynes; property of David Telfair & Co; amount due £44
Christopher Haynes; property of Andw Miller & Co; amount due £0.18
Wm Noblin; property of David Telfair & Co; amount due £14.16
John Brickill; property of George Wray, Virginia; amount due £26.13.4
Frederick Jones; property of David Telfair & Co; amount due £86.16
William Pass; property of David Telfair & Co; amount due £7.8.8
William Pass; property of Jno Thompson; amount due £6.4
John Rorie jr; property of David Telfair & Co; amount due £4
Ann Fort; property of David Telfair & Co; amount due £13.12.8
Joseph Borden; property of David Telfair & Co; amount due £5.13
Joseph Borden; property of Andw Miller & Co; amount due £9.18.4
Joseph Borden; property of Archd Hamilton & Co; amount due £6.16.4
    [subtotal] £1,228.15.4 owed

307W. [page 16]:
"Note"--ink blobs on the sheet are an accident   [signed] Wm Wooten
John Steptoe sr; property of David Telfair & Co; amount due £15.16.8
Arthur Pitman; property of David Telfair & Co; amount due £16.5.4

Sales of Confiscated Land

Arthur Pitman; property of Alexr Telfair & Co; amount due £17.17.6

Willie Jones; property of Archd Hamilton & Co; amount due £1,145.10.3

Willie Jones; property of Alston Young & Co; amount due £239.2.11

Willie Jones, as exr. of Robert Jones decd; property of Henry Murcot, exr of Richd Edwards decd; amount due
£324.17.8 + interest £81.19.5 = £406.17.1
[written below] £127.12.7

William Martin; property of Andw Miller & Co--3 Negroes = Will, Jack, & Hannah; amount due £[omitted]

William Martin; property of Henry Martin--part of a tract sold, money due Aug. 1780 1/6th of 600 ac in Granville
Co on waters of Nuttbush Cr, borders: Lemuel Simms; amount due £[omitted]

307X. [page 21]:

Joseph Gray; property of Alexr Telfair & Co--Negro girl Dinah; amount due £750

Joseph Gray; property of Andw Miller & Co; amount due £32.8.8

Joseph Gray; property of Jno Thompson; amount due £233.18.8

Joseph Gray; property of Murdock Hudson & Co; amount due £113.12

Joseph Gray; property of Alexr Telfair & Co; amount due £92.7

Peter Bird; property of David Telfair & Co; amount due £43.8

Holliday Packer; property of Cunnerson & Co; amount due £13

Edward Brantley; property of David Telfair & Co; amount due £5.12

Edward Brantley; property of John Thompson; amount due £2.4

Stephen Butler; property of John Doaks, Cross Creek; amount due £5

Stephen Butler; property of John Leggitt; amount due £0.18

Thomas Taylor; property of Cunnerson & Co; amount due £2.15
[subtotal] £4,493.1 owed

307Y. [page 22]:

Harris Taylor; property of Cunnerson & Co; amount due £6

Wm Coupland; property of John Thompson; amount due £5.19.6

Benjamin Sherwood; property of Cunnerson & Co; amount due £25.8.6

Benjamin Sherwood; property of Andw Miller & Co; amount due £130

William Coupland "self"; property of John Sim, Isle of Wright, Va; amount due £20

Wm Barksdale; property of Archd Hamilton & Co; amount due £31.6

Coupland Whitfield; property of Archd Hamilton & Co; amount due £13.3

Oliver Joyner; property of Andw Miller & Co; amount due £0.17

Lacy Simmons; property of Young Alston & Co; amount due £38.1.7

John Branch; property of David Telfair & Co--1 pr. small steelyards; amount due £33.9.4

John Branch; property of Alexr Telfair & Co; amount due £22

Caleb Moncrief; property of David Telfair & Co; amount due £13.12.8

Caleb Moncrief; property of Archd Hamilton & Co; amount due £2.9.4

307Z. [page 19]:

John Bradford esq; property of David Telfair & Co--1 pr. steelyards; amount due £20 [? hole in page]

John Bradford esq; property of Andw Miller & Co; amount due £8.13

Timothy Ives; property of David Telfair & Co; amount due £0.11

William Reid jr; property of John Thompson; amount due £010.6

Wm Ozbern; property of Andw Miller & Co; amount due £16.5

Drewry Harrington; property of Archd Hamilton & Co; amount due £367.10

Drewry Harrington; property of James McNeil; amount due £1.5

Joseph Edwards; property of Archd Hamilton & Co; amount due £75.12.8

Joseph Edwards; property of David Telfair & Co; amount due £3.10.8

Joel Walker; property of David Telfair & Co; amount due £28.10.4

Elisha Ward; property of David Telfair & Co; amount due £9.18.4

Sales of Confiscated Land

Thomas Drummond; property of David Telfair & Co; amount due £1.2.6
Thomas Drummond; property of Andw Miller & Co; amount due £6.4
John Long; property of Archd Hamilton & Co; amount due £273.12
John Long; property of David Telfair & Co; property of 4.15.9
   [subtotal] £5,833.8.8 owed

307AA. [page 20]:
William Moran; property of Archd Hamilton & Co; amount due £40.12
William Moran; property of David Telfair & Co; amount due £9.18.4
John Scoals; property of Archd Hamilton & Co; amount due £5.2
Joseph Daniell; property of James McNeil amount due £1.15
Elizabeth Hath; property of Archd Hamilton & Co; amount due £1.15
Elizabeth Hath; property of James McNeil; amount due £13
William Wright; property of James McNeil; amount due £21
William Wright; property of Archd Hamilton; amount due £20
Henry Perkins; property of Thos McKnight, Currituck; amount due £3
Shadrach Weaver; property of James McNeil; amount due £1.17.6
Mark Pitt; property of James McNeil amount due £14.17.4
Peter Robertson; property of John Thompson; amount due £178
Jesse Williams, as exr. of Wilson Williams; property of James McNei; amount due £25.1
Absalom Nicholson; property of David Telfair & Co; amount due £6.14
Absalom Nicholson; property of James McNeil; amount due £2.0

307BB. [page 23]:
Absalom Nicholson, as security of Nichs Lewis; property of James McNeil; amount due £5.10.5
Richard Hill; property of Archd Hamilton & Co; amount due £23.10
Joseph Wright Nicholson; property of James McNeil; amount due £21.1.4
Joseph Wright Nicholson; property of David Telfair & Co; amount due £22.4
Eli Williams; property of Archd Hamilton & Co; amount due £25.16.8
Eli Williams; property of James McNeil; amount due £25.16.8
Eli Williams; property of David Telfair & Co; amount due £4.10
Isaac Dean; property of Archd Hamilton & Co; amount due £25.15.9
Aaron Clark; property of David Telfair & Co; amount due £10.16
Aaron Clark; property of Archd Hamilon & Co; amount due £14.17
Thomas Mathis; property of Archd Hamilton & Co; amount due £79.1
John Powers; property of Archd Hamilton & Co; amount due £38.1.2
Presley Cox; property of Archd Hamilton & Co; amount due £20.13
John Stephens; property of Archd Hamilton & Co; amount due £11.7.4
   [subtotla] £6,463.6.4 owed

307CC. [page 24]:
Joel Hurt; property of Archd Hamilton & Co; amount due £200
Thomas Dunn; property of Andw Miller & Co; amount due £0.18
Phillip Kearney; property of Andw Miller & Co; amount due £10
Phillip Kearney; property of Archd Hamilton & Co; amount due £815
Thomas Ring; property of Archd Hamilton & Co; amount due £142.12
Cory Cox; property of Andw Miller & Co; amount due £30
Moses Reid; property of Andw Miller & Co; amount due £4.8.6
Wm Daniell; property of Andw Miller & Co; amount due £2.12
Wm Hurt; property of Archd Hamilton & Co; amount due £19.15.2
Benjamin Nevel; property of Archd Hamilton & Co; amount due £2.10
Benjamin Nevel; property of Andw Miller & Co; amount due £1

James Fawseit; property of Archd Hamilton & Co; amount due £5.11.8
Nicholas Lewis; property of Andw Miller & Co; amount due £2.18.7
John Powers; property of Archd Hamilton & Co; amount due £24.1.3

307DD. [page 25]:
Wm Burt; property of Archd Hamilton & Co; amount due £46.11.5
Wm Crabb; property of Archd Hamilton & Co; amount due £0.2
John Saxon; property of Archd Hamilton & Co; amount due £92.13
John Saxon; property of David Telfair & Co; amount due £3.5.6
James Hogg; property of Archd Hamilton & Co; amount due £8.12.8
James Hogg; property of James McNeil; amount due £4
Isaac Jackson; property of Archd Hamilton & Co; amount due £10.13.4
Isaac Jackson; property of Anthy Warwick & Co; amount due £5
Wm Mahony; property of John Thompson; amount due £13.10
Charles Blanton; property of Andw Miller & Co; amount due £6
Charles Blanton; property of Archd Hamilton & Co; amount due £17.3
Willis Alston; property of Archd Hamilton & Co; amount due £9
Willis Alston; property of Andw Miller & Co; amount due £41
Chrislun Morris; property of Anthoy Warwick & Co; amount due £10.10
Littleberry Green; property of Andw Miller & Co; amount due £3.0
Francis Williams; property of Anthy Warwick & Co; amount due £3.14.10
  [subtotal] £7,998.19.3 owed

307EE. [page 26]:
Richard Stevens; property of Archd Hamilton & Co; amount due £4.8
Richard Stevens; property of Archd Cunnerson & Co; amount due £3
Edward Good; property of John Thompson; amount due £5.15.5
Samuel Mattox; property of Andw Miller & Co; amount due £0.14
Drury King; property of Anthy Warwick & Co; amount due £0.5
Molton Carter; property of Anthy Warwick & Co; amount due £3.0
Holeman Southall; property of Anthy Warwick & Co; amount due £26.13.4
Sarah Williams; property of Anthy Warwick & Co; amount due £1.6.6
Richd Pemberton; property of John Thompson; amount due £3.8.10
Richd Pemberton; property of Anthy Warwick & Co; amount due £7.4
Richd Pemberton; property of Alexr Hamilton & Co; amount due £10
Richd Pemberton; property of Andw Miller & Co; amount due £27.3.8
James Mallory; property of Crawford & Co; amount due £9.7
James Mallory; property of Doctor Warren; amount due £2.13.4
James Mallory; property of Anthy Warwick & Co; amount due £5

307FF. [page G]:
Francis Mallory; property of Crawford & Co; amount due £19.16.8
Francis Mallory; property of Warren & Co; amount due £19.16.8
John Gunn; property of Anthy Warwick & Co; amount due £1.15
John Gunn; property of John Graham; amount due £16
Mary Ellis; property of McGeorge & Co; amount due £25
Benjamin Carter; property of Anthy Warwick & Co; amount due £13.1.1
John Justice esq; property of Andw Miller & Co; amount due £48.15
John Justice esq; property of Anthy Warwick & Co; amount due £40
Saml Norwood; property of Andw Miller & Co; amount due £17.5
Richd Norwood; property of John Thompson; amount due £2.12.6

Sales of Confiscated Land

Richd Norwood; property of Alexr Telfair & Co; amount due £1.10
Joseph Taylor; property of John Thompson; amount due £0.5
David Pugh; property of Archd Hamilton & Co; amount due £0.14
  [subtotal] £8,299.13.10 owed

307GG. [page H]:
Ephraim Merritt; property of Anthy Warwick & Co; amount due £0.14.8
Uriah Smith; property of John Thompson; amount due £21.10
Uriah Smith; property of Andw Miller & Co; amount due £2
Benjamin McCulloch; property of Archd Hamilton & Co--Oct. 10, 1777 "£1299"; amount due £1,279.18.11½
Benjamin McCulloch; property of Archd Hamilton & Co "bond"; amount due £5,700
Benjamin McCulloch; property of David Donald; amount due £53.6.8
Benjamin McCulloch; property of Andw Miller & Co; amount due £60
Benjamin McCulloch; property of Alexander & H Telfair & Co; amount due £55
Phillip Corlew; property of John Thompson; amount due £7.12
Richard Thompson; property of Archd Hamilton & Co; amount due £2.6
Mark Browning; property of Archd Hamilton & Co; amount due £25.16
Daniel Crawley; property of Andw Miller & Co; amount due £7
Joseph Dickin; property of Andw Miller & Co; amount due £23.4
Joseph Dickin; property of Archd Hamilton & Co; amount due £5.2.6
Joseph Ewbank; property of Andw Miller & Co; amount due £5

307HH. [page I]:
Elias Harris; property of Hamilton & Co [sic]; amount due £190.8
John Purnall; property of Archd Hamilton & Co; amount due £20
Henry Evans; property of Archd Cunnerson & Co; amount due £28.4.7
Josiah Sparks; property of Archd Hamilton & Co "bond"; amount due £46.15 "account" £6
Charles Moore; property of Alexr Telfair & Co; amount due £16
Charles Moore; property of John Thompson; amount due £5.13.4
John Daniell; property of Hamilton & Co; amount due £36
John Daniell; property of James McNeil; amount due £25.18
John B Ashe; property of McCloud; amount due £10
Col. Alexanr. McCulloch; property of Archd Hamilton & Co; amount due £300
Chas Pasteur; property of Andw Miller & Co; amount due £23
Chas Pasteur; property of Gibson & Co, Virginia; amount due £9.6.8
Chas Pasteur; property of Cunnerson & Co--for Hatchet; amount due £22
Chas Pasteur; property of Miller's estate, bond & interest; amount due £321
  [subtotal] £16,608.10.2½ owed

307II. [page J]:
Egbert Haywood; property of Andw Miller & Co; amount due £7.8
William Dilliard; property of Andw Miller & Co; amount due £7.8
John Gaskins; property of David Telfair & Co; amount due £20.6
William Hall; property of Alexr Telfair & Co; amount due £287.5.10
William Hall; property of John Thompson; amount due £58.5.1
William Hall; property of Archd Cunnerson & Co; amount due £21.19.2
William Hall; property of Wm McClellan, Tarbo.; amount due £8.2
Chas Mitchell; property of David Telfair & Co; amount due £2
Chas Mitchell; property of John Thompson; amount due £3.7.6
John Phillips; property of David Telfair & Co; amount due £10
William Merritt; property of David Telfair & Co; amount due £12.6.8
William Merritt; property of Alexr Telfair & Co; amount due £13.12

Sales of Confiscated Land

William Merritt; property of Archd Cunnerson & Co; amount due £43.4
    [subtotal] £17,137.16.5½ owed

307JJ. [page K]:
John Merritt; property of David Telfair; amount due £1.10
Thomas Hill sr; property of James McNeil--9 Negroes & increase & 3 tracts of land; amount due £ [omitted]
Col. Nicholas Long "made improvements"; property of Andw Miller & Co--100 ac near the town of Halifax, 500
    or 600 ac on Quonkie Cr, houses & lots in Halifax town with 30 ac; amount due £ [omitted]
Col. Jno Whitaker "Informd."; [former] "owner unknown supposed to have been plundered--a Negro boy claimed
    by Benjamin Waller & proved to satisfaction of Wm Wooten
[signed] Wm Wooten and Wm Montfort, "Com. C. P."

[page L]:
Wm Wooten, "C Ct", certifys the foregoing is a true copy of the book kept by Halifax Commissioners of Confiscated
Property; [signed] Wm Wooten;   "David Short, exr. of Saml Weldon in No hampton; Will Montfort--Onslow"

308. [two copies of the following list] State of North Carolina account with Will Montfort, Halifax Co Commissioner
of Confiscated Property:
cash received of "sundrie" people	£2,246.14.7	
cash "ditto" of Henry Montford	£3,500	
	[total]	£5,746.14.7

cash paid Col. Nichs Long	£4,200	
"ditto" Wm Wooten, Commr	£ 974.4	
"ditto" John Geddy for paper	£ 40	
"ditto" cash per balance	£ 532.10.7	
[total]	£5,746.14.7	

Halifax Co Nov. session 1783 the foregoing was examined in Court.   [signed] Jno Geddy & H Montfort
Halifax Co Nov. session 1783 the foregoing was examined in Court by John Geddy & H Montfort, esqs & approved
and Commissioner allowed 2%.   [signed] Wm Wooten, "C Ct"

309. [two copies of the following list] State of North Carolina in account with Wm Wooten:
Jul. 2, 1789 cash paid Col. Nichs Long	£4,150	
balance due the State	£1,703.3.4	
	[total]	£5,853.3.4
Jul. 1780 cash received of sundry persons	£4,878.19.4	
Jun. 1780 cash received of Will Montfort, Comr.	£ 974.4	
	[total]	£5,853.3.4
balance due the State	£1,703.3.4	

Halifax Co Nov. session 1783 the foregoing was examined in Court. [signed] Jno Geddy & H Montfort
Halifax Co Nov. session 1783 the foregoing was examined in Court by John Geddy & Henry Montfort, exqs, &
approved and Commissioner allowed 2%.   [signed] Wm Wooten, C Ct.

310. Account of Confiscated Property sold by Nichs Long that belonged to the "State of" Jas McNeale:
143 ac on the road from Halifax to Culpepper's Bridge over Fishing Cr £2,000
a black horse   £40.5
a grey horse   £5.10
Negro Jacob--£377.1, Negro Phill--£740.7, 1 "Bofald"--£50.6 [total] £1,167.4
381 ac on Swift Cr in Nash Co £2,600
208 ac on Beaverdam Swamp in Nash Co £320
Negro George £735.1   [total] £6,850.10

Sales of Confiscated Land

deduct Court's allowance for wife of said McNeale--£2,283.10

311. Halifax Co Court (at Halifax town) third Monday in Aug. (or Aug. 15), 1785: Fanny, wife of Jams McNeale, asked the Court for provision out of estate of James McNeale, the same being confiscated, & the Court ordered she is to get a third before estate is sold. [signed] Wm Wooten, C Ct.

312. Receipt [no number] Dec. 2, 1785 to Christopher Hayns [or Haynes], Halifax Co surveyor, £24 for 12 surveys.

313. Receipt No. 475 May 4, 1787 to Christopher Haynes, Halifax Co surveyor, £4 for surveying one tract & a lot in Halifax.

314. [two copies of this list: one has prices indicated as certificates or bonds as well as total price, the other has only total price]   Sept. 19, 1785 Account of sales of Confiscated Property in Halifax Co:
a) 341 ac on N side of Quankey Cr in Halifax Co; formerly property of Andrew Miller & Co; bought by Nicholas Long for £350 certificates
b) 24 ac joining Halifax town; formerly property of Andrew Miller & Co; bought by John Geddy for £382 bond
c) 108 ac on Simms Meadow; formerly property of Andrew Miller & Co; bought by John Clayton for £606.5 certificates
d) lot 3, improved, in Halifax town; formerly property Andrew Miller & Co; bought by John Ponns for £320 certificates
e) lot 63 in Halifax town; formerly property Andrew Miller & Co; bought by John Geddy for £290 bond
f) lot 64, improved, in Halifax town; formerly property Andrew Miller & Co; bought by John Ponns for £636 certificates
g) lot 65, improved, in Halifax town; formerly property Andrew Miller & Co; bought by John Ponns for £1,651.6
h) Negro Mungale; formerly property Andrew Miller & Co; bought by John Baptist Ashe for £725 bond
i) Negro Cesar; formerly property Andrew Miller & Co; bought by Fanifold Green [or James West Green--on second list] for £1,010.1 bond
j) Negro Bob; formerly property Andrew Miller & Co; bought by Robert Freear for £800 certificates
k) Negroes Will & Hannah; formerly property Andrew Miller & Co; bought by John Geddy for £378 bond
l) a black horse; formerly James McNeel's property; bought by John Geddy for £378 bond
m) a black horse; formerly James McNeel's property; bought by Jesse Read for £5.10 certificates
n) 172 ac on Marsh Swamp; sold in 1777 by Archd Hamilton & Co to Edwd Moore; bought by John Baptist Ashe for £164 certificates
o) 143 ac on Jenito Br; sold in 1777 by Archd Hamilton & Co to Edwd Moore; ought by John Baptist Ashe for £200 certificates
p) 138 ac on N side of Marsh Swamp; "convey'd as aforesd"; bought by John Baptist Ashe for £110 certificates
q) 275 ac on Burnt coat Swamp; "convey'd as aforesd"; bought by James Carstaphan for £150 certificates
r) a Negro Jack; formerly James McNeel's property; bought by James Carstaphan for £377.1 certificates   [on first list & not the second list]
s) 2 pr. tobac. screws; formerly Andr Miller's property; bought by John Geddy for £32
t) Negro Phil; formerly James McNeel's property; bought by Thos Armstrong for £740.7 certificates
u) a corner "bofett" etc; formerly James McNeel's property; bought by Jeremiah Nelms for £50.6 certificates
[total]   £6,160.15 certificates + £2,857.6 bonds = £9,018.1

315. Mar. 1, 1786 surveyed 0.5 ac lot No. 37 in Halifax town; formerly James Milner's property; plat shows lot is on the corner of St. David's St & Dobbs St; [signed] "X"pher Haynes, surveyor; [on back] Lunsford Long.

316. Mar. 1, 1786 surveyed 478 ac; formerly James Milner's property; on Cowhall Swamp; border: Marmaduke Young, Solomon Turner, & Charles Johnson; [signed] "X"pher Haynes, surveyor; [on back] Honore Gerroud.

317. May 28, 1785 surveyed 336 ac; No. 67; formerly property of Andrew Miller & "others"; on N side of Little Quankey Cr; [signed] "X"pher Haynes, surveyor; [on back] Nicholas Long.

318. Jun. 14, 1785 surveyed 0.5 ac lot No. 3 in Halifax town on Roanoak R; formerly Andrew Miller & Co's property; on the corner of Dobbs St & St. Georges St; No. 68; [signed] "X"pher Haynes, surveyor; [on back] John Ponns.

319. Jun. 14, 1785 surveyed 0.5 ac lot No. 63 in Halifax town on Roanoak R; formerly Andrew Miller & Co's property; on King St "or" Main St; No. 66; [signed] "X"pher Haynes, surveyor; [on back] John Geddy.

320. Jun. 14, 1785 surveyed 0.5 ac lot 64 in Halifax town; formerly Andrew Miller & Co's property; on Kings St "or" Main St; No. 69; [signed] "X"pher Haynes, surveyor; [on back] John Ponns

321. Jun. 14, 1785 surveyed 0.5 ac lot No. 65 in Halifax town; formerly Andrew Miller & Co's property; on the corner of Kings "or" Main St and St. George's St and on Roanoak R; No. 63; [signed] "X"pher Haynes, surveyor; [on back] John Ponns.

322. Jun. 14, 1785 surveyed 105 ac; formerly Andrew Miller & Co's property; border: John Clayton and Eelbeck; No. 61; [signed] "X"pher Haynes, surveyor; chain carriers Paul Meecham & Jas Kendall; [on back] John Clayton.

323. Jun. 15, 1785 surveyed 21 ac; formerly Andrew Miller & Co's property; border: James Leslie's lower corner on S side of Roanoak R, runs up the river to lower corner of Halifax town, along the town line to upper corner of lot 106, & joins Willie Jones' line; No. 65; [signed] "X"pher Haynes, surveyor; [on back] John Geddy.

324. Jun. 15,1785 surveyed 336 ac; formerly Andrew Miller & Co's property; on N side of Quankey Cr; No. 62; [signed] "X"pher Haynes, surveyor; [on back] Nicholas Long.

325. Sept. 6, 1785 surveyed 138 ac; formerly property of John Hambleton & "others"; on N side of Marsh Swamp; border: Pryor Gardiner's corner in Clemment's line, Joseph Edmonson, & the mouth of Geneto Br; No. 1; [signed] "X"pher Haynes, surveyor; chain carriers Pryor Gardiner & Robt Harris [two copies of this survey].

326. Sept. 7, 1785 surveyed 143 ac; formerly property of John Hambleton & "others"; on S side of Marsh Swamp; border: George Heleofer, Joseph Gardiner, & Meeting Stone Br; No. 3; [signed] "X"pher Haynes, surveyor; chain carriers John Wood & Robt Harris [two copies of this survey].

327. Sept. 7, 1785 surveyed 172 ac; formerly property of John Hambleton & "others"; on N side of Marsh Swamp; border: the mouth of Geneto Br, John Wood, & John Hairgroves; No. 2; [signed] "X"pher Haynes, surveyor; chain carriers John Wood & Robt Harris [two copies of this survey].

328. Sept. 8, 1785 surveyed 275 ac; formerly property of John Hambleton & "others"; on head of Jacket Swamp; border: Taylor Flewellin, Cone, Samuel Smith, & Willm Pearman; No. 60; [signed] "X"pher Haynes, surveyor; chain carriers Lewis Daniel & Shadrick Rogers; [on back] Jas Cathstaphen [sic].

HERTFORD COUNTY
329. a petition by James Baker (of Hertford Co) to the Legislative Committee on Petitions: in 1787 Baker bought from Col. Hardy Murfree, Edenton Dist. Commissioner of Confiscated Property, two tracts of 320 ac each, "reported by" Tyrrel Co surveyor as confiscated, for £3,360 by bond; prior to the sale, the land was entered by John Hooker and a grant obtained; due to writ of "enquiry" and jury verdict, the land was found to belong to Hooker; Col. Murfree says the land was returned as property of James Craven decd, a citizen of this State, "who" informed the Commissioner that "he" could "contend" the land as "his undoubted right", if he could find the grant to his father; the Committee finds that if "Mr. Craven" can't find the grant and the land belonged to no one prior to Hooker's entry, then the land is out of reach of the Confiscation law and belongs to Hooker; Committee recommends following resolution: (1) the Commissioner is to dismiss a suit he instituted in Hertford Co Court "on" Baker's bond "for" said purchase money when Baker pays the cost "thereof" [the Court suit], (2) either cancel or deliver the bond to him [Baker], and (3) the

Sales of Confiscated Land

Comptroller is to "credit" the Commissioner's account that amount. [signed] Fredk Harget, chairman; read & concur--in Senate Dec. 8, 1790 and in House Dec. 11, 1790.

330. Receipt No. 153 Dec. 29, 1785 to Samuel Bell £6 for surveying two tracts and a town lot.

331. Receipt No. 300 Oct. 12, 1786 to Samuel Bell £2 [or £0.40] for surveying a lot.

332. Account of Confiscated Property sold in Hertford Co:
a) a lot in Winton, unimproved, No. 45; formerly John Agnew's property; bought by Thomas Brickell for £130 certificate
b) 640 ac, improved, on Meherin Cr; formerly Hartly & Nicholson's property; bought by Josiah Collins for £1,360
c) 102 ac, unimproved, on Meherin Cr; formerly Hartly & Nicholson's property; bought by Josiah Collins for £405
[total] £1,895 [signed] H Murfree, Comr

333. Aug. 12, 1786 surveyed 0.5 ac lot No. 22 in Winton, unimproved; formerly John Agnew's property; border: on N side of Back St; 150' by 150'; [signed] Samuel Bell, surveyor; chain carriers Mathias Brickell jr & Samuel Bell; [on back] Hardy Murfree.

334. Nov. 5, 1785 surveyed 102 ac; part of a tract known as Mt. Sion; formerly Messrs. Hartley & Nicholson's property; border: James Wright & "the" pecoson; [signed] Samuel Bell, surveyor; chain carriers William Walton & James Copeland; [on back] Josiah Collins jr.

335. Nov. 5, 1785 surveyed 640 ac; known as Mt. Sion; formerly Messrs. Hartley & Nicholson's property; border: James Wright, Ozias Beeman, James Copeland, a branch, Elm Swamp, & Jackson; [signed] Samuel Bell, surveyor; chain carriers William Walton & James Copeland; [on back] Josiah Collins.

336. Nov. 27, 1785 surveyed 0.5 ac, unimproved, lot No. 45 in Winton; formerly John Agnew's property; border: fronts on Main St, Wynns St, & Ferry St; 300' on Wynns St and 75' on Main & Ferry Streets; [signed] Samuel Bell, surveyor; chain carriers Mathias Brickell jr & Samuel Bell; [on back] Thos Brickell.

HYDE COUNTY
337. Receipt No. 326 Nov. 22, 1786 to Southe Rue, Hyde Co surveyor, £22 for 11 surveys.

338. Mar. 15, 1785 surveyed 400 ac due to order of James Armstrong, Edenton Dist Commr of Confiscation; in Mattemaskeet [Swamp] on W side of Wesockin Cr; formerly William Piat's property; border: SE corner of a place known as Mulberry Ridge; [signed] Southy Rue, surveyor; [on back] Dec. 22, 1785 by James Armstrong, Newbern Dist. Comr. of Confiscation, to John Cooper esq of Virginia for £401.

339. Aug. 30, 1785 surveyed 640 ac; formerly Robert Palmer esq's property; on "the" ridge of Mattamaskett [Lake]; border: the lake and the Indian's survey; [signed] Southy Rue, surveyor; [on back] No. 2 Dec. 22, 1785 sold by Col. James Armstrong, Comr., to Col. Joseph Leech for £76.

340. Aug. 30, 1785 surveyed 500 ac; formerly Robert Palmer esq's property; "in" the ridge of Mattamaskett Lake; border: "his" other survey, Gibbs esq, & the lake; [signed] Southy Rue, surveyor; [on back] No. 3 Dec. 22, 1785 sold by James Armstrong, Newbern Dist. Comr. of Confiscation, to John Cooper esq of Virginia for £150.

341. Aug. 30, 1785 surveyed 640 ac; formerly Robert Palmer esq's property; in New Currituck Swamp; border: "his" own corner in John Smith's line, Anthony Tooley, John Tooley, Giddin, & John Slade; [signed] Southy Rue, surveyor; [on back] No. 4 Dec. 22, 1785 sold by Col. James Armstrong, Comr., to Joseph Leech for £370.

Sales of Confiscated Land

342. Aug. 30, 1785 surveyed 300 ac; formerly Robert Palmer esq's property; on S side of Mattamaskite Lake; border: Caleb Swindel and the lake; [signed] Southy Rue, surveyor; [on back] No. 5 Dec. 22, 1785 sold by James Armstrong, Newbern Dist. Comr. of Confiscation, to John Cooper esq of Virginia for £95.

343. Aug. 30, 1785 surveyed 200 ac; formerly Robert Palmer esq's property; in New Currituck [Swamp] on the head of Chappel Cr; border: a branch that makes out of Chappel Cr, Thomas Easter, & William Easter; [signed] Southy Rue, surveyor; [on back] No. 6 Dec. 22, 1785 sold by James Armstrong, Newbern Dist. Comr. of Confiscation, to James Jesper for £202.

344. Aug. 30, 1785 surveyed 400 ac; formerly Robert Palmer esq's property; on the ridge of Mattamaskett Lake on NW side; border: the land and the swamp; [signed] Southy Rue, surveyor; [on back] No. 1 Dec. 22, 1785 sold by Col. James Armstrong, Comr., to Joseph Leech for £91; [the following in very small writing] "Thos Thornton bought part of the above".

345. Sept. 1, 1785 surveyed 640 ac; formerly Robert Palmer esq's property; in Mattamaskett [Swamp] on N side of the lake and back of Fort Point; border: William Swindel's "outer" corner and James Clayton's back line; [signed] Southy Rue, surveyor; [on back] No. 8 Dec. 22, 1785 sold by James Armstrong, Newbern Dist. Comr. of Confiscation, to John Alderson for £304.

346. Sept. 2, 1785 surveyed 260 ac; formerly Robert Palmer esq's property; on S side of Mattamaskett Lake; border: Bartholomew Cain's NW corner on the lake "formerly" called William Cradle's corner; [signed] Southy Rue, surveyor; [on back] Dec. 22, 1785 sold by James Armstrong, Newbern Dist. Comr. of Confiscation, to John Cooper of Virginia for £205.

LENOIR COUNTY
347. Apr. 1, 1794 received of William White £10, my fee in a suit of ejectt. brought by Newbern Dist. Commissioner of Confiscated Property for recovery of Tower Hill land in Lenoir Cr; [signed] Bl. Baker.

348. Jul. 16, 1787 received of Charles Markland sq £181 in certificates for lot No. 29 in Kinston; formerly Samuel Cornell's property; [signed] James Armstrong, Newbern Dist. Commissioner of Confiscated Property.

349. Apr. 9, 1794 surveyed 0.5 ac No. 29 in Kinston, due to "certificate" from Newbern Dist. Commissioner of Confiscated Property to Charles Markland; border: Caswells, Herritages, & Gordens Streets and joins the Chappel lot; [signed] Lamuel Byrd, surveyor.

LINCOLN COUNTY
350. a bond Apr. 17, 1781 John Caruth, Joseph Dickson, Thomas White, & Samuel Espey; £250,000 for John Caruth to be commissioner. Signed John Caruth, Joseph Dickson, Thomas White, & Samuel Espey. Witness D Dnney [or D D Hkey], John Barber, & Samuel White.

351. a bond Apr. 17, 1781 John Barber, James White, Robert Alexander, & Frederick Hambright; £250,000 for John Barber to be commissioner. Signed John Barber, James White, Robt Alexander, & Fred Hambright. Witness D D Hkey, Thos White, & John Caruth.

352. a bond Apr. 17, 1781 Thomas Espey, Adam Niell, James Huggins, & Jacob Money; £250,000 for Thomas Espey to be a commissioner. Signed Thos Espey, James Huggins, Jacob Money's mark, & Adam Niell. Wintess D D Hkey, Frederick Hambright, & Jas White.

353. Report Oct. session 1783 by Thomas Espey, John Barber, & John Carruth:
a) from the estate of Nicholas Warlock--5,700 wt of beef delivered to County commr. Robt Alexander esq $313
b) and a horse from said estate--appraised at £25 specie delivered to Col. Dickson for use of State Troops
c) sold from the estate of said Nicholas Warlock £27,016 currency

Sales of Confiscated Land

    "plantation" and mill rented to   £ 2,500 curry.

    a Negro wench hired at   £   45 curry.

d) from the estate of William Ramsey--1,000 wt of beef delivered to County   Commr. $55

e) from the estate of Jacob Mauny jr--570 wt of beef delivered to County   Commr. $31

f) from the estate of Peter Carpinter--520 wt of beef delivered to County   Commr. $28.75

g) from the estate of John Alexander--520 wt of beef delivered to County   Commr. $28.75

h) sold of the estate of Bickerstaff & Robinson £2,170 curry.

i) from the estate of Abel Beatey--1,000 wt of beef delivered to County Commr. $55;   rent of the plantation & Negroes £1,060 currency

j) by order of Col. Dickson delivered to Hugh Polk "DC" for the hospital at Charlotte--a number of cattle appraised at £19,020 curry.

k) sold at vendue--the property of Nicholas Welch £700 curry.

l) delivered to County Commr.--57 head of cattle appraised at £29,300 curry.

m) sold at vendue--estate of Moses Moore £29,828 curry.; land rented @ £425 curry.

n) sold at vendue--estate of Peter Costner decd. £43,403 curry.

o) sold at vendue--estate of Prestin Goforth decd. £4,507 curry.

p) sold at vendue--estate of Solomon Bason decd. £11,757 curry.; and a horse appraised at £30 specie delivered for public service

q) hired at public sale--3 Negroes, property of Bickerstaff, hired at £60

r) hired at public sale--6 Negroes £515

s) hired at public sale--a Negro wench, property of John Richop, hired at £260

t) Solomon Bason's land rnted at £1,910

u) Pinkney's land rented at 25 bushels of corn

[signed] Jo Dickson, c. c.

354. [The following is similar to #353 above and is from Lincoln Co Pleas & Quarter Sessions Court Mintues--CR 060.301.1 pages 135 & 136.]

Lincoln Co October session 1785 [sic]

    The Committee to whom was referred the settlement of the "accompts" of the Commissioners of Confiscated Property for said county report as follows: vizt. it is their "oppinion" that all the property of the disaffected persons sold by the Commissioners and not collected the notes and bonds be returned to the owner or owners and the specie notes be paid in specie indents according to the intent at the time of taking them and the currency notes in currency or by the scale and that all the cattle, provisions, etc. which the Commissioners "sized" being the property of disaffected persons which they actually gave to the public be confiscated to the use of the same. [signed] Robert Alexander, James Logon, & John Wilson

    Court concurred with said report and ordered the same to be entered on their minutes.

According to the direction of the above Committee, the said "comms" came into Court and exhibited the following accounts:

State Dr.	State Crt.
a) delivered to Robert Alexander, County Commr.,	from widdow Warlock
5,700 wt of beef £125.4	5,700 wt of beef £125.4
a horse delivered to Joseph Dickson for	
public service £25.0	by one horse £25
b) delivered to Robert Alexander, County Commr.,	
1,000 wt of beef from Wm Ramsey	by 1,000 wt beef £22
c) delivered to Robt Alexander, County Commr.,	
520 [wt of beef] from Peter Carpinter £11.4	by 520 wt beef £11.4
d) delivered to Robt Alexander, County Commr.,	
520 wt of beef from John Alexander £11.4	by 520 wt beef £11.4
e) Jun. 8, 1781 delivered to Robt Alexander,	
County Commr., 57 head of cattle appraised	by 57 head of cattle

Sales of Confiscated Land

£29,300   £29,300

f) May 31, 1781 delivered to Hugh Polk, D. Comy,   by 36 head of cattle
     36 head of cattle appraised to   £19,980   £19,980

g) Jan. 1782 received by the Commissioners from
     the amount of the sales of Bickerstaff's and   by cash in currency
     Robinson's estates   £2,170 currency   £2,170

h) Jan. 1782 received by the Commrs. cash from
     the sales of the estate of Nicholas Welch in   by cash in currency
     currency   £700   £700

The following property ordered by Court to be returned to the former owners:

i) recd. by the Commrs. notes & bonds from the
     sale of the estate of Moses Moore to the
     ammount of currency   £30,263

j) to cash from the sale of the estate of Peter
      Costner in currency notes   £43,403

k) to cash from the sale of Prestin Goforth's estate in currency notes   £4,507

l) to cash from the sale of the estate of Solomon Beson in currency   £11,757
     and a horse at £30 specie   £30

m) to cash from the hire of 3 Negroes from the
     estate of Benn Bickerstaff in currency notes   £60

n) to cash for the hire of 6 Negroes the property
     of Lenard Saylor in currency notes   £515

o) to the hire of one Negro the property of John Richop in currency   £260

p) to the rent of Solomon Besson's land in currency   £1,910

q) to the estate of Abel Beatey for beef an indent in specie   £22

r) to the estate of Jacob Mauny for beef an indent in specie   £12.8

s) to the rent of Pinkby's [or Pinkly] land in specie   £3.2.6

Lincoln Co October session 1785: Thomas Espie, John Barber, & John Carruth came into Court and made oath in due form of law that the accounts by them exhibited to Court as they stand stated are just & true. Sworn in open Court, test. [signed] Jo Dickson, clk.

354t. [The following is in NC Archives CR 060.928.1 Lincoln Co Miscellaneous file]

Dec. 21, 1782 An order to Lincoln Co sherriff: You are commanded to summon:

Philip Earhart	Adam Killyon	Michal Ingle
Martin Keener	George Romener	Michal Miller
George Fink	Peter Linebarger	Peter Snyder
Lemal Sanders	Fredrick Heager	Ritchard Beel
Robert Johnston	Thomas Beaty	Sherod Stroud
Thomas Anderson sr	James Cronester	Henry Hoover
Henry Slinkard	Philip Clonenger	Christian Syke
Adam Dyke	Michal Cloninger	John Shegal
George Heager	George French	John Binnom
Jacob Sits	Arther Bynam	Lenard Killon
George Sits	Gilbert Bynam	John Beel jr
Abraham Earhart	Peter Finger sr	David Abernethy jr
George Dick	Gasper Club	John Stroud jr
James Reed	John Saylor	Simon Hager sr
David Hutchason	John Stroud sr	

to appear before the Justices of the County Court of Pleas & Quarter Sessions to be held at the Court house on the first Monday in January next to show cause if any why their estate shall not be deemed forfieted.   [signed] Thomas Espey, comr.

also summon:

Jacob Forney sr	Elizabeth Wamack	Meary Morrison
John Bowers	James Ross	Esther King
Ann Brown	Meary Elexander	Abner Wamack
Susannah Forney sr	Meary Walker	Robert Caruthers

to appear before the Justices of the County Court of Pleas to give evidence in behalf of the estate of Philip Earhart, Abraham Earhart, & others.

[on back] Philip Earhart & Martin Keener in the Conental forces under M J Green; Thomas Anderson in Burke Co; John Shegal not found; Adam Dyke, Adam Killyon, Fredrick Heager, Michal Ingle, Henry Hoover, & Jams Cronester are gone with the enemy; Nicholas Holerman was summoned by Wm Armstrong constable; the remainder summond; Meary Walker is in Mecklenburg Co; the remainder of the evidence is summoned.   [signed] Joseph Henry H S F.

354u. [The following is also in CR 060.428.1 sited in #353A above.]
Lincoln Co, NC   A return of men summoned by order of the Commissioners of Confiscated Property to show cause why their estates shall not be confiscated agreeable to act of Assembly:

Fredrick Sumey	John Bumgarner	Henry Crase
Peter Peker	John Hekleman	John Crase
Thomas Hoover	Jacob Hekleman	Christian Cras
Jacob Lotts	Andrew Craislay	George Havner
William Keener	John Kenor	Daniel Kingery
Barney Snayder	Robert Blackburn	John Miller
Conrad Hekelman	Antony Holman	

ordered by the Court that the following persons be summoned to appear at next Court to be held for said county to be "tryed" respecting their characters as enemies to the United States.

[on back] "Tory citation"   5 supoenas   £0.13.4
                                  tryal by jury   £0. 9.4
                                  copies   £0. 8.0   [total] £1.6.8

354v. Lincoln Co   Names of those supposed to come under the Confiscation act:

Petter Carpenter	Phillip Warlack	Henry Roads
Abel Beaty	Thomas Wasson	Jacob Sides "little"
Thomas Casner	Jacob Glance	Henry Hoover
George Hovis	Fredrick Heager	Henry Reynolds
John Reed	Jn Richop	Christian Rinehart
George Dick	Jn Alexander on	Petter Eaker sr
Adam Dick	Indian Cr	Jacob Money
Lenard Saylor	Andrew Hoyl	Henry Williams
Fredrick Propes	Jn Hoyl	Valuntine Warlick
Valuntine Koon	Thomas Beaty	and

Petter Eaker jr, Jacob Carpenter jr, Mical Eaker, Jn Hofstotlar, Jn Eaker, & Mical Hofstotlar.   The last six took Thos Espey, John Espey, & Saml Espey prisoner and delivered them to the enemy of this and the Untied States at Ramsour's. Sept. 19, 1782 addressed to Lincoln Co sheriff--You are commanded to take [rest of sheet lost].

MARTIN COUNTY
355. State of North Carolina account with Samuel Smethwick, Francis Ward, & Thos Hunter, Commissioners of Confiscated Property:
Sept. 10, 1781--cash paid Samuel Smethwick, Commissioner of Specific Tax,

for 1781 by order of Court per rect. £3,707.17.11

Dec. 1780--cash recd. by Samuel Smethwick or debts due sundry British
merchants £1,000

        cash recd. of Thomas Hunter for "ditto", as per acct. rendered £2,188

        cash recd. of Wm Caskeet for a debt due Young, Miller & Co £40

        cash recd. of Francis Ward for "ditto"   £256.4

        cash recd. of Francis Watson for "ditto"   £5 [page torn]

        cash recd. of John Garrot for "ditto"   £8.0

        cash recd. of John Battery for "ditto"   £9.12

        cash recd. of Cathbyrd Phelps for "ditto"   £7.1.3

        cash recd. of Martin Griffin's admrs. for "ditto" £117.6

        cash recd. of William Hinson for "ditto"   £29.17.4

        cash recd. of Benjamin Hardison for "ditto"   £32.11.4

        cash recd. of Thomas Beasley for "ditto" £30.14 [written over £33.18]

        [total] £3,707.17.11

"excepted" pr. Thos Hunter, Saml Smethwick, & Francis Ward, Comrs.

Martin Co Mar. session 1781 Above account settled with Commissioners of Confiscated Property; [signed] Thos Hunter, c. c.

MECKLENBURG COUNTY

356. Account of Capt. James Reep, Commissioner of Confiscated Property for Mecklenburg Co:

from Col. George Alexander £ 804.4.0

from Col. Robert Smith   £1,308.5.10

from Col. Thos Harris   £ 148.14.10

  [total] £2,261.4.8 [written over £2,261.5.6]

Apr. 19, 1784 sworn by James Reep to Robt Harris, JP. [signed] Ja Rees, c cr

357. Oct. 4, 1784 recd of Capt. James Reese, Commissioner of Confiscated Property for Mecklenburg Co £2,261.4.8 "in dollar bills". [signed] Wm Locke; "Memorandum" Wm Locke has credited this sum in his account settled with me. [signed] Frans. Child, Comptr.

358. Receipt No. 54 Jan. 20, 1792 to Joseph Graham, on account of William Black, Mecklenburg Co surveyor, £64 for 32 surveys; plats returned to Salisbury Dist Commissioner of Confiscated Property in 1791.

MONTGOMERY COUNTY

359. Jun. 5, 1786 sold 300 ac to Frances Ledbetter [write over] for £1,202; No. 32; on both sides of Mountain Cr & on S side of Pee Dee R. [not signed]. sworn chain carriers Menzey Thomas & John Thomas. [on back] "confiscated Dec. 1792 Newbern".

360. Jun. 5, 1786 sold 56 ac to William Saunders for £36; No. 14; at the mouth of Long Cr & on N side on Rocky R; formerly Henry Eutace McCulloh's property; [signed] Charles Bruce, CCPSD; sworn chain carriers James Irby & Averit Irby.

361. Jun. 5, 1786 sold 54 ac to William Saunders for £29; No. 10; on N side of Rocky R; formerly Henry Eustace McCulloch's property; [signed] Charles Bruce, CCPSD; sworn chain carriers John Clark & Jesse Brooks.

362. Jun. 5, 1786 sold 120 ac to William Saunders for £40; No. 13; on both sides of Island Cr of Rocky R; formerly Henry Eustace McCulloch's property; border: a gravelly hill side; [signed] Charles Bruce, CCPSD; sworn chain carriers William Brooks & Joseph Johnson.

Sales of Confiscated Land

363. Sept. 20, 1786 sold 222 ac to Jesse McClendon for £500.10; No. 12; on NE side of Pee Dee R; formerly Henry Eustace McCulloch's property; [signed] Charles Bruce, CCPSD; sworn chain carriers Coleby Randle & John Davidson [two copies of this survey].

364. Jun. 5, 1786 sold 35 ac to William Saunders for £17; No. 16; on N side of Rocky R; formerly Henry Eustace McCulloch's property; [signed] Charles Bruce, CCPSD; sworn chain carriers Exodus Whitley & John Gilbert sr.

365. Jun. 5, 1786 sold 149 ac to William Kindal for £321; No. 31; on both sides of Rocky R in Montgomery & Anson Cos; formerly Henry Eustace McCulloch's property; border: John Hill and "the" thoroughfare; plat shows an island; includes Henry Stokes' improvement; [signed] Charles Bruce, CCPSD.

366. Jun. 5, 1786 sold 174 ac to Thomas Clark for £6s; No. 19; on waters of Glady fork of Beaverdam Cr; formerly Henry Eustace McCulloch's property; [signed] Charles Bruce, CCPSD; sworn John Crump & James Crump.

367. Sept. 20, 1786 sold 300 ac to John Hopkins for £121; No. 15; on NE side of Pee Dee R and W of Little R; formerly Josiah Martin's property; border: a hill about 10 poles from Rocky Cr of Little R; [signed] Charles Bruce, CCPSD.

368. Jun. 5, 1786 sold 160 ac to Mark Allen for £10; No. 20; on waters of Davids Cr of Pee Dee R; formerly Josiah Martin's property; border: 3 pines on upper side of lower fork of said creek which is a corner of No. 17, 18, & 11 and joins John Cheek; [signed] Charles Bruce, CCPSD; sworn chain carriers Gabriel Davis & Isaac Davis.

369. Jun. 5, 1786 sold 160 ac to Alexander Fraser for £31.15; No. 17; formerly Josiah Martin's property; border: an oak in fork of "said" creek; [signed] Charles Bruce, CCPSD; sworn chain carriers Gabriel Davis & Issac Davis.

370. Jun. 5, 1786 sold 160 ac to Mark Allen for £20; No. 11; on waters of Davids Cr of Pee Dee R; formerly Josiah Martin's property; border: 3 pines above said creek being a corner of No. 17, 18, & 20; [signed] Charles Bruce, CCPSD; sworn chain carriers Gabriel Davis & Isaac Davis.

371. Jun. 5, 1786 sold 160 ac to Mark Allen for £17.10; No. 18; on waters of Davids Cr of Pee Dee; formerly Josiah Martin's property; border: 2 pines & 2 hickorys on lower side of Davids Cr being corner of No. 17, Ham's place, William Barnes, & 3 pines on said creek being a corner of tracts No. [blank]; [signed] Charles Bruce, CCPSD; sworn chain carriers Gabriel Davis & Isaac Davis.

372. Receipt No. 338 Dec. 9, 1786 to Mark Allen, Montgomery Co surveyor, £22 for 11 surveys; [on back] "pay the within to James Glasgow" [signed] John Palmer for Mark Allen.

373. Montgomery Co Dec. session 1779: Henry Mounger esq, Col. Drury Ledbetter, & Peter Randle are appointed Commissioners of Confiscated Property. [signed] Jas Allen, c c c. "a true copy" [signed] Geo Davidson, c c c.
Mar. session 1780 (a) Henry Mounger esq's bond with James Crump, John Baker, David Penington, Joseph Bell, James Allen, & John Jeffery securities; (b) Col. Drury Ledbetter's bond with William Loftin, Robert Moss, Edward Moore, Job Calliway, & Peter Jackson securities; (c) Peter Randle's bond with Charles Ledbetter, Capt. West Harris, Etheldread Harris, & George Kirk securities. [signed] James Allen, c c c "a true copy" [signed] Geo Davidson, c c c; [on back] Mar. 1780.

374. Mar. 28, 1780 [1779--lined out] a bond by Col. Drury Ledbetter, William Loftin, Robert Moss, Edward Moore, Job Calliway, & Peter Jackson for £100,000 [£150,000--lined out] for Ledbetter to be Commissioner of Confiscated Property. Signed Drury Ledbetter, Robert Moss, Edd Moore, Job Calliway, Peter Jackson, & William Lof[page torn]. Witness Jas Allen; [on back] "settled with the Court and did my business".

Sales of Confiscated Land

375. Mar. 28, 1780 a bond by Henry Mounger, James Crump, John Baker, David Penington, Joseph Bell, James Allen, & John Jeffery for £100,000 for Mounger to be Commissioner of Confiscated Property. Signed Henry Mounger, James Crump, John Baker, David Penington's mark, Joseph Bell, Jas Allen, & Jno Jeffery.

MOORE COUNTY
376. Receipt No. 260 May 30, 1786 to William Finley, Moore Co surveyor, £44 for 22 surveys.

377. May 15, 1786 Account of sales of Confiscated Property in Moore Co:
a) John Overton "to" 480 ac; formerly Gregg & Doud's property; No. 1--£15
b) Milton Glass "to" 100 ac; formerly John McNiell's property; no. 2--£10.5
c) G J McRee & Curtis Ivy "to" 100 ac; formerly Laughlin Beaton's property; No. 3--£5.0
d) G J McRee & Curtis Ivy "to" 200 ac; formerly Conner Doud's property; No. 4--£10.0
e) G J McRee & Curtis Ivy "to" 100 ac; formerly Fred Grigg's property; No. 5--£13.0
f) G J McRee & Curtis Ivy "to" 200 ac; formerly John McNiell's property; No. 6--£91.0
g) G J McRee & Curtis Ivy "to" 400 ac; formerly Fred Gregg's property; No. 7--£40.0   [total] £184.5   [written over £185.5]
"errors excepted" [signed] G J McRee

378. Jun. 21, 1785 surveyed 200 ac; formerly James McNeil's property; plat shows land on both sides of Lendons Cr; [signed] W Finley, surveyor; chain carriers John Gilmore & Matthew Kitching; purchased for £91 by G J McRee & C Ivy.

379. Jun. 21, 1785 surveyed 100 ac; formerly James McNeil's property; on boh sides of Juniper Br of McLendons Cr; [signed] W Finley, surveyor; chain carriers John Gilmore & Matthew Kitching; purchased for £10.5 by Milton Glass.

380. Jun. 22, 1785 surveyed 100 ac; formerly Laughlin Beaton's property; on W side of McLendons Cr; border: summit of a hill; [signed] W Finley, surveyor; chain carriers John Gilmore & Matthew Kitching; purchased for £5 by G J McRee.

381. Jul. 2, 1785 surveyed 200 ac; formerly Coner Doud's property; on both sides of Pocket Cr; border: Montgomery's line on W side of said creek; [signed] W Finley, surveyor; chain carriers John Gilmore & Matthew Kitching; purchased for £10 by G J McRee & Curtis Ivy.

382. Jul. 1, 1785 surveyed 100 ac; formerly Fredrick Greg's property; on both sides of Pocket Cr; border: summit of a hill by a branch of Pocket Cr and William Goyns [sic]; [signed] W Finley, surveyor; chain carriers John Gilmore & Matthew Kitching; purchased for £13 by G J McRee & Curtis Ivy.

383. Jul. 3, 1785 surveyed 480 ac; formerly Fredrick Greg & Coner Doud's property; on both sides of Pocket Cr; [signed] W Finley, surveyor; chain carriers John Gilmore & Matthew Kitching; purchased for £15 by John Overton.

384. Jul. 8, 1785 surveyed 400 ac; formerly Fredrick Greg's property; on waters of Pocket Cr; [signed] W Finley, surveyor; chain carriers John Gilmore & Matthew Kitching; purchased for £40 by G J McRee & Curtis Ivy.

NASH COUNTY
385. Receipt No. 77 Dec. 5, 1785 to William Lancaster, Nash Co surveyor, £10 for 5 surveys.

386. Sept. 29, 1785 Account of sales of property "suggested" to be Confiscated in Nash Co [two copies of this list: one has total price only, the other has prices in bonds or certifictes]:
a) 247 ac on waters of Sappony Cr; formerly James Cary's property; bought by   Micajah Thomas for £121 certificates
b) 673 ac on S side of Tar R; formerly George Brown's property; bought by   Dixon Martial for £240.5 bond
c) 720 ac on N side of Tar R; formerly John Grunlies' [sic] property; bought   by Dixon Martil for £150.1 bond

Sales of Confiscated Land

d) 381 ac on waters of Swift Cr; formerly James McNeil's property; bought by Thomas Armstrong for £2,600 certificates
e) a Negro George; formerly James McNeil's property; bought by William Aven for £735.1 bond
  [total] £2,721 certifictes + £1,125.7 bond = £3,346.7

387. Sept. 29, 1785 received of William Lancaster, Nash Co surveyor, 5 "double" plotts of confiscated property. [signed] Nichlas Long, Comr.

388. Sept. 6, 1785 surveyed 249 ac; due to orders of Halifax Dist. Commissioners; formerly James Cary's property; on N side of Sapponer Cr; border: Willm Bennitt; [signed] Willm Lancaster, surveyor; sworn chain carriers Solomon Collins & George Sutton; [on back] Micajah Thomas.

389. Sept. 7, 1785 surveyed 673 ac; due to orders of Halifax Dist. Commissioners; formerly George Brown's property; on S side of Tar R; border: Duncan Lemmon, Crowell, & Pridgion; [signed] Willm Lancaster, surveyor; sworn chain carriers Philander Williams & Brittain Smith; [on back] Dixon Marshall £240.

390. Sept. 8, 1785 surveyed 720 ac; due to orders of Halifax Dist. Commissioners; formerly John Grunlies' property; Benjm Barnns' corner on Great Br, David Bunn, Benjm Bun, Cattail Marsh, Duncan Lemmon, Lewis Joyner, John Barnns, & Jacob Barnns; [signed] Willm Lancaster, surveyor; sworn chain carriers Benjm Barnns & Fulgum Wester; [on back] Dixon Marshall £150.

391. Sept. 15, 1785 surveyed 208 ac; due to orders of Halifax Dist. Commissioners; formerly James McNeal's property; on S side of Beaverdam Swamp; border: Josiah Nicholson and Capt. Whitehead; [signed] Willm Lancaster, surveyor; sworn chain carriers Josiah Nicholson & Willibay Powell; [on back] Famy McNeil £304

392. Sept. 16, 1785 surveyed 381 ac; due to orders of Halifax Dist. Commissioners; formerly James McNeal's property; on N side of Swift Cr; border: William Battle, Willm Avent, the mouth of a branch of Swift Cr, an old mill on said creek, & a swamp; [signed] Willm Lancaster, surveyor; sworn chain carriers Capt. Willm Battle & Thomas Kerney; [on back] Thos Armstrong.

393. Nov. 21, 1795 surveyed 342 ac for Peter Arrington; formerly James McNiel's property; on N side of Swift Cr; border: William Battle's corner on the creek, Allen Mann, & a spring branch; pruchased by Thomas Armstrong from Nicholas Long, Halifax Dist. Commissioner of Confiscated Property, and sold by Nash Co sheriff, as said Armstrong's property, to Peter Arrington; [signed] Joseph Arrington, surveyor; sworn chain carriers Elias Boon & Henry Simmons; [on back] No. 549 Nov. 3, 1795 [sic].

NEW HANOVER COUNTY
394. 1786   Account of sales of Confiscated Property in New Hanover Co:
Jun. 7   John Kingsborough--part of lot No. 1; [formerly] Danl Southerland [property]; £5,050.0
     James Read--a Negro fellow called Glasgow; formerly Federick
     Gregg's property; £670.0   [total] £5,720.0
Oct.   James Read--lot No. 27; [formerly] John McDonnell's [property];   £2,250.0
     James Logan--a Negro fellow Will Seul [or Seall]; [formerly] Jno
     McDowell's [property]; £800
[grand total] £8,770.0 "errors excepted" G J McRee

395. [no dated] surveyed part of lot 1 on N side of Market St in Wilmington; formerly Danil Sotherlin's property; 33' on the street and 27' back; improved with a dwelling house two stories high; [signed] Thos Dwane, surveyor; [sold to] John Kingsborough £5,050.

396. [no date] surveyed part of lot 1 on S side of Market St in Wilmington; formerly George Parker's property; 26' 10" on the street and 71' back; improved with a two story brick dwelling house, with a cellar under it, & "another" out house; [signed] Thos Dwane, surveyor; [on back] John Kingsberry "grant issd." Oct. 1788.

Sales of Confiscated Land

397. May 18, 1785 surveyed 250 ac; formerly William Tryon esq's property; border: upper corner of said Tryon's 450 ac survey on S side of Rockfish Cr, a pond, "the" main road, Benjn Fussle, & a bridge; [signed] Jo Dickson, surveyor; [on back] No. 2 David Jones,   Phill Jones £345.

398. May 25,1785 surveyed 180 ac; formerly William Tryon esq's property; below the Welch tract Road; border: upper corner of said Tryon's 450 ac survey at a pond, "the" great road, Benjn Fussle's old line, & a branch, & Ferguson; [signed] Jo Dickson, surveyor; [on back] No. 1 David Jones,   Ph Jones.

399. May 25, 1785 surveyed 450 ac; formerly William Tryon esq's property; on S side of Rockfish Cr; includes "a large" number of old Boxed trees and a litle improvement of James Padget's; border: where Rockfish Cr joins "the" river, lower end of James Padget's field on a high bluff, & a pond; [signed] Jo Dickson, survey; [on back] Phil Jones £345,   No. 3 David Jones.

400. Jun. 7, 1785 surveyed   a lot and house on Market St in Wilmington; formerly property of Geo [John--lined out] Parker, a subject of Great Britain; between the houses of David James & William Campbel; house is 26' 10" in front and 28' back and lot is 43' "further"; house is 3 stories: first story--2 front rooms fronting on Market St & a back room with a "fier" place in it and likewise in one of the front rooms, second story--a large front room and a back room both with "fier" places, third story--3 small rooms one of which has a "fier" place; house has a cellar under it with apartment "one" of the apartments having a "fier" place in it; [signed] Thos Dwane, surveyor; purchased by J Kingsborough for £3,000; [on back] John Parker's house and lot Market St No. 1 on South side; John Kingsberry [sic].

401. Jun. 8, 1785 surveyed a house and lot No. 27 on Dock St in Wilmington; formerly Edward Bridgin's property; house is 31' 9" in front, lot extends 10' further, & lot is 71' back; [signed] Thos Dwane, surveyor; Peter Bacot £2,100.

402. Jun. 8, 1786 surveyed a lot No. 176 on N side of Castle St in Wilmington; formerly John McDonnel's property; border: a stake in the river on SW corner of said lot, runs E on N side of Castle St to Front St at SE corner of said lot, N 66' on Front St to NE corner, W parallel to Castle St to the river, Cape Fear R on W, Castle St on S, Front St on E, & a dividing line with "another" lot on N; improved with a warf; [signed] Thos Dwane, surveyor; [on back] James Read.

NORTHAMPTON COUNTY
403. Receipt No. 2 May 30, 1782 £200 received in payment of confiscated property sold except property sold to defray salaries of the delegates in Congress agreeable to a resolve passed in General Assembly at Hillsborough Apr. 1782. [signed] Saml Lockhart; [on back] Jos Spruill, E T, to the treasurer Nathanel Allen and Com [hole in page] Spruill, E T, Nov. 6, 17[hole in page] £200 + £7.3.4 = £217.3.4.

ORANGE COUNTY
404. Jan. 18, 1783 Orange Co, NC Devalt Mock's oath to John Taylor, Orange Co JP; Devalt says sometime in Feb. 1780 he purchased a "tract or entry" from George Houke; land was "originally" entered in Lord Granville's Office Jan. 17, 1763 by William Spurgen who "conveyed" it to said Houke; on waters of Abbotts Cr, head waters of Reedy Run, & crosses a waggon road; since them Frederick Miller "as this deponent believes" entered part of the land and had it surveyed "taking away some of his" houses and improvement; Devault asks to have Miller's grant suspended until an "impartial investigation" can be made and asks for a caveat to issue from Rowan Co Court. [signed] Dewoeld Mock and John Taylor, JP; [on back] Jun. 10, 1783 to Honble. James Glasgow, Secretary, suspend the grant & issue a caveat in Rowan Co Court [signed] Alex Martin; caveat issued Jan. 18, 1783 by Henderson, fees paid. [This is evidently a suspension of a grant and doesn't relate to confiscated land.]

Sales of Confiscated Land

405. Feb. term 1780 Orange Co Court proceeded to appoint Commissioners for "taking in hand and disposing" of Confiscated Property in Orange Co; appointed: Joshua A Potts, James Carrington, & John Ray, who entered performance bonds accordingly; Apr. 20, 1784 "a true copy" [signed] Jos Bonton, c c.

406. Receipt No. 107 May 17, 1783 to Thomas Mulhollan, Orange Co surveyor, £108 for 54 surveys.

407. Receipt No. 126 Dec. 22, 1785 to Thomas Mulhollan, Orange Co surveyor, £128 for 64 surveys.

408. Sept. 6, 1780 Orange Co Commissioners of Confiscated Property to State of North Carolina:
a) to cash by them received   £994
   to bonds now in their hands of sundry people on demand   £1,191
   [total] £2,185
b) by cash paid for paper £40
   by commissioners @ 2%   £43.14   [total] £83.14
   balance due the State   £2,101.6 = £2,185- £83.14
c) "also" bonds payable No. 30 next for hire of Negroes formerly propbery to
   Thos McKnight "concerning which the above account is drawn" £4,161
   Doctor Bark "also owes"   £100
   due 3 months "hence" [total] £4,261
   Cr. by commissioners at that time £85.4.4
   balance then £4,175.15.8   "errors excepted" pr. Joshua A Potts, c c.

409. Joshua A Potts, Orange Co Commissioner of Confiscated Property, Settlement Aug. 1783; received Apr. 24, 1784 [8 sheets]:
"Ledger" to the Proceeding Journal:
page 1 [a double sheet]: "State of North Carolina"

409A. dept.:

Apr. 15, 1780 to Joshua Potts "2" £25	credit: Aug. 30, 1780 by James Carrington "3" £225
Aug. 30 to Joshua Potts "2" £15	[no date] Joshua Potts "2" £366
Sept. 22 to Joshua Potts "2" £730	Aug. 31 Joshua Potts "2" £403
Oct. 3 to Joshua Potts "2" £247	Sept. 12 Joshua Potts "2" £135
ditto for commissions "2" £232.3	Sept. 14 Joshua Potts "2" £113
Apr. 16, 1782 ditto for amount of bonds sent to Auditors, "now" to be sent to Solicitor £3,872	Dec. 15 & 18 Joshua Potts "2" £325
"ditto" for balance paid [at] 210 to 1 equal to specie £2 to be delivered to the Treasurer "2" £417.17 [total] £5,539	Joshua Potts amount of bonds on hand £3,872 Jan. 31, 1781 by Joshua Potts "2" £100 [total] £5,539

page 2 [a double sheet]: "Joshua Potts"

409B. dept.:

Aug. 30, 1780 to State of NC "1" £366	credit: Apr. 15, 1789 by State of NC "1" £25
Aug. 31 to State of NC "1" £403	Aug. 30 by State of NC "1" £15
Sept. 12 to State of NC "1" £135	Sept. 11 by State of NC "1" £730
Sept. 14 to State of NC "1" £113	Oct. 3 by State of NC "1" £247
Dec. 15, 1780 "ditto" sundries "Jourl 4" £550	Aug. 16, 1782 "ditto" bonds offered up "1" £3,872
Jan. 1, 1781 "ditto" amount bonds on hand "1" £3,872	"ditto" for commissions "1" £232.3
Jan. 31 "ditto" "1" £100	Jan. 31, 1781 by balance due the State paid [at] 210 to 1 equal to

Sales of Confiscated Land

[total] £5,539   £2 to be delivered to Orange Co
                                         Solicitor £417.17
                                         [total] £5,539

page 3 [left half of page; right half of page is "409K" below]:
"James Carrington"
409C. dept.:
Aug. 30, 1780 to State of NC "1" £225
[a sheet was cut out of the booklet here]

page 1 of "Journal":
409D. To Orange Co Court: A Journal of transactions of Joshua Potts, John Wray, & James Carrington, Orange Co Commissioners of Confiscated Property. John Wray esq declined to act "of course" [so] the business devolved to Joshua Potts and James Carrington.
Apr. 15, 1780 State of NC dep. "1/2" Joshua Potts for 1½ quires good writing paper to be used in the business £25
May 27 hired the following Negroes which were all that could be collected
   [had--lined out] of estate of Thomas McKnight [no money mentioned]: Davey, Toney sr, Toney jr, Sam, Sambo, Sandy, Dorias, Nancy, Jim, Jim's wife, Jenney, Seasor, Choe & 6 children, Grace & 3 children, & Edy & a child--
   total 25 Negres hired until Aug. 30 next.

page 2 of "Journal":
409E. Aug. 30, 1780 James Carrington dep. "3/1" State of NC for hire of Negro Davy for past 3 months £150
   "ditto" for 3 months insuing being hired to him "this" day £120 [total] £225
Joshua Potts dep. "2/1" received the hire of Toney sr by hands of Thomas Bailey £235
   "do" received hire of Dorias by hand of William Galbreath for John Allen £131 [total] £366
State of NC dr "1/2" Joshua Potts for ¼ quire of writin paper £15 hired said Negroes to sundry people who are to return them with their hire on or before Nov. 30 next and took their bonds accordingly [no money amount]

page 3 of "Journal":
409F. Aug. 30, 1780 "Joshua Potts dr 2/1":
State of NC received the hire of Edy & child £112
"ditto" of Nancy formerly hired to John Rews £65
"ditto" for Grace & 3 childen by hand of Ben Leonard for Mrs. White £39
Sept. 1 "ditto" of Sam by Mark Patterson £187 [total] £403
Sept. 11 State of NC dr "1/2" Joshua Potts paid cash to Mathew Jones, Treasurer per receipt £730
Sept. 12 Joshua Potts dr. "2/1" State of NC, for hire of Negro Dorias, from Mr. Shaw for John Allen £135

page 4 of "Journal":
409G. Sept. 14, 1780 Joshua Potts dr "2/1" State of NC, for hire of Grace received from Stephen Hart £113
Oct. 3 State of NC dr "1/2" Joshua Potts paid to Matthew Jones, Treasurer, see receipt £247
Dec. 15 Joshua Potts dr "2/1" State of NC, for hire of Negro Grace, received from Col. Hugh Tining £205
Dec. 18 received for hire of Grace & children from John Taylor "Town" £120
Jan. 1, 1781 Received of James Carrington the full of his public account £225 [total for this page] £550

page 5 of "Journal":
409H. On Nov. 30, 1780 Joshua Potts resigned [as] Commissioner with respect to Confiscated Property and "the people" not delivering the Negroes according to their bonds, they remain in their hands or possession liable to be recalled agreeable to Act of Assembly.
   See the names of different persons from whom money was received "as by" entries in the Journal, and for reminder of the Negroes refer to the various bonds "herewith" returned, a list of which is inserted on the "other" [next] page.

Sales of Confiscated Land

A list of said Negroes and respective people in whose care they were on "my" resignation "I" delivered [list to] Orange Co sheriff.

page 6 of "Journal":
409I. Bond No. 1 by Thomas Hart esq for hire of--(a) Sambo, Jim & wife & child, Sandy, Jenny, and (b) Seasor and Chole & 6 children "for Doct. Burk" £1,056 "paper money" due Aug. 30, 1780
Bond No. 2 by Thomas Bailey for hire of--Sandy Nov. 1780 £400 "paper money" due Aug. 30, 1780
Bond No. 3 by Thomas Bailey for hire of--Toney £400 "paper money" due Aug. 30, 1780
Bond No. 4 by William Galbreath for hire of--Toney a boy £655 "paper money" Aug. 30, 1780
Bond No. 5 by William Galreath for hire of--Darcus £131 "paper money" due Aug. 30, 1780
Bond No. 6 by Joseph Thompson for hire of--Sambo £405 "paper money" due Aug. 30, 1780
Bond No. 7 by Joseph Thompson for hire of--Jenney £310 "paper money" due Aug. 30, 1780
Bond No. 8 by Robert McIntire for hire of--Nancy £205 "paper money" due Aug. 30, 1780
Bond No. 9 by Mark Patterson for hire of--Sam £310 "paper money" due Aug. 30, 1780
[total] £3,872 with interest "by" people of Orange Co

page 7 of "Journal":
409J. Jan. 31, 1781 Joshua Potts dr "2/1" State of NC received of Enoch
   Collis, or hire of Seasor, Chole & 6 children to Doctr. Burke, in whose care those Negroes were left £100
[no date] State of NC dr "1/2" Joshua Potts, commissions 4% on amount of money and bonds that passed through his hands as inserted in the Journl vizt £5,804 £232.3
"NB" This 4% commission includes 2% for Joshua Potts and 2% for James Carrington
Apr. 16, 1782 State of NC dr "1/2" Joshua Potts for amount of bond sent £3,872

409K. [right half of page 3, see 409C above]: "credit": Jan. 1, 1781 by Joshua Potts "2" £225

[no page number]:
409L. Aug. 11, 1783 Halifax Co, NC, oath by Joshua Potts before John Geddy, Halifax Co JP: Joshua says the within account is just and says the balance due Orange Co Commissioner of Confiscated Property on Jan. 31, 1781 was "only" £417.17 "paper currency". [signed] John Geddy at Halifax
Orange Co Aug. term 1783: the enclosed account came to Orange Co Court this term and ordered recorded. [signed] Jos Bonton, c c. Dec. 1783 "a true copy" [signed] Jos Bonton, c c.

410. Mar. 1788 Account of sales of Orange Co Confiscated Property:
#54   357 ac on Alamance Cr; formerly H E McCulloch's property; bought by Thomas Mulhollan for £61.6
#47   159 ac on Eulias Cr; formerly H E McCulloch's property; bought by Joseph Dickson for £16.10.9
#30   168 ac on Willis's Cr; formerly H E McCulloch's property; bought by Hardy Parkins for £141
#43   184 ac on Varnals Cr; formerly H E McCulloch's property; bought by James Godfrey for £55
#31   173 ac on Willis's Cr; formerly H E McCulloch's property; bought by Tilman Dixon for £151
#35   70 ac on Varnals Cr; formerly H E McCulloch's property; bought by Eli McDonnald for £105
#30   200 ac on Enoe R; formerly H E McCulloch's property; bought by Stephen Moore for £101
#19   208 ac on Little R; formerly H E McCulloch's property; bought by Wm Sheppard for £437.10
 [total] £1,068.6.9
[on back] land sold by A Lytle, Commissioner Hillsborough Dist.

411. [no date] Account of sales of Orange Co Confiscated Property:
lot 23 in Hillsborough; formerly Edd Fanning's property; bought by Wm Lytle for £1,022
lot 12 in Hillsborough; formerly Edd Fanning's property; bought by Josiah Watts for £726
lot 15 in Hillsborough; formerly Edd Fanning's property; bought by Wm Watters [or Walters] for £535
lot 22 in Hillsborough; formerly Edd Fanning's property; bought by Memucan Hunt for £1,001
lot 33 in Hillsborough; formerly Edd Fanning's property; bought by Wm Shepperd for £550
lot 21 in Hillsborough; formerly Edd Fanning's property; bought by Roswell Hustnyton [sic] for £501

Sales of Confiscated Land

part of lot 25 in Hillsborough; formerly Edd Fanning's property; bought by George Doherty for £4,558

3/4ths of lot 35 in Hillsborough; formerly Edd Fanning's property; bought by George Doherty for £835

lot 34 in Hillsborough; formerly Edd Fanning's property; bought by George Doherty £601

lot 31 in Hillsborough; formerly Edd Fanning's property; bought by Absalom Tatom for £223.1

lot 32 in Hillsborough; formerly Edd Fanning's property; bought by Wm Shepperd for £405

#2 300 ac on W of Hillsborough; formerly Edmund Fanning's property; bought by John Esties for £801

#1 143 ac on N of Hillsborough; formerly Young, Miller & Co's property; bought by John Taylor for £1,000

#3 64 ac on Enoe R; formerly James Milner's property; bought by Wm Cabe for £450

#4 186 ac on Enoe R; formerly James Milner's property; bought by John Flintham [or Flutham] for £841

#5 180 ac on waters of [blank]; formerly [blank] property; bought by Tilman Dixon for £1,110

#33 102 ac on waters of Haw R; formerly H E McCulloch's property; bought by Tilman Dixon for £216.2

#32 172 ac on waters of Haw R; formerly H E McCulloch's property; bought by Wm Shepperd for £311

#36 50 ac on waters of Haw R; formerly H E McCulloch's property; bought by James Thomson for £102

#37 33 ac on waters of Haw R; formerly H E McCulloch's property; bought by James Thomson for £100

#38 23 ac on waters of Haw R; formerly H E McCulloch's property; bought by Jno McDaniel for £100

#34 140 ac on waters of Haw R; formerly H E McCulloch's property; bought by Saml Campbell for £80

#40 146 ac on waters of Haw R; formerly H E McCulloch's property; bought by Martin Cole for £305

#42 116 ac on waters of Haw R; formerly H E McCulloch's property; bought by Michael Mozer for £227

#41 112 ac on waters of Haw R; formerly H E McCulloch's property; bought by Philip Mozer for £150

#45 240 ac on waters of Haw R; formerly H E McCulloch's property; bought by John Courts for £305.10

#46 208 ac on waters of Haw R; formerly H E McCulloch's property; bought by Saml Parker for £401

#50 115 ac on waters of Haw R; formerly H E McCulloch's property; bought by James Williams for £122

#44 108 ac on waters of Haw R; formerly H E McCulloch's property; bought by James Williams for £110.10

[subtotal] £17,689.3

[The following are on the back of same sheet:]

#9 292.5 ac on waters of Alamance Cr; formerly H E McCulloch's property; bought by George Doherty for £307

#10 115 ac on waters of Alamance Cr; formerly H E McCulloch's property; bought by Henry Cooke for £51

#48 230 ac on waters of Alamance Cr; formerly H E McCulloch's property; bought by Joseph Noey for £231

#39 69 ac on waters of Alamance Cr; formerly H E McCulloch's property; bought by Wm McCawley for £125

#52 90 ac on waters of Alamance Cr; formerly H E McCulloch's property; bought by Wm Ray for £166

#51 60 ac on waters of Alamance Cr; formerly H E McCulloch's property; bought by Henry Thomson for £120

#53 200 ac on waters of Alamance Cr; formerly H E McCulloch's property; bought by Wm Oneal for £325

#49 225 ac on waters of Alamance Cr "on Little R"; formerly H E McCulloch's property; bought by Wm Lythe for £325

#54 569 ac on waters of Alamance Cr "on Little R"; formerly H E McCulloch's property; bought by Wm Lythe for £1,270

[total] £20,609.3 [£20,599.3--lined out]

412. Nov. 26, 1782 surveyed 560 ac; No. 1; formerly Henry Eustace McCulloh's property; on waters of Flat R; border: Charls. Roberts, Arthur Mangum, Robert Dickens, William Wait, "another" tract of McCulloh's, & Rocky Cr; [signed] Thos Mulhollan, surveyor; sworn chain carriers Jno M Farling & Wm Smallwood; [on back] sold to Thos Burk [signed] Jas Mebane, Commissioner; Gow Burk [sic] £636; Thomas Burk.

413. Nov. 26, 1782 surveyed 325 ac; No. 2; formerly Henry Eustace McCulloh's property; on waters of Flat R; border: Arthur Mangum, William Smallwood, & said McCulloh; [signed] Thos Mulhollan, surveyor; sworn chain carriers Jno M Farling & Wm Smallwood; [on back] sold to John Estes [signed] Jas Mebane, Commissioner, £420

414. Nov. 27, 1782 surveyed 235 ac; No. 3; formerly Henry Eustace McCulloh's property; on waters of Flat R; border: Charls. Roberts, said McCulloh, & Rocky Cr; [signed] Thos Mulhollan, surveyor; sworn chain carriers Jno M Farling & Wm Smallwood; [on back] sold to John Taylor & James Mebane [signed] James Mebane, Commissioner.

415. Nov. 27, 1782 surveyed 347 ac; No. 4; formerly Henry Eustace McCulloh's property; on NE side of Flat R; border: Charles Roberts, Wm Roberts, said McCulloh, & Rocky R; [signed] Thos Mulhollan, surveyor; sworn chain carriers Jno M Farling & Wm Smallwood; [on back] sold to John Taylor & James Mebane [signed] James Mebane, Commissioner.

416. Nov. 28, 1782 surveyed 400 ac; No. 5; formerly Henry Eustace McCulloh's property; on NE side of Flat R; border: John Duke, James Vaughn, & said McCulloh; plat also shows land is on both sides of Cedar Cr running into Flat R; [signed] Thos Mulhollan, surveyor; sworn chain carriers Jno M Farling & Wm Smallwood; [on back] sold to John Taylor & James Mebane [signed] James Mebane, Commissioner.

417. Nov. 28, 1782 surveyed 296 ac; No.6; formerly Henry Eustace McCulloh's property; on waters of Flat R; border: James Vaughn, William Smallwood, & said McCulloh; plat also shows land is on both sides of Dry Cr; [signed] Thos Mulhollan, surveyor; sworn chain carriers Jno M Farling & Wm Smallwood; [on back] sold to John Taylor & James Mebane [signed] James Mebane, Commissioner.

418. Nov. 28, 1782 surveyed 117 ac; No. 7; formerly Henry Eustace McCulloh's property; on S side of Flat R; border: William Horton, Reason Rickets, John Duke, & said McCulloh; [signed] Thos Mulhollan, surveyor; sworn chain carriers Jno M Farling & William Smallwood; [on back] sold to Nicholas Long [signed] James Mebane, Commissioner.

419. Nov. 29, 1782 surveyed 484 ac; No. 10; formerly Henry Eustace McCulloh's property; on waters of Little R; border: Johnston, Deningham, Charls. Horton, William Rea, & Patrick Clark; [signed] Thos Mulhollan, surveyor; sworn chain carriers Jas Vaughn & Thos King; [on back] sold to William Johnston [signed] James Mebane, Commissioner.

420. Dec. 2, 1782 surveyed 461 ac; No. 11; formerly Henry Eustace McCulloh's property; on waters of Little R; border: Charles Horton, Patrick Clark, William Rea, & "another" of McCulloh's tracts; [signed] Thos Mulhollan, surveyor; sworn chain carriers Thos King & Reason Rickets; [on back] sold to James Williams [signed] James Mebane, Commissioner.

421. Dec. 3, 1782 surveyed 226 ac; No. 12; formerly Henry Eustace McCulloh's property; on waters of Flat R; border: John Duke and said McCulloh; [signed] Thos Mulhollan, surveyor; sworn chain carriers Thos King & Reason Rickets; [on back] sold to James Williams [signed] James Mebane, Commissioner.

422. Dec. 4, 1782 surveyed 214 ac; No. 13; formerly Henry Eustace McCulloh's property; on waters of Little R; border: John Duke, Nehemiah Edge, Thos King, & said McCulloch; [signed] Thos Mulhollan, surveyor; sworn chain carriers Thos King & Reason Rickets; [on back] sold to James Williams [signed] James Mebane, Commissioner.

423. Dec. 4, 1782 surveyed 560 ac; No. 54; formerly Henry Eustace McCulloh's property; on Rock Cr of Eno R; border: Charls. Roberts and Arthur Mangum; [signed] Thos Mulhollan, surveyor; sworn chain carriers Jno M Farling & Wm Smallwood; May 6, 1786 sold to William Lytle for £1,270 [signed] Archd Lytle, Comr.

424. Dec. 6, 1782 surveyed 264 ac; No. 15; formerly Henry Eustace McCulloh's property; on waters of Little R; border: John Tilley, Archer Herris, & Thos King; [signed] Thos Mulhollan, surveyor; sworn chain carriers Jno Duke & Jas Vaughn; [on back] sold to Andrew Ross for £151 [signed] James Mebane, Commissioner.

425. Dec. 6, 1782 surveyed 204 ac; No. 16; formerly Henry Eustace McCulloh's property; on S side of Little R; border: William Rea and "another" of McCulloh's tracts; [signed] Thos Mulhollan, surveyor; sworn chain carriers Wm McClellin & Jesse Veazy; [on back] sold to John Eustice for £443 [signed] James Mebane, Commissioner.

Sales of Confiscated Land

426. Dec. 7, 1782 surveyed 335 ac; No. 17; formerly Henry Eustace McCulloh's property; on S side of Little R; border: "another" of McCulloh's tracts; [signed] Thos Mulhollan, surveyor; sworn chain carriers Wm Rea & Lazareth Tilley; [on back] sold to James Thackston for £803 [signed] James Mebane, Commissioner.

427. Dec. 9, 1782 surveyed 380 ac; No. 18; formerly Henry Eustace McCulloh's property; on N side of Little R; border: John Tilley, "another" of McCulloh's tracts, & William Rea's corner on the river; [signed] Thos Mulhollan, surveyor; sworn chain carriers William Rea & Lazareth Tilley; [on back] sold to Jacob Richards for £301 [signed] [signed] James Mebane, Commissioner; "entered" by Thos Mulholan, Wm Mebane, & Jas Mebane.

428. Dec. 10, 1782 surveyed 208 ac; No. 19; formerly Henry Eustace McCulloh's property; on N side of Little R; border: George Horner [or Homer], Mr. Smith, & said McCulloh; [signed] Thos Mulhollan, surveyor; sworn chain carriers Wm Rea & Lazareth Tilley; [on back] sold to Thos Burk [signed] James Mebane, Commissioner; [entered by Wm Veazey--lined out].

429. Dec. 10, 1782 surveyed 225 ac; No. 20; formerly Henry Eustace McCulloh's property; on N side of Little R; border: Mr. Smith and other tracts of McCulloh; [signed] Thos Mulhollan, surveyor; sworn chain carriers William Rea & Lazareth Tilley; [on back] [sold to] James Thackston [signed] James Mebane, Commissioner; [entered by Wm Veazey--lined out].

430. Dec. 12, 1782 surveyed 270 ac; No. 21; formerly Henry Eustace McCulloh's property; on both sides of Stinken Quarter Cr; border: Peter Gortner, Petter Helton, & said McCulloh; [signed] Thos Mulhollan, surveyor; sworn chain carriers Leonard Kimbro & Christian Long; [on back] sold to Thos Mulhollan for £105 [signed] James Mebane, Commissioner.

431. Dec. 13, 1782 surveyed 292.5 ac; No. 9; formerly Henry Eustace McCulloh's property; on S side of Haw R & on waters of Great Alamance Cr; border: Capt. Wm Rogers; [signed] Thos Mulhollan, surveyor; sworn chain carriers Wm Philips & M Regin; May 8, 1786 sold to George Doherty for £307 [signed] Archd Lytle, Comr.

432. Dec. 13, 1782 surveyed 270 ac; No. 22; formerly Henry Eustace McCulloh's property; on waters of Stinken Quarter Cr; border: Peter Hilton, Jacob Anthony, & said McCulloh; [signed] Thos Mulhollan, surveyor; sworn chain carriers Leonard Kimbro & Christian Long; [on back] sold to James Williams [signed] James Mebane, Commissioner.

433. Dec. 14, 1782 surveyed 258 ac; No. 23; formerly Henry Eustace McCulloh's property; on both sides of Stinken Quarter Cr; border: Christian Long, Michael Fogleman, said McCulloh, & a "centril" corner of four tracts; [signed] Thos Mulhollan, surveyor; sworn chain carriers Leonard Kimbro & Christian Long; [on back] sold to John Eustice [signed] James Mebane, Commissioner.

434. Dec. 14, 1782 surveyed 270 ac; No. 24; formerly Henry Eustace McCulloh's property; on waters of Stinken Quarter Cr; border: Michael Fogleman, Michael Shofner, said McCulloh, & "centril" corner of four tracts; [signed] Thos Mulhollan, surveyor; sworn chain carriers Leonard Kimbro & Christian Long; [on back] sold to John Eustice for £502 [signed] James Mebane, Commissioner.

435. Dec. 14, 1782 surveyed 140 ac; No. 45; formerly Henry Eustace McCulloh's property; on both sides of Stinken Quarter Cr of Great Allamance Cr; border: Philip Snoterly; [signed] Benjamin Rainey, D surveyor; sworn chain carriers William Phillips & George Fridle; entered by Henery Cook; [on back] sold to Henrey Cook [signed] James Mebane, Commissioner.

436. Dec. 15, 1782 surveyed 255 ac; No. 25; formerly Henry Eustace McCulloh's property; on waters of Stinken Quarter Cr; border: Adam Smith, Tobias Smith, John Graves, said McCulloh, & great road from Hillsborough to Salisbury; [signed] Thos Mulhollan, surveyor; sworn chain carriers George Kimbrow & Conrood Kimbrow; [on back] sold to Thos Hardy Pirkens [signed] James Mebane, Commissioner.

Sales of Confiscated Land

437. Dec. 15, 1782 surveyed 212 ac; No. 26; formerly Henry Eustace McCulloh's property; on wates of Stinken Quarter Cr; border: Samuel Suthen, Philip Foust, Tobias Smith, said McCulloh, Adam Smith, & on both sides of the great road from Hillsborough to Salisbury; [signed] Thos Mulhollan, surveyor; sworn chain carriers George Kimbrow & Conrood Kimbrow; [on back] sold to Nicholas Long for £324 [signed] James Mebane, Commissioner.

438. Dec. 16, 1782 surveyed 357 ac; No. 27; formerly Henry Eustace McCulloh's property; on both sides of Great Allemance Cr; border: Jacob Rich, Henry Cook, & said McCulloh; [signed] Thos Mulhollan, surveyor; sworn chain carriers Joseph Noey & Wm Graves; [on back] sold to Thos Burk for £317 [signed] James Mebane, Commissioner.

439. Dec. 17, 1782 surveyed 184 ac; No. 28; formerly Henry Eustace McCulloh's property; on S side of Great Alamance Cr; border: George Friddle, Conrod Pile, & said McCulloh; [signed] Thos Mulhollan, surveyor; sworn chain carriers James Noey & Wm Graves; [on back] sold to John Eustice for £102 [signed] James Mebane, Commissioner.

440. Dec. 17, 1782 surveyed 253 ac; No. 36; formerly Henry Eustace McCulloh's property; on waters of Stinking Quarter Cr; border: Malchia Fogleman and Malchia Isles; [signed] Benja Rainey, D surveyor; sworn chain carriers William Phillips & George Fridle; [entered by John Butler--lined out]; [on back] sold to Thos Mulhollan [signed] James Mebane, Commissioner.

441. Dec. 17, 1782 surveyed 292 ac; No. 39; formerly Henry Eustace McCulloh's property; on waters of Little Alamance Cr; border: William Rogers; [signed] Benja Rainey, D surveyor; sworn chain carriers Wm Phillips & John Holt; [on back] sold to William Rogers for £75 [signed] James Mebane, Commissioner.

442. Dec. 18, 1782 surveyed 152 ac; No. 29; formerly Henry Eustace McCulloh's property; on waters of Great Alamance Cr; border: Jacob Rich and said McCulloh; [signed] Thos Mulhollan, surveyor; sworn chain carriers Joseph Noey & Wm Graves; [on back] sold to James Williams [signed] James Mebane, Commissioner.

443. Dec. 18, 1782 surveyed 163 ac; No. 38; formerly Henry Eustace McCulloh's property; on waters of Gun Cr; border: Ludwick Albright & Christian Huffman; [signed] Benja Rainey, D surveyor; sworn chain carriers William Phillips & Joseph Pivy; [on back] sold to Andrew Ross £101 [signed] James Mebane, Commissioner.

444. Dec. 18, 1782 surveyed 111 ac; No. 46; formerly Henry Eustace McCulloh's property; on waters of Gun Cr; border: John Shaddey; [signed] Benja Rainey, D surveyor; sworn chain carriers Wm Phillips & Philip Albright; [on back] sold to James Williams [signed] James Mebane, Commissioner.

445. Dec. 19, 1782 surveyed 230 ac; No. 31; formerly Henry Eustace McCulloh's property; on waters of Great Alamance Cr; border: Jacob Boon, Adam Whisel, Barnet Troehsler, & James Lett; [signed] Thos Mulhollan, surveyor; sworn chain carriers Jas Lett & Nicholas Holt; [on back] sold to John Eustice [signed] James Mebane, Commissioner.

446. Dec. 19, 1782 surveyed 295 ac; No. 35; formerly Henry Eustace McCulloh's property; on Stinking Quarter Co on Great Allamance Cr; border: George Fridle & Meluia Isley; [signed] Benjamin Rainey, D surveyor; sworn chain carriers William Phillips & George Fridle; entered by Conroad Pile; [on back] sold to Jal Mebane & Thos Mulhollan [signed] James Mebane, Commissioner.

447. Dec. 19, 1782 surveyed 100 ac; No. 37; formerly Henry Eustace McCulloh's property; on waters of Little Allamace Cr of Great Allamance Cr; border: William Oneal and Rueben Holt [or Hett]; [sigend] Benjamin Rainey, D surveyor; sworn chain carriers   William Phillips & Benja Phillips; entered by John Butlar; [on back] sold to Jal Mebane & Thos Mulhollan [signed] James Mebane, Commissioner.

448. Dec. 19, 1782 surveyed 370 ac; No. 43; formerly Henry Eustace McCulloh's property; on waters of Little Allamance Cr; includes Big "Medow"; [signed] Benjamin Rainey, D surveyor; sworn chain carriers William Phillips

Sales of Confiscated Land

& Benja Phillips; entered by John Butlar; [on back] sold to Thos Burk for £181 [signed] James Mebane, Commissioner.

449. Dec. 20, 1782 surveyed 159 ac; No. 30; formerly Henry Eustace McCulloh's property; on N side of Great Allemance Cr; border: Joseph Houseman and said McCulloch; [signed] Thos Mulhollan, surveyor; sworn chain carriers Joseph Noey & Wm Graves; [on back] sold to John Eustice [signed] James Mebane, Commissioner; "supposed to be" entered by William Graves.

450. Dec. 21, 1782 surveyed 270 ac; No. 33; formerly Henry Eustace McCulloh's property; on waters of Great Allemance Cr; border: Michael Charles, Shadrick Holt, Jacob Willhite, & Guilford Co line; [signed] Thos Mulhollan, surveyor; sworn chain carriers Jacob Willhite & Nicholas Holt; [on back] sold to John Eustice [signed] James Mebane, Commissioner; [entered by Thomas Hamilton--lined out].

451. Dec. 21, 1782 surveyed 180 ac; No. 34 ac; formerly Henry Eustace McCulloh's property; on waters of Great Allemance Cr; border: Jacob Wilhite, Shadrich Holt, & Guilford Co line; [signed] Thos Mulhollan, surveyor; sworn chain carriers Jacob Willhite & Nicholas Holt; [on back] sold to John Eustice [signed] James Mebane, Commissioner; [entered by Thomas Hamilton--lined out].

452. Dec. 22, 1782 surveyed 132 ac; No. 41; formerly Henry Eustace McCulloh's property; on Varnels Cr of Haw R; border: Peter Woolf; [signed] Thos Mulhollan, surveyor; sworn chain carriers Wm Rogers & Peter Woolf; "not entered"; [on back] sold to Nicholas Long [signed] James Mebane, Commissioner.

453. Dec. 26, 1782 surveyed 500 ac; No. 9; formerly Henry Eustace McCulloh's property; on both sides of Camp Cr and both sides of Orange & Granvil Co line; border: Mr. Rose; [signed] Thos Mulhollan, surveyor; sworn chain carriers Fred Rose & Alexr Moore; [on back] sold ato Andrew Ross [signed] James Mebane, Commissioner.

454. Dec. 26, 1782 surveyed 146 ac; No. 47; formerly Young, Miller & Co property; on waters of Eno R; border: NE corner of town of Hillsborough, a field, & Mr. Hogg; [signed] Thos Mulhollan, surveyor; sworn chain carriers Andrew McEntier & James Hunter; [on back] sold to Thos Burk & James Hogg "for the College of Hillsborough" [signed] James Mebane, Commissioner.

455. Dec. 27, 1782 surveyed a "small" part of lot 25 in Hillsborough; known as the Blue House, a corner house "of" Churtin St & King St and on upper side of King St; "said to be" Miller & Co's [Edmond Fanning--lined out] property; [no dimentions]; [signed] Thos Mulhollan, surveyor; [on back] sold to Patrick Saint Lawrence [signed] James Mebane, Commissioner "for" Col. Moore.

456. Dec. 27, 1782 surveyed 1 ac a lot in Hillsborough; No. 59; "said to be" James Miller's property; a corner lot "of" Churtin St & Tryon St and on upper side of Tryon St; 250 links by 400 links; [signed] Thos Mulhollan, surveyor; [on back] sold to Andw Ross [signed] James Mebane, Commissioner.

457. Dec. 27, 1782 surveyed 1 ac a lot in Hillsborough; No. 60; "said to be" James Miller's property; a corner lot "of" Churtin St & Queen St and on upper side of Queen St; 250 links by 400 links; [signed] Thos Mulhollan, surveyor; [on back] sold to John Alison [or Elleson] [signed] James Mebane, Commissioner.

458. Dec. 27, 1782 surveyed 1 ac a lot in Hillsborough; No. 83; "said to be" Miller & Co's property; 250 links by 400 links; [signed] Thos Mulhollan, surveyor; [on back] sold to George Huskins [signed] James Mebane, Commissioner; [two copies of this survey].

459. Dec. 27, 1782 surveyed 1 ac a lot in Hillsborough; No. 136; "said to be" Gov. Tryon's property; on lower side of Margreatt Lane and W side of Wake St; 250 links by 400 links; [signed] Thos Mulhollan, surveyor; [on back] sold to Jas Williams [signed] James Mebane, Commissioner.

Sales of Confiscated Land

460. Dec. 27, 1782 surveyed 1 ac a lot in Hillsborough; No. 137; "said to be" Gov. Tryon's property; on lower side of Margaret Lane and W of Wake St; 250 links by 400 links; plat has a wiggly double line [not called a creek] running diagonally through the lot; [signed] Thos Mulhollan, surveyor; [on back] sold to James Williams [signed] James Mebane, Commissioner.

461. Dec. 27, 1782 surveyed 1 ac a lot in Hillsborough; No. 138; "said to be" Gov. Tryon's property; on lower side of Margarett St and W of Wake St; 250 links by 400 links; [signed] Thos Mulhollan, surveyor; [on back] sold to James Williams [signed] James Mebane, Commissioner.

462. Dec. 27, 1782 surveyed 1 ac a lot in Hillsborough; No. 139; "said to be" Gov. Tryon's property; a corner lot on Wake St & Margaret Lane and on lower side of said land; 250 links by 400 links; [signed] Thos Mulhollan, surveyor; [on back] sold to James Williams [signed] James Mebane, Commissioner.

463. Dec. 28, 1782 surveyed 1 ac a lot in Hillsborough; No. 79; "said to be" James Miller's property; a corner lot on Churtin St & Tryon St and on upper side of Tryon St; 250 links by 400 links; [signed] Thos Mulhollan, surveyor; [on back] sold to Jacob Richards [signed] James Mebane, Commissioner.

464. Apr. 4, 1783 surveyed 640 ac; No. 934; formerly David Edwards' property; on both sides of Collins Cr of Haw R; border: Jno Edwards sr and Jno Edwards jr; being a survey formerly made for John Edwards sr; [signed] Thos Mulhollan, surveyor; sworn chain carriers Jno Stroud & Thos Hatwell; [on back] Sept. 4, 1783 David Edwards.

465. May 13, 1783 surveyed 60 ac; No. 51; formerly Henry Eustace McCulloch's property; on S side of Haw R and waters of Little Allimance Cr; border: Peter Cotner; [signed] Thos Mulhollan, surveyor; sworn chain carriers Fredrick Kimbrough & Petor [sic] Cotner; [on back] May 8, 1786 sold to Henry Thomson for £120 [signed] Archd Lytle, Comr.

466. May 13, 1785 surveyed 90 ac; No. 52; formerly Henry Eustace McCulloch's property; on S side of Haw R and on waters of Little Allimance Cr; border: Adam Smith; [signed] Thos Mulhollan, surveyor; sworn chain carriers Fredrick Kimbrough & Petor Cotner; May 8, 1786 sold to William Rea for £166 [signed] Archd Lytle, Comr.

467. May 14, 1785 surveyed 200 ac; No. 53; formerly Henry Eustace McCulloh's property; on both sides of Great Alamace Cr; border: Barnet Troxler and Michael Holt; [signed] Thos Mulhollan, surveyor; sworn chain carriers Jno Boon & Michl Holt; [on back] May 8, 1786 sold o William Oneal for £325 [signed] Archd Lytle, Comr.

468. May 15, 1785 surveyed 159 ac; No. 47; formerly Henry Eustace McCulloch's property; on S side of Haw R; border: Philip Eulias and on waters of Eulias Cr; [signed] Thos Mulhollan, surveyor; sworn chain carriers Andrew Mulhollan & John Boon; Mar. 1787 sold to Joseph Dickson for £17.10.9 [signed] Archd Lytle, Comr.

469. May 15, 1785 surveyed 230 ac; No. 48; formerly Henry Eustace McCulloch's property; on S side of Haw R and on waters of Eulias Cr; border: tract No. 47; [not signed]; sworn chain carriers Andrew Mulhollan and John Boon; May 8, 1786 sold to Joseph Noey for £231 [signed] Archd Lytle, Comr.

470. May 15, 1785 surveyed 225 ac; No. 49; formerly Henry Eustace McCulloh's property; on waters of Eulias Cr; border: tract No. 48; [signed] Thos Mulhollan, surveyor; sworn chain carriers Andrew Mulhollan & Jno Boon; May 8, 1786 sold to William Lytle for £325 [signed] Archd Lytle, Comr.

471. May 18, 1785 surveyed 208 ac; No. 46; formerly Henry Eustace McCulloh's property; on both sides of Stinken Quarter Cr; border: Ezekiel Boggs and Thos McCulloh; [signed] Thos Mulhollan, surveyor; sworn chain carriers Peter Hitten & Jno Coones; May 8, 1786 sold to Samuel Parker for £401 [signed] Archd Lytle, Comr.

472. May 19, 1785 surveyed 240 ac; No. 45; formerly Henry Eustace McCulloh's property; on both sides of Stinken Quarter Cr; border: Peter Hilton [on Hitton]; [signed] Thos Mulhollan, surveyor; sworn chain carriers Peter Hilton & Jno Coones; May 8, 1786 sold to John Counts for £305.10 [signed] Archd Lytle, Comr.

Sales of Confiscated Land

473. Jun. 10, 1785 surveyed 33 ac; No. 51; formerly Henry Eustace McCulloh's property; on S side of Haw R and on waters of Vernals Cr; border: Robert Hunter; [signed] Thos Mulhollan, surveyor; sworn chain carriers Jno McDaniel & Jas Godfrey; May 8, 1786 sold to James Thomson [or Thompson] for £100 [signed] Archd Lytle, Comr.

474. Jun. 11, 1785 surveyed 50 ac; No. 36; formerly Henry Eustace McCulloh's property; on S side of Haw R and on waters of Varnels Cr; border: tract No. 37 and William Clendenin [or Clendenning]; includes par of the improvement of James Thompson; [signed] Thos Mulhollan, surveyor; sworn chain carriers Jno McDaniel & Jas Godfrey; May 8, 1786 sold to James Thomson [or Thompson] for £102 [signed] Archd Lytle, Comr.

475. Jun. 11, 1785 surveyed 23 ac; No. 38; formerly Henry Eustace McCulloh's property; on S side of Haw R; border: tract No. 51 and Eli McDaniel esq; [signed] Thos Mulhollan, surveyor; sworn chain carriers Jno McDaniel & Jas Godfrey; May 8, 1786 sold to John McDaniel for £100 [signed] Archd Lytle, Comr.

476. Jun. 12, 1785 surveyed 140 ac; No. 34; formerly Henry Eustace McCulloh's property; on waters of Vernals Cr; border: Peter Woolf, Robert Homes, & "nigh the" great road; [signed] Thos Mulhollan, surveyor; sworn chain carriers Jno McDaniel & Jas Godfrey; May 8, 1786 to Samuel Campbell for £80 [signed] Archd Lytle, Comr.

477. Jun. 12, 1785 surveyed 70 ac; No. 35; formerly Henry Eustace McCulloh's property; on waters of Varnels Cr; border: tract No. 34 and Peter Woolf; [signed] Thos Mulhollan, surveyor; sworn chain carriers Jno McDaniel & Jas Godfrey; [no date] sold to Eli McDaniel for £105 [signed] Archd Lytle, Comr.

478. Jun. 12, 1785 surveyed 184 ac; No. 43; formerly Henry Eustace McCulloh's property; on S side of Haw R and on both sides of Vernals Cr; border: James Homes, Drury Hunnicut, Brown's field, & a branch; includes Jas Godfrey's improvement; [signed] Thos Mulhollan, surveyor; sworn chain carriers Jno McDaniel & Jas Godfrey; Feb. 26, 1788 sold to James Godfrey for £55 [signed] Archd Lytle, Comr.

479. Jun. 12, 1785 surveyed 108 ac; No. 44; formerly Henry Eustace McCulloh's property; on S side of Haw R; border: tract No. 43 and a branch; [signed] Thos Mulhollan, surveyor; sworn chain carriers Jno McDaniel & Jas Godfrey; plat shows land is on both sides of a double wiggly line, not called a creek; May 8, 1786 sold to James Williams for £110.10 [or £110] [signed] Archd Lytle, Comr.

480. Jun. 12, 1785 surveyed 115 ac; No. 50; formerly Henry Eustace McCulloh's property; on waters of Vernals Cr; includes Benjamin McGemery's improement; border: Peter Woolf; [signed] Thos Mulhollan, surveyor; sworn chain carriers Jno McDaniel & Jas Godfrey; May 8, 1786 sold to James Williams for £122 [or £120] [signed] Archd Lytle, Comr.

481. Jul. 18, 1785 surveyed 155 ac; No. 10; formerly Henry Eustace McCulloh's property; on both sides of Stinken Quarter Cr; includes the improvement where Henry Cook lives; [signed] Thos Mulhollan, surveyor; sworn chain carriers Jacob Holt & Peter Holt; May 8, 1786 sold to Henry Cooke for £51 [signed] Archd Lytle, Comr.

482. Jun. 25, 1785 surveyed 64 ac; No. 3; formerly John Milner's property; on N side of Enoe R; border: William Cabe's corner on the river; [signed] Thos Mulhollan, surveyor; sworn chain carriers Wm Cabe & Jno Flinthem; May 8, 1786 sold to William Cabe for £450.1 [signed] Archd Lytle, Comr.

483. Jun. 25, 1785 surveyed 186 ac; No. 4; formerly John Milner's property; on S side of Enoe R; border: John Flinthim; [signed] Thos Mulhollan, surveyor; sworn chain carriers Wm Cabe & Jno Flinthem; May 8, 1786 sold to John Flinthim for £841 [signed] Archd Lytle, Comr.

484. Jun. 25, 1785 surveyed 180 ac; No. 5; formerly John Milner's property; on S side of Enoe R; border: tract No. 4 on N and a corner of No. 4 on the river; [signed] Thos Mulhollan, surveyor; sworn chain carriers Wm Cabe & Jno Flinthem; May 8, 1786 sold to Tilman Dixon for £1,110 [signed] Archd Lytle, Comr.

Sales of Confiscated Land

485. Oct. 20, 1785 surveyed 168 ac; No. 30; formerly Henry Eustace McCulloh's property; on waters of Wells's Cr; border: tracts No. 31 & 32 and Danl Freeman's land; [signed] Thos Mulhollan, surveyor; sworn chain carriers   James Neal & Wm Wells; Mar. 1788 sold to Thos H Perkins for £141 [signed] Archd Lytle, Comr.

486. Oct. 20, 1785 surveyed 173 ac; No. 31; formerly Henry Eustace McCulloh's property; on waters of Wells Cr; border: tracts No. 30, 32, & 33 and Joseph Wells' land; [signed] Thos Mulhollan, surveyor; sworn chain carriers James Neal & [no first name] Wells; Mar. 1788 sold to Tilman Dixon for £151 [signed] Archd Lytle, Comr.

487. Oct. 21, 1785 surveyed 170 ac; No. 32; formerly Henry Eustace McCulloh's property; on waters of Wells Cr; border: tracts No. 30, 31, & 33 and James Stoneman's land; [signed] Thos Mulhollan, surveyor; sworn chain carriers Jas Neal & Wm Wells; May 8, 1786 sold to William Shepperd for £311 [signed] Archd Lytle, Comr.

488. Oct. 21, 1785 surveyed 102 ac; No. 33; formerly Henry Eustace McCulloh's property; on waters of Wells Cr; border: tracts No. 31 & 32 and Jos Wells' land; [signed] Thos Mulhollan, surveyor; sworn chain carriers Jas Neal & Wm Wells; May 8, 1786 sold to Tilman Dixon for £206.2 [signed] Archd Lytle, Comr.

489. Oct. 25, 1785 surveyed 69 ac; No. 39; formerly Henry Eustace McCulloch's property; on S side of Haw R and on waters of Little Alamance Cr; border: tract No. 40 and Thomas Mulholan; [signed] Thos Mulhollan, surveyor; sworn chain carriers Rubin Holt & Robt McCulloh; May 1, 1786 sold to William McCawley for £125 [signed] Archd Lytle, Comr.

490. Oct. 25, 1785 surveyed 146 ac; No. 40; formerly Henry Eustace McCulloch's property; on S side of Haw R and on waters of Little Allamance Cr; border: tract No. 39 and Rubin Holt; [signed] Thos Mulhollan, surveyor; sworn chain carriers Rubin Holt & Robt McCulloh; May 8, 1786 sold to Martin Cole for £305 [signed] Archd Lytle, Comr.

491. Oct. 26, 1785 surveyed 116 ac; No. 42; formerly Henry Eustace McCulloch's property; on S side of Haw R and on waters of Rock Cr; border: tract No. 41, Joseph Albright, & Ben Picket; [signed] Thos Mulhollan, surveyor; sworn chain carriers Jas Godfrey & M Moser; May 8, 1786 sold to Michoael Mozer for £227 [signed] Archd Lytle, Comr.

492. Feb. 7, 1786 surveyed 143 ac; No. 1; formerly Young Miller & Co's property; on N side of Hillsborough and on waters of Eno R; border: Mr. Hooper; [signed] Thos Mulhollan, surveyor; sworn chain carrier Wm Cummins; May 8, 1786 sold to John Taylor esq for £1,000 [signed] Archd Lytle, Comr.

493. Feb. 7, 1786 surveyed 300 ac; No. 2; formerly Edmund Fanning's property; on W side of Hillsborough and on both sides of Eno R; border: side of Oconenky Mountain, the town line, & Courts' line; [signed] Thos Mulhollan, surveyor; sworn chain carriers Wm Cummins & Ben Nunham; "NB" the "other" plan says sold to John Estes for £801 [signed] Archd Lytle, Comr; [on back] May 8, 1786 sold to John Estes for £801 [signed] Archd Lytle, Comr.

494. May [omitted], 1786 surveyed 200 ac; No. 30; formerly Henry Eustace McCulloch's property; on waters of Enoe R; border: widow Brittain, Wm Dunnegan, & "the" great road; [signed] Thos Mulhollan, surveyor; sworn chain carriers   Matt Cate & Ben Cate; Mar. 1788 sold to Stephen Moore for £101 [signed] Archd Lytle, Comr.

495. [no date] surveyed 1 ac lot No. 12 in Hillsborough; formerly Edmond Fanning's property; border: 400 links on King St and 250 links deep; [signed] Thos Mulhollan, surveyor; May 8, 1786 sold to Josiah Watts for £726 [signed] Archd Lytle, Comr.

496. [no date] surveyed 1 ac lot 15 in Hillsborough; formerly Edmond Fanning's property; border: fronts of King St; 250 links by 400 links; [signed] Thos Mulhollan, surveyor; May 8, 1786 sold to William Watters for £535 [signed] Archd Lytle, Comr.

Sales of Confiscated Land

497. [no date] surveyed 1 ac lot No. 21 in Hillsborough; formerly Edmond Fanning's property; a corner lot on Kings St and Wake St; 250 links by 400 links; [signed] Thos Mulhollan, surveyor; May 8, 1786 sold to Roswell Huntington for £501 [signed] Archd Lytle, Comr.

498. [no date] surveyed 1 ac lot No. 22 in Hillsborough; formerly Edmund Fanning's property; 400 links by 250 links; [signed] Thos Mulhollan, surveyor; May 8, 1786 sold to Memucan Hunt for £1,001 [signed] Archd Lytle, Comr.

499. [no date] surveyed 1 ac lot No. 23 in Hillsborough; formerly Edmond Fanning's property; 400 links by 250 links; [signed] Thos Mulhollan, surveyor; May 8, 1786 sold to William Lythe [written over Shepperd] for £1,022 [signed] Archd Lytle, Comr.

500. [no date] surveyed [acres omitted]; part of lot 25 in Hillsborough; formerly Young Miller & Co's property; a corner lot on Churtin St and King St; border: 210' front on Churtin St and 81' front on King St; plat shows lot is 264' by 156' with a notch 84' by 54' out of a corner, evidently the corner of Churtin & King Sts; [signed] Thos Mulhollan, surveyor; May 8, 1786 sold to George Doherty for £4,558 [signed] Archd Lytle, Comr.

501. [no date] surveyed 1 ac lot 31 in Hillsborough; formerly Edmund Fanning's property; a corner lot on Wake St and Tryon St; 400 links by 250 links; [signed] Thos Mulhollan, surveyor; May 8, 1786 sold to Absalom Tatom for £223.1 [signed] Archd Lytle, Comr.

502. [no date] surveyed 1 ac lot 32 in Hillsborough; formerly Edmond Fanning's property; fronting on Tryon St; 400 links by 250 links; [signed] Thos Mulhollan, surveyor; May 8, 1786 sold to William Shepperd for £450 [signed] Archd Lytle, Comr.

503. [no date] surveyed 1 ac lot 33 in Hillsborough; formerly Edmond Fanning's property; fronting on Tryon St; 400 links by 250 links; [signed] Thos Mulhollan, surveyor; May 8, 1786 sold to William Shepperd for £550 [signed] Archd Lytle, Comr.

504. [no date] surveyed 1 ac lot 34 in Hillsborough; formerly Edmond Fanning's property; fronting on Tryon St; 400 links by 250 links; [signed] Thos Mulhollan, surveyor; May 8, 1786 sold to George Doherty for £601 [signed] Archd Lytle, Comr.

505. [no date] surveyed 0.75 ac part of lot 35 ac in Hillsborough; formerly Edmund Fanning's property; a corner lot on Church St and Tryon St; border: 200 links of Church St and 125 links on Tryon St; plat shows lot is 400 links by 250 links with a notch 200 links by 125 links out of a corner, evidently the corner of Church & Tryon Sts; [signed] Thos Mulhollan, surveyor; May 8, 1786 sold to George Doherty for £835 [signed] Archd Lytle, Comr.

506. Oct. 26, 1786 surveyed 112 ac; No. 41; formerly Henry Eustace McCulloch's property; on S side of Haw R; border: tract No. 42, Mr. Moser, & Ben Picket; includes Moser's improvement; [signed] Thos Mulhollan, surveyor; sworn chain carriers Jas Godfrey & M Moser; [on back] May 8, 1786 sold to Philip Mozer for £150 [signed] Archd Lytle, Comr.

507. [no date] surveyed 357 ac; No. 56; formerly Henry Eustace McCulloch's property; on both sides of Great Alamance Cr; [signed] Thos Mulhollan, surveyor; sworn chain carriers Jos Noe & Wm Graves; Feb. 26, 1788 sold to Thos Mulhollen for £61 [signed] Archd Lytle, Comr.

508. [no date] surveyed 208 ac; No. 19; formerly Henry Eustace McCulloch's property; on waters of Little R; border: George Horner & John Tilley; [signed] Thos Mulhollan, surveyor; sworn chain carriers Wm Ray & Jno Tilley; Feb. 1788 sold to William Shepperd for £437.10 [signed] Archd Lytle, Comr.

509. Jan. 20, 1804 surveyed 210 ac on waters of Enoe R; border: Chesenhall Harris & Forester; [signed] Saml Bradford, S. O. C.; [on back] plat is a tract formerly Henry Eustace McCulloch's property in Orange Co & sold Jul.

Sales of Confiscated Land

29, 1804 at Orange Co Court house to Gen. Samuel Benton for £102 by Henry Shepperd, Hillsborough Dist. Commissioner of Confiscated Property [signed] H Shepperd; No. 540 Aug. 20, 1804.

510. Jul. 24, 1804 surveyed 350 ac on waters of Gun Cr; border: Henry Bracker; [signed] Jas Patterson, d. s. "certified by" Saml Bradford, S. O. C.; sworn chain carriers Wm B Grove & N B Rose; [on back] plat is a tract formerly Henry Eustace McCulloch's property in Orange Co & sold at Orange Co Court house Jul. 29, 1804 to William B Grove esq for $89 by Henry Shepperd, Hillsborough Dist. Commissioner of Confiscated Property [signed] H Shepperd; No. 539 Aug. 6, 1804.

PASQUOTANK COUNTY

511. "claim"--executors of William Actchison vs State of North Carolina--jurors: Peter Wynns, Joseph Perry, Benja Jones, Hardy Hunter, Joshua Tarhington, David Askew, William Littlejohn, Isaac Carter, Demsey Jackson, Solomon Pool, Peter Morrisett, & Edmund Blount; jury find the facts to be true in the "certificate" from Pasquotank Co Court relative to the claim of Alexander Diack, executor of estate of William Actchison, for 1/4th of the stock and profits of "the" copartnership; the stock & profits follow: 400 ac called Newfield, a lot & "houses" thereon in Winfield on lease from Thomas Relfe, Negroes--Patience, Phillip, Pompey, Setar, Rachel & her 3 children, Simon, Ned, Lydia & her 2 children, Job, & Miriam & her 3 "or" 4 children, household furniture at Winfield, horses, cattle, hogs, sheep, plantation utensils at Winfield, and sundry merchandize & outstanding debts at Winfield; said Diack has a right to apply for 1/4th of the stock & profits due to the will of said deceased. [signed] Peter Wynns, foreman; "a true copy" [signed] Charles Bondfield, c s c.

 Dec. term 1779 Pasquotank Co the justices order Commissioners of Confiscated Property deliver to Alexander Diack 1/4th of the stock & profits from the estate of William McCormick & Co "an absentee of this State" after deducting commissions and 1/4th of the stock & profits to Margaret Parker after being sold by the Commissioners at public auction before Feb. 15 next; and lay their proceedings before this Court; "a true copy" [signed] Enoch Relfe, c c c.

512. "claim"--Margaret Parker vs State of North Carolina--jury: Peter Wynns, Joseph Perry, Benjamin Jones, Hardy Hunter, Joshua Tarhington, David Askew, William Littlejohn, Isaac Carter, Demsey Jackson, Solomon Pool, Peter Morrisett, & Edmund Blount; the above jury find Margaret Parker's claim to be true and say James Parker has 2 "infant" sons--one in "some part" of Great Britain since before Independence of this State and the other taken away by his father last Summer; if James Parker had remained a subject of this state would be entitled to 1/4th of "original" stock & profits of "the" copartnership mention "therein" [Margaret Parker's claim]; the stock & profits now are [see No. 511 above]; under a clause of the sixth section of an Act entitled "an Act to carry into effect an act passed at Newbern in 1777 entitled an act for Confiscating Property of all such persons as are inimical to the United States and of such persons as shall not in a certain time therein mentioned appear and submit to the State whither they shall be received as Citizens thereof and of such persons as shall so appear and shall not be admitted as Citizens and for other purposes therein mentioned & for other purposes is to be considered as having died intestate" that his [James Parker's] 1/4th of said stock & property is to be distributed among his wife & "such other of his representatives as would have had a legal claim to his estate if he had died intestate & [are] a subject of this State". [signed] Peter Wynns, foreman; Dec. term 1779 Pasquotank Co the justices order Commissioners of Confiscated Property delivered to Alexander Diack 1/4th of the stock & profits from estate of William McCormick & Co "an absentee of this State" after deducting commissions and 1/4th of stock & profits to Margaret Parker after being sold by Commissioners at public auction before Feb. 15 next and lay their proceedings before this Court; "a true copy" [signed] Enoch Relfe, c c c.

513. Jun. term 1779 Pasquotank Co the justices, on motion of James Iradel esq, order that a claim of Margaret Parker wife of James Parker merchant "an absentee coming within the description of the Confiscation Act", on behalf of herself & her infant child to a part of the estate of William McCormick & Co, might be received & certified in Superior Court agreeable to the description of the Act of Assembly; and claim of Alexander Diack, executor of William Actchison merchant deceased, to part of the same estate is received & certified in the same manner; also the proceedings of the Commissioners of "forfeited" estate is suspended for the estate of William McCormick & Co until determination is made about the claim by Superior Court; "a true copy" [signed] Enoch Relfe, c c.

Sales of Confiscated Land

514. Jonathan Allen's account vs Cornell's confiscated estate: M Isler [or Ister], M Macon, M Bryan, M J Wms [sic], & M Baker:

to my services as overseer & manager of the estate from Dec. 12,1778 to Mar.

31, 1779 = 110 days @ 40/ per day	£220
to "a boy" 110 days @ 20/ per day	£110
to 3 horses 110 days @ 48/	£264
to making 11 pair Negroes britches @ 32/	£17.12
to making 4 jackets @ 32/	£ 6.8
to 2 bushels of salt @ £4	£ 8
to 1 pair of shoes @ £6	£ 6
to the midwife for 2 Negro women "laying inn" & necessarys found	£40
to a gallon of rum for the sick Negroes	£ 4
to a gall of "molasses" for "do"	£ 0.16
to 5 bushels of oats @ £4	£20
to the blacksmith	£10

Jonathan Allen   [total]   £698.16   [written over £698.6.8]

[no date] Craven Co Jonathan Allen swears to Wm Bryan, JP, that the above account is just & true.

515. Feb. 19, 1780 received of John Richardson, Commissioner for disposing confiscated property in Pasquotank Co   £6,282.4

Mar. 24   received of "ditto in further part"   £3,732.8

Apr. 8   received of Jonathan Banks "in further part"   £7,030.16
          [total]   £17,045.8

Apr. 22, 1780   these sums accounted for in my statement with Committee of Accounts [signed] "W Lk"; [on back] Thos Harvey.

516. Aug. 4, 1788 To the Comptroller--Thomas Harvey esq, Commissioner of Confiscated Property in Pasquotank Co; today paid in full the Comptroller's Report against Banks, Harvey, Richardson, Commissioners "aforesaid"; their account should therefore be "tallad" [or land]. [signed] J Haywood, Treasurer.

PITT COUNTY

517. To Comr. of Confiscated "Perty." Majr. Gen. Caswell esq Dobbs Co--Oct. 2, 1783 Pitt Co: Sir, I received your letter to me, dated Aug. 15, on Sept. 23 and "observe the contents thereof"; I don't have a single shilling in my hands of confiscated property, nor any papers relative thereto, no never had; Mr. Ed Salter [or Satter] and Mr. Fredrick Bryan were appointed Commissioners by the County Court, but they never qualified or acted in any manner, there being no business of that kind in our county; just before the sale at Newbern on Dec. 30 last, Gen. Simpson observed Col. Shepherd's advertisements at the Court house door and informed me there were 3 lots in the town of Martinborough property of Wm Brimage; I informed Col. Shepherd of them, and he sold them on the second day of the sale to Col. James Armstrong for about £30.   This is all the information I can give of any confiscated property in this county. [signed] David Perkins, shf.

518. Receipt No. 48 Jan. 5, 1792 to William Moye £0.40 [or £2] for one survey in Pitt Co.

519. May 28, 1787 surveyed 240 ac; by order of James Armstrong, Commissioner of Confiscated Property for Newbern Dist; all of a grant Mar. 9, 1759 to Robert Parmer esq; on W side of Little Contentnea Cr; border: Daniel Demsey Moss's corner on the creek swamp, Moses Mannen, & the mouth of a branch; [signed] Wm Moye, c surveyor; chain carriers Ephraim Spivey & Daniel Demsy Moss; [on back] formerly Robert Parmer's property; Saml Simpson.

RANDOLPH COUNTY

520. [no date] Randolph Co: certified that no account has ever been settled by said county's Commissioners of Confiscated Property, no person having acted in that capacity; [signed] A Sann [or Lann], c c.

Sales of Confiscated Land

521. Receipt No. 58 Sept. 15, 1785 to John Collier, Randolph Co surveyor, £60 for 30 surveys; [on back] Apr. 3, 1786 received the within order of Thomas Clark, collector, [signed] Jno Collier.

522. Dec. 26, 1782 surveyed 298 ac on Uwarie R at the mouth of Jacksons Cr; border: crosses Uwarrie R & Moor's Road and joins Fuller; [signed] John Collier; sold to James Roberts.

523. May 4, 1785 surveyed 243 ac; No. 1; on Carraway Cr; formerly Henry Eustace McCulloch's property; border: a white oak marked "M C" on W side of said creek and crosses the creek; [signed] John [page torn]; May 1, 1786 sold to Patrick Travers for £534 [signed] Archd [page torn].

524. May 1785 surveyed 243 ac; No. 2; formerly Henry Eustace McCulloch's property; on Carraway Cr; border: tract No. 1 and crosses the creek; [signed] John Collier c s; May 1, 1786 sold to Patrick Travers for £410 [signed] Archd Lytle, Comr.

525. May 1785 surveyed 243 ac; No. 3; formerly Henry Eustace McCulloch's property; on Carraway Cr; border: tract No. 2 and crosses the creek; [signed] John Collier, c s; May 1, 1786 sold to William Pickett for £471 [signed] Archd Lytle, Comr.

526. May 1785 surveyed 243 ac; No. 4; formerly Henry Eustace McCulloch's property; on Carraway Cr; border: tract No. 3 and crosses the creek; [signed] John Collier, c s; May 1, 1786 sold to William Pickett for £471 [signed] Archd Lytle, Comr.

527. May 1785 surveyed 243 ac; No. 5; formerly Henry Eustace McCulloch's property; on Carraway Cr; border: tract No. 4 and crosses the creek; [signed] John Collier, c s; May 1, 1786 sold to Patrick Travers [William Shepperd--lined out] for £381 [signed] Archd Lytle, Comr.

528. May 1785 surveyed 243 ac; No. 6; formerly Henry Eustace McCulloch's property; on Carraway Cr; border: tract No. 5 and crosses the creek; [signed] John Collier, c s; May 1, 1786 to William Lytle for £215 [signed] Archd Lytle, Comr.

529. May 1785 surveyed 243 ac; No. 7; formerly Henry Eustace McCulloch's property; on Carraway Cr; border: tract No. 6, Moor's Road, & crosses the creek; [signed] John Collier, c s; May 1, 1786 sold to William Bailey [or Bayley] for £253 [signed] Archd Lytle, Comr.

530. May 1785 surveyed 243 ac; No. 8; formerly Henry Eustace McCulloch's property; on Carraway Cr; border: Moor's Road, crosses the creek at the mouth of Back Cr, & tract No. 7; [signed] John Collier, c s; May 1, 1786 sold to William Bailey for £452.1 [signed] Archd Lytle, Comr.

531. May 1785 surveyed 169 ac; No. 9; formerly Henry Eustace McCulloch's property; on Carraway Cr; tract No. 8 and crosses Carraway Cr; [signed] John Collier, c s; May 1, 1786 sold to Patrick Travers for £276.11.6 [signed] Archd Lytle, Comr.

532. May 1785 surveyed 260 ac; No. 10; formerly Henry Eustace McCulloch's property; on Carraway Cr; border: below Frohock's tract and crosses the creek; [signed] John Collier, c s; May 1, 1786 sold to Francis Arnold for £452 [signed] Archd Lytle, Comr.

533. May 1785 surveyed 260 ac; No. 11; formerly Henry Eustace McCulloch's property; on Carraway Cr; border: Bailey, tract No. 10, & crosses the creek; [signed] John Collier, c s; May 1, 1786 sold to Patrick Travers for £360.1.6 [signed] Archd Lytle, Comr.

Sales of Confiscated Land

534. May 1785 surveyed 75 ac; No. 12; formerly Henry Eustace McCulloch's property; on Warie R below the mouth of Carraway Cr; border: Bailey, Fuller, crosses said river, & Susanah McGee; [signed] John Collier, c s; May 1, 1786 sold to William Bell for £151 [signed] Archd Lytle, Comr.

535. May 1785 surveyed 272 ac; No. 13; formerly Henry Eustace McCulloch's property; on Warie R; border: Bailey, a former survey, & crosses said river; [signed] John Collier, c s; May 1, 1786 sold to William Bell for £403.3 [signed] Archd Lytle, Comr.

536. May 1785 surveyed 290 ac; No. 14; formerly Henry Eustace McCulloch's property; on Warie R; border: Sloan's line and Toms Cr; [signed] John Collier, c s; May 1, 1786 sold to Patrick Travers [William Shepperd--lined out] for £400.3 [signed] Archd Lytle, Comr.

537. Jun. 1785 surveyed 250 ac; No. 15; formerly Henry Eustace McCulloch's property; on Warie R; border: Hill's corner on W side of the river and crosses the river; [signed] John Collier, c s; May 1, 1786 sold to Alexr Nelson for £315 [signed] Archd Lytle, Comr.

538. Jun. 1785 surveyed 250 ac; No. 16; formerly Henry Eustace McCulloch's property; on Warie R; border: tract No. 15, crosses Two Mile Br, & crosses said river; [signed] John Collier, c s; May 1, 1786 sold to William Lytle for £501 [signed] Archd Lytle, Comr.

539. Jun. 1785 surveyed 250 ac; No. 17; formerly Henry Eustace McCulloch's property; on Warie R; border: tract No. 16, crosses the river above the mouth of Hannah's Cr, & on Bundys Cr; [signed] John Collier, c s; May 1, 1786 sold to Patrick Travers [William Shepperd--lined out] for £1,000 [signed] Archd Lytle, Comr.

540. Jun. 1785 surveyed 250 ac; No. 18; formerly Henry Eustace McCulloch's property; on Warie R; border: crosses the river and crosses Hannahs Cr; [signed] John Collier, c s; May 1, 1786 sold to William Lytle for £1,366.13.4 [signed] Archd Lytle, Comr.

541. Jun. 1785 surveyed 160 ac; No. 19; formerly Henry Eustace McCulloch's property; on Warie R; border: Robbins and crosses the river; [signed] John Collier, c s; May 1, 1786 sold to John Stanfield for £355 [signed] Archd Lytle, Comr.

542. Jun. 1785 surveyed 136 ac; No. 20; formerly Henry Eustace McCulloch's property; on Second Cr waters of Warie R; border: Hill's line on N side of said creek; [signed] John Collier, c s; May 1, 1786 sold to John Clarke for £181 [signed] Archd Lytle, Comr.

543. Jun. 1785 surveyed 270 ac; No. 21; formerly Henry Eustace McCulloch's property; on Jacksons Cr; border: Godfree Ridge's corner and crosses said creek; [signed] John Collier, c s; May 1, 1786 sold to John Clarke for £212 [signed] Archd Lytle, Comr.

544. Jul. 11, 1785 surveyed 397 ac; No. 1; formerly Henry Eustace McCulloch's property; part of [McCulloch's] tract No. 10; on S fork of Uwarrie R; border: original line of [McCulloch's] tract No. 10 run by Gen. Rutherford and Samuel Park's corner; [signed] John Collier, c s; plat shows land is on both sides of the road to Salisbury; May 1, 1786 sold to Samuel Parke for £751 [signed] Archd Lytle, Comr.

545. Aug. 10, 1785 surveyed 438 ac; formerly Henry Eustace McCulloch's property; "of the" richlands of Warie R; border: "the" original line and tract No. 5; [signed] John Collier, c s; May 2, 1786 sold to William Lytle for £481 [signed] Archd Lytle, Comr.

546. Aug. 10, 1785 surveyed 438 ac; formerly Henry Eustace McCulloch's property; "of the" richlands of Warie R; border: tracts No. 2 & 4; [signed] John Collier, c s; chain carriers John Merrel & Dan Merrel; May 2, 1786 sold to William Lytle for £1,405 [signed] Archd Lytle, Comr.

547. Aug. 10, 1785 surveyed 381 ac; No. 7; formerly Henry Eustace McCulloch's property; in the richlands of Uwarie R; border: tract No. 6 and "the" old line; [signed] John Collier, c s; chain carriers John Merrel & Dan Merrel; May 2, 1786 sold to John Clarke for £1,905 [signed] Archd Lytle, Comr.

548. Oct. 1785 surveyed 200 ac; No. 22; formerly Henry Eustace McCulloch's property; on Stinking Quarter Cr; border: McGee, Barton, & the county line; [signed] John Collier, c s; May 1, 1786 sold to Wm Yorke for £231 [signed] Archd Lytle, Comr.

RICHMOND COUNTY
549. Sept. 20, 1787 sold to Thomas Clark 200 ac for £270; No. 1; on N side of Pee Dee R; formerly Samuel Williams and Henry Williams' property; border: Jacob Falconbery's lower corner, William Bluit's upper corner, & Pee Dee R; [signed] Charles Bruce, CCPSD.

ROWAN COUNTY
550. Receipt No. 246 May 20, 1786 to Griffith Rutherford, Rowan Co surveyor, £10 for 5 surveys.

551. Receipt No. 361 Jan. 5, 1787 to Griffith Rutherford, Rowan Co surveyor, £20 for 10 surveys.
552. Oct. 14, 1809 to Lewis Beard, Rowan Co Commissioner of Confiscated Land, letter from Ed Jones, Solicitor General: two suits were brought by Lewis Beard as commissioner in Rowan Co--(a) against Hugh Cunningham and (b) against John Sloane, in Salisbury Dist. Superior Court and suits are "now" pending in Rowan Co Superior Court; Court of Conference [or N C Supreme Court] has judged [? hole in page] a case of the University vs. Foy; the Court held that Act of Assembly passed in 1800 at Raleigh to direct the trustees of the University "of the land" vested in them by previous acts of the Legislature, was unconstitutional and void [see N C Reports vol. 5 p. 57-66 for trustees of the University vs. Foy and Bishop]; it didn't affect the trustee's title to land previously granted by the Legislature; this decision will govern the suits you've instituted against Cunningham and Sloane since the "supreme judicial Authorits" [hole in page] have decided against the State's claim and title for the land you've brought suit as aforesaid. It becomes unnecessary to prosecute those suits further. The Act of Assembly under which you're appointed Commissioner directs the suits you've instituted to be prosecuted by me as Solicitor General; so I direct you to dismiss the suits. [signed] Ed Jones, sol. genl.

553. [on back] Maj. Mountflorence to Spruce Macay--Confiscated Property:
[on front] Salisbury Jan. 7, 1782 Qt. M. Dept. articles confiscated:
1 bridle & 1 saddle of James Turner
1 bridle & 1 saddle of Edd. Turner and one hatter
1 wagon & 2 gear of rope--John Wood sr
1 gear of rope of Richard Barns & 1 pair swingle trees, one clovise [or clavise], & a single line--of Richard Barns
1 saddle & 1 gear of rope--Jno Wood jr
1 bridle & 2 gears iron traces of Philip Peck & 3 straw collars & 3 "grease" bags of Peck
2 forage bags--Jacob Burley
1 bridle & 1 saddle of Jacob Blessing
3 bags, 1 pair of stillyards, & 3 gears of Jacob Ham
"34 of Graham"
2 bags of Kenery
1 gear iron traces of Jacob Ham
an axe of James McDonald
an axe of Keners
an axe of Thos White & hanks of thread of Cortridger
Recd. of Maj. Spruce Mc Coye [sic], one of Rowan Co Commissioners of
    Confiscated Property, the above articles which I am to account for with
    "Qt. Mr. Genl." Department. [signed] Jas Cole Mountflorene D. Qt. My. No.
    Car.

554. Salisbury Jan. 7, 1782 Comy. Depot:
30 bushels of corn of Jno Wood sr
26 bushels of corn of Edd. Turner
30 bushels of corn of Richd. Turner
110 lbs of flour of David Burlay
100 lbs of flour of Christian Smith
10 bushels of wheat of Philip Peck
3   bushels of wheat of Jacob Buley
12 bushels of wheat of Jacob Blessing
100 lbs of flour of Philip Grub
18 bushels of corn of Boyd McCrary
5 beeves of [blank] Minse [written over Minze]   899 lbs of meat
1 [beef] of Edd. Turner 180 lbs of meat
2 [beeves] of Thos White   359 lbs of meat
[total] 104 bushels of corn, 310 lbs of flour, 25 bushels of wheat, & 1,438 lbs of meat
Received of Majr. Spruce McCoye, one of Rowan Co Commissioners of Confiscated Property, 104 bushels of con,
310 lbs of flour, 25 bushels of wheat, 8 head of beef cattle "where" weight in meat was found to be 1,438 lbs, which
I am to account for with Commissary General's Department.   [signed] Jas Cole Mountflorence, St. Qt. My. No. Carl.

555. Jan. 1783 received of George Henry Berger esq & Joseph Cunningham, Rowan Co Commissioners of Confiscated
Property, £18,476.191 certificates and bonds due to sale of confiscated land and Negroes in Rowan Co agreeable to
Act of Assembly in 1782 "commonly called" Confiscation Act.   [signed] Griffith Rutherford, Supr. Comr.; [on back]
voucher No. 4.

556. George Henry Berger and Joseph Cunningham, Rowan Co Commissioners of Confiscated Property, in account
with State of North Carolina:
a) Dec. 15, 1782 amount of sales of land & Negroes per voucher No. 1-- £18,476.19.1
Feb. 1783 amount of notes taken for rented property and not yet collected per   voucher No. 2--£51.18.0
Feb. 1783 amount of notes taken for rented property and not collected per   voucher No. 3--£138.6.2
 [total] £18,667.3.3
b) by General Rutherford's receipt for certificates and bonds per voucher No.   4--£18,476.19.1
by notes taken and not collected--£190.4.2   [total] £18,667.3.3
by commissions of 2 commissioners @ 4%--£746.12.8
"for a proper statement" of this account see Comptroller's Ledger B folio 117   [signed] F Child.

Nov. session 1784 Rowan Co: the within account settled per order of Court and accepted   [signed] Ad Osborn, c. c.

557. George Henry Berger and Joseph Cunningham, Rowan Co Commissioners of Confiscations:
Dec. 15, 1782 to amount of sales of sundry tracts of land and Negroes as per   voucher No. 1   £18,676.19.1 [sic]
Feb. 1783 to amount of notes taken for rented property not yet collected
    [voucher] No. 2   £52.18
            to amount of notes taken for rented property not collected
    [voucher] No. 3   £138.6.2   [total] £18,867.3.3
to balance due Berger & Cunningham   £540.1.6
[grand total]   £19,407.4.9

by sundry certificates an bonds paid into hands of General Rutherford per voucher No. 4   £18,476.19.1
by amount of sundry notes taken but not collected   £191.4.2
by commissions of two Commissioners on £18,476.19.1 @ 2% each per Act of   Assembly passed Oct. 1779
  Chapter 11 [see State Records 24 p.281-282]   £739.1.6
[total]   £19,407.4.9

Sales of Confiscated Land

"errors excepted"   [signed] George H Berger

Dec. 1, 1787 above account proved before me. [signed] Frnas Child, Comptr.
[on back] "charge Genl. Rutherford with certificates & bonds paid him"

558. Rowan Co sales of property "suggested" to be confiscated:
Sept. 18, 1786 half of lot 18 in W square of Salisbury; formerly James Kerr's
    property; bought by Lewis Beard for £525.
"to error" in 202 ac on waters of Swearng. Cr; No. 12; formerly Henry E
    McCulloh's property; bought by James Malloy for £3.0.

Montgomery Co   Jun. 5, 1786
[no date] 56 ac on N side of Rocky R at the mouth of Long Cr; No. 14; "in
    possession" of William Irby; formerly Henry E McCulloh's property; bought
    by William Sanders for £37.
"to error" in 81 ac on both sides of Richardsons Cr; joining Hudson's line;
    includes Myles improvement "Anson"; No. 4; formerly Henry E McCulloh's
    property; bought by Thomas Clark for £10.
[total] £887 + "to interest received from sundries" £36.12 = £923.12

Charles Bruce, Commissioner of Confiscations Salis. Dist., settled Jun. 3, 1791.

559. Rowan Co, NC   A list of the sales of the Confiscated property of said county held at the Court house Salisbury
on Dec. 15, 1782 and continued from day to day until sold [prices--"currency at 150 to 1"]:

559A. 1. 119 ac bought by John Lewis Beard & Walln Beller for £200.13.1
2. 316 ac bought by Robert McKee for £346
3. 216 ac bought by Andrew Bostion for £282
4. 124 ac bought by Andrew Bostion for £133
5. 192 ac bought by Abraham Womack for £201
6. 159 ac bought by Spruce McCay for £262
7. 167 ac bought by David Smith for £167.10
8. 152 ac bought by Elijah Merrill for £170
9. 237 ac bought by Umphrey Brooks for £392
10. 237 ac bought by Umphrey Brooks for £267.5
11. 220 ac bought by Andrew Bostion for £107
12. 202 ac bought by Andrew Bostion for £101
13. 218 ac bought by Andrew Bostion for £204.10
14. 208 ac bought by Andrew Bostion for £417
15. 193 ac bought by Mathew Lock for £258
16. 238 ac bought by George Henry Barger for £238
17. 274 ac bought by Lewis Winkler for £76
18. 373 ac bought by Lewis Winkler for £130
19. 310 ac bought by Joseph Coningham for £210
20. 416 ac bought by Samuel Cummins for £503
21. 180 ac bought by William Milsaps for £45
22. "sold by McCulloh"
23. 287 ac bought by John Lopp for £348
24. 155 ac bought by Beacham Helton for £115
25. 175 ac bought by Anthony Newnan for £277
26. 200 ac bought by Anthony Newnan for £227
27. 305 ac bought by Conrad Bream for £392

Sales of Confiscated Land

28. 400 ac bought by Joseph Cunningham for £351
29. 154 ac bought by John Ford for £200   "refused to give bond"
30. 244 ac bought by Richard Pearson for £346   "refused to give bond"
31. 175 ac   "sold by McCullock"
32. 343 ac bought by Benjamin Abbot for £43.9
33. 425 ac bought by William Brandon for £301
34. 425 ac bought by Mathew Locke for £204
35. 343 ac bought by Jacob Utzman for £100
36. 375 ac bought by John Lewis Beard for £200
37. 375 ac bought by John Lewis Beard for £301
38. 375 ac bought by David Craige for £150.10
39. 375 ac bought by William Brandon for £101
40. 367 [written over 275] ac bought by Thomas Carson for £100
41. 275 ac bought by John Claver for £100.1
42. 266 ac bought by John Billings for £120.1
43. 193 ac bought by Andrew Baird for £71.1   [subtotal £8,450.0.1]
44.   "not to be found"
45. 201 ac bought by Benjamin Rounsavall for £203
46. 231 ac bought by Benjamin Rounsavall for £151
47. 366 ac bought by Maxwell Chambers for £428
48. 147 ac bought by Abraham Lewis for £100.8
49. 113 ac bought by Abraham Lewis   "bought of McCulloh"
50. 189 ac bought by Maxwell Chambers for £236
51. [blank] ac bought by Thomas McCarty   "sold by McCulloh"
52. 126 ac bought by Spruce McCay for £301
53. 278 ac bought by Spruce McCay for £301
54. [blank] ac bought by William Penny   "sold by McCulloh"
55. 265 ac James Scrivner for £202   [subtotal £1,922.8]
[total] £1,922.8 + £8,450.0.1 = £10,372.8.1
[numbers 1-55 above on North side of Yadkin River--see similar list in #561 below]

559B. "the land on the South side of the Yadkin River":
1.   "sold by execution at the suit of Thomas Frohock"
2. 336 ac bought by Valentine Beard for £826
3. 370 ac bought by James Craige for £226
4. 308 ac bought by James Craige for £385
5. 253 ac bought by Henry Horah for £310
6. 200 ac bought by Robert Martin for £230.10
7.   "Barren land not sold"
8. 115 ac bought by Peter Faust for £117
9. 200 ac bought by Francis Lock for £200.10
10. 340 ac bought by Radford Ellis for £341.10
11. 263 ac bought by David Woodson for £420
12. 482 ac bought by John Lewis Beard for £200
13. 282 ac bought by David Craige for £291
14. 299 ac bought by John Steele for £300
15. 146 ac bought by David Woodson for £150
16. 213 ac bought by David Woodson for £300
17. 355 ac bought by David Craige for £256
18. 365 ac bought by Francis Lock for £266
19. 314 ac bought by Joseph McConnehe for £352
20. 110 ac bought by David Craige for £67.0.4

21. 96 ac bought by David Craige for £52.0.8
22. 247 ac bought by Francis Lock for £200
23. 202 ac bought by William Brandon for £203
24. 200 ac bought by Francis Lock for £306
25. 109 ac bought by William Brandon for £110   [total] £6,109.11.0
[total of both sales:] £10,72.8.1 + £6,109.11 = £16,481.19.1

559C. Samuel Bryant's Negroes:

1 Negro woman sold for continental officer's certificates	£ 135.0
one Negro boy for specia certificates	£1,150.0
one "ditto	£ 710.0
[grand total]	£18,476.19.1
"add for so much short cash in page 'K'"	£200
[grand total]	£18,676.19.1

[on back] "voucher No. 1" Messrs Bergers & Cunningham

560. [on a sheet] "the sail begun and hel in the month of December 1784"   [this may apply to #561 below].

561. [The following is a list on two sheets; the first sheet has "voucher No. 1" at bottom; the second sheet has "No. 2" written on it.]

561A. 1. "Nems South side of Yedgen [R]":

2. Voltine Berd £826	15. David Wodson £150
3. Jeoms Creek £226	16. David Wodson £300
4. Jeoms Creek £335	17. David Creek £256
5. Henry Hurow £385	18. Francis Lock £266
6. Roberd Martin £231	19. Juguvay McConky £352
7. Henry Suel £163	20. David Creek £67.0.4
8. Peter Fast £117	21. David Creek £52.0.8
9. Col. Francis Lock £200.10	22. Francis Lock £200
10. Rotford Allos £341.10	23. William Brondon £203
11. David Woodson £420	24. Francis Lock £360
12. John Luis Berd £260	25. William Brondon £110
13. David Creek £291	
14. John Stell £300	

561B. "North scid" [of Yadkin R]:

1. John Lws. Berd & Wolder Bello £200.13.1	
2. Roberd McKey £326	29. "J. F." [blank]
3. Andray Bostion £282	30. Richmon Porson £346
4. Andray Bostion £133	31. [blank]
5. [omitted on this list]	32. [blank]
6. Sprus McCay £201	33. Willan Brondon £301
7. David Smith £167.10	34. Jacob Judsman £100
8. Eley Merrel £170	35. John Luis Berd £200
9. Omfros Brucks £392	36. John Luis Berd £301
10. Onfros Brucks £267.5	37. Devid Creek £150
11. Andray Bostion £107	38. William Brendon £100
12. Andray Bostion £107	39. [blank]
13. Andray Bostion £204.10	40. Thomes Corson £100
14. Andray Bostion £417	41. John Clever £100.1
15. Matha Lock £258	42. John Bellen £120.1

Sales of Confiscated Land

16. George Henry Berger £238
17. Lodwik Wenkler £76
18. Lodwik Wenkler £180
19. Joseph Conkem £200
20. Samuel Gomins £503
21. Willom Milsaps £45
22. [blank]
23. John Wilson £348
24. Bukom Hilton £155
25. Anton Nunen £277
26. Anton Numen £327
27. Conrad Brem £392
28. Joseph Conekem £351

43. Andray Berd £71.1
44. [blank]
45. Benjemin Rounsifond £203
46. Benjemin Rounsifond £151
47. Max Chemer £428
48. Abrahm Luis £100.8
49. Abrahm Luis [blank]
50. Max Chemer £238
51. [blank]
52. Sprus McCay £301
53. Sprus McCay £301
54. [blank]
55. Jeoms Channer £202
[subtotal] £16,988.11

561C. one "nero" £ 135.0
     "dito" £1,150
     "dito" £ 750 [subtotal] £1,995.0
[grand total] £16,988.11 + £1,995.0 = £18,983.15.1

561D. [second sheet which is marked "No. 2"]:
"Aconmpt of Jeoms Kerr lots and neros"
[Robert Hays £25.5.0--lined out]
Elizabeth Kerr £31.5.0
Arek [or Auk] Kerr £7.0.6
"dito" £3.16.0

"Wenhlos Miller nero winch"
Vollentin Berd £12.0.0

"John Mithel lots"
Roberd Hays £25.5.0
Capt. Garbreuyeh £9.0.0
Merey McDonel £1.12.0
John Nelson £33.6.8
George Elled £3.6.8 [total for this sheet] £126.11.10

562. Rowan Co, NC A list of notes taken by Joseph Cunningham as Commissioner for the rents of confiscated lands rented in Feb. 1783:

1. Abednigo Mackatee £4.3
2. John Baker £3.4
3. Barnhart Michael £1.1
4. Jacob Byerley £2.6
5. William Wood £1.1
6. Jacob Wike £1.0
7. Joseph Davis £1.12
8. Joseph Garland £3.7
9. Henry Weyman £1.4
10. William Weyar £1.1
11. Melchar Derr £1.2
12. Fredreck Raker £1.4

13. Luke White £1.11
14. John Davis £5.5
15. Anthony Hinkle £2.11
16. Jacob Beck £1.4
17. William Spurgan £1.1
18. David Byailey £4.4
20. the widow Sapenfield £1.12
21. Edward Williams £5.1
    "proved lost"
[total] £51.18
"skeet cast" or
   "shut east" £1
[grand total] £52.18

Sales of Confiscated Land

"Not collected and a doubt whether they ["it"--lined out] an account of the law passed next session session of the General Assembly"
[on back] "No. 2"

563. A "list of platts and certificates of confiscated lands which have been surveyed and sold, but the purchase money not paid, except such as are certified for the purchasers in" [this list evidently relates to Charles Bruce's sale #291 above in Guilford County folder]

563A. Rowan County:
1. John Armstrong   162 ac sold Sept. 18, 1786
3. Henry Ghiles   216 ac sold Sept. 18, 1786
4. Henry Ghiles   124.75 ac sold Sept. 18, 1786
11. James Mulloy   220 ac sold Sept. 18, 1786
12. James Mulloy   202 ac sold Sept. 18, 1786
13. John Armstrong   218 ac sold Sept. 18, 1786
14. John Armstrong   208 ac sold Sep. 18, 1786
50. Edward Yarbrough   216 ac sold Feb. 13, 1786
[page torn] Edward Yarbrough   69 ac sold Feb. 13, 1786

563B. in Anson County:
2. Thomas Clark   64 ac sold Jun. 8, 1786
3. Thomas Clark   100 ac sold Jun. 8, 1786
4. Thomas Clark   81 ac sold Jun. 8, 1786
5. Thomas Clark   54 ac sold Jun. 8, 1786
6. Sampson Lanier   150 ac sold Jun. 8, 1786
7. Thomas Clark   30 ac sold Jun. 8, 1786
8. Thomas Clark   30 ac sold Jun. 8, 1786
9. Patrick Boggan   300 ac sold Sept. 22, 1786
10. William Wood   400 ac sold Sept. 22, 1786
13. Anthony Sharpe   200 ac sold Sept. 22, 1786

563C. in Montgomery County:
10. William Saunders   54 ac sold Jun. 5, 1786
11. Mark Allen   160 ac sold Jun. 5, 1786
12. Jesse McClendon   222 ac sold Sept. 20, 1786
13. William Saunders   120 ac sold Jun. 5, 1786
14. William Saunders   56 ac sold Jun. 5, 1786
15. John Hopkins   300 ac sold Sept. 20, 1786
16. William Saunders   35 ac sold Jun. 5, 1786
17. Alexander Fraser   160 ac sold Jun. 5, 1786
18. Mark Allen   160 ac sold Jun. 5, 1786
19. Thomas Clark   174 ac sold Jun. 5, 1786
20. Mark Allen   160 ac sold Jun. 5, 1786
[signed] Charles Bruce, [page torn--probably "CCPSD"]

564. Nov. 23, 1782 sold 110 ac to David Craig; No. 20; on S side of Yadkin R; formerly Henry Eustace McCulloch's property; border: tract No. 19 and a line of the "old manner" [McCulloch's] tract No. 6; plat shows land is on both sides of Cran Cr; [signed] Charles Bruce, CCPSD; sworn chain carriers   George Basinger & Lewis Calor.

565. Nov. 26, 1782 sold 96 ac to David Craig; No. 21; on S side of Yadkin R; formerly Henry Eustace McCulloch's property; in the fork of Crane Cr; border: tracts No. 20, 19, & 23, a line of the "old manner" [McCulloch's] tract No.

Sales of Confiscated Land

6, & George Fraley; plat shows land is on both sides of S fork of Crane Cr; [signed] Charles Bruce, CCPSD; sworn chain carriers George Basinger & Lewis Calor.

566. Nov. 26, 1782 surveyed 109 ac for William Brandon; No. 25; formerly Henry Eustace McCulloch's property; on S side of Yadkin R; border: a poplar on W bank of Yadkin R in a line of the "old manner" [McCulloch's] tract No. 11 and widow Hartmon's field; [signed] David Woodson for Griffith Rutherford, surveyor; sworn chain carriers George Basinger & Lewis Calor.

567. Feb. 13, 1786 sold 216 ac to Edward Yarborough for £475; No. 50; on Brushy fork of Abbots Cr; formerly Matthias Sappingfield's property; border: a corner of Felix Clodfelter and crosses the fork; [signed] Charles Bruce, CCPSD; sworn chain carriers Anthony Hinkle & William Boatinhamer.

568. Feb. 13,1786 sold 69 ac to Edward Yarborough for £320; No. 51; on Brushy fork of Abbots Cr; formerly Matthias Sappingfield's property; border: NE corner of another of Sappingfield's tracts and crosses said fork; [signed] Charles Bruce, CCPSD; sworn chain carriers Anthony Hinkle & Luke White.

569. Sept. 18, 1786 sold 162 ac to John Armstrong for £1,205; No. 1; on N side of Yadkin R; formerly Edward Turner's property; border: John Doty's corner beech on N bank of said river, Joseph Goss, runs down a branch that empties into Sandy Cr, & down the creek to Yadkin R; [signed] Charles Bruce, CCPSD; chain carriers Moses Doty & Joshua Story.

570. Sept. 18, 1786 sold 202 ac to James Mulloy for £525; No. 12; on waters of Swearing Cr; formerly Henry Eustace McCulloch's property; border: a corner of tract No. 11, Cathrine Shavers, corner of tract No. 3, & corner of tract 10; [signed] Charles Bruce, CCPSD; sworn chain carriers Henry McKee & Thomas Coyl.

571. Sept. 18, 1786 sold 220 ac to James Mulloy for £515; No. 11; on waters of Swearing Cr; formerly Henry Eustace McCulloch's property; border: corner of No. 10 and a heap of stones; [signed] Charles Bruce, CCPSD; sworn chain carriers Henry McKee & Thomas Coyl.

572. Sept. 18, 1786 sold 124.75 ac Henry Ghiles for £1,000; No. 4; on W side of Swearing Cr; formerly Henry Eustace McCulloch's property; border: William Lynn, Robert Simeson, Jacob Wiseman, Joseph Bowen, & tract 3; [signed] Charles Bruce, CCPSD; sworn chain carriers Henry McKee & Thomas Coyl.

573. Sept. 18, 1786 sold 208 ac to John Armstrong for £1,160; No. 14; on waters of Swearing Cr; formerly Henry Eustace McCulloch's property; border: a hickory corner of tract No. 13, Hugh Davis, Meyers, & tract No. 9; [signed] Charles Bruce, CCPSD; sworn chain carriers Henry McKee & Thomas Coyl.

574. Sept. 18, 1786 sold 216 ac to Henry Ghiles for £1,050; No. 3; on both sides of Swearing Cr; formerly Henry Eustace McCulloch's property; border: Joseph Bowen, corner of tract No. 5, tract No. 2, & William Lynn; [signed] Charles Bruce, CCPSD; sworn chain carriers Henry McKee & Thomas Coyl.

575. Sept. 18, 1786 sold 218 ac to John Armstrong for £1,015; No. 13; on waters of Swearing Cr; formerly Henry Eustace McCulloch's property; border: corner oak of tract No. 12, corner of tract No. 14, & corner of tract No. 9; [signed] Charles Bruce, CCPSD; sworn chain carriers Henry McKee & Thomas Coyl.

576. Sept. 25, 1787 sold 640 ac to Edward Yarborough for £5,066.1; No. 50 [sic]; on both sides of Yadkin R; formerly Henry Eustace McCulloch's property; border: John Sloan's corner on N side of said river, Radford Ellis's corner, John L Beard, crosses the mouth of Horah's Br, said river, & Island, William Hudgins, & Fosters Br; plat shows Shoemakers Br and part of an island; [signed] Charles Bruce, CCPSD; [on back] "made acct. and to be recorded from Feb. 22, 1790 date No. 479."

RUTHERFORD COUNTY
[following lists #577 & 578 are from Morgan Dist. Superior Court Miscellaneous Records--DSCR 205.428.2]:

Sales of Confiscated Land

577. Rutherford Co Pleas & Quarter Sessions Court second Monday in Jul. 1782 before William Gilbert, James Withrow, Jonathan Hampton, & "other justices" a Grand Jury say the following people, all late of Rutherford Co planters, "aided and joined" the army of Maj. Ferguson and are convicted as Tories "a true bill" [signed] William Porter, foreman, before Felix Walker, c c:

William Mills	Alexander Coulter	Elias Brock
William Going	Joseph Moore	Daniel Singleton
Arthur Taylor	William Morgan	William Henry
Moses Whitly	David Morgan	William Green
Thomas Townsend	Elias Morgan sr	Samuel Moore
Philemon Hawkins	James Cook sr	Abel Sangham [or
Joseph McDaniel	John Goodbread	Langham]
Jeremiah McDaniel	Thomas Goodbread	Jonas Bedford
John McDaniel	Phillip Goodbread jr	Mumphord Wilson
James Kelly	Federick Jones	Isaac Cooper
James Lemar	Isham Revis	Benjamin Biggerstaff
William Adams sr	George Revis	Peter Dills
William Adams jr	Allbros Mills	Shadrach Alley
Benjamin Adams	George Davice	Caleb Taylor
Benjamin Adams jr	George Davice jr	George Cox
John Morgan	John Davice	George Cox jr
Moses Wright	James Chitwood sr	John Cox
Giles Williams	Joseph Chitwood	Joel Cox
Essex Capshaw	Richard Chitwood	Arthur Ownsby
Robert Taylor	Gideon Rucker	John Felts
"Whiteoak"	John Richardson	John Jones
John Owins	Benjamin Moore	Freeman Jones
Thomas Gore	Joseph Lawrence	David George
William Thomason	William Battle	Stephen Shelton
Joseph Clark	Andrew Poor	Samuel Hendrix
Isaih Blackwell	Stephen Langford	John Hendrix
William Webb	John Morris	William Nettle jr
John Webb	Joseph Underwood	Shadrach Nettle
Jeremiah Webb	Tho Whiteside	Jesse Nettle
John Camp	John Hutson	James Upton
James Camp	Mark Powel	John King
John Camp jr	William Hall	Barna King
Thomas Camp	Giles Reynolds	William Hinson sr
Wm Hinson jr	William Duning	Samuel Thompson
Brock Davice	Jonn Thomason	Neel Tolly
Joseph Baily	James Patterson	John Walburt
Stophel Walburt	Edward Francis	William Shephard
Micajah Proctor	James Capshaw	William Capshaw

all aided and joined the army of Maj. Ferguson.

578. [the following is only a partial list; part of sheet is lost]
A petition mentioned for a case between William Gilbert vs.

Gideon Rucker	Mark Powel	Jonas Bedford
John Ashworth	Jeremiah McDaniel	Ambros Mills
John Thomason	Joseph McDaniel	William Nattle
George Thomason	Peter Dills	John Edenton
Barnaba King	William Robins	Simeon [hole in

Sales of Confiscated Land

Benjamin Biggerstaff	Joseph Underwood	page] Hovis
Samuel Biggerstaff	Thos Robinson	Thomas Baker
Thomas Welch of Sandy Run	Thomas Townsend	Joseph Clark
John Camp	Vesey Husbands of	
Thomas Camp	Burke Co	

& "others" unknown on Sept. 6, 1780 by "boyonets and pistols came to the dwelling house of the petitioner" [petition ends here, rest of sheet lost].

[the following are from Rutherford Co Pleas & Quarter Sessions Court minutes CR 086.301.1 and 086.301.2]

579. October 1781:
579A. p. 40: Ordered by Court that the sheriff summon all suspected persons supposed to be guilty of treason against the State to appear at next Court and answer charges.

579B. p. 41: Ordered by Court that the Captains in each Company in this county do make a return of all suspected persons in his Company supposed to be guilty of treason [against] the State and to the Clerk of Court immediately.

579C. p. 42: On motion of William Gilbert esq and testamony produced by the Court it is ordered that the opinion of the Court be entered on the records to wit--it is the opinion of the Court that the said William Gilbert is not guilty of the charge laid against him to the General Assembly and we do certify that W Gilbert never plundered nor was guilty of plundering to our knowledge.

580. January 1782:
580A. p. 46: On petition of James Cook in open Court against the Commissioner of Confiscated property setting forth their selling some confiscated property, contrary to law; ordered by the Court that James Withrow and Robert Porter, Commissioners be cited to appear at our next Court to answer the charge.

580B. Ordered that Letters of Administration issue to Ann Mills, widow of James Miller, on estate of Ambrose Mills decd. She gave bond of £1,000 specie with John Earle & William Gilbert security.

580C. Robert Taylor, summoned to appear at this Court on charge of being an enemy of the State, upon enquiry the Court are of the opinion that he be discharged and his property returned to him

580D. p. 48: Ordered by Court that William Robins who was summoned to appear at this Court to answer charge of High Treason, did enter into the service of this State for 18 months and tht his property be restored to him and remain in peaceable possession of his family; he producing surety for his entering said service John McClure and Geo Winters his sureties to £200 specie

580E. On enquiry made by the Court respecting William Mills, charge of treason against the State, it appearing to the Court that said Mills is now in "actual" service of this State, the Court therefore are of the opinion that his property is protected by law, and it is ordered that the property of said Mills remain in peaceable possession of his family til the law shall otherwise direct.
James Miller being obligated to the Court that the estate now in the possession of said Mills shall not be entered [or embereld] bound in the sum of £500 specie.

580F. p. 49: Samuel Carpenter summoned to this Court to answer a charge of treason against the State, upon enquirey it is the opinion of the Court that he be discharged and have the privileges of a Citizen.

580G. Jno McAdams summoned to appear at this Court to answer a charge of treason against the State; upon enquirey it is the opinion of the Court that he be discharged and have the privileges of a Citizen.

Sales of Confiscated Land

580H. John McKiney summoned to appear at Court to answer a charge of treason against the State; upon enquirey it is the [opinion of] Court that he be discharged and admitted to the privileges of a Citizen.

580I. p. 52 Micajah Proctor sr to appear at the Court to answer the charge of treason against the State; upon inquiry the Court are of the opinion that he be acquitted and discharged and privilege of a citizen allowed.

581. April 1782:
581A. p. 55 Benjamin Hyder cited to appear at Court to answer charge of treason against the State; on enquiry it is the opinion of the Court that he be acquitted of the charge nothing appearing against him and he [be] restored to the privilege of a citizen.

581B. p. 56 John Childers brought into Court on a charge of words spoken against the State; on enquiry it is the opinion of the Court tht he be bound on security for his good behavior.

582. July 1782:
582A. p. 58 Ordered by Court James Miller, Colonel of the county do order sufficient guard of Militia to guard the officers and Justices of this Court during this term.

582B. p. 60 Ann Mills and James Miller, administrator of the estate of Ambrose Mills decd, return an Inventory of said estate and prays an order of sale; granted.

582C. p. 63 Jurors find a Bill of Profacturas treason against William Mills and others. John Goodbread, one charged in said bill appeared & pleads not guilty.

582D. On motion James Cook, agent for William Henry, moved to make an enquiry whither the estate of William Henry shall be confiscated agreeable to the bill found by the Grand Jury against him this term agreeable to law. Accordingly the following jury were impaneled and sworn to try enquire the above estate: Thomas Welch, William Callahan, James Armstrong, Alex McFadin, John Twity, Robert Lewis, Wm Neel, Jno Russel, James Beaty, Jacob MClinden, Thomas Morris, & Jacob Vinsant.
p. 64 The jury find the defendant guilty of the Felony & treason laid in the enquisition and that all his goods & chattels, lands & tenements are forfeited to the State & Confiscated.

582E. p. 66 Grand Jury returned inquisition of treason, forfeiture, & confiscation against estate of Isham Revis & others; Isham Revis request to traverse the inquisition & have a trial by jury.
p. 67 The State vs. Isham Revis--following jury sworn: Thomas Welch, James Armstrong, Alex McFadin, John Twitty, Robert Lewis, Wm Neel, John Russel, James Beaty, Jacob McClenden, Thomas Morris, & Jacob Vinsant; jury finds defendant guity of charge and that all his goods, chattels, lands, & tenements are forfeited to the State & confiscated.

582F. Grand Jury returns an inquisition of treason forfeitures against Thomas Mills and others; jurors for the State present and find a bill against William Withrow and others; Grand Jury dismissed.

582G. p. 70 Ordered all the goods in possession of Wm Gilbert "supposed to be" the property of Mary Magauchy shall be restored to the "proper" owner in lawful "prog".

582H. p. 72 Joshua Taylor appeared on charge of treason against the State and prays a "tryal"; ordered that it be laid over til next Court.
582I. Ordered that all persons returned in the inquisition by the Grand Jury for treason, forfiture, & "C" against the State may apply to the Clerk of this Court who is ordered to issue subpoenas to all persons on application to enforce the attendance of their witnesses if any to appear at our next [Court] be prepared for tryal.

582J. Robert Taylor and John Goodbread appeared under charge of treason and applied for tryal; ordered to be laid over to next Court.

582K. Ordered that Jean Henry, wife of William Henry decd, be given possession of all and singular the goods, chattels, lands & tenements, rights & credits of her late husband William Henry decd. Confiscated this term agreeable to act of General Assembly in that case made & provided.

582L. page 73 Ordered that depositions of John Neil, William Smart sr, & David Huddleston jr respecting the lands of James Marlin & Samuel Andrews be recorded.

582M. Celia Taylor, in behalf of Arthur Taylor decd, came into Court and prays tryal on the estate of said Arthur; laid over til next Court.

582N. Ordered by the Court that the Commissioners of Confiscated Property advertise all persons returned in the enquisition by the Grand Jury for treason, forfeiture, confiscation against the State to appear at next Court to answer the charges; to advertise sixty days before next Court.

583. October 1782:
583A. p. 76 John Webb appeared on a charge of treason against the State for trial; ordered that it be laid over til next Court.

583B. p. 77 Petition of Charles McKnight against Alexander McCooper enemies of the State; judgment by default.

583C. Fornigreen Norman appeared on charge of treason against the State; ordered that his trial be laid over til next Court.

583D. Joel Dogget presents a Power of Attorney in open Court from his father Bushart Dogget impowering said Joel to take into his possession certain Negroes, the property of his father, proved to be his property by affidavits to the satisfaction of the Court and now in the hands of Commissioners of Confiscated Property.
p. 78 Ordered by the Court that said Commissioners deliver to said Joel Dogget 2 Negroes, viz--Cloe and Syell, property already proved to be the property of his father Busherd Dogget.

583E. p. 79 Petition of James Withrow against Wm Thomason & "others"--judgment by default.

583F. p. 80 Petition of Thomas Morris against James Chitwood--judgment by default.

583G. Petition of John Smith against Thomas Davice [Thomas Reynolds--lined out]--judgment by default.

583H. Petition of Jonathan Hampton against William Nettles and George Davice and "others", enemies of the State--judgment by default.

583I. p. 81 Petition of Thomas Welch against Wm Thomason, Abe Langham, William & Nicholas Welch and "others", enemies of the State--judgment by default.

583J. Petition of David Miller against John Morgan, Esex Capshaw, James Capshaw, & "others", enemies of the State--judgment by default.
583K. Joshua Hawkins came into Court on supposition of some charge that might be laid against him for treason and against the State; upon examination, there appears nothing against him; & it is opinion of Court that he be discharged and acquitted as Citizen.

583L. John Stanford, George Tubbs, & Thomas Baker appeared in open Court on a supposition of some charge laid against them for treason against the State.
p. 82 On examination, it appears there is nothing against them, and it is opinion of Court that they be discharged and acquitted as Citizens.

583M. Petition of George Black against Alexander Coulter, George Russel, & "others", enemies of the State--judgment by default.

583N. Petition of John Anderson against Robert Davis, Thomas Davice, & "others", enemies of the State--judgment by default.

583O. On petition of Ann Adjutant, it's ordered by Court that all and every part of the property both real & personal of her husband Scroup Adjutant, who is now in actual service of this State, be and remain in the possession of said Ann Adjutant agreeable to Act of Assembly in that case provided.

583P. Jeremiah Webb appeared on a charge of treason against the State ordered laid over til next Court.

583Q. Petition of William Gilbert against Gedian Rucker and James Chitwood and "others", enemies of the State--judgment by default against all except Jno Goodbread, who pleads not guilty in person.

583R. p. 83 Petition of Charles Lewis against Thomas Miller and Alexander Coulter, enemies of the State--judgment by default.

583S. Petition of George Winters against George Thomason and "others", enemies of the State--judgment by default.

583T. On application, it's ordered by Court that property & estate of David George decd, who died in service of his country, be & remain in the possession of Bethne George, widow of said deceased agreeable to law.

583U. Christopher Walbert jr appears in person for his father Christopher Walbert on a charge of treason against the State; ordered that it be laid over til next Court.

583V. William Webb appeared on a charge of treason against the State; ordered laid over til next Court.

583W. Joshua Taylor, returned in the enquistion of the Grand Jury for treason and felony against the State, came into Court and prays to traverse the inquisition
p. 84 and have a trial by Jury; accordingly granted and ordered that a Jury come; jury was summoned, impaneled, & sworn to try the inquiry, do find the defendant not guilty of the charge and acquitted according to law.

583X. Petition of Graves Eves against Nathan Proctor and John Robertson, enemies of the State--judgment by default.

583Y. Ordered by Court that Celia Taylor be and is hereby possessed of all the estate of Arthur Taylor decd, who died in the service of his country, except such part of his estate as said Arthur Taylor conveyed in his lifetime.

583Z. p. 85 John Goodbread, returned in the enquisition by the October Grand Jury for treason and felony against the State, appeared and prays to traverse the enquistion and have a trial by Jury; granted by Court; James Adair, Alexander Grant, Alexander McKey, Robert Young, Thomas Morris, George Winters, Abel Lewis, James Wilson, Robert Gilky, Robert Prince, John Huddlestone, & John Russel were summoned, impaneled, & duly sworn to try the enquiry, and find that John Goodbread is guilty of that felony and treason laid against him; and that all his goods and chattels, lands, & tenements are forfeited to the State & Confiscated.

584. October 1782 [second part]:
584A. Ordered by Court that Joshua Taylor be and is to be possessed of all and singular his goods & chattels, lands, & tenements, and every part and parcel of his estate whatsoever; and that it be given up to him by any person who may have the same in possession.

Sales of Confiscated Land

584B. p. 86 Daniel Shipman, Samuel Blackburn, James Blackburn, John Tubbs, Jno Fisher, Aaron Gage, Micajah Proctor, Elias Morgan, Benjamin Bracket, Isaac Hinton, & George Revis appeared on charge of treason against the State for trial; ordered that their several trials be laid over til next Court.

584C. p. 87 Petition of James Miller against Joseph McDaniel, Giles Williams, & "others"--judgment by default.

584D. Petition of William Morrison against Jeremiah [and ?] Joseph McDaniel and "others"--judgment by default.

584E. Petition of Andrew Hampton against Jeremiah McDaniel and "others", enemies of the State--judgment by default.

584F. Ordered by Court that Mary Goodbread, wife of John Goodbread whose estate was confiscated this term, be given and granted and is to be possessed of 200 ac of land; including the "planation" whereon John Goodbread now lives; including the cleared land and all the stock of horses, cattle, & hogs and household furniture that she is possessed of, 2 Negroes--woman named Ran [or Nan] and a fellow Tax [or Lax]; given and granted to her as her dower in said estate.

584G. p. 88 Ordered by Court that the Commissioners of Confiscated Property, after paying John Miller what he has found from himself and by his purchase for the use and consumption of the late expedition against the Cherokee Indians, is ordered and "requested" to deliver to James Holland, County Commissioner, all the residue of the corn that shall arise from the rents of lands by them rented in consequence of the confiscation law.

584H. Petition of Michael McKlewrath against James Robbins and "others", enemies of the State--judgment by default.

584I. Petition of James Cook against George Thomason and "others", enemies of the State--judgment by default.

584J. p. 89 Petition of John Russel against Amros Mills and "others", enemies of the State--judgment by default.

584K. Petition of Anthony Dickey against Mark Powel and "others", enemies of the State--judgment by default.

584L. Petition of David Miller against William Adams and "others", enemies of the State--judgment by default.

584M. Ordered by Court that Mary Biggerstaff, widow of Aaron Biggerstaff decd, be allowed all her moveable property except Negroes, and all the lands possessed by her deceased husband in his lifetime, and the rents of her land for the present year. On application of Mary Biggerstaff, it's ordered that the trial of Aaron Biggerstaff for forfiture treason be laid over till next Court.

584N. p. 91 Ordered that an order of sale issue to Ann Mills and James Miller, administrators on the estate of Ambros Mills decd; accordingly Ordered by Court that James Miller and Ann Mills have authority [to] take into their possession all the estate of Ambrose Mills decd in this State where to be found.

584O. Petition of James Adair against Thomas Townsend and "others", enemies of the State--judgment by default.

584P. Petition of Michael McKlewarth against John Morris an enemy of the State--judgment by default.

584Q. On application of William Willis, ordered that the enquistion found by the Grand Jury for felony and treason against William Willis decd be heard next Court.

584R. State vs Micajah Proctor and "others" on the enquisition of treason and ordered by the Court that a nole prosogee [nolle prosequi] be entered unto said Micajah Proctor
p. 92 he having been acquitted and discharged last January term as appears of record.

Sales of Confiscated Land

584S. William Hall, William Lively, William Capshaw, Essex Capshaw, Gillian Lively, William Going, John Price, Fredrick Price, William Lusk, Edward Francis appeared on a charge of treason against the State and ordered that their trials be referred till next Court.

584T. Petition of Martha Dickey against Joseph Underwood and "others", enemies to the State--judgment by default.

584U. Petition of Stephen Willis against Wm Robins and "others", enemies of the State--judgment by default.

584V. p. 93   John Goodbread, returned in the inquisition by the Grand Jury, appeared and prays to traverse enquisition and have a trial by jury.   Granted by Court and order that a jury be impaneled and sworn.   James Adair, Alexander Grant, Alexander McKey, Robert Young, Thomas Morris, George Winters, Abel Lewis, James Wilson, Robert Gilky, Robert Prince, Jno Huddlestone, & Jno Russel were impaneled & sworn to try enquiry and find John Goodbread is guilty of the charge of treason and that all his goods, chattels, lands, & tenements are forfeited to the State.   [same man tried in #583Z, same term of Court].

584W. Jurors for the State present find a bill against William Lusk, Peter Quin, & David Baily for treason against the State.

584X. Ordered by the Court that Joshua Taylor be possessed of all his boods, chattels, lands, & tenements of estate of every kind whatever and that the Commissioners of Confiscated [Property] are to deliver the property of said Taylor on application.

585. January 1783:
585A. p. 97   William Gilbert vs John Russel--judgment by default.

585B. p. 99   On petition of Nancy Lawrence, praying that the estate of her late husband Joseph Lawrence who was found guilty of treason felony and against the State by the Grand Jury, may be brought to trial; accordingly it was granted by Court and James Gray, Ralph Wilson, Thomas Donelson, John Wherry, Stephen Willis jr, Jesse Nevil, Abel Lewis, & John Fleming were summoned, sworn as jurors to try the enquiry and find the said Joseph Lawrence if guilty of all that felony and treason found against him by the Grand Jury, and all his goods, chattels, lands, & tenements are forfeited to the State and confiscated.

585C. p. 102   Daniel Shipman, William Johnson, James Patterson, William Webb, Peter Quinn, Samuel Blackburn, William Robins, Thomas Herrod, John Fisher, & John Tubbs appeared on a charge of treason against the State; it's ordered that their trials be continued.

585D. p. 103   William Gilbert on petition vs:

Gideon Bucker	Thomas Welch of	Joseph Clark
John Answorth	Sandy Run	Ursy Husbands of
John Goodbread	John Camp	Burke Co
Richard Ledbetter	Thomas Camp	Jonas Bedford
James Chitwood	Mark Powel	Ambros Mills
Joshua Chitwood	Jeremiah McDaniel	William Nettles
William Thomason	Joseph McDaniel	Shadrack Nettles
John Thomason	Peter Dills	John Eggerton
George Thomason	William Robbins	Simeon Harris
Barnaba King	Joseph Underwood	
Benjamin Biggerstaff	Thomas Robinson	
Samuel Biggerstaff	Thomas Townsend	

and "others"--judgment by default; James Gray, George Anderson, Joseph Young, David Moore, John Miller, Rodger Carson, James Hamilton, John Huddleston, James Armstrong, James Wilson, Alexander McFadin, & Patrick Watson

Sales of Confiscated Land

summoned, impaneled, & sworn to try the enquiry; find for the plaintiff against the several defendants and assess damages to £1,206 specia and costs.

585E. p. 104   Ordered that a didimas postestatum be granted in behalf of Stephen Fuller to any justice of the peace in the State of Georgia to take examination of witnesses in his suit with Isham Revis. [related to #582E above ?]

585F. p. 105   John Walker esq on petition vs Ambros Mills, Elias Brock, Thomas Townsend, Jeremiah McDaniel, Joseph McDaniel, Benjamin Biggerstaff, Stephen Langford, Jonas Bedford, James Chitwood, Abram Green, & William Green.   William Morrison, William Porter, William Withrow, Thomas Welch, James Adair, Robert Rankin, Stephen Willis jr, James Gray, James McDaniel of "the" Cove, John Twitty, James McDaniel of Broad R, & James Armstrong summoned, impaneled, & duly sworn to try the enquiry; find for the plaintiff against the several defendants and assess damages to £540 specia & costs.

585G. p. 106   Catherine Sides, widow of John Sides decd, came into Court on suspection of a charge being exhibited against her late husband for treason, and there appearing no charge, it is considered by the Court that she be dismissed with priviledges of law on said Sides' estate.
p. 107   Ordered by the Court that letters of administration issue to Catherine Sides on the estate of John Sides decd. She gave bond of £200 specia with William Callahan & Jacob Vinsant securities; administrator sworn.

585H. Richard Ledbetter returned by the Grand Jury for treason against the State came into Court and prays that his trial be continued; granted.

585I. Petition of John McClaine agains Ambros Mills and "other" enemies of the State--judgment by default.

585J. p. 108   Robert Taylor came into Court and produced the record of an acquittance and discharge on a former trial concerning the forfiture of his property the same charge being continued in an inquisition against him.   It is considered by the Court that all further proceedings on the said inquisition be dismissed and set asaide as to Robert Taylor, and he be entirely freed and acquitted from the said charge and he go without.   It is ordered by the Court that his property be restored to him.

585K. p. 109   On consideration, it's ordered by the Court that Nancy Lawrence, wife of Joseph Lawrence whose estate was confiscated this term, be given and granted all that tract of 250 ac in said county whereon she lives on Camp Cr; also she gets all of the moveable property belonging to said estate, except such as have already been sold by the Commissioners of Confiscated Property according to a late act of Assembly made for the wives and widows.

585L. On motion of the attorney for the estate of William Willis decd, praying that the estate which came under the "denomination" of the confiscation law, might be brought to trial by jury.   Ordered that a jury be sworn.   Accordingly a jury was summoned to enquire the charge; find that the estate is "clear" and is acquitted from said charge, and the estate doesn't come under the purview of confiscation law; agreeable to law.

585M. p. 110   William Gilbert vs John McAdams--judgment by default; a jury impaneled and sworn; not agreed and dismissed, continued.

585N. Ordered by the Court that William Willis, executor on the estate of Willis decd, do proceed on said estate according to law.

585O. p. 111   Petition of John Miller againast William Thomason and "others"--judgment by default.

585P. Petition of John McClure against Jonas Bedford and "others", enemies of the State--judgment by default.

585Q. Petiton of Hugh Kilpatrick against Joseph & Jeremiah McDaniel and "others"--judgment by default.

94

Sales of Confiscated Land

585R. Ordered by Court that all services [executions--lined out] done by the Officers of this Court for any estates under the "denomination" of the confiscation law be paid out of the estates that are or may be confiscated, and all estates or parts of estates granted to wives or widows be secure against any executions that may issue for said services.

585S. p. 112   On considertion, it's ordered by the Court that Executions [issued against any--lined out] in consequence of any judgment obtained on petition in this Court issued against any estates that haven't been condemned and confiscated provided such persons as may own said estates have applied for trial or entered their appearance of record.

585T. p. 115-118   Whereas summons have issued to the sheriff to notify the following persons to appear and answer an inquisition of treason, felony, & forfiture found against them by the Grand Jury to wit:

Long Tom Welch	Shadrack Ally	John Camp jr
Robert Moore	George Cox	William Moore
James Shepard	Arthur Ownby	Samuel Hendrix
John Lusk	John Jones	William Nettle jr
James Chitwood	Samuel Younge	John King
Shadrack Chitwood	Thomas Reynolds	William Henson
Daniel Chitwood	John Harris	William Duning
William Hermon	Joseph Cartwright	John Thomason
Abednego Green	Arthur Osborne	John Baily
Shadrack Green	Jeremiah Gage	William Capshaw
Richmond Fleming	Essex Capshaw	John Goforth
James Norman	Andrew Poor	Philemon Hawkins
Abraham Clements	Stephen Langford	Jeremiah McDaniel
Grandshaw Camp	Joseph Underwood	William Adams
Edward Dickes	Thomas Whiteside	William Adams jr
John Dickes	Mark Powel	Robert Taylor
James McIntire	Elias Brock	Whiteoak
John McNiss	Samuel Moore	Thomas Gore
Joseph Langly	Jonas Bedford	Joseph Clark
Lewis Price	Isaac Cooper	James Camp
Charles Roper	Peter Dills	Joseph Moore
William Jolly	Calub Taylor	Stephen Shelton
William Hanah sr	George Cox	John Hendrix
William Hanah jr	John Felts	James Upton
Thomas Davice	John Sanders [or	Barnaba King
Allen Davice	Landers]	William Henson jr
James Cook sr	William Welch	Brock Davice
Thomas Goodbread	Nicholas Welch	Neel Tolly
George Davice	Lewis Harris	James Capshaw
Ambros Mills	Benjamin Malone	Elijah Davice
George Davice jr	Michael Osborne	David Baily
John Davice	John Robertson	John Chitwood jr
Robert Collins	Joseph Chitwood	Charles Mullin
Gideon Rucker	Thomas Swafford	John Richardson
Moses Whitty	Benjamin Moore	Joseph McDaniel
William Battles	James Kelly	John Hutson
James Lemar	Giles Reynolds	Giles Williams
William Green	John Owen	Abel Langham
William Thomason	Mumphord Wilson	John Camp

and now being solemly called "shew" cause why their property should not be confiscated, failed to appear or "shew" any cause.   It is therefore considered by the Court that their property be adjudged forfieted.

585U. p. 119   On motion, it's ordered by Court that Mary Biggerstaff, widow of Benjamin Biggerstaff decd, is to be securely possessed of all that part of her late husband's estate lately granted to her by the Court and some other Book Accounts belonging to said estate; she is impowered to sell or collect said Accounts; & together with all the rest granted as before, she's entirely secure against all judgments or executions obtained against her late husband's estate.

585V. p. 120   The State vs Thomas Townsend--on motion of the attorney for the State, a jury was impaneled and sworn to enquire whether the estate of Thomas Townsend should be confiscated; the said jury finds Thomas Townsend guilty of treason and all his goods & chattels, lands & tenaments are forfieted to the State & confiscated.

585W. p. 122   On motion, it's ordered by the Court that Mercy Bedford, wife of Jonas Bedford whose estate was confiscated this term, be given and to be possessed of the following part of her late husband's estate, to wit: a certain tract of land on Floids Cr formerly sold to Jonas Bedford by George Winters, a third of all the land belonging to said estate, and all the moveable property now in her possession & elsewhere to be found, agreeable to an act of Assembly made for provision of wives & widows.

586. April 1783:
586A. p. 130   Court ordered James Miller, one of the administrators on the estate of John Battles decd, deliver unto John Fergus, guardian of the orphans of the said Jno Balllte decd, all the property, bonds, & debts that he has in possession by virtue of his administration belonging to said estate; and James Miller is hereby acquitted, discontinued, & discharged as administrator on said estate.

586B. p. 132   The clerk read at the door of the Court House the certioraris from the Superior Court to this Court to stop the proceedings of indictment or inquisitions found by the Grand Jury July term last.
p. 133   Ordered that all the proceedings on said indictments or inquistions be entirely stopped until the Superior Court shall determine otherwise.

586C. p. 135   Ordered the Clerk of this Court do serve David Miller with a list of all persons found in the inquisition guilty of treason by the Grand Jury.

587. July 1783:
587A. p. 142   Ordered by Court that Letters of Administration issue to James Withrow and Sarah Lusk on the goods, chattels, lans, & tenaments of John Lusk decd, except so much of said estate as have already been taken by lawful authority.   They gave Wallace Beaty as security for £200 specia.

587B. p. 147   Ordered by Court that citations issue to the sheriff to summon James Miller, James Withrow, & Robert Porter, Commissioners of Confiscated property to settle with this Court respecting their office on Thursday July 17 this present term, agreeable to resolve of General Assembly in that case made & provided.

587C. p. 148   Agreeable to a citation issued yesterday to summon to appear and settle with the Court his day, James Miller, commissioner, came into Court and refused to settle agreeable to said order except the law were produced to enforce such settlement; the Court allowed him longer time if he "chosed".   [this same statement also written on p. 149]

587D. p. 156   James Withrow and Robert Porter, Commissioners of Confiscated Property, came into Court agreeable to the citation and order made for a settlement with this Court respecting their office.   Ordered by the Court that Felix Walker, Clerk of the Court, be appointed to settle with said commissioners and to receive their returns anytime before September 1 next, who agreed in open Court.

587E. p. 157   John Angel [or Angle], a British deserted, came into Open Court and took the oath of allegience to the State.

Sales of Confiscated Land

587F. Ordered by Court that Elizabeth Younge, wife of Samuel Younge, be and is to be possessed of all the estate real and personal of said Samuel Younge; and also the Commissioners of Confiscated Property are hereby ordered to pay to the said wife all monies & sums of money arising from any part of the estate of Samuel Younge sold by virtue of their commission agreeable to an act of Assembly in that case made & provided.

588. [The following is in Morgan Dist. Land Records DSCR 205.408.1 (folder for 1783-1788).] Sept. 12, 1787 writ of restitution: William Gilbert of Rutherford Co vs John Goodbread, John Ashworth, Joseph Underwood, Thomas Townsend, John Camp, Richard Ledbetter, & Thomas Camp; a judgment of £742.19 was issued; this writ issued due to an "error in the proceedings"; William Gilbert is to return: (a) a Negro wench & child property of John Ashworth, (b) a Negro wench of Joseph Underwood, (c) 3 tracts of land to Thomas Townsend on main Broad R, (d) a "plantion" of Richard Ledbetter, (e) a waggon of John Camp, & (f) a tract of Jno Camp at the high shoals on Second Broad R. [signed] Wm W Erwin, clk.

[The following are in Morgan Dist. Criminal Action papers DSCR 205.326.1 file for 1783 and are grouped together even though there from different counties.]
589. Sept. 1783 a suit vs Thomas Mills (of Rutherford Co)--on Sept. 10, 1780, he was a captain in the King's Army; evidence: Wm Gilbert, Ben Cleveland, Geo Black, & Saml Hunter; "not a true bill".

590. Mar. 1783 a suit vs Joseph Lawfield (of Surry Co)--on Oct. 20, 1781 he was in the loyal militia in Wilkes Co; evidence: John Franklin & Ben Cleveland; "a true bill".

591. Sept. 1783 a suit vs John Camp, planter (of Rutherford Co)--on Sept. 10, 1780, he took a commission and was a captain in the King's Army; evidence: Willm Grant & George Black; "a true bill".

592. Mar. 1783 a suit vs David Lorance (late of Burke Co)--on Jun. 15, 1780, in Lincoln Co, he aided the King's "cause" with 200 other people; evidence: Peter Henley, Isaac Robertson, & Jacob Shook; "not a true bill".

593. Mar. 1783 a suit vs Benjamin Hyrndon (late of Wilkes Co)--in 1779 he "screened" Isaac Daniel & Pritchet Alexander from "punishment"; suit brought by William Terril Lewis; "not a true bill".

594. Jan. 11, 1783 a suit vs George Sides--he's accused of treason in a summons for Mar. 1783 Court from Jos Dickson, clerk; witnesses Jacob Forney, Richard Jones, & Joseph Abernathy.

595. Mar. 1783 a suit vs John Thompson (late of Rutherford Co) & John Walbert (Rutherford Co)--on Sept. 10, 1780 with 500 other people as tories in the loyal militia assisted the King's troops under command of Maj. Forgison [sic]; witness John Anderson, Saml King, David Miller, Somer [or Tomer] Walker, & John Somel; "a true bill".

596. Aug. 19, 1783 a bond by widow Mills, wife of Ambros Mills, & Wm Wills to Wm Gilbert for £250 each for Thomas Mills to appear to answer charges as captain under Maj. Forgison at Kings Mountain.

SAMPSON COUNTY
597. Receipt No. 5 Dec. 16, 1785 to Enoch Herring £30 for 15 surveys in Sampson Co.

598. May 4, 1785 surveyed 130 ac on W side of Six Runs Cr & N side of N prong of Marsh Br; part of a "large" survey of land formerly property of Thomas Cristia, of Ireland; border: Joseph Burch, John Eason, & Christia's old line; [signed] Enoch Herring, surveyor; chain bearers Benja Eason & Willm Whitley; [on back] Saml Oats No. 13.

599. May 5, 1785 surveyed 106 ac; part of a "large" survey formerly property of Thomas Cristia, of Ireland; on W side of Six Runs Cr; border: Samuel Oats and Nathan Jones; [signed] Enoch Herring, surveyor; chain bearers Samuel Oats & John Wester; [on back] No. 6 John Wester.

Sales of Confiscated Land

600. May 5, 1785 surveyed 101 ac; part of a "large" survey formerly property of Thomas Christia, of Ireland; on W side of Six Runs Cr; border: Cristia's line and John Wester; [signed] Enoch Herring, surveyor; chain bearers Benja Easton & Willm Whitley; [on back] No. 10 Jas Spiller.

601. May 9, 1785 surveyed 461 ac; part of a "large" survey formerly property of Thomas Christia, of Ireland; border: Stephen Blackman, Cristia's line, Roger Snell, & Ivy; [signed] Enoch Herring, surveyor; chain bearers Rice Blackman esq & Stephen Blackman; [on back] No. 11 Jas Spiller.

602. May 6, 1785 surveyed 330 ac; part of a "large" survey formerly property of Thomas Christia's, of Ireland; on W side of Six Runs Cr; border: Joseph Burch, John Hay, Unity McDade, Cristia's line, William Fryer's old corner, & John Easom; plat shows land includes a pond; [signed] Enoch Herring, surveyor; chain bearers Benja Eason & Willm Whitley; [on back] No. 4 Jas Spiller

603. May 11, 1785 surveyed 107 ac; part of a "large" survey formerly late Gov. Dobbs' property; on W side of Six Runs Cr & N side of lower Beverdam Swamp; border: Thomas Karr, Jonathan Talow, & Beverdam Swamp; [signed] Enoch Herring, surveyor; chain bearers Nehemiah Scott & Elisha Turlington; [on back] No. 2 Thos Carr.

604. May 11, 1785 surveyed 62 ac; part of a "large" survey formerly late Gov. Dobbs' property; on W side of Six Runs Cr & N side of lower Beverdam Swamp; border: Jonathan Talow's corner on Beverdam Swamp; [signed] Enoch Herring, surveyor; chain bearers Nehemiah Scott & Elisha Turlington; [on back] No. 3 Jonathan Taylor.
605. May 11, 1785 surveyed 110 ac; part of a "large" survey formerly late Gov. Dobbs' property; border: on N side of Jonathan Talow's "plantation" and said Talow's corner of Casons Br; [signed] Enoch Herring, surveyor; chain bearers Nehemiah Scott & Elisha Turlington; [on back] No. 9 Jas Spiller.

606. May 11, 1785 surveyed 407 ac; part of a "large" survey formerly late Gov. Dobbs' property; on W side of Six Runs Cr & S side of lower Beverdam Swamp; [signed] Enoch Herring, surveyor; chain bearers Nehemiah Scott & Elisha Turlington; [on back] No. 8 Curtis Ivy & G J McRee.

607. May 12, 1785 surveyed 159 ac; part of a "large" survey formerly late Gov. Dobbs' property; on W side of Six Runs Cr; border: Jonathan Karr, Casons Br, Jonathan Talow's corner on the branch, & John Hay; [signed] Enoch Herring, surveyor; chain bearers Nehemiah Scott & Elisha Turlington; [on back] No. 12 Jonathan Carr.

608. May 12, 1785 surveyed 292 ac; part of a "large" survey formerly late Gov. Dobbs' property; on W side of Six Runs Cr and between upper & lower beverdams; border: Scott, John Hay, Thomas Karr, & Talow; [signed] Enoch Herring, surveyor; chain bearers Nehemiah Scott & Elisha Turlington; [on back] No. 14 Thos Carr.

609. May 18, 1785 surveyed 201 ac; formerly property of William Forbes, son of Edward Forbes jr of Liverpool, Great Brittain; on W side of Six Runs Cr & S side of Gilmore's Swamp; border: Benjn Easom's upper corner on Gilmores Cr, "the" old line, Hardy Holmes, & John Hay; [signed] Jo Dickson, surveyor for Enoch Herring surveyor; [on back] No. 15 Hardy Holmes.

610. May 27, 1785 surveyed 82 ac; part of a "large" survey formerly Gov. Dobbs' property; on W side of Six Runs Cr & N side of Beverdam Swamp; border: W edge of Casons Br and Jno Holmes; [signed] Enoch Herring, surveyor; chain bearers Col. Jas Moor & Capt. Hardy Holmes; [on back] No. 5 Jonathan Taylor.

611. May 27, 1785 surveyed 72 ac; part of a "large" survey formerly Gov. Dobbs' property; on W side of Six Runs Cr & N side of lower Beverdam Swamp; border: John Holms; [signed] Enoch Herring, surveyor; chain bearers Capt. Hardy Holmes & Mjr. Jonathan Talow; [on back] No. 7 James Moore.

612. May 28, 1785 surveyed 571 ac; part of a "large" survey formerly Gov. Dobbs' property; on W side of Six Runs Cr & N side of lower Beverdam Swamp; John Hay, Jonathan Karr's corner on E side of Gilmoors Beverdam Swamp,

Sales of Confiscated Land

Casons Br, & John Holmes; [signed] Enoch Herring, surveyor; chain bearers Hardy Holmes esq & Benjamin Easom; [on back] No. 1 Curtis Ivy & Griffith J McRee.

613. Aug. 31, 1803 surveyed 60.5 ac; within a grant to Arthur Dobbs; on E side of Beverdam Swamp; border: David Bunting, widow Carr, Laban Taylor, main run of Beaverdam [Swamp], & edge of "the mud" of Beaverdam Swamp; [signed] John Thomas, D surveyor [for] E Herring, surveyor; [on back] Mar. 24, 1804 sold by James Marley, Fayetteville Dist Commissioner of Confiscated Property, to David Bunting for £0.3.6 per acre at Sampson Co Court house, [signed] J Marley, comr; No. 1   No. 549.

614. Aug. 31, 1803 surveyed 69.75 ac; within a grant to Arthur Dobbs; on E side of Beaverdam Swamp; border: widow Carr and Laban Taylor; [signed] John Thomas, D surveyor [for] Enoch Herring, surveyor; [on back] May 24, 1804 sold by James Marley, Fayetteville Dist Commissioner of Confiscated Property, to Theophilus Carr for £0.3.6 per acre at Sampson Co Court house, [signed] J Marley, comr; No. 2   No. 543

615. Oct. 6, 1803 surveyed 176 ac; within a large grant to T Christy; on W side of Six Runs Swamp; border: a corned of Arthur Dobbs & Christy's 2 large surveys on main runs of Six Runs [Swamp], Joseph Esom, a water oak marked "Y I" on main run of Six Runs Swamp near a corner of Easom's old 500 ac survey; [signed] John Thomas, D surveyor [for] Enoch Herring, surveyor; chain bearers Sampson Young & Bennit Ballard; [on back] May 14, 1805 sold by James Marley, Fayetteville Dist Commissioner of Confiscated Property, to Adam Marley for $725 at Sampson Co Court house, [signed] J Marley, cmr; No. 4   No. 551 dated Nov. 26, 1805.

616. Oct. 15, 1803 surveyed 198.5 ac; within a large grant to T Christy; on W side of Six Runs Swamp; border: "the giving" line of Esom's 500 ac survey and the main runs of Six Runs [Swamp]; [signed] John Thomas, D surveyor [for] Enoch Herring, surveyor; chain bearers Sampson Young & Bennit Ballard; [on back] Mar. 24, 1804 sold by James Marley, Fayetteville Dist Commissioner of Confiscated Property, to James Marley for £21 per acre at Sampson Co Court house, [signed] J Marley, cmr; No. 5   No. 548.

617. Oct. 15, 1803 surveyed 444 ac; within a large grant to T Christy; on E side of Six Runs Swamp; border: the main run of said swamp, a branch, Marley's field, R Snell's field, a "sliew run" of Six Runs Swamp; [signed] John Thomas, D surveyor [for] Enoch Herring, surveyor; chain bearers Sampson Young & John Bush; [on back] Mar. 24, 1804 sold by James Marley, Fayetteville Dist Commissioner of Confiscated Property, to James Marley for £0.10 per acre at Sampson Co Court house, [signed] J Marley, cmr; No. 8   No. 547.

618. Oct. 16, 1803 surveyed 39.5 ac; within a large grant to T Christy; on E side of Six Runs Swamp; border: a corner of Michael King sr's 711 ac survey and Marley; [signed] John Thomas, D surveyor [for] Enoch Herring, surveyor; chain bearers Sampson Young & John Bush; [on back] Mar. 24, 1804 sold by James Marley, Fayetteville Dist Commissioner of Confiscated Property, to Stephen Slocumb for £0.5 per acre, [signed] J Marley, cmr; No. 7   No. 545.

619. Oct. 16, 1803 surveyed 64 ac; within a large grant to Arthur Dobbs; on W side of Beaverdam Swamp; border: Ben Carr's corner on "the" runs of Beaverdam [Swamp], James Rhodes, & Scott's old line of a 160 ac survey; [signed] John Thomas, D surveyor [for] Enoch Herring, surveyor; chain bearers Sampson Young & Bennit Ballard; [on back] May 14, 1805 sold by James Marley, Fayetteville Dist Commissioner of Confiscated Property, to John Barfield for £108.7.7 at Sampson Co Court house, [signed] J Marley, cmr; No. 9   No. 552 dated Apr. 9, 1809.

620. Oct. 25, 1803 surveyed 101 ac; within a large grant to Arthur Dobbs; on W side of Beaverdam Swamp; border: John Blackman, Jesse Carr, & on the run of Beaverdam Swamp below Carr's mill; [signed] John Thomas, D surveyor [for] Enoch Herring, surveyor; [on back] Mar. 24, 1804 sold by James Marley, Fayetteville Dist Commissioner of Confiscated Property, to James Blackman for £0.17.6 per ac, [signed] J Marley, cmr; No. 3   No. 542 dated Feb. 23, 1805.

Sales of Confiscated Land

621. Nov. 5, 1803 surveyed 67 ac; within a "large" grant to T Christy; on E side of Six Runs Swamp; border: the main run of Six Runs Swamp, a dividing line between Slocomb & Ballard, "the given" line of Michael King sr's 711 ac survey, & said King's last corner; [signed] John Thomas, D surveyor [for] Enoch Herring, surveyor; chain bearers Sampson Young & John Bush; [on back] Mar. 24, 1804 sold by James Marley, Fayetteville Dist Commissioner of Confiscated Property, to Stephen Slocomb for £0.10 per acre, [signed] J Marley, cmr; No. 10   No. 544.

622. Nov. 5, 1803 surveyed 34 ac; part of a "large" grant to T Christy; on W side of Six Runs Swamp; border: Stephen King's upper corner, runs on the main runs of Six Runs Swamp to where the first "sliew" makes out on E side, & R Snell; [signed] John Thomas, D surveyor [for] Enoch Herring, surveyor; chain bearers Sampson Young & John Bush; [on back] Mar. 24, 1804 sold by James Marley, Fayetteville Dist Commissioner of Confiscated Property, to Stephen King for £0.2.6, [signed] J Marley, cmr; No. 11   No. 546.

SURRY COUNTY
623. a bond Feb. 19, 1780 Matthew Brooks, Wm Shepperd, Wm Dobson, & Jno Armstrong to Gov. Richard Caswell for £300,000; condition Matthew Brooks to perform the job as Commissioner of Confiscated Property for Surry Cr. Signed Matthew Brooks, Wm Shepperd, Wm Dobson, & Jno Armstrong. Witness Jo Williams, c c.   Wit. oath Feb. 1780 acknowledged. "a true copy" [signed] Jo Williams, c c.
624. a bond Feb. 19, 1780 Joseph Phillips, Wm Shepperd, Wm Dobson, & Jno Armstrong to Gov. Richard Caswell for £300,000; condition Joseph Phillips to perform the job as Commissioner of Confiscated Property for Surry Co. Signed Joseph Phillips, Wm Shepperd, Wm Dobson, & Jno Armstrong. Witness Jo Williams, c c. Wit. oath Feb. 1780 acknowledged. "a true copy" [signed] Jo Williams, c c.

625. a bond Feb. 19, 1780 Richard Varnall, Wm Shepperd, Wm Dobson, & Jno Armstrong to Gov. Richard Caswell for £300,000; condition Richard Varnall to perform the job as Commissioner of Confiscated Property for Surry Co. Signed Richard Varnall, Wm Shepperd, Wm Dobson, & Jno Armstrong. Witness Jo Williams, c c. Wit. oath Feb. 1780 acknowledged. "a true copy" [signed] Jo Williams, c c.

626. a bond Aug. 16, 1781 James Shepperd, Wm Shepperd, Wm Underwood, Wm Cook, & James Gaines to Gov. Thomas [James--lined out] Burke for £500,000; condition James Shepperd, appointed "this day", to perform the job as Commissioner of Confiscated Property for Surry Co. Signed Jams. Shepperd, Wm Shepperd, Wm Underwood, Wm Cook, & Jams. Gaines. Witness Jno Thos Longino. Wit. oath Aug. 1781 acknowledged. "a true copy" [signed] Jno Williams, c c.

627. a bond Aug. 17, 1782 James Gaines, Sam Cummins, & Matthew Moore (of Surry Co) to Gov. Alexander Martin for £5,000 [sic]; condition James Gaines', appointed "this day", to perform the job as Commissioner of Confiscated Property for Surry Co.   Signed Jams. Gaines, Saml Cummins, & Mattw Moore. Witness Jno Thos Longino. Wit. oath Aug. 1782 acknowledged.

628. a bond Aug. 17, 1782 Reuben Dodson, Wm Meridith, & George Deatherage (of Surry Co) to Gov. Alexander Martin for £5,000; condition Reuben Dodson, appointed "this day", to perform the job as Commissioner of Confiscated Property for Surry Co. Signed Reuben Dodson, Wm Meridith, & George Deatherage. Witness Jno Thos Longino. Wit. oath Aug. 1782 acknowledged.

629. second Monday in Aug. 1790 Surry Co Pleas & Quarter Sessions Court at the court house--petition William Robinson vs James Roberts, whose estate was confiscated; plaintiff preferred his petition agreeable to an act of Assembly and the Court entered a judgment by default; jury--Richard Horn, Johnson Summers, Andrew Martin, John Williams, William N Cook, William Johnson, Reuben Wheless, Jacob McCraw, Jonathan Haines, John Summers, Micajah Oglesby, & West Moseley--find for the plaintiff and find damages £175.10.4¼ and cost. "signed" Joseph Williams, clerk of Court Aug. 12, 1790; [signed] Jo Williams, c c.

Sales of Confiscated Land

630A. second Monday or Feb. 14, 1780 Surry Co Pleas & Quarter Sessions Court: Joseph Phillips esq was appointed a Commissioner to dispose of Confiscated Property; Mary 17, 1788 Joseph Williams, clerk certifys this is a true copy of the Court records. [signed] Jo Williams, c c.

630B. Mar. 17, 1788 Joseph Phillips; persuant to his appointment to sell confiscated property and collect debts from citizens of this State due to "sundrie" persons subjects of Great Brittain and others who removed themselves from "this" or the United States; Joseph Phillips certifys he has received "among other debts" for the use of this State from (1) Robert Lenair, on account of Lenair & Williams, £2,440 a debt & interest due John Hamilton & Co and (2) £857.4 from John Hedgpeth for debt & interest due William Hamilton & Co. Signed Joseph Phillips, coms.

631. [no date] List of Commissioners of Confiscated Property for Surry Co:
Feb. session 1780 Matthew Brooks, Joseph Philips, & Richard Varnal were appointed [commissioners], entered into bond, & qualified.
Aug. session 1781 James Shepperd was appointed Commissioner of Confiscated Property in room of Richd Varnall, who was killed at Kings Mountain.
Aug. session 1782 Matthew Brooks & Joseph Philips resigned and James Gains & Reuben Dobson were appointed Commissoners of Confiscated Estates in their room; "also" James Shepperd was suspended from acting as Commissioner of Confiscated Property for neglect of duty. [signed] Jo Williams, c c.

632. [no date] Committee to whom was referred the petition of William T Lewis & Joel Lewis, formerly of Surry Co, report:
By the petition and testimony "adduced" to the committee, it appears William T Lewis and Joel Lewis bought a tract from Salisbury Dist Commissioner of Confiscated Property, which was previously James Roberts' property whose estate was "particularily" confiscated; the commissioner never made a deed nor has a grant issued from the Secretary's Office; so the committee recommends the following resolution: the Secretary is to issue a grant to William Armstrong (of Surry Co) who purchased said 500 ac from William Terril and Joel Lewis (of Surry Co) which land was legally sold by the confiscation of this State, and the Secretary is to observe the "requisitions" of the law. [signed] J G Blount, chairman. Nov. 27, 1795 read & resolved in Senate; Nov. 28, 1795 concur in House of Commons; [on back] £930 G M O No. 545 executed Nov. 29, 1795.

633. Jun. 16, 1785 List of receipts taken and money paid by Col. Joseph Philips, Surry Co Commissioner of Confiscated Property, to Robert Lanier, late Treasurer of Salisbury Dist:
a) Jun. 3, 1780 paid into the treasury per Robert Lanier's rect. £200.0
b) Aug. 26   "do do"   £2,440.0
c) Oct. 13   "do do"   £ 800.0
d) Jun. 3, 1782 "do do"   £ 800.0 [total] £4,240
"Received the above mentioned [page torn] given by" [rest of page lost].

634. Jun. 3, 1780 received of Maj. Joseph Phillops, Surry Co commissioner, £200 "part of" confiscated money in his hands. Signed Robt Lanier, treasr. Salisbury Dist; [on back] No. 1.

635. Aug. 26, 1780 received of Col. Joseph Phillips, Surry Co Commissioner of Confiscated Property, £2,440 "money he has received" by virtue of his office. [signed] Robt Lanier, treasr. Salisbury Dist; [on back] No. 2.

636. Oct. 13, 1780 received of Col. Joseph Phillips, Surry Co Commissioner of Confiscated Property, £800. [signed] Robt Lanier, treasr. Salisbury Dist; [on back] No. 3.

637. Jun. 3, 1782 received of Col. Jos Phillips, Surry Co commissioner, £800 "which is placed to his credit on the books". [signed] Robt Lanier, treasr. Salisbury Dist; [on back] No. 4.

638. List of persons who rendered on oath to Surry Co Commissioners of Confiscated Property an account of debts they owed by bond, accounts, etc to Messrs. Archibald & John Hamilton & Co, merchants late of North Carolina, which sums were confiscated & paid to the commissioners for use of the Public of North Carolina:
a) [William Moore--lined out]   £9,400

Sales of Confiscated Land

[Lannier & Williams--lined out]   £2,440
[John Hedgepeth--lined out]   £857.4   [total] £12,697.4
b) William Moore   £3,000
  Messrs. Moore & Tatum   £1,400
  Lenair & Williams   £2,440
  Jno Hedgepeath   £857.4   [total] £7,697.4
[Names under "b" were added later & in different handwriting.]
"there appears from returns made by commrs. that they also received from Will Moore a debt due Thomas Multer [or Matter] & Co £5,000"
[no date] Francis Child, Comptroller of Public Accounts, certifys the foregoing list "totaling £12,697.4" were paid to the treasury and this is a true copy, signed at Hillsborough.

639. "1783" Col. Joseph Phillips, Surry Co Commissioner of Confiscated Property, for 1780 and 1781:
a) Account of State of North Carolina
  Jun. 3, 1789 to cash received of John Hudspeth   £800
  Aug. 26   to "do" received of Robert Lanier   £2,440
  Jun. 3   to "do" received of Robert Lanier   £800
b) Jun. 3, 1780 by cash paid Robt Lanier, treasurer per receipt No. 1   £200
  Aug. 26   by "do" paid Robt Lanier, treasurer per receipt No. 2   £2,440
  Oct. 13   by "do" paid Robert Lanier, treasurer per receipt No. 3   £800
  Jun. 3, 1782 by cash paid Robert Lanier, treasurer per receipt No. 4   £800
  [total] £4,240 - £4,040 = £200 cr. by balance due
Nov. term 1783 Joseph Phillips, Surry Co Commissioner of Confiscated Property, "tendered" the above statement and there's a balance due him of £200. [signed] Mar. Armstrong, Wm T Lewis, & Ja Martin; "a true copy" [signed] Jo Williams, c c.

640. Account of committee appointed to settle with Commissioners of Confiscated Property:
"1784" Matt Brooks to State of North Carolina due to his being Surry Co Commissioner of Confiscated Property:
a) to corn received of Richard Thomerson for rent of Wm Applewhite's
   "plantation" 10 bushels
b) to corn recieved of Ro Lanier for rent of Jno & Wm Null's "plantation"
   36 bushels
c) to rent of John Denney's "plantation"   90 [bushels of corn]
d) to rent of Henry Burches "plantation"   19.5 [bushels of corn]
e) to rent of Reuben Jackson's "plantation"   5 [bushels of corn]
f) to rent of Barney Dempsey's "plantation"   3 [bushels of corn]
g) to rent of George Turner's "plantation"   3 [bushels of corn]
h) to rent of John Pace's "plantation"   3 [bushels of corn]
i) to rent of John Jervis's [or Jerrus'] "plantation" 5 [bushels of corn]
j) to rent of Leflet Jervis' "plantation"   5 [bushels of corn]
k) to rent of Isam Thompson's "plantation"   8 [bushels of corn]
l) to rent of Wm Ramsey's "plantation"   50 [bushels of corn]
m) to rent of West Moseley's "plantation"   5 [bushels of corn]
n) to rent of John Slace's "plantation"   11 [bushels of corn]
o) to rent of Richard Horn's Negro & "plantation"   112 [bushels of corn]
p) to rent of Wm Lackey's "plantation"   12.5 [bushels of corn]
q) to rent of Thomas Skidmore's "plantation"   12 [bushels of corn]
r) to rent of George Gunter's "plantation"   4.5 [bushels of corn]
   [total]   394.5 bushels of corn
s) to cash received of James Badget due Gideon Wright £500
t) to cash received of John Lynch "as he gave on account in his hands as
   liable to be taken for public use" £273.15.4

Sales of Confiscated Land

The above 394.5 bushels of corn for public use and the above £773.15.4 has been paid to the Treasurer May session 1784 Surry Co; we, the committee appointed to settle with Commissioners of Confiscated Property, certify the above account was proved before us. [signed] Jo Winston & Ben Watson "a true copy" [signed] Jo Williams, c c.

641. Oct. 27, 1795 "resurveyed" 500 ac for William Armstrong on both sides of Lovins Cr & middle fork of Tarrat R; border: crosses Bridges Cr; [signed] J A Word [or Wond], D surveyor; chain carriers William Word & Joshua Word; [this probably refers to No. 904 above].

TYRRELL COUNTY
642. Receipt No. 303 Oct. 12, 1786 to Hezekiah Spruill, Tyrrell Co surveyor, £18 for 9 surveys.

643. Receipt No. 37 Dec. 7, 1793 to Humphrey Hardy £2 for surveying 450 ac in Tyrrell Co formerly property of Gov. White of the West Indies.

644. Oct. 9, 1783 a return of confiscated property in Tyrrell Co: a black horse, property of Edward Vandaniel, and a saddle; the horse was taken by "the commanding officer" of said county and put into service of said State under "the conduct of" Capt. Joseph Swift; said horse wasn't returned in April 1780 and is "yet in custody" and to be sold 29th "of this inst." [signed] Stephen Swain & Jno Anderson, commissioners; Oct. term 1783 proved in open Court by the above commissioners. "a true copy" [signed] J Mackey, c c.

645. Nov. 25, 1791 received of Hardy Murfree, Commissioner of Confiscated Property, £4 for cryers fees for Tyrrell Co confiscated property. [signed] E Blount, shf.

646. Hardy Murfree esq. Nov. 25, 1791 to Hodge & Wells:
to advertise confiscated property in Tyrrell Co 8 weeks £1.16
to advertise confiscated property in Edenton 9 times £2 [total] £3.16
Received the above amount from Commissioner of Confiscated Property Nov. 27, 1791. [signed] A Hodge for Co.

647. Aug. 9, 1785 surveyed 282 ac; No. 4; formerly Henry Eustace McCulloch's property; of the richland of Warie R; [signed] John Collier, c surveyor; chain carriers John Merrel & Dan Merrel; May 2, 1786 sold by A Lytle, commr, to William Bell for £1,005; [this land is most probably in Randolph Co, not Tyrrell Co].

648. Aug. 9, 1785 surveyed 282 ac; No. 5; formerly Henry Eustace McCulloch's property; of the richlands of Warie R; border: tract No. 4; [signed] John Collier, c surveyor; chain carriers John Merrel & Dan Merrel; May 2, 1786 sold by A Lytle, commr, to William Bell for £1,031; [this land is most probably in Randolph Co, not Tyrrell Co].

649. Aug. 9, 1785 surveyed 282 ac; No. 6; formerly Henry Eustace McCulloch's property; of the richlands of Warie R; border: tract No. 6 and an old field; [signed] John Collier, c surveyor; chain carriers John Merrel & Dan Merrel; May 2, 1786 sold by A Lytle, commr, to William Bell for £1,151; [this land is most probably in Randolph Co, not Tyrrell Co].

650. Aug. 25, 1787 surveyed 360 ac in two adjoining parts: No. 3 is 190 ac and No. 4 is 170 ac; on W side of Kendricks Cr and S side of Bakers Swamp; formerly property of Gov. White of the West Indies; border: Buncomb's line at the creek, head of a large branch, & SW corner of [tract] No. 2; surveyed due to order of Hardy Murfree, Edenton Dist. Commissioner of Confiscated Property; [signed] H Hardy, D S; chain carriers Thomas Knott & Theophilis Reddit; [on back] Humphrey Hardy.

651. Aug. 25, 1787 surveyed 250 ac due to order of Hardy Murfree, Edenton Dist. Commissioner of Confiscated Property; No. 5; formerly property of Gov. White of the West Indies; on S side of Barkers Swamp; border: on S by Thomas Buncombe, NW corner of tract No. 2 at the mouth of a large branch, tract No. 4, Baker's line, & tract No. 6; [signed] H Hardy, D surveyor; chain carriers Micaijah Stubbs & Thomas Knott; [on back] Nehemiah Long.

Sales of Confiscated Land

652. Aug. 25, 1787 surveyed 200 ac due to order of Hardy Murfree, Edenton Dist. Commissioner of Confiscated Property; No. 6; on S side of Baker's Swamp; formerly property of Gov. White of the West Indies; being the upper part of Baker's land "so called"; border: a corner of tract No. 5 at Bakers Swamp, Thomas Buncombe, Deep Run, & the head of Baker's Swamp; [signed] H Hardy, D surveyor; chain carriers Micaijah Stubbs & Thomas Knott; [on back] Nehemiah Long.

653. Dec. 15, 1785 surveyed 0.5 ac a lot No. 79 in Windsor; no improvements thereon; formerly McKitrick's property; surveyed due to order of Hardy Murfree, Edenton Dist. Commissioner of Confiscated Property; "back of lot" [blank]; plat shows lot is 105' by 210'; [signed] Humpy Hardy, surveyor; [on back] Benjn Bryar; [this land is most probably in Bertie Co].

654. Dec. 15, 1785 surveyed 0.5 ac lot No. 81 in Windsor; formerly McKitrick's property; surveyed due to order of Hardy Murfree, Edenton Dist. Commissioner of Confiscated Property; no improvements thereon; back of Benja Bryar; plat shows lot is 105' by 210'; [signed] Humpy Hardy, survey; [on back] Benjn Bryar; [this land is most probably in Bertie Co].

655. Sept. 2, 1786 surveyed 320 ac; No. 7; formerly James Craven's property; on E side of Scoperlong R & known as Hendericks Point; border: a "larrall" on the river in Buzzard Bay, Hendericks Point, & the sound; [signed] Hez Spruill, surveyor; [on back] Jas Baker.

656. Sept. 2, 1786 surveyed 320 ac; No. 8; formerly James Craven's property; on E side of Scoperlong R & side of Albermarl Sound; known as Poperwells; border: Chapman and the sound; [signed] Hez Spruill; [on back] James Baker.

657. Dec. 13, 1786 surveyed 165 ac; No. 9; formerly Stephen Hooker decd's property and willed to his son John Hooker; on E side of Scuperlong Bay; known as Grapvine Neck; border: Nehemial Spruill's corner on the bay and a branch than divides said land from Frans Nathan Hooker's land; [signed] H Spruill, surveyor; chain bearers Jno Swinn & Jno Newberrey; [on back] Nathan Hooker.

WAKE COUNTY
658. Receipt May [hole in page], 1783 to John Humphries £22 for 11 surveys; [on back] No. 18; No. 72; received the within "conts" [signed] B Sanders [or Sandes], sheff.

659. Sept. 29, 1785 received of Capt. Thomas Armstrong £2,600 for 381 ac on Swift Cr sold due to confiscation law; formerly James McNeil's property; [signed] Nicholas Long, comr; witness Matt Ramsy.

660. On Jan. 1, 1783 "or thereabouts" at a confiscated estate sale for Hillsborough Dist, 400 ac on Terrels Br of Little Lick Cr in Wake Co was sold to James Moore for £101; formerly Henry E McCulloch's property; two-thirds of the money was paid; "nearly" on Jan. 8, I appeared by appointment at Hillsborough to give bond for the remaining balance, but the commissioner refused to receive the certificates, so I gave my bond & "full" sum of £101 on 5 years credit with 6% interest annually with John Humphries, [of] Virga., as security; I haven't received a grant for the land & haven't paid any of the purchase money; in 1789 a suit was brought against me & James Moore and by security John Humphries in Hillsborough Superior Court by State Treasurer for £101 principal & interest; before a judgment was made, General Assembly begun the first Monday in No. 1789 at "Fayatville" passed a resolution giving "the privilege" to those people who have bought confiscated property and gave bond to "repare to" the Treasury's Office and pay two-thirds of their bonds in certificates providing they would "confes judgment" for the remaining one-third in "acutal cash" at Hillsborough Superior Court in Apr. 1790; "at which time" my security John Humphries "appeared" and paid two-thirds of £101 or £66.13.4 with interest due or a total of £96.11.6 as per Treasurer's receipt "in the hands of" John Humphries, and the judgment for remaining one-third and interest or £48.5.9 in "actual money" as per record of said Court; so to secure John Humphries, James Moore (of Wake Co) empowers the Secretary of State to grant said 400 ac to John Humphries (of Virginia) and Moore given up his claim of title. [signed] Apr. 26, 1790 Jas Moore; witness Saml High, Henry Warren, & David Halliburton; wit. oath Sept. 1790 by Henry Warren; [on back] Oct. 26, 1790

Sales of Confiscated Land

(Wake Co) John Humphries assigns his rights to John Hinton since John Hinton has paid the Treasurer of North Carolina "the full purchase price" as per receipt. [signed] Jno Humphries; witness J Lane & H Lane.

661. Dec. 23, 1782 surveyed 200 ac; No. 1; formerly McCulloch's property; on both sides of Little Lick Cr below the mouth of "Chunk a pipe" Cr; border: crosses the creek near the mouth of Tims Br; [signed] John Humphries, surveyor; chain bearers Thomas Nichols & Henry Massey; [no date] sold to William Moore.

662. Dec. 23, 1782 surveyed 400 ac; No. 2; formerly McCulloch's property; on both sides of Terrels Br & Gum Br; border: tract No. 1 and an old corner; [signed] John Humphries, surveyor; chain bearers Thomas Nichols & Henry Massey; [no date] sold to James Moore; [evidently the same as No. 660 above].

663. Dec. 23, 1782 surveyed 330 ac; No. 3; formerly McCulloch's property; on both sides of Little Lick Cr & Chunk's pipe Cr; border: an old corner and crosses Little Lick Cr below the mouth of Chuck a pipe Cr, & a ridge near an old path; plat also shows Tims Br; [signed] John Humphries, surveyor; chain bearers Thomas Nichols & Henry Massey; [no date] sold to William Moore.

664. Dec. 23, 1782 surveyed 330 ac; No. 4; formerly McCulloch's property; on both sides of Little Lick Cr; border: a ridge near an old path on S side of the creek and crosses Little Lick Cr near the mouth of Cedar Cr; [signed] John Humphries, surveyor; chain bearers Thomas Nichols & Henry Massey; [no date] sold to William Moore.

665. Dec. 24, 1782 surveyed 208 ac; No. 5; formerly McCulloch's property; on both sides of Little Lick Cr; border: the first corner of [tract] No. 1 and an old line; [signed] John Humphries, surveyor; chain bearers Thomas Nichols & Henry Massey; [no date] sold to Lewis Bledsoe; "entered" by Benjn Clark.

666. Dec. 24, 1782 surveyed 164 ac; No. 6; formerly McCulloch's property; on Rocky Run of Little Lick Cr; border: a corner of [tract] No. 5 in an old line and Brasfield; [signed] John Humphries, surveyor; chain bearers Thomas Nichols & Henry Massey; [no date] sold to Wm Moore; "entered" by L Moore.

667. Dec. 28, 1782 surveyed 244 ac; No. 7; formerly McCulloch's property; on S side of Neuse R; border: Alston and the river; plat also shows "a" spring; [signed] John Humphries, surveyor; chain bearers Amos Reynolds & James Bowdown; [no date] sold to William Moore.

668. Dec. 28, 1782 surveyed 291 ac; No. 8; formerly McCulloch's property; on S side of Neuse R and both sides of Rockey Br; border: [a corner of No. 7--lined out] on the river; [signed] John Humphries, surveyor; chain bearers Amos Reynolds & James Bowdown; [no date] sold to Nicholas Long.

669. Dec. 28, 1782 surveyed 341 ac; No. 9; formerly McCulloch's property; on N waters of Little Lick Cr; border: an old line and first corner of tract No. 1; plat shows Tims Br and land is on both sides of Flat Br of Little Lick Cr; [signed] John Humphries, surveyor; chain bearers Amos Reynolds & James Bowdown; [no date] sold to "Virginia" John Humphries.

670. Dec. 28, 1783 surveyed 372 ac; No. 10; formerly McCulloch's property; on both sides of Little Lick Cr; border: first corner of [tract] No. 1 on N side of said creek; [signed] John Humphries, surveyor; chain bearers Amos Reynolds & James Bowdown; [no date] sold to William Moore.

671. Dec. 28, 1783 surveyed 372 ac; No. 11; formerly McCulloch's property; on both sides of Little Lick Cr; border: a corner of [tract] No. 10 on N side of said creek; [signed] John Humphries, surveyor; chain bearers Amos Reynolds & James Bowdown; [no date] sold to William Moore.

672. Jul. 2, 1783 surveyed 345 ac in Granville & Wake Counties; formerly Henry E McCulloch's property; on both sides of Beaverdam & Smiths Creeks; border: the low ground, near Wagstaff Canaday's fence, near Mary Patterson, Wake Co line, & crosses Cowpen fork of Beaverdam Cr; [signed] Micajah Bullock, surveyor; sworn chain carriers

Sales of Confiscated Land

Harwood Nance & Philip Bullock; [on back] Mar. 1788 sold to Jeremiah Bailey for £221 certificates, [signed] Archd Lytle, comr.

673. Jul. 2, 1786 surveyed 129 ac in Granville & Wake Counties; formerly Henry E McCulloch's property; on both sides of Smiths Cr; border: near Wagstaff Canaday's fence and Wake Co line; [signed] Micajah Bullock, surveyor; sworn chain carriers Harwood Nance & Philip Bullock; sold Mar. 1788 to James Bailey for £141 certifictes, [signed] Archd Lytle, comr.

NO COUNTY OR MORE THAN ONE COUNTY
674. The Committee of Propositions & Grievances "No. 1" report on petition of Thomas Callender: Parker Quince levied an attachment on a house & lot of Daniel Southerland to recover on said Southerland's note £399.8.4 and £8.0.5 cost; pending the suit, the Commissioner of Confiscated Property seized said house & lot and rented it for a year to said Quince, who gave bond of £45 with the petitioner as security; "afterwards" the Commissioner sold said house & lot for £5,050 as appears by his return to the Comptroller due to the ninth section of Chapt. 5 of Laws of 1779; the petitioner is entitled to his petition; therefore the committee proposes the following resolution: Treasurer is to release Thomas Calander from the amount of a judgment agains him due to the bond for £45 and interest from Jan. 7, 1785, and Treasurer to pay Thomas Calander, executor of Parker Quince, the amount of judgment & cost recovered against Southerland after deducting the mount of the "judgment released to said Calander"; [signed] Jno M Benford, chairman; Dec. 22, 1797 read & concur in Senate; Dec. 22, 1797 concur in House of Commons; [on back] £328.6.9 paid Hill + £79.2 paid to Lockhart as collector of arears = £407.8.9 "good in the Treasurer's settlement for the last". [This is probably from New Hanover Co since Calender and Quince lived there.]

675. The Committee of Propositions & Grievances "No. 1" report on petition of Robert Smith & George Alexander: the petition should be granted but the petitioners should only get the "value of the money at the time it was paid" to the Commissioners of Confiscated Property with interest and propose the following resolution: Treasurer is authorized to pay Robert Smith & George Alexander £171.16.4; [signed] John Moore, chairman; Dec. 19, 1803 concur in House of Commons; Dec. 19, 1803 passed in Senate; Dec. 20, 1803 second reading in both houses; Dec. 20, 1803 third reading in both houses.

676. Receipt No. 37 Oct. 15, 1791 to Griffith Rutherford £7.3.6, his commission on sale in 1782 of land in Rowan & Anson Counties & 3 Negroes formerly property of Samuel Bryant of Salisbury Dist, as per Comptroller's receipt; [on back] No. 456.

677. Statement of balance due on Robt Long's bond for confiscated property:
a) Robert Long with Job Garretson bond dated Jun. 19, 1792 £1,190.9.9
   interest due Dec. 1, 1793   £485.15.4
   payment in part of principal Apr. 1, 1793   £396.16.7
   pl. due   £793.13.2 + interest £485.15.11 = £1,279.9.7
b) Robert Long with Job Garretson bond dated Jun. 23, 1792 £309.9.11
   interest due Dec. 1, 1793   £23.9.10
   payment in part of principal Apr. 22, 1793   £88.4.9
                              Nov. 30, 1793   £14.18.7   [total] £103.3.4
   principal due £206.6.7 + £23.9.10 = £229.16.5
c) part of the bond of £1,190.9.9 due Dec. 1, 1793   £79.7.5
   due for interest on said bond to Dec. 1, 1793   £485.15.11 [total] £565.3.4
d) part of £309.9.11 bond due Dec. 1, 1793   £20.12.8
   due for interest on said bond to Dec. 1, 1793   £23.9.10   [total] £44.2.6
   interest due on £79.7.5 + £20.12.8 from Dec. 1, 1793 "until paid"
[signed] B Harwood Apr. 23, 1793; [on back] Apr. 24, 1794 Wm Marbury, D agent, certifys the bond of £1,190.9.9 dated Jun. 19, 1792 was for real & personal property of Principio Company and bond of £309.9.11 dated Jun. 23, 1792 was for personal property of Nottingham Company.

Sales of Confiscated Land

678. Oct. 11, 1794 Treasury Office: a list of monies due on the Books of Old Arrers received and paid to the Office in behalf of several people "herein after named" by Mr. Lewis Beard, Collector of Arrears for Salisbury Dist. & Morgan Dist:

Jun. 30, 1794 paid in behalf of David Craig for confiscated property purchased £218.7

Jun. 30, 1794 paid in behalf of David Craig for confiscated property purchased £220.4.11

Jun. 30, 1794 paid in behalf of Conrad Brem for confiscated property purchased £97.14.9

Jun. 30, 1794 paid in behalf of David Woodson for confiscated property purchased £86.18.4

Jun. 30, 1794 paid in behalf of Jonathan Hampton, sheriff of Rutherford Co, £57.14.7

Jun. 30, 1794 paid in behalf of Jacob [Hufman ? hole in page]man for confiscated property sold £26.16.8

Jun. 30, 1794 paid in behalf of Peter Faust for confiscated property sold £25.2.7

[total] £732.18.10 - Mr. Beard (commissioner on £732.18.10 due) at 8% £58.12.8 = £674.6.2

Oct. 11, 1794 Lewis Beard, Collector of Arrears for Salisbury & Morgan Dists, swears the above is "just", [signed] Wm Duffy, clk Treasy.

Oct. 11, 1794 Treasury Office: received of John Haywood, public Treasurer, £58.12.8 in full of above commissions, [signed] Ls Beard, Col. Arrears.

679. State of North Carolina in account with John Hawks:

a) to 14 certificates Nos. 366, 111, 1871, 1819, 265, 266, 919, 971, 678,
247, 467, 905, 1766, & 466 totaling £132.0.6 delivered herewith in payment of this account £131.13.6
to balance due the State £0.6.6 [total] £132.0

b) by 4 years rent of a "plantation" formerly Timothy Clear decd's property at £33 per ac being the price it was rented for at public vendue £132

"Er. Esd." John Hawks New Bern Apr. 9, 1783 sworn before Thos Sitgreaves, JP

State of North Carolina in account with John Hawks:

c) to 14 certificates Nos. 366, 111, 1871, 1819, 265, 266, 919, 971, 678, 247, 467, 905, 1766, & 466 totaling £131.13.6 delivered herewith in payment of this account £131.13.6
by 4 years rent of a "plantation" formerly Timothy Clear decd's property at £33 per ac being the price it was rented for at public vendue £132

"Er. Esd." John Hawks New Bern Apr. 9, 1783 sworn before Thos Sitgreaves, JP

[the following added] to amount of certificates brought down £131,13.6

to balance due the State £0.6.6 [total] £132

[on back] entered Jun. 23, 1794 R C Comptr, examined.

680. Dec. 29, 1785 in the House of Commons: Resolved that the final settlement certificates issued by John Pearce, auditors certificates, county commissioners, & comptrollers certificates be received by the present Commissioner of Confiscated Property for property hereafter sold which shall be allowed by them in their "setlements". [signed] Richd Dobbs Spaight, S C; "by order" J Hunt, clk; "by order" J Haywood, clk; Dec. 29, 1785 concur in Senate [signed] Alex Martin; [on back] "final settlement certificates to be recd. for confiscated property"

681. Sept. 20, 1786 Jesse McClendon, Coleby Randle, & James Tindal to Gov. Richard Caswell; a bond for £1,001; condition McClendon, Randle, & Tindal to pay Charles Bruce, Commissioner of Confiscated Property, £500.10 in 12 months. [signed] [Jesse McClendon, Coalbe Randle, & James Tindel--all lined out]; witness Edmd Lilly jr & Cary Pritchard; [on back] Mar. 19, 1788 received £443.14 Charles Bruce; Sept. 23, 1788 received £47 C Bruce; Mar. 21, 1789 received £56.16.5 [no name].

682. grants sent to Col. Glasgow by Probate [sic] Collier Jan. 22, 1787:

a) 210 for Rowan Co and 16 for Edgecomb Co "confiscated land" [total] 226

b) remaining now in the Office at Kingston:

Rowan	157	Wayne	103
Gates	19	Duplin	7
Anson	31	Bladen	7

Sales of Confiscated Land

Washington 77
Dobbs 14
Sampson 15 [written over 18]
[total] 313

Guilford 8
Bertie 8
Currituct 6
New Hanover 3
Burke 1
Pitt 1 [total] 144

[grand total] 313 + 144 = 457
[signed] Winston Caswell [Gov. Richard Caswell's secretary]

683. Received Jun. 28, 1787 for the Secretary's Office the following grants for Confiscated Property:

Thos Clark 54 ac
Thos Clark 81 ac
Thos Clark 100 ac
Thos Clark 30 ac
Thos Clark 30 ac
Thos Clark 174 ac
Thos Clark 64 ac

John Alcorn 141 ac
James Mulloy 220 ac
James Mulloy 202 ac
Robert Shaw 223 ac
Josiah Watts 1 ac
William Dick 156 ac
William Oneal 200 ac [signed] Jas Mulloy

684. A list of [certificates] numbers and amounts [on two sides of a small sheet]:

1941 [blank]
1942 & 1943 £23.17
48 £1.8
1945 & 1946 £1.7.1
59 £63.15.8
806 £30.19
257 £39.12
1777 £74.8
79 £504.2

256 £37.10
1199 £9.4
922 £9.4.6
1779 £170.19
31 £1.16.4
250 £39.9
814 £10.14
1947 £4.7.4
960 £14.12

854 £13.14
1597 £17.5
867 £66.13
73 £3.1
973 £14.12.6
149 £87.14.2
[total on
front of sheet] £1,240.5.9

[on back of sheet]:

927 £11.5
987 £6.1.6
1668 £32.3.6
737 £162
1124 £15
1770 £127.11.6
1920 £9.2
817 £262.11
83 £46.6

1222 £162.0
1217 £51.12.10
218 £49.19
1694 £13.10
81 £51.9
898 £30.7.7
1716 £22.10
1713 £1.2.6
1686 £18.0

963 £14.12.6
1682 £15.15
1711 £3.16.6
1701 £8.6.6
1661 £28
1703 £7.17.6
1664 £18
943 £24.7.6
1659 £84.0

[total] £2,517.12.8 "Oneal" No. 6 [Note: there was Oneal who was a colonel in Orange Co.]

685. "No. 3" Thos Burk esq £1,105.5 specie:

No. 802 £816.10.9
No. 735 £240
No. 698 £5.10   [total]
No. 192 £9
[total] £1,071.0.9   [total]

£1106
- £1071.0.9
£ 34.19.3
- £ 25.11
£   9.8.3

No. 1214 £25.11
No. 1076 £7.3
No. 291 £1.12 [total] 1,105

Sales of Confiscated Land

686. specie certificates received of Col. Moore   £3,900.14.5   "No. 8"
List of specie certificates:

£1150.12.0	£127.16.0	£5.9	£18.6
£582.17.4	£82.18.3	£5.9	£26.8
£575.15.8	£39.15.0	£12.0	£6.1.6
£426.12.0	£22.8.8	£20.13.6 [total]	£3,900.14.5
£418.13.4	£24.10.8	£14.12.6	
£316.6.5	£4.8.1	£19.2.6	

687. received of John Humphries on account of Confiscated Property "lislee" [or a squiggle]; [probably in Wake Co].

688. Taylor No. 4   £482.6.4

No. 523 $14 £5.12	No. 187 $261 3/8 £104.10.8
No. 649 £6.2	No. 140 [written over 240] $138 £55.4
No. 734 £28.0	No. 446 £4.15
No. 392 £2.6	No. 1188 £43.0
No. 797 $13 1/8 £5.5	No. 1187 £61.4
No. 540 $13 6/8 £5.10	[total] £435.1
No. 541 £10.0	No. 16, 125, & 70 £46.7
No. 108 $261 3/8 £104.10.8	[total] £482.6

689. Interest received on bonds taken for confiscated property sold:

to Saml McDill £22.19	Geo Parks £2.18.1
Roddy Hanna £38.6.8	John Hopkins £7.5.2
Thos Clark £24.16.4	John Brevard £144.12
Edward Yarborough £69.11.3	Thomas Archor £8.9.8 [subtotal] £922.15.7
Anthony Sharpe £11.14.4	William Kendal &
James Bell £29.17.10	Mark Allen £30.14
Patrick Boggan £6.6	Richard Tindal £163.14.2
John Armstrong £195.4	Peter Brown £0.17.1
Will Saunders £110.7	[total] £918.0.10
Thos Clark £22.2.1	Daniel McKindley £51.18
Ro Hunter Martin £2.1	[grand total] £972.18.10
William Wood £26.11.2	

to cash received for Aulding Moor for rent of ferry   £3.0

690. [no date] Sub committee on Revenue No. 3 to examine accounts of Commissioners of Confiscated Property, their sales produce, & settlements.   Messrs. W Jones, B Williams, Skinner, Barnes, & J P Williams.

Salisbury	C Bruce	£17,901.15.11
Edenton	Murfree	£12,332.9.3
Hillsborough	Lytle	£19,012.18.11
Wilmington	McRee	£26,466.1.10 [total] £75,713.5.11

691. Received of Benjamin Sheppard, esq Commissioner of Confiscated Property:

John Craddock £32	Peter Bacot £32
John Daves £40	Patrick Campbell £120
John Patten £40	Samuel Chapman £40
John Craddock £48	William Powell £32
Thomas Dudley £40	David Hall £32
John Vance £16	Miles Knight £8
Peter Bacot £60	[total £664--lined out]
Peter Bacot 100	[on back] £664.16 [sic]

Sales of Confiscated Land

[probably Wilmington Dist]

692. Col. William Oneal "Dr" to Negroes £2,821
    received in certificates   - £2,528.14.9
                [total]   £   292.5.3

No. 1073 £24.3	No. 40 £10.12	No. 295 £7.16
No. 879 £20	No. 43 £6.12	No. 255 £4.2
No. 206 £9.8	No. 284 £13.1	No. 212 £8.16
No. 1215 £3.12	[or 254]	No. 225 £5
No. 299 £4.8	No. 296 £6.12	[No. 297 £6.19--lined out]
No. 348 £4.7	No. 44 £1.6	No. 272 £1.5
No. 726 £9.6	No. 9 £3	[subtotal] £283.12
No. 927 £6.0	No. 710 £4.19	No. 227 £4
No. 913 £6	No. 341 £4.4	No. 209 £1.10
No. 199 £10.6	No. 340 £4.16	No. 374 £1.10
No. 41 £6.12	No. 342 £13.1	No. 236 £0.9
No. 43 £6.8	No. 56 £5.1	[total] £291.1 "10½ bol"
No. 13 £9	No. 343 £9.5	"add" No. 228 £1.8
No. 42 £10.4	No. 219 £9.14	[total] £292.9
No. 15 £8.12	No. 193 £3.0	
No. 46 £3.0	No. 202 £4.12	
	No. 105 £6.3	

288.16 + 7.9 + 1.8 = 297.13   [it's not clear if this applies to the above]
[on back] £297.13 "Oneal"; "Col. Oneal in this bundle £292.9"

693. [no commissioner's name for following list; evidently the number of certificate and date certificate was received; some of these are also in Treasurer & Comptroller's Military Papers vol. 3 page 105 folio 4 and page 106 folio 1 under "certificates drawn by Timothy McCarthy out of Office of Comm. to liquidate accounts of Continental Line of NC"]
No. 99 John Kingsborough £500 No. 15, 1785
No. 100 John Kingsborough £500 Nov. 15, 1785
No. 98 John Kingsborough £690 Nov. 15, 1785
No. 128 Robert Raiford £300 May 22, 1780
No. 1170 David Aitkins £170.15.6 Nov. 12, 1785
No. 1174 Robt Bradly £170.15.6 Nov. 12, 1785
No. 1165 William Stewart £170.15.6 Nov. 12, 1785
No. 741 Thomas Skepton £138.9.3 Jan. 1, 1786
No. 333 Charles Grimsley £139.19.6 Jan. 1, 1786
No. 334 Andrew Pool £139.19.6 Jan. 1, 1786
No. 335 Andrew Andrews £139.19.6 Jan. 1, 1786
No. 751 Alexander Daugharty £72.18.0 Jan. 1, 1786
No. 153 Thomas Cullas £139.5.6 Jan. 1, 1786
No. 225 Benja Willis £139.5.6 Jan. 1, 1786
No. 738 James Britt £138.19.3 Jan. 1, 1786
No. 161 George Wilkins £80.8 Jan. 1, 1786
No. 162 Solomon Willis £80.8 Jan. 1, 1786
No. 742 Samuel Water £138.19.3 Jan. 1, 1786
No. 12 William Gouch £21.19.8 Jan. 1, 1786
No. 489 Etheldred Woodam £138.19.3 Oct. 5, 1786
No. 490 Francis Woodruff £138.19.3 Oct. 5, 1786
No. 491 Abner Halbe £139.0.3 Oct. 5, 1786
No. 404 Edward Smythick £42.14.1 Oct. 5, 1786

Sales of Confiscated Land

No. 1141 Ambrose Towle £15.11.11 Oct. 5, 1786
No. 492 Jesse Teel [or Jeil] £139.0.3 "do"

694. A list of notes taken Feb. 1783 for tory property rented etc not collected and a doubt arising whether "they ought on account" of the law passed next session of General Assembly:

Mickel Wallar £1.10
Henry Agener £2.0
Lenerd Crider £2.0.6
William Smitern £3.0
Conruth Frock £5.12
John Labwoder £1.5
Andray Brown £1.10
Peter Littel £2.0
 [subtotal] £18.17.6

Volenten Berd £12.0
Agebl Kerr £7.0.6
Roberd Hays £25.4
Edmen Yarbery £9.0
Mr. Kerr £31.5
Mr. M Diel £1.12
John Nelsson £33.6.2
      [total] £138.6.2

[on back] "No. 3" [Evidently this is voucher number 3 from Rowan County; see Nos 556 and 557 above.]

695. State of North Carolina in account with Jona Banks, Thomas Harvey, & John Richardson, commissioners:
a) Feb. 1, 1780   to paper £8.0
                commissions on sales £3,086.2.11
                sheriff's "do"   £771.16.0
        cash paid to Alexr. McClain on Miles Gale's account £459.17.6
                balance due £47,109.9.7   [total] £51,435.6.0
        by half amount of sales of William McCormeck's estate £51,435.6
                "by balance per contra" £47,109.9.7

b) Jun. 19, 1780 to commissions on £496.12.10--£29.15.11
                sheriff's commissions £12.8.3
                balance £454.7.10   [total] £496.12
                by account of sales of John Donlop's estate £496.12
                "ball. per contra" £454.7.10
[on back]   copy of sales of John Dunlop & Wm McCormick's estates; "account current".

696. List of certificates to Archd Lytle, Commissioner of Confiscated Property [date of certificate, amount, and interest--when indicated]:
696A. Reason Rickels   dated Aug. 1, 1783 £43.3.6
Henry Hill   dated Aug. 1, 1783 £31.6.4
"No. 2" Peter Piland   dated Aug. 1, 1783 £30.7.9
Milchar Tar   dates Aug. 1, 1783 £29.11.5
Maltar Turner   dated Aug. 1, 1783 £29.11.15
Jno Elliot   dated Aug. 1, 1783 £53.14.8
Jacob Watson   dated Aug. 1, 1783 £92.4
Jno Mires   dated Aug. 1, 1783 £84.17.10
Jno Reddin   dated Aug. 1, 1783 £61.3.10
Jams. Fogarty   dated Aug. 1, 1783 £79.10.6
Wm Sinklair   dated Aug. 1, 1783 £17.10.1
Asse Jenkins   dated Aug. 1, 1783 £77.14
Corns Ryan   dated Aug. 1, 1783 £69.12.9
Howel Herrod   dated Aug. 1, 1783 £29.11.5
Jno Sullivant   dated Aug. 1, 1783 £42.12
Davis Benton   dated Aug. 1, 1783 £29.11.5
Jas Rowland   dated Aug. 1, 1783 £13.15.2

Sales of Confiscated Land

Jas Rowland   dated Aug. 1, 1783 £13.14.1 [turned in] by Wm Lytle
Joel Lewis   dated Aug. 1, 1783 £437.8.9
[total]   £1,267.1.11 + interest   £209.0.11 = £1,476.2.10

696B. Moses McWhorter   dated Sept. 3, 1783 £29.4 + interest £3.17.4
Moses McWhorter   dated Mar. 15, 1784 £8 + interest £1.0
Robt March   dated £4.10 + interest £1.0
George Morgan   dated Jun. 25, 1782 £319.0 + interest £73.6.3
Jno Newton   dated "Mar. 16" £11.1 + interest £1.14.4
Jams Hammond   dated "Aug. 28" £11.17 + interest £2.11.6
Hezekiah Childs   dated Jun. 10, 1785 £11.5 + interest £0.16.10
Andw McBride   dated Aug. 1, 1783 £22.15.11 + interest £3.15.2
William Clark   dated Aug. 1, 1783 £22.15.10 + interest £3.15.2
William Clark   dated Aug. 1, 1783 £22.15.10 + interest £3.15.2
[subtotal] principal £1,939.7.6 + interest £95.11.9
Ben Debow   dated Jun. 6, 1784 £1.12 + interest £0.4
Thos Roundtree   dated Dec. 12, 1781 £2.6.3 + interest £0.11.6
Jams Laughter   dated Sept. 17, 1783 £7.18 + interest £1.3.10
Wm Nells   dated Apr. 19, 1782 £10.10.8 + interest £1.5.2
Jno Wallace   dated Jun. 14, 1786 £40.10 + interest [blank]
Edward Burke   dated Sept. 22, 1784 £56.8 + interest £5.7.1
Nathan Blackburn   dated "Jun. 5" £9.2 + interest £1.1
Jno Dauley   dated "Aug. 23" £9.2 + interest £1.0
Nicholas Jones   dated Sept. 4, 1783 £11.2 + interest £1.15.4
David Cochran   dated Sept. 21, 1784 £3.10 + interest £7.0
Wm Rhoads   dated Aug. 20, 1783 £2.13.4 + interest £7.6
Phillip Allen   dated Feb. 14, 1782 £2.4 + interest £11.0
Thos Williams   dated Apr. 17, 1786 £15.5 + interest [blank]
Nicholas Bechell   dated Jun. 20, 1782 £12.0 + interest £2.17.4 [turned in] by Wm Lytle
James Kerby   dated Aug. 20, 1783 £9.3 + interest £1.9.4 [turned in] by Wm Lytle
Henry Kelly   dated Apr. 10, 1784 £9.2 + interest £1.2
George Michele   dated Aug. 8, 1783 £13.10 + interest £14.4
Daniel Parker   dated Aug. 20, 1783 £9.3 + interest £1.9.4
Joseph Griffin   dated Sept. 9, 1783 £9.0 + interest £1.8
Daniel Banch   dated Oct. 1, 1783 £13.10 + interest £2.0.5
James Gunter   dated Aug. 20, 1783 £9.3 + interest £1.9.4
Timothy Landrum   dated Sept. 1, 1784 £20.5 + interest £1.18.2
Thos Brummage   dated Aug. 31, 1784 £20.5 + interest £2.0
Andw Harrison   dated Sept. 1, 1784 £20.5 + interest £1.18.2
[total] £2,256.16.9 + interest £128.1.7 = £2,384.18.4   "Wm Lytle"

696C. Jno McVay   dated Aug. 1, 1783 £17.11.4
Drury Hyrne   dated Aug. 1, 1783 £38.9
Jno Baker   dated Aug. 1, 1783 £13.3.10
Peter Rheme   dated Aug. 1, 1783 £97.16.6
Theops. Pevis [or Purce]   dated Aug. 1, 1783 £24.6.6 [turned in] by "sundries"
Wm Harris dated Aug. 1, 1783 £30.7.9
Wm Steel dated Aug. 1, 1783 £33.8.9
Jno Rice   dated Aug. 1, 1783 £18.14.11
Thomas Parks   dated Aug. 1, 1783 £30.7.9
Joseph Aldrige   dated Aug. 1, 1783 £30.7.9
[subtotal] principal £333.14.1 + interest £55.4.3

Mathew Cates   dated Aug. 1, 1783 £80.13.3
Morris Richards   dated Aug. 1, 1783 £30.7.9
Jno McKoy   dated Aug. 1, 1783 £131.2.4
Wm Brickly   dated Aug. 1, 1783 £19.4.6
Ephm Etherige   dated Aug. 1, 1783 £19.4.3
Jno Henry   dated Aug. 1, 1783 £131.2.4
Jos McAllister   dated Aug. 1, 1783 £38.4.6
Jos McAllister   dated Aug. 1, 1783 £38.4.5
Jno Wood   dated Aug. 1, 1783 £30.8.2
Geo Wilky   dated Aug. 1, 1783 £30.7.9
Jno Montgomery   dated Aug. 1, 1783 £30.7.9
Jno Mitchel   dated Aug. 1, 1783 £19.4.6
Thos Allen   dated Aug. 1, 1783 £20.17.1
Jams Johnston   dated Aug. 1, 1783 £19.19
Wm Jackson   dated Aug. 1, 1783 £26.21 [turned in] by "sundries"
Jno Scarf   dated Aug. 1, 1783 £133.2.6
Hudson Ray   dated Aug. 1, 1783 £9.2 + interest £9.9.9
Wm Hilton   dated Aug. 1, 1783 £135.11.3
Math McAlley   dated Aug. 1, 1783 £181.17.1
Thos Padon   dated Aug. 1, 1783 £79.7.6 + interest £0.8.6
Jno Baily   dated Aug. 1, 1783 £31.6.4
Jno Cavan   dated Aug. 1, 1783 £31.6.4
Jacob Steelwell   dated Aug. 1, 1783 £46.8.4
Wm Jackson   dated Aug. 1, 1783 £30.8.2
Jno Forge   dated Aug. 1, 1783 £31.6.4
Jams Dyell   dated Aug. 1, 1783 £116.18.9
Aaron Springfield   dated Aug. 1, 1783 £31.6.4
Ben Hestor   dated Aug. 1, 1783 £31.6.4
Tew [or Lew] Bogsby   dated Aug. 1, 1783 £61.3
Richd Bradley   dated Aug. 1, 1783 £23.0
Jams Brisly   dated Aug. 1, 1783 £56.14.6
"short cast £20"
[total principal] £1,675.14.8 + £2,719.12.5 = £4,395.7.1
[total interest]   £276.19.8 + £55.3.11 = £332.3.11
[grand total]   £4,727.11.0

696D. Peter Mallet   dated Nov. 30, 1781 £439.4 + interest £116.11
Daniel McCahan   dated Aug. 10, 1782 £203.7 + interest £32.10.8
Jno Griffen   dated Apr. 1786 £317.7.5 + [blank]
Jno. Campbell   dated Aug. 20, 1783 £86.0 + interest £13.15.1
Anthy Staford   dated "Jun. 10" £55.19 + interest £9.7.8
Jno Coble   dated "Oct. 1" £4.0 + interest £0.12.2
Tobia Smith   dated "Jun. 10" £20.9 + interest £3.6
James Thompson   dated "Aug. 20" £13.10 + interest £2.2.6
Joseph Dickson   dated Mar. 3, 1784 £114.17.6 + interest £14.4.1
Dudley Rundles   dated Jan. 10, 1785 £9.16.2 + interest £3.10
Wm Newcam   dated Jun. 12, 1783 £11.7.6 + interest £1.18.10
Jas McAllister   dated "Aug. 20" £6.0 + interest £0.18.2
Jno Davis   dated Jan. 10, 1785 £9.12 + interest £0.4
James Hughes   dated Jan. 10, 1785 £9.12 + interest £0.4
Nathl Read   dated Jan. 10, 1785 £9.12 + interest £0.4 [turned in] by "sundries"
Owen Lee   dated Jan. 10, 1785 £9.12 + interest £0.4 [turned in] by "sundries"

Sales of Confiscated Land

[last four] "short in interest £0.45.4"
Rl Allison   dated Apr. 22, 1784 £9.0 + interest £1.3
Wm Warton   dated Oct. 1, 1783 £14.8 + interest £2.3.4   "£0.9.4 too much"
Laurce Friddle   dated "Apr. 30" £10.14 + interest £2.0
Jno McDonnald   dated "Jun. 10" £13.10 + interest £23.10
Elic McDonnald   dated "Jun. 10" £48.0 + interest £8.13
Thos Ragan   dated Aug. 23, 1784 £9.2 + interest £0.18.2
Stephin Potts   dated Sept. 5, 1783 £48.0 + interest £8.3.8   "£0.7 too much"
Jos Dickson   dated Sept. 26, 1781 £18.15 + interest £5.2
James Hugans   dated Sept. 25, 1782 £49.0.6 + interest £10.10
Ehram Tarr   dated "Jul. 23" £23.4 + interest £5.3.3   [turned in] "by £123.4" [sic]
Wm Hunt   dated Aug. 27, 1783 £114.0 + interest £16.8   "£0.26.7 short"
Bernd Cabe   dated "Jun. 10" £110.11.4 + interest £18.6   "£0.19 short"
Absm Cleveland   dated "Jun. 19" £47.7.4 + interest £7.16.9
Geo Vogleman   dated Aug. 27, 1782 £39.3.10 + interest £8.12.3
Jno McClain   dated "Dec. 25" [written over Sept.] £11.2 + interest £2.8
Jno Hawkins   dated Oct. 3, 1784 £84.5 + interest £7.13.8
Nathan Horneday   dated Oct. 1, 1783 £13.13 + interest £2.1
Jno Groves   dated Sept. 24, 1784 £8.6.6 + interest £0.15
[total] principal £6,719.16.1 + interest £307.7.1 = £7.27.3.2   "No. 2"

697. "bond of County Commissioners of Confiscated Property in the different counties"; "1782"--both written on a form letter [not signed] dated Jan. 1, 1793 from the Comptroller to revenue receiving officers to pay accounts once per year.

698. Received of James Roberts on account of his bond given for confiscated property £93.13.4   "listed Jan." [on one side of a sheet and the following is on the other side:]
W Searcy   £38 + £2.5.7 interest
A Faodes [or Taodes]   £3.6.8 + £1.4.8 interest
J Rooks   £9.4 + £4.4 interest
O Cox   £3.0 + £0.15 interest
W Elred   £11.4 + £4.0 interest
J Bablock   £5.17 + £1.18.6 interest
J Mullen   £11.5 + £2.6 interest
[the following totals lined out:]
£81.16.8 principal + £16.13.9 interest = £98.10.5 - "total" £93.19.1 =   £4.17.1 - £4.11.4 = £0.5.9

HENRY EUSTACE McCULLOCH folder
699. Oct. 19, 1802 Micajah Ferril (of Wake Co) to brother & friend William Ferril (same); power of attorney to "do my business" relating to a tract on Alebeys Cr; known as Lewis Howell's tract; mortgaged by said [? hole in page] Howell to [sic] Henry Eustis McCulloh and sold by Howell to Alexr Clark whose heirs sold to Micajah Ferril and Micajah has "settled with the commissioners of the University" for said land; William Ferril is to get a deed from the commissioners for Micajah due to an act of Assembly; Micajah (a) assigns one deed to James Wood for 71 ac of said tract on N side of Flat Rock Br and (b) assigns to George Carrington 86 ac the remainder of the tract which Micajah has already sold and William Ferril is to deed the land.   Signed Micajah Ferel. Witness James Latta.

700. Jan. 29, 1805 Nicholas Iler (of Mecklenburg Co) to George McCulloh (of Rowan Co); power of attorney to receive from Adlai Osborne, agent & commissioner for trustees of University of North Carolina, money due Nicholas. Signed Nicholes Iler. Witness Ls Beard.

Sales of Confiscated Land

701. Jan. 30, 1805 Thomas Weer (of Mecklenburg Co) to George McCulloh (of Rowan Co); power of attorney to receive form Adlai Osborne, agent & commissioner for trustees of University of North Carolina, money due to Thomas. Signed Thomas Weir. Witness Ls Beard.

702. Apr. 23, 1805 George Nicholson (of Mecklenburg Co) to George McCulloh (of Rowan Co); power of attorney to receive from Adlai Osborne, agent & commissioner for trustees of University of North Carolina, money due to George. Signed George Nickelson [or Nickeson]. Witness Ls Beard.

703. Jun. 25, 1809 Jacob Grans (of Orange Co) to Archibald D Murphey (same); power of attorney to receive from North Carolina's Treasurer the money paid by me to the trustees of University of North Carolina for land originally Henry E McCulloh's and by him sold to me, but no deed was made, so land was confiscated and the money Jacob paid [to the trustees] went from the trustees to the Treasurer; this case falls under Court of Conference case of [George] McCulloh vs [Richard] Ray [see North Carolina Reports vol. 1 p. 510-513]. Signed Jacob Grans [in german]. Witness R Wood, Malacay Cerley, & John Noe; [on back] amount of principal £154.10 + interest £119 paid to Treasurer by Gain Alves, treasurer of University of North Carolina, being the money Jacob Grans paid to said treasurer for land "supposed" to be confiscated but falls under the case of McCulloh & Ray decided by Court of Conference £165.19.0 + interest from Apr. 5, 1805 £42.6.1 = £208.5.1.
Jul. 17, 1809 Received from John Haywood, Public Treasurer, £208.5.1 for Jacob Grans. Signed A D Murphey, attorney for Jacob Grans.

704. Jul. 27, 1796 received of Geo Nicholson £19.15 in part of his bond to trustees of University. Signed Ad Osborn, com. & attorney.

705. Jan. 23, 1797 received of Willm Flannegan £41.4 principal + £0.24.8 interest of his bond to trustees of University of North Carolina. Signed Ad Osborn.

706. Jul. 1801 received of Geo Nicholson £19.15 + £0.55.6 interest; balance of his bond to the trustees. Signed Ad Osborn.

707. Jul. 20, 1801 received of Maycager Ferrell £35 in two different payments due to Henry Ustes McColloh by mortgage deed made by Howell to said McCulloch "which I think said Ferrell ought to have the prefference of Compromes after paying the balance". Signed Wm Shepperd, comr. Witness Wm Ferrell.

708. Trustees vs. Wm Flannigan: Jul. 26, 1803 received £50 in part of judgment. Signed Ad Osborn, attorney for trustees. £50 paid in 100 d[hole in page] S C Bank No. 242.

709. Jul. 29, 1803 received from Wm Fleneken £4.5.5 cost in the suit of the trustees against him. Signed Isaac Alexander, attorney.

710. Oct. 27, 1803 received of William Flennegon $88 in part of execution in suit of Trustees vs William Flannigan. Signed Wm Beaty, shff.

711. Jan. 25, 1804 received of William Flanigan £22.16.7 balance in full of judgment in suit of Trustees vs Wm Flanigan. Signed Wm Beaty, shff.

712. Aug. 17, 1805 received of Thomas Bingham £0.45 being my fees and commission in an execution [due to suit] of Trustees of University vs. said Bingham. Signed J Lane, shff.

713. Payments made to Thomas Bingham (of Randolph Co) due to an act of Assembly entitled "An act to relieve certain inhabitants of Mecklenburg Co & other citizens of the State" [see Laws of North Carolina Dec. 1794 Chapt. 3, p. 2-3]:
interest on £60.9.6 from May 1797   £28.18

Sales of Confiscated Land

interest on cost of suit   £2.3.6
interest on amount shff. received for coms.   £2.18
[principal]   £60.9.6
"bill of costs"   £8.1.8
attos. fees for defendant   £5.0
clerk for copy of record   £0.11.0   [total] £108.1.8 paid this day out of North Carolina treasury to Thomas Bingham (of Randolph Co). Apr. 1805 [signed] John Haywood.
[no date] Thomas Bingham (of Randolph Co) acknowledges he received £108.1.8 from John Haywood. [signed] Thomas Bingham's mark. Witness H Branson.

714. Payments made to George McCulloch, esq (of Rowan Co), attorney of George Nicholson (of Mecklenburg Co) due to an act of Assembly entitled "An act to relieve certain inhabitants of Mecklenbury Co & other citizens of the State":
interest on £19.5.0 from Jul. 1796   £10.5.2
interest on £22.10.6 from Jul. 1801   £5.6
[total principal] £41.15.6 + [total interest] £15.11.2 = £57.6.8
Jun. 8, 1805 paid £57.6.8 this day to George McCulloch, esq, attorney of George Nicholson.   [signed] John Haywood, treasurer.
[no date] George McCulloch (of Rowan Co), attorney of George Nicholson (of Mecklenburg Co), acknowledges he received the money.   [signed] G McCulloh. Witness B W Goodman [hole in page].

715. Payments to Wm Flannaken (of Mecklenburg Co) due to an act of Assembly entitled "An act to relieve certain inhabitants of Mecklenburg Co & other citizens of the State":
principal £42.8.8 + interest [since] Jan. 23, 1797   £21.12.6
principal £50.0 + interest [since] Jul. 26, 1803   £5.18.9
principal £44.0 + interest [since] Oct. 27, 1803   £4.9.10
principal £22.16.7 + interest [since] Jan. 25, 1804   £2.0. [hole in page]
principal £4.5.5 + interest [since] Jul. 29, 1803   £0.10
[total]   £198.1.10
Jul. 18, 1805 paid £198.1.10 this day to William Flannakin (of Mecklenburg Co). [signed] John Haywood, public treasurer.
[no date] William Flannakin (of Mecklenburg Co) acknowledges he received £198.1.10. [signed] Wm Flenniken. Witness Will White.

716. Payments to Obediah Green (of Orange Co) through his attorney John Haywood jr (of Franklin Co) due to an act of Assembly entitled "An act to relieve certain inhabitants of Mecklenburg Co & other citizens of the State":
principal   £26.18.3
interest from Aug. 30, 1799 to Sept. 30, 1805   £10.4.3
principal   £26.18.3
interest from Aug. 30, 1799 to Sept. 30, 1805   £10.4.3
principal   £26.18.3
interest from Aug. 30, 1799 to Sept. 30, 1805   £10.4.3
principal   £23.18.8
interest from May 1, 1797 to Sept. 30, 1805   £11.17.10   [total]   £110.1.6
Oct. 1805 paid £110.1.6 "today" to John Haywood jr.   [signed] John Haywood, public treasurer.
[no date] John Haywood (of Franklin Co) acknowledges receipt of the money. [signed] J Haywood. Witness [none].

717. Payments made to Micajah Ferrell (of Wake Co) due to an act of Assembly entitled "An act to relieve inhabitants of Mecklenburg Co & other citizens of the State":
interest on £35 from Jul. 20, 180[hole in page] to Dec. 3, 1805   £9.3.9
[total]   £35 + £9.3.9 = £44.3.9
Dec. 3, 1805 paid £44.3.9 today to Micajah Ferrell. [signed] John Haywood, public treasurer.

Sales of Confiscated Land

[no date] Micajah Ferrell acknowledges receipt of the money. [signed] Micajor Fearell by his attorney W Fearell. Witness Garvin Alves.

718. a bond May 1, 1796 in Orange Co by Obediah Green & Nicholas Holt to trustees of University of North Carolina; bond for £47.17.4; condition: Obediah & Nicholas to pay trustees £23.18.8 by May 1, 1797. [signed--cut off the page]. Witness [hole in page] Shepperd.

719. a bond May 1, 1786 in Orange Co by Obediah Green & Nicholas Holt to trustees of University of North Carolina; bond for £47.17.4; condition: Obediah & Nicholas to pay trustees £23.18.4 by May 1, 1799. [signed] Obed Green & Nicholas Holt's mark "H". Witness H Shepperd; [on back] Hillsboro May 31, 1799 received of Joseph Clendenning £26.18.3 [signed] Gavin Alves, treasurer; interest on £26.18.3 from May 31, 1799 to Sept. 30, 1805 is £10.4.3.

720. a bond May 1, 1786 in Orange Co by Obediah Green & Nicholas Holt to trustees of University of North Carolina; bond for £47.17.4; condition: Obediah & Nicholas to pay trustees £23.18.4 by May 1, 1798 [sic]. [signed] Obed Green & Nicholas Hart's mark "H". Witness H Shepperd; [on back] Hillsboro May 31, [hole in page] received of Joseph Clendenning £8.19.5 and of Nicholas Holt £17.18.10 [total] £26.18.3. [signed] Gavin Alves, treasurer; interest on £26.18.3 from May 1799 to Sept. 30, 1805 is £10.4.3.

721. a writ: Apr. [hole in page], 1799 from Leonard Henderson, clerk of Hillsborough Dist. Superior Court, to Randolph Co sheriff to arrest Thomas Bingham & Nathaniel Steed to be brought to Hillsborough Dist. Superior Court on Oct. 6 "next" to answer a suit by trustees of University of North Carolina for £120.19.4 debt "to the damage of the trustees £60". [signed] Leo Henderson; issued Jul. 20, 1799
Writ returned to Hillsborough Court Oct. 1799 [signed] J Lane, sheriff.
Defendants attorney is William Norwood; case continued until Apr. 1800 and jury found a verdict for £120 "to be discharged" on payment of £60.9.6 with interest from May 1, 1797; the following writ issued: Apr. 6, 1800 from Leonard Henderson, clerk of Hillsborough Dist. Superior Court, to Randolph Co sheriff to collect £120.19 and £8.1.8 cost from Thomas Bingham & Nathaniel Steed. [signed] Leo Henderson; issued Jul. 10, 1800.
Fee bill & judgment £120.19.0 to be discharged on payment of £60.9.6 with inerest from May 1, 1797 "til paid".

bond & process	£0.14
determination	£0.18
execution	£0.5
tax	£0.10 [subtotal] £2.7
shff. Lane	£0.14.8
attorney fees	£5.0
[total]	£8.1.8

The foregoing writ returned Oct. 1800 with endorsement--"the money paid by the defendants to William Norwood since the execution issued". [signed] J Lane, shff
"a true copy" Samuel Benton, clerk Hillsborough Dist. Superior Court [signed] Apr. 4, 1805 S Benton by A B Bruce. "I was employed by Thomas Bingham in the foregoing suit" and received a fee of £5 from him. [signed] Wm Norwood.

722. Jun. 12, 1805 Mecklenburg Co Isaac Alexander, C M C, certifys that the trustees of the University by Adlai Osborn esq brought a suit against William Flenniken on a bond given by William Flenniken to Adlai Osborn, as attorney of said trustees, for £123.12 on Jul. 25, 1795 payable in three annual installments with interest from Jul. 25, 1796 when first installment was due; in Apr. term 1803, Adlai Osborn obtained a judgment against William Flenniken for £81.3.4 or the last two installments and £32.11 for 6 years 9 months interest; execution was returned satisfied to Jan. term 1804 and £4.12.11 cost. [signed] Isaac Alexander; [on back]:

judgment	£83.3.4
interest at time of judgment	£32.11.0
cost of suit	£4.12.11
sheriff's cost	£3.6.10

Sales of Confiscated Land

[total]   £121.14.1
first installment paid Jan. 23, 1797 - £42.8.8
[total owed]   £104.2.9
[see also #987 above]

723. Jun. 17, 1805 Lewis Hernedy swears that land sold by Henry Eustace McCulloch to Wm Bolton "were left for some time" by the heirs of Bolton intestate until the heirs agreed to sell to Obed Green; John [hole in page, maybe "Albright"] was the guardian of Bolton's heirs; Green delt with the trustees and gave a bond with consent of "said" Albright; bond and mortgage was with Obediah Green & Nicholas Holt; Green sold to Lewis Hernedy after paying all but £17 of the money; the £17 was paid and £12 was paid by Holt or a total of £23.18.8 "each"; Lewis Hernedy asks John Haywood to receive the funds due him. [signed] Lewis Hernedy's mark "H". Witness J Winslow & Wm Armstrong.

724. Sept. 15, 1785 surveyed 350 ac for John Willis; No. 1; on waters of Great Alimance Cr in Guilford Co; formerly Henry Eustace McCulloch's property; border: crosses a branch; includes Robt Smith's improvement; [signed] A Philips; sworn chain carriers Jesse McCalister & John McCalister; [on back] No. 123 £350.

725. Sept. 15, 1785 surveyed 332 ac for John Willis; No. 2; on waters of Great Alimance Cr in Guilford Co; formerly Henry Eustace McCulloch's property; border: William Shaver, Christian Isley, & tracts 3, 1, & 6; [signed] A Philips; sworn chain carriers Jesse McCalister & John McCalister; [on back] No. 115 £615.15.

726. Sept. 16, 1785 surveyed 262 ac for John Willis; No. 3; formerly Henry Eustace McCulloch's property; on both sides of Ceder Cr in Guilford Co; border: Thomas Hamilton jr's field and tracts 2 & 6; [signed] A Philips; sworn chain carriers Jesse McCalister & John McCalister; [on back] No. 117 £700.

727. Sept. 16, 1785 surveyed 374 ac for John Willis; No. 4; formerly Henry Eustace McCulloch's property; on both sides of Ceder Cr waters of Great Alimance Cr in Guilford Co; border: a post oak marked "H M", crosses a branch, crosses Hillsborough Road, joins tracts 2 & 5, & crosses Cedar Cr; includes Thomas Hamilton sr's improvement; [signed] A Philips; sworn chain carriers Jesse McCalister & John McCalister; [on back] No. 118 £1,065.

728. Sept. 16, 1785 surveyed 394 ac [plat & survey say 395 ac & "394 ac" on the back] for John Willis; No. 5; formerly Henry Eustace McCulloch's property; on waters of Alimance Cr in Guilford Co; border: a post oak corner of tract 6, joins a corner of tracts 3 & 4, & runs on a line of tract 4; [signed] A Philips; sworn chain carriers Jesse McCalister & John McCalister; [on back] No. 120 £1,400.

729. Sept. 16, 1785 surveyed 276 ac for John Willis; No. 6; formerly Henry Eustace McCulloch's property; on waters of Alimance Cr in Guilford Co; border: a corner post oak of tract 5, crosses a branch, & joins tracts 1, 3, & 5; [signed] A Philips; sworn chain carriers Jesse McCalister & John McCalister; [on back] No. 119 £725.

730. Nov. 17, 1785 surveyed 372 ac for James Williams; No. 10; formerly Henry Eustace McCulloch's property; on both sides of Back Cr in Guilford Co; border: tract 9, Orange Co line, & tract 5; [signed] A Philips; sworn chain carriers Jesse McCalister & William Pursell; [on back] No. 131 £728.

731. Nov. 18, 1785 surveyed 330 ac for James Williams; No. 11; formerly Henry Eustace McCulloch's property; on N side of Great Alimance Cr in Guilford Co; border: George Ingles, crosses Hermons Br, & Peter Low; [signed] A Philips; sworn chain carriers Jesse McCalister & William Pursell; [on back] No. 130 £741.

732. Nov. 19, 1785 surveyed 328 ac for James Willis; No. 12; formerly Henry Eustace McCulloch's property; on waters of Alimance Cr and both sides of Hermons Br in Guilford Cr; border: Findly [or Findley] Stewart, crosses "said" Stewarts Br, & Peter Low; [signed] A Philips; sworn chain carriers Jesse McCalister & William Pursell; [on back] No. 121 £920.

Sales of Confiscated Land

733. Dec. 6, 1785 surveyed 234 ac for John Willis; No. 14; formerly Henry Eustace McCulloch's property; on waters of Alimance Cr in Guilford Co; border: tracts 13 & 19 anc crosses a branch; includes where John McBride resides [or includes John McBride's improvement]; [signed] A Philips; sworn chain carriers William Cuningham & Sampson Lanier; [on back] No. 453; No. 128 £453.

734. Dec. 8, 1785 surveyed 324 ac for John Willis; No. 16; formerly Henry Eustace McCulloch's property; on both sides of Alimance Cr in Guilford Co; border: Hugh Shaw; [signed] A Philips; sworn chain carriers Sampson Lanier & William Cuningham; [on back] No. 125 £623 [Thomas Henderson--lined out] John Willis.

735. Dec. 8, 1785 surveyed 261 ac for John Willis; No. 17; formerly Henry Eustace McCulloch's property; on both sides of Great Alimance Cr in Guilford Co; border: tracts 16 & 18; [signed] A Philips; sworn chain carriers Sampson Lanier & William Cuningham; [on back] No. 116 £637; £667 [sic] John Willis.

736. Dec. 9, 1785 surveyed 256 ac for John Willis; No. 18; formerly Henry Eustace McCulloch's property; on S side of Great Alamance Cr and both sides of a fork thereof in Guilford Co; border: tract 17 and crosses a branch; [signed] A Philips; sworn chain carriers Sampson Lanier & Wiliam Cuningham; [on back] No. 122 £256; John Willis £587 [sic].

737. Jun. 20, 1786 sold 350 ac to John Willis for £850 [sic]; No. 1; [same as #724 above]; [signed] Charles Bruce, CSCPSD; sworn chain carriers Sampson Lanier & William Cuningham;.

738. Jun. 20, 1786 sold 332 ac to John Willis for £615 [sic]; No. 2; [same as #725 above] [signed] Charles Bruce, CSCPSD; sworn chain carriers Jesse McCalister & John McCalister.

739. Jun. 20, 1786 sold 262 ac to John Willis for £700; No. 3; [same as #726 above]; [signed] Charles Bruce, CSCPSD; sworn chain carriers Jesse McCalister & John McCalister.

740. Jun. 20, 1786 sold 374 ac to John Willis for £1,065; No. 4; [same as #727 above]; [signed] Charles Bruce, CSCPSD; sworn chain carriers Jesse McCalister & John McCalister.

741. Jun. 20, 1786 sold 394 ac to John Willis for £1,400; No. 5; [same as #728 above; [signed] Charles Bruce, CSCPSD; sworn chain carriers Jesse McCalister & John McCalister.

742. Jun. 20, 1786 sold 276 ac to John Willis for £725; No. 6; [same as #729 above]; [signed] Charles Bruce, CSCPSD; sworn chain carriers Jesse McCalister & John McCalister.

743. Jun. 20, 1786 sold 268 ac to James Hamilton for £801; No. 9; on both sides of Cedar Cr in Guilford Co; formerly Henry Eustace McCulloch's property; border: Martin Boon, Orange Co line, & tracts 4 & 5; [signed] Charles Bruce, CSCPSD; sworn chain carriers Jesse McCalister & William Pursell.

744. Jun. 20, 1786 sold 372 ac to James Williams for £741; No. 10; [same as #730 above]; [signed] Charles Bruce, CSCPSD; sworn chain carriers Jesse McCalister & William Pursell.

745. Jun. 20, 1786 sold 330 ac to James Williams for £728; No. 11; [same as #731 above]; [signed] Charles Bruce, CSCPSD; sworn chain carriers Jesse McCalister & William Pursell.

746. Jun. 20, 1786 sold 328 ac to John Willis for £920 ac; No. 12; [same as #732 above]; [signed] Charles Bruce, CSCPSD; sworn chain carriers Jesse McCalister & William Pursell.

747. Jun. 20, 1786 sold 234 ac to John Willis for £453; No. 14; [same as #733 above]; [signed] Charles Bruce, CSCPSD; sworn chain carriers William Cunningham & Sampson Lanier.

Sales of Confiscated Land

748. Jun. 20, 1786 sold 324 ac to John Willis for £623; No. 16; [same as #734 above]; [signed] Charles Bruce, CSCPSD; chain carriers [omitted].

749. Jun. 20, 1786 sold 261 ac to John Willis for £667; No. 17; [same as #735 above]; [signed] Charles Bruce, CSCPSD; sworn chain carriers Sampson Lanier & William Cunningham.

750. Jun. 20, 1786 sold 256 ac to John Willis for £687; No. 18; [same as #736 above]; [signed] Charles Bruce, CSCPSD; sworn chain carriers Sampson Lanier & William Cunningham.

751. Jun. 20, 1786 sold 240 ac to James Bell for £560; No. 22; formerly Henry Eustace McCulloch's property; on a fork of Alimance Cr in Guilford Co; [signed] Charles Bruce, CSCPSD; sworn chain carriers Sampson Lanier & William Cunningham.

752. Jun. 20, 1786 sold 204 ac to Rodda Hanna for £550.1; No. 23; formerly Henry Eustace McCulloch's property; on both forks of Alamance Cr in Guilford Co; border: tracts 22 & 24 and John Hardin; [signed] Charles Bruce, CSCPSD; chain carriers [omitted].

753. Jun. 20, 1786 sold 156 ac to William Dick for £513; No. 24; formerly Henry Eustace McCulloch's property; on Great Alamance Cr in Guilford Co; border: crosses Alamance Cr, a corner of tracts 22 & 23, & joins tract 23; [signed] Charles Bruce, CSCPSD; sworn chain carriers Sampson Lanier & William Cunningham.

754. Jun. 20, 1786 sold 141 ac to John Alcorn for £283 ac; No. 28; formerly Henry Eustace McCulloch's property; on waters of Great Alamance Cr in Guilford Co; border: George Clapp; [signed] Charles Bruce, CCPSD; sworn chain carriers Sampson Lanier & William Cunningham.

755. Sept. 18, 1786 sold 216 ac to Henry Ghiles for £1,050; No. 3; formerly Henry Eustace McCulloch's property; on both sides of Swearing Cr in Guilford Co; border: Joseph Bowen, tracts 2 & 5, & William Lynn; [signed] Charles Bruce, CCPSD; sworn chain carriers Henry McKee & John McKee.

756. May 28, 1786 surveyed 300 ac in Granville Co; formerly Henry E McCulloch's property; on the streams of Ledge of Rocks Cr; border: Peter Cash & Tounsend; [signed] Micajah Bulloch, C surveyor; sworn chain carriers John Williams & Joseph Carnes; [on back] No. 4 sold Mar. 1788 to John Brown for £260 certificates [signed] Archd Lytle, comr.

757. Jun. 1, 1786 surveyed 365 ac in Granville Co; No. 6; formerly Henry E McCulloch's property; on streams of Ceader Cr; border: a pine on E & W line of "the Ceader Tract" and Bullock; [signed] Micajah Bulloch, C surveyor; sworn chain carriers John Williams & Joseph Carnes; Mar. 11, 1788 sold to Phil Hawkins for £111 certificates [signed] Archd Lytle, comr.

758. Jun. 1, 1786 surveyed 283 ac in Granville Co; No. 10; formerly Henry E McCulloch's property; on E side of Cedar Cr; border: a pine 74 poles E of Cedar Cr, Burford's path, & E and W line of "the Great Meadow Tract"; [signed] M Bulloch, surveyor; sworn chain carriers John Williams & Edmund Carns; Mar. 11, 1788 sold to Phillemon Hawkins jr for £55 certificates [signed] Archd Lytle, comr.

759. Jun. 1, 1786 surveyed 320 ac in Granville Co; No. 11; formerly Henry E McCulloch's property; on both sides of Cedar Cr; border: a drean of Cedar Cr; [signed] Michael Bulloch, surveyor; sworn chain carriers John Williams & Edmund Carns; Mar. 11, 1788 sold to Phillemon Hawkins jr for £253.10 certificates [signed] Archd Lytle, comr.

760. Jun. 5, 1786 surveyed 310 ac in Granville Co; No. 8; formerly Henry E McCulloch's property; on the streams of Cedar Cr; border: Wheelar; [signed] Michael Bulloch, surveyor; sworn chain carriers John Williams & Edmund Carns; Mar. 11, 1788 sold to Col. Phil Hawkins for £200 certificates [signed] Archd Lytle, comr.

Sales of Confiscated Land

761. Jun. 6, 1786 surveyed 175 ac in Granville Co; No. 45; formerly Henry E McCulloch's property; border: Wallar's and Veazey's coner; [signed] M Bulloch, surveyor; sworn chain carriers John Wallar & Joseph Wallar; Mar. 1788 sold to Isaac Eastwood for £131 certificates [signed] Archd Lytle, comr.

762. Jul. 2, 1786 surveyed 127 ac in Granville Co; No. 33; formerly Henry E McCulloch's property; on both sides of Smiths Cr; includes the greater part of "the" old field; border: John Hooker; [signed] Michael Bulloch, surveyor; sworn chain carriers Harwood Nance & Philip Bullock; Mar. 11, 1788 sold to Phil Hawkins jr for £201 certificates [signed] Archd Lytle, comr.

763. Jul. 6, 1786 surveyed 240 ac in Granville Co; No. 44; formerly Henry E McCulloch's property; border: Wallar's & Veazey's corner; [signed] Michael Bulloch, surveyor; sworn chain carriers John Wallar & Joseph Wallar; [on back] Mar. 1788 sold to John Howard for £160 certificates [signed] Archd Lytle, comr.

764. [no dated] surveyed 154.25 ac in Granville Co; No. 41; formerly Henry E McCulloch's property; on Little Ledge of Rocks Cr; border: Richard Banks' corner on the creek; [signed] Michael Bulloch, surveyor; sworn chain carriers Hermon Bagley & Epharim Emry; [on back] for Jeremiah Bullock.

765. [no date] surveyed 250 ac in Granville Co; No. 1; formerly H E McCulloch's property; on both sides of Tarborough Road; border: Townsend, James Cash, & Wallace; [signed] Michael Bullock, surveyor; sworn chain carriers John Williams & Edmund Carnes; [on back] Aug. 2, 1803 sold by H Shepperd, Hillsborough Dist. Commissioner of Confiscated Property, to John Forsyth at Granville Co Court house for $50 [signed] H Shepperd, commr; No. 541 dated Nov. 1, 1804.

Following in Treasurer & Comptroller's Records Box 6
first folder [#766-776]:
766. Payments made to Nicholas Iler (of Mecklenburg Co) due to an act of Assembly entitled "An Act to relieve certain inhabitants of Mecklenburg Co & other citizens of the State":
interest on £33 from Apr. 30, 1796   £17.9.6
[total]   £33 + £17.9.6 = £50.9.6
Feb. 27, 1805 John Haywood, Public Treasurer, paid £50.9.6 to George McCulloch esq (of Rowan Co), attorney of Nicholas Iler.
[no date] George McCulloch acknowledges receipt of money as attorney of Nicholas Iler. [signed] G McCulloh, attorney for Nicholas Iler.

766B. Jun. 22, 1795 Nicholas Iler & William Polk (of Mecklenburg Co) to the trustees of University of North Carolina; a bond for £53.10 for 1 year. [signed] [cut off the page]. Witness Isaac Cook.

767. Payments made to Thomas Wair (of Mecklenburg Co) due to an act of relieve certain inhabitants of Mecklenburg Co & other citizens of the State:
interest on £28 for Jul. 27, 1803   £2.13.1
[total]   £28 + £2.13.1 = £30.13.1
Feb. 27, 1805 John Haywood, Public Treasurer, paid £30.13.1 George McCulloch esq (of Rowan Co), attorney of Thomas Wear.
Feb. 27, 1805 George McCulloch acknowledges receipt of the money. [signed] G McCulloch, attorney for Thomas Weir. Witness Ls Beard.

767B. Jul. 27, 1803 Ad Osborn received $40 "in part interest" on judgment of Trustees vs Tho Weir; "formerly received $16". [signed] Ad Osborn.

768. Payments to James Maxwell (of Mecklenburg Co) due to an act of relieve certain inhabitants of Mecklenburg Co & other citizens of the State:
interest on £206.12.4 from Jul. 1802   £31.16.6

Sales of Confiscated Land

[total] £206.12.4 + £31.16.6 = £238.8.10
Feb. 27, 1805 John Haywood, Public Treasurer, paid £238.8.10 to George McCullock esq (of Rowan Co).
Feb. 27, 1805 George McCullock acknowledges receipt of the money. [signed] G McCulloch, attorney for Robert Maxwell, son & attorney of James Maxwell. Witness Ls Beard.

768B. Jan. sessions 1797 Trustees vs James Maxwell sr & Gordon Potter: judgment for £390 to be discharged upon payment of £194 or £64.13.4 with interest, £64.13.4 due Aug. 1 next with interest, & £64.13.4 due Aug. 1, 1798 with interest; execution for £64.13.4 which was continued until Oct. 1798 and suspended and revived to a judgment at Apr. term 1801 for total of £194.0 + £8.19.6 cost = £202.19.6; execution was issued and continued until Jul. term 1802 and returned satisfied "added cost" £0.15 + sheriff's cost £2.17.10 = £206.12.4 [grand total] "exclusive of interest". Feb. 7, 1805 "a true copy". [signed] Isaac Alexander, clerk of Mecklenburg Co.
768C. Feb. 1, 1805 Robert Maxwell, attorney of James Maxwell (of Mecklenburg Co) to George McCulloh (of Rowan Co); power of attorney to get the money paid by James Maxwell to Adlai Osborne, agent & commissioner of Trustees of University of North Carolina, agreeable to act of Assembly. [signed] Robert Maxwell, attorney for Leus Maxwell [sic]. Witness Ls Beard.

769. Payments to Joseph Bigham (of Mecklenburg Co) due to an act of relieve certain inhabitants of Mecklenburg Co & other citizens of the State:
interest on £119 from Jun. 23, 1796   £62.10.8
[total] £119 + £62.10.8 = £181.10.8
Feb. 27, 1805 John Haywood, Public Treasurer, paid £181.10.8 to George McCulloch esq (of Rowan Co), attorney of Joseph Bigham.
Feb. 27, 1805 George McCulloch acknowledges receipt of the money. [signed] G McCulloch, attorney for Joseph Bigham. Witness Ls Beard.

769B. Jun. 23, 1795 Joseph Bingham, John Montgomery, & William Orr (of Mecklenburg Co) to Trustees of University of North Carolina; a bond for £238; condition: bond void if Bingham, Montgomery, or Orr pay £119 in 3 annual installments as follows--£39.13.4 on Jun. 23, 1796 and same amount in 1797 & 1798 with interest from Jun. 23, 1796. [signed] [Joseph Bingham, John Montgomery, & William Orr--lined out]. Witness Isaac Cook. [hole in page] "my for" Ad Osborn; [on back] Jos Bingham's bond for portion of Jno McClure's mortgage in pursuance of an obligation made by said Jno McClure to Jas Montgomery to make a deed for 200 ac of the mortgaged premises; "NB" I have given a memo not to [hole in page] till letter made "A. O."; pay Jun. 23, 1796 "N B" the [hole in page] case executed and now taken up "A. O." [and some random numbers].

769C. Jan. 31, 1805 Joseph Bingham (of Mecklenburg Co) to G McCulloh (of Rowan Co); power of attorney to get money Joseph Bingham paid to Adlai Osborne, agent & commissioner of trustees of University of North Carolina, agreeable to an act of Assembly. [signed] Joseph Bingham. Witness Ls Beard.

770. Payments to George McCulloch esq (of Rowan Co), attorney for James McCaleb, executor of Archibald Houston (of Cabarrus Co) due to an act of relieve certain inhabitants of Mecklenburg Co & other citizens of the State:
interest on £50.0 from Dec. 1796   £25.11
[total] £50 + £25.11 = £75.11
Jun. 18, 1805 John Haywood, Public Treasurer, paid £75.11 to George McCulloch esq, attorney of James McCaleb, executor.
Jun. 18, 1805 George McCulloch acknowledges receipt of the money. [signed] G McCulloch, attorney for Jas McCaleb, executor of Archd Houston. Witness B W Goodman.

770B. Dec. 1, 1796 Ad Osborn received £50 from Archibald Houston "credit to" his bond of £120 due to the Trustees.

770C. Mar. 26, 1805 James McCaleb, executor of Archibald Houston (of Cabarrus Co) to George McCulloh (of Rowan Co); power of attorney to get money Archibald Houston paid to Adlai Osborne, agent & commissioner of trustees of University of North Carolina, agreeable to an act of Assembly. [signed] Jeams McCealeb [sic]. Witness Ls Beard.

771. Payments to George McCulloh esq (of Rowan Co), attorney to James Houston, attorney of James Reese (of Iredell Co) due to an act of relieve certain inhabitants of Mecklenburg Co & other citizens of the State:
interest on £30.1 form May 1796   £16.7
[total]   £30.1 + £16.7 = £46.8
Jun. 18, 1805 John Haywood, Public Treasurer, paid £46.8 to George McCulloch, attorney of James Houston, attorney of James Rees (of Iredell Co).
Jun. 18, 1805 George McCulloch acknowledges receipt of the money. [signed] G McCulloch, attorney for James Houston, attorney of James Reese. Witness B W Goodman.

771B. May 23, 1796 Ad Osborn, attorney for the Trustees, received of James Houston, attorney of James Rees (1) 2 "single" bills made by William McCree & Joshua Baker to James Rees for £21.6 principal payable Nov. 8, 1793 and (2) "an order" on James Cannon for £8.15 with interest due to James Rees; both to be credited to James Rees's buying 106 ac formerly Henry E McCulloh's property and sold by Trustees of University of North Carolina.

771C. Mar. 26, 1805 James Houston, attorney of James Reese (of Iredale [sic] Co) to Geroge McCulloh (of Rowan Co); power of attorney to receive money James Houston paid to Adlai Osborne, agent & commissioner of trustees of University of North Carolina, agreeable to an act of Assembly. [signed] Jam. Houston. Witness Ls Beard.

772. Payment to George McCulloch (of Rowan Co), agent of Samuel Montieth (of Burke Co), due to an act of relieve certain inhabitants of Mecklenburg Co & other citizens of the State:
interest from Jun. 2, 1796   £53.15.1
[total]   £97.0 principal + £53.15.1 = £150.15.1
Oct. 9, 1805 John Haywood, Public Treasurer, paid £150.15.1 to George McCulloch.
[no date] George McCulloch acknowledges receipt of the money. [signed] G McCulloch, attorney for Saml Monteith [sic]. Witness David Ruth.

772B. Jun. 22, 1795 Samuel Montieth & William Montieth (of Mecklenburg Co) to Trustees of University of North Carolina; a bond for £228; condition: bond void if Samuel or William pay £114 in 3 installments: £38 on Jun. 22, 1796 and the same in 1797 & 1798 with interest from Jun. 22, 1796. [signed] Saml Mentieth & William Menteth. Witness Wm B Alexander & J McK Alexander; [on back] credit £17 per Jno McK Alexander's affidavit and an order of the Trustees [signed] Ad Osborn; Sept. 27, 1805 Ad Osborn certifys, after deducting £17, the balance of principal & interest paid.

772C. Sept. 5, 1805 Samuel Montieth (of Burke Co) to George McCulloh (of Rowan Co); power of attorney to get the money Samuel Montieth paid to Adlai Osborne, agent & commissioner of trustees of University of North Carolina, agreeable to an act of Assembly. [signed] Saml Mentieth. Witness Ls Beard.

773. Payment to Nathaniel Steed (of Randolph Co) due to an act of relieve certain inhabitants of Mecklenburg Co & other citizens of the State:
interest on £107 from Dec. 20, 1799 to Oct. 1805   £37.5.1
interest on £95.3 from Jan. 1800 to Oct. 1805   £35.15
principal £202.3 + £37.5.1 + £35.15 = £272.3.1
Oct. 9, 1805 John Haywood, Public Treasurer, paid £272.3.1 to George McCulloh (of Rowan Co), agent of Nathaniel Steed.
[no date] George McCulloch acknowledges receipt of the money. [signed] G McCulloch, attorney for Nathaniel Steed. Witness David Ruth.

773B. Sept. 18, 1799 Nathaniel Steed & Micajah Lasseter to Trustees of University of North Carolina; a bond for Nathaniel or Micajah to pay £202.3 in 60 days. [signed] Nathaniel Steed & Micajah Lasseter. Witness J Clark; [on

Sales of Confiscated Land

back] Feb. 1, 1805 (Orange Co) Wm Shepperd, commissioner for Trustees, acknowledges receipt of payment of within note [signed] Wm Shepperd. Witness C Steed; [no date] received $55 of the within bond [not signed]; [no date] received $55 of within bond [not signed]; Dec. 20, 1799 received £51.17 and 30¢ of within bond [not signed]; Jan. 16, 1800 received £95.3 of within bond [not signed]. [revenue impression for 10 cents North Carolina on this sheet].

773C. Feb. 24, 1805 Nathaniel Steed (of Randolph Co) to George McCulloch (of Rowan Co); power of attorney to receive £202.3 with interest from North Carolina's Treasurer paid by Nathaniel Steed to William Shepperd, agent of Trustees of University of North Carolina, for part of a tract sold Apr. 6, 1774 by Thomas Frohock to John Blalock & due to a late decision of Court of Conference and late act of Assembly. [signed] Nathll. Steed. Witness Abner Steed & Thomas Winslow. [the following added] George McCullah, please appropriate the above sum "to the use of" Micajah Lasseter's bond [signed] Nathaniel Steed.

773D. Aug. 7, 1805 Benjamin Steed, Clayton Steed, & Colin Steed, executors of will of Nathaniel Steed decd (of Randolph Co) to George McCulloh (of Rowan Co); power of attorney to received the money Nathaniel Steed paid to William Shepperd, agned & commissioner of Trustees of University of North Carolina, agreeable to act of Assembly. [signed] Benjamin Steed, Clayton Steed, & Colin Steed. Witness Samuel Lewis, Thomas Kuran, & Jesse Shaw; [on back] Mr. McCulloh credit whatever is received to Michale Lasseter's & Thomas Winslow's bond "to him" [signed] Benjamin Steed, Clayton Steed, & Colin Steed.

774. Payments to George McCulloh, agent of James Osborne (of Mecklenburg Co), due to an act of relieve certain inhabitants of Mecklenburg Co & other citizens of the State:
£32.19 principal + £7.18 interest = £40.17
Oct. 9, 1805 John Haywood, Public Treasurer, paid £40.17 to George McCulloh, agent of James Osborne.
[no date] George McCulloch acknowledges receipt of the money. [signed] G McCulloch, attorney for James Osborne. Witness David Ruth.

774B. Nov. 10, 1801 Mecklenburg Co   Ad Osborn, agent of the Trustees, received of James Osborne £27 in full of judgment obtained by the Trustees against him for £20.12.6.

774C. Apr. session 1802 Trustees of University vs James Osborn & Fredk Shaffer: judgment for £40 discharged upon payment of £20.12.6 with interest from Jul. 25:
debt   £21.10
court costs   [hole in page]
sheriff's services [hole in page] [total] £32.19
The above execution of £32.19 returned satisfied Oct. term 1801. [signed] Feb. 6, 1805 Isaac Alexander, clerk Mecklenburg Co.

774D. Jan. 31, 1805 James Osburne (of Mecklenburg Co) to George McCulloh (of Rowan Co); power of attorney to get the money James Osburne paid to Adlai Osborne, agent & commissioner of trustees of University of North Carolina, agreeable to an act of Assembly. [signed] James Osburn. Witness Ls Beard.

775. Payment to Samuel Mitchell, agent of James Glass (of Mecklenburg Co), due to an act of relieve certain inhabitants of Mecklenburg Co & other citizens of the State:
£71 principal "3 annual installments"
+ interest from Jan. 1798 to Oct. 1805   £32.16.5 = £103.16.5
Oct. 9, 1805 John Haywood, Public Treasurer, paid £103.16.6 to George McCulloh (of Rowan Co), agent of James Glass.
[no date] George McCulloch acknowledges receipt of the money, due to power of attorney from Samuel Mitchell, Wm Robb, & Margret Glass, executors of James Glass. [signed] G McCulloch, attorney for executors of Jas Glass. Witness David Ruth.

775B. Jan. 24, 1797 Samuel Mitchell, James Milwee, & James Glass (of Mecklenburg Co) to Trustees of University of North Carolina; a bond for £142; condition: bond void if Samuel, John, or James pay £71 to the Trustees in 3 annual

installments: £23.13.4 on Jan. 24, 1798 and the same amount in 1799 and 1800 with interest from first installment. [signed] Samuel Mitchell, John Millwee, & James Glass. Witness Ad Osborn; [on back] Jan. 23, 1798 credit this bond £23.13; Jan. 31, 1799 credit £17.11; Apr. 25, 1799 £7.10 [signed] "A O"; balance:
[total principal] £71 - £23.13 - £17.11 - £7.10 = £22.6
[total interest] (on £17.11) £2.16.8 + (on £7.10) £0.9 + (on £23.13) £4 = £7.5.8; [grand total] £22.6 (principal) + £7.5.8 (interest) = £29.11.8
£29.11.8 + cost of £3.16 = £33.7.8.
Received of Elijah Alexander by Ad Osborn; "bale of int. provinces" bond to McCulloh land made to Jam. Glass per assignments; writ issued "to" Aug. 1802 "E J O"; Oct. 9, 1805 G McCulloh certifys "to the best of my recollection & belief" [that] Adlai Osborne esq, agent for the Trustees, said Samuel Mitchel acted as agent for James Glass and did not pay in his own right but as agent for Glass, and I presume Osborne's statement is "lodged with" Gavin Alves, Treasurer for the Trustees; interest on £71 from Jan. [hole in page] 1798 to Oct. 7, 1805 (7 years 8.5 months) £32.16.5.

775C. a deed Jan. 24, 1797 Adlai Osborn (of Iredell Co), commissioner & attorney for Trustees of University of Northa Carolina, to James Glass (of Mecklenburg Co); for £71 sold 130 ac on McCalpins Cr in Mecklenburg Co; border: James Boys' corner, crosses the creek, an old field, & a small hickory by the house; formerly Henry Eustace McCulloch's property & confiscated due to an act of Assembly at Raleigh Feb. 6, 1795 and "granted" to the Trustees for the benefit of the University; being a tract sold by Thomas Polk, agent for Henry E McCulloh, to John Province. [signed] Ad Osborn. Witness Samuell Mitchell. Wit. oath Jan. 1797 acknowledged. recorded in Book 14 p. 245 Feb. 24, 1797 [presently in Mecklenburg Co deed Book 15 p. 245].

775D. Feb. 1, 1805 William Robb, executor, & Margret Glass, executrix of James Glass decd, (of Mecklenburg Co) to George McCulloh (of Rowan Co); power of attorney to get the money the executor & executrix paid to Adlai Osborne, agent & commissioner of trustees of University of North Carolina, agreeable to an act of Assembly. [signed] Wm Robb & Margaret Glass's mark. Witness Ls Beard.

776. Payments to Robert Shields (of Mecklenburg Co) due to an act of relieve certain inhabitants of Mecklenburg Co & other citizens of the State:
£21 principal + £2.3 interest from Jan. 1804 to Oct. 1805 = £23.3
Oct. 18, 1805 John Haywood, Public Treasurer, paid £23.3 to George McCulloh (of Rowan Co), agent of Robert Shields' executors.
[no date] George McCulloch acknowledges receipt of the money. [signed] G McCulloch, attorney for Thos Huson & Jno H. Orr, executors of Robt Shields. Witness David Shields.

776B. Jan. 27, 1804 Wm Beaty, sheriff, received of Robt Shields £21 in part of judgment obtained by Col. Orsborn [sic], trustee of the University, vs Robt and Wm Shields.

776C. Jul. 25, 1805 Isaac Alexander, clerk Mecklenburg Co, certifys the Trustees of University by their attorney Adlai Osborn esq recovered a judgment against William Sheilds and Robert Shields at Apr. term 1803:
principal £38.14 + interest £15.8 = £54.2 + costs £4.12.11.
Execution issued which the sheriff returned to Jan. term 1804 "levied" £21 "costs satisfied" and £15 of debt paid to the attorney.

776D. Jul. 24, 1805 Thomas Huson & John H Orr, executors of will of Robt Shields heir [sic] of John Shields decd (of Mecklenburg Co) to George McCulloh (of Rowan Co); power of attorney to get the money Robert Shields paid to Adlai Osborne, agent & commissioner of trustees of University of North Carolina, agreeable to an act of Assembly. [signed] Thos Huson & John H Orr. Witness Ls Beard.

second folder [#777-802]:
777. Petition of John Johnston esq--"your" [Legislative] Committee report: John Johnston ought to have his title to the land when he pays the Treasurer or gives bond payable to the governor for the use of the State £1,088 being the original price agreed on between John Johnston an Henry Eustace McCulloh after deducting 6 years interest, which

Sales of Confiscated Land

by act of Assembly is taken off all debts due a person who resided in Great Britain during the late war; by act of Assembly, he is released from obligation he gave Commissioner of Confiscated Property of Edenton Dist. [signed] Thomas Person, chm. Dec. 24, 1787 Tarborough S Haywood, clerk of Senate, certifys this is a true copy of a report concurred with by both houses of Assembly.

778. Payments to Henry Charles (of Mecklenburg Co) due to an act of relieve certain inhabitants of Mecklenburg Co & other citizens of the State:
interest on £30 from Jan. 26, 1803   £3.15
interest on £5 from Aug. 28, 1803   £11.0
interest on £14.2 from Jul. 26, 1803   £1.6.9
interest on £2.1.9 from Jan. 31, 1805   £0.0.1
total principal £51.3.9 + total interest £5.12.10 = £56.16.7
Feb. 27, 1805 John Haywood, Public Treasurer, paid £56.16.7 to George McCulloh esq (of Rowan Co), attorney for Henry Charles.
Feb. 27, 1805 George McCulloch acknowledges receipt of the money. [signed] G McCulloch, attorney for Henry Charles. Witness Ls Beard.

778B. Jan. 1803 Ad Osborn received of John McRaven, by Henry Charles, $60 part of a judgment of Trustees vs Jno McRaven.
Apr. 28, 1803 Ad Osborn received of Henry Charles $10 [£5--written in a corner] part of a judgment of Trustees vs Jno McRaven.
Apr. 1803 "A O" due to Trustees by H Charles   £15.7.

778C. Trustees vs Henry Charles: debt £15.7 + cost £1.6.9 = amount £16.13.9
credit on execution by sheriff Jno Ca[hole in page]
   for money paid to him   £14.2
balance   £2.1.9
Jan. 31, 1805 Wm Beaty, sheriff, received £2.1.9 in full of above balance.

778D. Feb. 2, 1805 Henry Charles (of Mecklenburg Co) to George McCulloh (of Rowan Co); power of attorney to recieve the money Henry Charles paid to Adlai Osborne, agent & commissioner of trustees of University of North Carolina, agreeable to an act of Assembly. [signed] Henrich Cael [or Carl] (in German). Witness Ls Beard.

779. Payments to Lewis Griffin (of Randolph Co) due to an act of relieve certain inhabitants of Mecklenburg Co & other citizens of the State:
interest on £177.9 from [hole in page] 15, 1800   £51.15
[total] £177.9 + £51.15 = £229.4
Feb. 27, 1805 John Haywood, Public Treasurer, paid £229.4 to George McCulloch esq (of Rowan Co), attorney of Lewis Griffin.
Feb. 27, 1805 George McCulloch acknowledges receipt of the money. [signed] G McCulloch, attorney for Lewis Griffin. Witness Ls Beard.

779B. Oct. 12, 1799 Lewis Griffin and [page torn] to Trustees of University of North Carolina; a bond to pay £177.19 in 12 months. [signed] Lewis Griffin's mark and [page torn]. Witness Wm Shepperd & J Clark   [sheet has a 20¢ North Carolina revenue stamp or coin impressed on the page]; [on back] "Apr. 15" Wm Shepperd received of Thos Winslow £177.9 "within bond" [signed] Wm Shepperd. Witness Gavin Alves; "In. to be charged form Apr. 1800".
779C. Jan. 28, 1805 Lewis Griffen (of Randolph Co) to George McCulloh (of Rowan Co); power of attorney to get the money Thomas Winslow paid William Shepperd, attorney of Trustees of University of North Carolina, due to my bond with said Sheppard for part of the land sold Apr. 6, 1774 by Thomas Frohock, agent for Henry Eustace McCulloh, to John Blalook as appears by bond, & due to late decision by Court of Conference and an act of Assembly. [signed] Lewis Griffin's mark. Witness Micajah Lasseter & Henry Winslow; Jan. 28, 1805 Lewis Griffin asks George

126

Sales of Confiscated Land

McCulloh to "appropriate" the above sum to Thomas Winslow [signed] Lewis Griffin's mark. Witness Micajah Lasseter & Henry Winslow.

780. Payments to James Osborn, administrator of "John" (of Mecklenburg Co), due to an act of relieve certain inhabitants of Mecklenburg Co & other citizens of the State:
interest on £184.4 from [hole in page--Jul.] 27, 1803   £17.9.11
[total] £184.4 + £17.9.11 = £201.13.11
Feb. 27, 1805 John Haywood, Public Treasurer, paid £201.13.11 to George McCulloh esq (of Rowan Co), attorney of James Osborn, administrator of John Osborn (late of Mecklenburg Co).
Feb. 27, 1805 George McCulloch acknowledges receipt of the money. [signed] G McCulloch, attorney for James Osborne. Witness Ls Beard.

780B. Jul. 27, 1803 Ad Osborn, attorney for the Trustees, received "now & at sundry times heretofore" of James Osborn, administrator of John Osborn, £184.4 principal and interest of his bond on, behalf of heirs of John decd, to the Trustees.

780C. Jan. 30, 1805 James Osborn, administrator of Jno Osborne decd, (of Mecklenburg Co) to George McCulloh (of Rowan Co); power of attorney to get the money James Osborn paid to Adlai Osborne, agent & commissioner of trustees of University of North Carolina, agreeable to an act of Assembly. [signed] James Osburn. Witness Ls Beard.

781. Payments to Gordon Potter (of Mecklenburg Co) due to an act of relieve certain inhabitants of Mecklenburg Co & other citizens of the State:
interest on £4 from Jul. 1801   £0.17
interest on £15.14 from Jan. 1804   £1.1.11
interest on £28.10 from Apr. 1804   £1.11.4
interest on £15 from Jul. 1803 "Osborn recpt"   £1.10
interest on £70 from Mar. 1802 "Osborn's recpt"   £12.06
interest on £35 from Jan. 1803 "Osborn's recpt"   £4.11
[total] £168.4.6 principal + £21.7.3 interest = £190.1.9
Feb. 27, 1805 John Haywood, Public Treasurer, paid £190.1.9 to George McCulloch esq (of Rowan Co), attorney of Gordon Potter.
Feb. 27, 1805 George McCulloch acknowledges receipt of the money. [signed] G McCulloch, attorney for Gordon Potter. Witness Ls Beard.

781B. Mar. 15, 1802 Ad Osborn received of Gordon Potter $140 part payment for execution of the Trustees vs Gordon Potter in Mecklenburg Co Court.
Jan. 1803 Ad Osborn received of Gordon Potter £35 in part payment of his bond to the Trustees on which a judgment is taken in Mecklenburg "C C"; "balance from Jan. 15   £81 [hole in page].
Jun. 25, 1803 the Trustees vs Gordon Potter "by him self" £10; Jul. 2, 1803 Ad Osborn received £5   [total] £15.

781C. Mecklenburg Co Apr. session 1797 the Trustees of University vs Gordon Potter and Jas Maxwell: judgment for £270 to be discharged on payment of £135 in 3 installments: (1) £45 with interest on whole principal until paid, (2) £45 Aug. 1 next with inerest, & (3) £45 with interest "of the balance" Aug. 1, 1798.
execution   £135 and continued until Jul. 1801 when sheriff returned attorney fee paid   £4.0; execution continued until Jan. 1804 [hole in page] sheriff returned costs satisfied   £6.17.4 and debt £8.7.2 of debt paid [to] A Osborn.
Apr. term 1804   two tracts of land executed and sold for $57; "suspended" Jul. term 1804: payments--(1) Jul. term 1801   £4, (2) Jan. 1804   £15.4.6, (3) land sold Apr. 1804   £28.10;   "paid in all" £47.14.6.
[on back] Feb. 6, 1805 Isaac Alexander, clerk of Mecklenburg Co, certifys the within is a true statement of suit of Trustees vs Gordon Potter & James Maxwell.

127

Sales of Confiscated Land

781D. Jan. 30, 1805 Gordon Potter (of Mecklenburg Co) to George McCulloh (of Rowan Co); power of attorney to get the money Gordon Potter paid to Adlai Osborne, agent & commissioner of trustees of University of North Carolina, agreeable to an act of Assembly. [signed] Gordon Potter. Witness Ls Beard.

782. Payments to Beaty McCoy (of Mecklenburg Co) due to an act of relieve certain inhabitants of Mecklenburg Co & other citizens of the State:
interest on £12.10 from Jul. 29, 1796   £6.8.9
interest on £13.5 from Jul. 30, 1802   £2.0
interest on £73.17.11 from Apr. 1803   £8.2.6
[total] £99.12.11 principal + £16.11.3 interest = £116.4.2
Feb. 27, 1805 John Haywood, Public Treasurer, paid £116.4.2 to George McCulloch esq (of Rowan Co), attorney of Beaty McCoy.
Feb. 27, 1805 George McCulloch acknowledges receipt of the money. [signed] G McCulloch, attorney for James [sic] McCoy. Witness Ls Beard.
[no date] John Haywood, Public Treasurer, says James & Beaty McCoy were jointly in a bond; James made payments to Osborne; Alves, the treasurer, credited in the name of "Beaty" only; this will account for variation in power of attorney and the "caption" of this account.

782B. Apr. 27, 1787 Ad Osborn received of Beaty McCoy, by hands of Jas McCoy, two receipts of H E McCollok and Thomas Frohoh £32.10 to be credited to Joseph Priest's mortgage bond and deducted from B McCoy's bond to the Trustees for balance of said mortgage.
Jul. 29, 1796 Ad Osborn received of James McCoy for Beaty McCoy £12.10 part of the first installment of "his" bond with the Trustees.
Jul. 30, 1803 Ad Osborn received of James McCoy $23 [£11.10 + £1.5 = £13.5--on the corner of the sheet] in part of his bond with Beaty McCoy to the Trustees.

782C. Jan. term 1803 Trustees of the University vs James McCoy & Beaty McCoy: judgment of £67.6.8 + £6.11.3 = £73.17.11; Feb. 6, 1805 Isaac Alexander, clerk of Mecklenburg Co, certifys an execution for the above debt and cost was returned satisfied by James McCoy to Apr. session 1803.

782D. Jan. 30, 1805 James McCoy (of Mecklenburg Co) to George McCulloh (of Rowan Co); power of attorney to get the money James McCoy paid to an act of relieve certain inhabitants of Mecklenburg Co & other citizens of the State: J McCoy. Witness Ls Beard.

783. Payments to Frederick Kembrow (of Orange Co) due to an act of relieve certain inhabitants of Mecklenburg Co & other citizens of the State:
interest on £24.11 from Feb. 24, 1802   £4.8.3
interest on £15 from May 1, 1802   £2.9
interest on £138 from Jan. 20, 180   £17.5.2
interest on £48.12.6 from Aug. 26, 1803   £4.8.6
[total]   £226.3.6 principal + £28.10.11 = £254.14.5
Feb. 27, 1805 John Haywood, Public Treasurer, paid £254.14.5 to Lewis Beard (of Salisbury), attorney of Frederick Kembrow.
Feb. 27, 1805 Lewis Beard acknowledges receipt of the money. [signed] Ls Beard, attorney of Frederick Kembrow. Witness G McCulloh.
783B. Apr. 8, 1800 Federick Cimbow [sic] & Jacob Graves to Trustees of University of North Carolina; a bond for £204 to be paid as follows: a third in 6 months, a third in 18 months, & a third in 2 years 6 months with interest beginning in 6 months. [signed] Federick Cimbow's mark & Jacob Grives; [a 20¢ North Carolina revenue stamp, or coin, impressed on this sheet]; [on back] Feb. 24, 1802 Wm Shepperd credits the bond with $49 & a shilling [£24.11--written in the corner] paid by Mr. Kimbrow; May 31, 1802 Hillsborough   Gavin Alves received $30 "or" £15 of within bond; Jan. 20, 1803 Hillsborough   Gavin Alves received £138 "or" $276; Aug. 26, 1803 Hillsborough Gavin Alves received £48.12.6 in full of the within bond & interest from Mr. Kimbrough.

Sales of Confiscated Land

783C. Feb. 24, 1802 Wm Shepperd received $49 and a shilling [£24.11--written in a corner] to credit to a bond to the Trustees by Mr. Cimbrow & Jacob Graves.
May 31, 1802 Hillsborough   Gavin Alves, treasurer, received $30 "or" £15 from Frederick Kimbrough part of a bond by him & Jacob Graves to the Trustees for £204.
Jan. 20, 1803 Hillsborough   Gavin Alves, treasurer of University of North Carolina, received of Frederick Kimbrough $276 "or" £138 in part of bond by him & Jacob Graves to the Trustees for £204 [dated] Apr. 8, 1800; "separate receipt given on back said note" and "I" calculate Kimbrough owes a balance of £46.18.9 with interest.

783D. [The following on one side of a small sheet; some adding is on the back of the same sheet:]
Bond for   £204
[interest Apr. 8, 1801 to Feb. 24, 1802] + £10.14.2 = £214.4.2
[by cash Feb. 24, 1802]   - £24.11   = £190.3.2
[interest on £190.3.2 Feb. 24, 1802 to May 31] + £3.1.11 = £193.5.1
[by cash May 31]   - £15   = £178.5.1
[interest on £178.5.1 May 31, 1802 ato Jan. 20, 1803] + £6.13.8 = £184.8.9
[by cash Jan. 20, 1803]   - £138   = £46.18.9
[interest from Jan. 20, 1803 to Aug. 26] + £1.13.9   = £48.12.6 [page torn]
"by ordinance of the Trustees [sic], bonds aren't to bear interest until the second year; the whole sum then due carries interest"

783E. Oct. 11, 1804 Fredrick Kimrow (of Orange Co) to Lewis Beard (of Salisbury, Rowan Co); power of attorney to get the money paid to William Shepperd, agent for the Trustees; for land sold in 1775 by Michael Holt, agent for Henry Eustace McCulloh, to my father Henry Kimrow as appears by bond given by Henry & Leonard Kimrow to Henry E McCulloh; trustees have "contrary to law" taken from Fredrick £226.3.6; due to a late decision of Court of Conference, Henry E McCulloh's agent should receive the money. [signed] Fredrick Kimrow's mark. Witness Michl Holt & Whitlock Arnold.

784. Payments to James McClughan (of Mecklenburg Co), executor of Andrew Ray decd, due to an act of relieve certain inhabitants of Mecklenburg Co & other citizens of the State:
interest on £17.8.4 from Mar. 1797   £8.12
[total]   £17.18.4 + £8.12 = £26.10.4
Feb. 27, 1805 John Haywood, Public Treasurer, paid to George McCulloh esq (of Rowan Co), attorney of James McClughan.
Feb. 27, 1805 George McCulloch acknowledges receipt of the money. [signed] G McCulloch, attorney for James McClughan, executor. Witness Ls Beard.

784B. Oct. 27, 1795 Andrew Ray & David Ray (of Mecklenburg Co) to Trustees of University of North Carolina; a bond for £53; condition: Andrew or David to pay £26.10 in one year. [signed] [cut off the page]. Witness J McK Alexander & Ad Osborn; [on back] Andw Ray's bond to Trustees for balance of mortgage [on] McCulloh land Mecklenburg Co;
£26.10 - £3.6 (credit per order of Trustees) = £23.4
by error of interest   - £5.5.8 = £17.18.4
Mar. 1, 1797 credit per Osborn   £15   [figuring stops here].

784C. Mar. 1, 1797 "Peg" [hole in page] Osborn received of Andrew Rai $30 in part of a bond due to Adlai Osborn.

784D. Jan. 30, 1805 James McClughan (of Mecklenburg Co), executor of Andrew Ray decd, to George McCulloh (of Rowan Co); power of attorney to get the money Andrew paid to Adlai Osborne, agent & commissioner of trustees of University of North Carolina, agreeable to an act of Assembly. [signed] James McClughan. Witness Ls Beard.

Sales of Confiscated Land

785. Payments to David Rea (of Mecklenburg Co) due to an act of relieve certain inhabitants of Mecklenburg Co & other citizens of the State:
interest on £26.9.6 from Jan. 25, 1797 per Osborne   £12.16.9
interest on £34.11 from Jan. 1803 per Osborne   £4.6.3
[total]   £61.0.6 principal + £17.3 = £78.3.6
Feb. 27, 1805 John Haywood, Public Treasurer, paid £78.3.6 to George McCulloch esq (of Rowan Co), attorney of David Rea.
Feb. 27, 1805 George McCulloch acknowledges receipt of the money. [signed] G McCulloch, attorney for David Rea. Witness Ls Beard.

785B. Oct. 27, 1795 David Ray & Andrew Ray (of Mecklenburg Co) to Trustees of University of North Carolina; a bond for £100; condition: David or Andrew to pay the Trustees £51.8 in 2 annual installments--(1) £25.14 in one year and (2) £25.14 in 2 years with interest after first year. [signed] [cut off the page]. Witness J McK Alexander & Ad Osborn; [on back] David Ray's bond for the balance of a mortgage [on] McCullok's land Mecklenburg Co; Jul. 25, 1797 credit interest £0.15.6 + principal £25.14 = £26.9.6; "issued to Jan. 1803 principal & interest"; Jan. 1803 Ad Osborn received balance of principal & interest of this bond also cost [? hole in page] "dismiss".

785C. Jan. 25, 1805 David Ray (of Mecklenburg Co), heir of John Ray decd, to George McCulloh (of Rowan Co); power of attorney to get the money David paid to Adlai Osborne, agent & commissioner of trustees of University of North Carolina, agreeable to an act of Assembly. [signed] David Rea. Witness Ls Beard.

786. Payments to Adam Ormand (of Mecklenburg Co) due to an act of relieve certain inhabitants of Mecklenburg Co & other citizens of the State:
interest on £28.0 from Jun. 23, 1796   £14.11.2
interest on £3.0.1 from Jan. 1797   £1.9.1
[total]   £31.0.1 principal + £16.0.3 interest = £47.0.4
Feb. 27, 1805 John Haywood, Public Treasurer, paid £47.0.4 to George McCulloh esq (of Rowan Co), attorney of Adam Ormand.
Feb. 27, 1805 George McCulloch acknowledges receipt of the money. [signed] G McCulloch, attorney for Adam Ormand. Witness Ls Beard.

786B. Jun. 23, 795 Adam Ormand & Samuel Lard Harris (of Mecklenburg Co) to Trustees of University of North Carolina; a bond for £28 to be paid by Jun. 23, 1796. [signed] Adam Ormand & Saml Ld Harris. Witness Will Polk; [on back] A Ormand & S L Harris' bond for £28 balance of Jas Ormand's bond to H E McCulloh with interest deducting T Frohock's receipt of £10.6 to the "trasters"; credit $47; credit interest £0.19.6 "part principal" £27.

786C. Jun. 23, 1795 Ad Osborn received of Adam Ormond, an heir of James Ormond decd, a receipt from Thomas Frohock agent for Henry E McCulloh & said Ormond's note "amounting to" the balance of James Ormond's futher bond and interest to this date and heirs of James Ormond are released from the bond given for purchase of his land from Henry Eustace McCulloh in Mecklenburg Co.

786D. Jan. session 1797 Trustees of the University vs Adam Ormond: judgment of £0.10 + cost £2.10.1 = £3.0.1 "satisfied not levied"; Feb. 6, 1805 Isaac Alexander, clerk of Mecklenburg Co, certifys the above is a true copy.

786E. Jan. 29, 1805 Adam Ormond (Mecklenburg Co) to George McCulloh (of Rowan Co); power of attorney to get money paid to Adlai Osborne, agent & commissioner of trustees of University of North Carolina, agreeable to an act of Assembly. [signed] Adam Ormond. Witness Ls Beard.

787. Payments to Frederick Shaver (of Mecklenburg Co) due to an act of relieve certain inhabitants of Mecklenburg Co & other citizens of the State:
interest on £42.0.4 from Jan. 24, 1797   £20.7.6
interest on £56.0 from Mar. 15, 1802   £9.16.6

interest on £13.1.3 from Jan. 25, 1803   £1.12.8
[total] £111.1.7 principal + £31.16.8 interest = £142.18.3
Feb. 27, 1805 John Haywood, Public Treasurer, paid £142.18.3 to George McCulloch esq (of Rowan Co), attorney of Frederick Shaver.
Feb. 27, 1805 George McCulloch acknowledges receipt of the money. [signed] G McCulloch, attorney for Frederick Shaver. Witness Ls Beard.

787B. Jan.2 4, 1797 Ad Osborn received from Fred Shaver £30.6.8 his first installment + £0.73.8 interest to this time + £9 part of second installment on his bond to Trustees; [following in a corner] £30.6.8 + 3.13.8 + £9 = £42.0.4.
Mar. 15. 1802 Ad Osborn received of Fredrick Shaffer $112 part of his bond to the Trustees.
Jan. 25, 1803 Ad Osborn received of Fredk Shaver £13.1.3 the balance of his bond with Trustees on judgment in Mecklenburg Co Court.

787C. Jan. 31, 1805 Frederick Shaver (of Mecklenburg Co), executor of Frederick Shaver sr decd, to George McCulloh (of Rowan Co); power of attorney to get the money Frederick Shaver decd paid to Adlai Osborne, agent & commissioner of trustees of University of North Carolina, agreeable to an act of Assembly. [signed] Frederic Shaver. Witness Ls Beard.

788. Payments to John Stewart (of Mecklenburg Co) due to an act of relieve certain inhabitants of Mecklenburg Co & other citizens of the State:
interest on £55.18.7 from Mar. 15, 1801   £9.15.8
interest on £7.10 from Jan. 1803   £0.19.4
[total]   £70.8.7 principal + £11.3.6 interest = £81.12.1
Feb. 27, 1805 John Haywood, Public Treasurer, paid £81.12.1 to George McCulloch esq, attoney of John Stewart.
Feb. 27, 1805 George McCulloch acknowledges receipt of the money. [signed] G McCulloch, attorney for John Stewart. Witness Ls Beard.

788B. Apr. session 1797 Trustees of the University vs Jno Stewart & James Osborn: judgment of £140.10 discharged on payment of £75.5 in 3 installments: (1) £23.8.4 with interest, (2) £23.8.4 due Jul. 31 next with interest, & (3) £23.8.4 with interest due Jul. 31, 1798; an execution was issued for £75.5 and continued until Jul. session 1802 when the Trustees' attorney said there remained due on the execution £28 with interest from Mar. 15, 1802 "costs satisfied" Jul. 1801 £8.13.7
[total] £75.5 + £8.13.7 = £83.18.7
execution for balance issued £28.0
credit at Jan. 1803   - £ 7.10
credit at Jan. 1804   - £ 7.0
balance unpaid   £13.10
"suspended Jul. term 1804" clerk's cost now due £2.0.6
[total]   £83.18.7 + £2.0.6 = £85.18.7;
[on back] Feb. 5, 1805 Isaac Alexander, clerk of Mecklenburg Co, certifys this is a true statement of the proceedings.

788C. Feb. 2, 1805 John Stewart (of Mecklenburg Co) to George McCulloh (of Rowan Co); power of attorney to get the money John Stewart paid to Adlai Osborne, agent & commissioner of trustees of University of North Carolina, agreeable to an act of Assembly. [signed] John Stewart. Witness Ls Beard.

789. Payments to George Hutcheson (of Mecklenburg Co) due to an act of relieve certain inhabitants of Mecklenburg Co & other citizens of the State:
interest on £4 form Jan. 26, 1797   £1.18.10
interest on £10.10 from Apr. 29, 1803   £1.3.1
[total]   £14.10 principal + £3.1.11 interest = £17.11.11
Feb. 27, 1805 John Haywood, Public Treasurer, paid £17.11.11 to George McCulloh esq (of Rowan Co), attorney of George Hutcheson.

Sales of Confiscated Land

Feb. 27, 1805 George McCulloch acknowledges receipt of the money. [signed] G McCulloch, attorney for George Hutcheson. Witness Ls Beard.

789B. Jun. 23, 1795 George Hutcheson to Trustees of University of North Carolina; a bond for £11 payable in [hole in page--one] "year" . [signed] Geo Hu[page torn]. Witness S McCoye & Ad Osborn; [written sideways on the page:] "judgment granted debt £19.9.8   cost £4.0"; [on back] Geo Hutcheson's note for £11 the balance of Willm McCullok's mortgage to Henry E McCulloh, pay Jun. 23, 1790, Jan. 26, 1797, or. by Geo Hutcheson "do", "assumed" Apr. 27, 1802 "A O"; principal of £11 due Jun. 23, 1796
interest until Jan. 26, 1797   £0.7.7
"then" paid   £4   [£11 - £4 = £7 still due]
interest 6 years 3 months til "this" time   £2.12.11 + £0.7.7 + £7 = £9.19.8

789C. Jun. 23, 1795 Ad Osborn received of William McCulloh [by] admr. George Hutcheson balance of sum secured by William's [sic] mortgage to Henry E McCulloh for land in Mecklenburg Co "received in one rect. by Thomas Polk" and his note for £11; mortgage released.

789D. Aug. 19, 1803 Wm Beaty, shff, received of Geo Hutchison £10.10 all of a judgment granted to Trustees of University of North Carolina Apr. 29, 1803 vs said Hutcheson.

789E. Jan. 31, 1805 George Hutchison, administrator of William McCulloch, (of Mecklenburg Co) to George McCulloh (of Rowan Co); power of attorney to get the money George Hutchison paid to Adlai Osborne, agent & commissioner of trustees of University of North Carolina, agreeable to an act of Assembly. [signed] Geo Hutchison. Witness Ls Beard.

790. Payments to William Steele (of Mecklenburg Co) due to an act of relieve certain inhabitants of Mecklenburg Co & other citizens of the State:
interest on £40 from Apr. 29, 1796   £21.4
interest on £20.4 from Aug. 27, 1798   £7.17.2
[total]   £60.4 interest + £29.12 = £89.5.2
Feb. 27, 1805 John Haywood, Public Treasurer, paid £89.5.2 George McCulloch esq (of Rowan Co), attorney of William Steele.
Feb. 27, 1805 George McCulloch acknowledges receipt of the money. [signed] G McCulloch, attorney for William Steele. Witness Ls Beard.

790B. Jun. 23, 1795 William Steele & Elias Alexander (of Mecklenburg Co) to Trustees of University of North Carolina; a bond for £116.10; condition: bond void if William or Elias pay £58.5 in 2 annual installments: (1) £29.2.6 on Jun. 23, 1796 and (2) £29.2.6 Jun. 23, 1797 with interest from Jun. 23, 1796. [signed] Wm [hole in page] Steele & Elias Alexander. Witness Isaac Cooke; [on back] Wm Steele & Elias Alexander's bond with the Trustees for the balance of William Steele's mortgage to H E McCulloh; Apr. 29, 1796 credit by cast £40 "A O"; Aug. 27, 1798 Ad Osborn recd of William Steel £20.4 the balance of bond & interest; £58.5 - £40 = £18.5 + £2.6.6 = £20.11.6 + £0.7.7 = £20.3.11; Aug. 27, 1798 (Salisbury, NC) Wm Steele to Col. Adlai Osborn--please pay George McCulloh esq £60 [sic] which is the sum I paid you; should "the matter in dispute" be in his favor, you will pay him the above sum; otherwise this is void. [signed] Wm Steele. Witness Ls Beard.

790C. Apr. 29, 1796 Ad Osborn received of Elias Alexander for part of his and William Steel's bond to the Trustees £40.

791. Payments to James Orr (of Mecklenburg Co) due to an act of relieve certain inhabitants of Mecklenburg Co & other citizens of the State:
interest on £95.13 from Jul. 27, 1803   £9.1.7
[total]   £95.13 principal + £9.1.7 = £104.14.7

Sales of Confiscated Land

Feb. 27, 1805 John Haywood, Public Treasurer, paid £104.14.7 to George McCulloch esq (of Rowan Co), attorney of James Orr.

Feb. 27, 1805 George McCulloch acknowledges receipt of the money. [signed] G McCulloch, attorney for James Orr sr. Witness Ls Beard.

791B. Jul. 27, 1803 Ad Osborn received £95.13 from James Orr "now and at sundry times heretofore" in full of principal & interest on his bond to Trustees "part of which" is in judgment.

791C. Jan. 30, 1805 James Orr (of Mecklenburg Co) to George McCulloh (of Rowan Co); power of attorney to get the money James paid to Adlai Osborne, agent & commissioner of trustees of University of North Carolina, agreeable to an act of Assembly. [signed] James Orr. Witness Ls Beard.

792. Payments to George Friddle (of Orange Co) due to an act of relieve certain inhabitants of Mecklenburg Co & other citizens of the State:
interest on £14.3.4 from May 1, 1797   £6.12.7
interest on £16.11 from Feb. 25, 1800   £4.19.4
interest on £16.11 from Feb. 25, 1800   £4.19.4   [sic]
[total]   £47.5.4 principal + £16.11.3 interest = £63.16.7
Feb. 27, 1805 John Haywood, Public Treasurer, paid £63.16.7 to George McCulloch esq (of Rowan Co), attorney of George Friddle.
Feb. 27, 1805 George McCulloch acknowledges receipt of the money. [signed] G McCulloch, attorney for George Friddle. Witness Ls Beard.

792B. May 1, 1796 Orange Co   George Friddle & H Shepperd to Trustees of University of North Carolina; a bond for £28.6.8; condition: bond void if George pays £14.3.4 by May 1, 1797 with interest beginning in one year. [signed] George Friddle's mark   & H Shepperd. Witness Josiah Teril.
May 1, 1796 Orange Co   George Friddle & Henry Shepperd to Trustees of University of North Carolina; a bond for £28.6.8; condition: bond void if George pays £14.3.4 by May 1, 1798 with interest beginning in one year. [signed] George Friddle's mark & H Shepperd. Witness Josiah Teril; "2 bonds of £14.3.4 is £28.6.8"; [on back] Feb. 25, 1800 Hillsborough   Gavin Alves, treasurer, received £16.11 of George Friddle.
May 1, 1796 Orange Co   George Friddle & Henry Shepperd to Trustees of University of North Carolina; a bond for £26.6.8; condition: bond void if George pays £14.3.4 by May 1, 1799 with interest beginning in one year. [signed] George Friddle's mark & H Shepperd. Witness Josiah Teril; [on back] Feb. 25, 1801 Hillsborough   Gavin Alves, treasurer, received £16.11 of George Friddle.

792C. Feb. 20, 1805 George Friddle (of Orange Co) to George McCulloh (of Rowan Co); power of attorney to get the money George Friddle paid to William Shepperd, agent of Trustees of University of North Carolina.   [signed] George Friddle's mark. Witness Ls Beard.

793. Payments to Robert Parks (of Mecklenburg Co) due to an act of relieve certain inhabitants of Mecklenburg Co & other citizens of the State:
interest on £34.3 from Apr. 26, 1797   £16.0.6
interest on £40.0 from Jan. 30, 1802   £7.8
interest on £41.8.8 from Oct. 28, 1802   £5.15.10
[total]   £115.8.11 principal + £29.4.4 interest = £144.13.3
Feb. 27, 1805 John Haywood, Public Treasurer, paid £144.13.3 to George McCulloch esq (of Rowan Co), attorney of Robert Parks.
Feb. 27, 1805 George McCulloch acknowledges receipt of the money. [signed] G McCulloch, attorney for Robert Parks. Witness Ls Beard.

Sales of Confiscated Land

793B. Jan. session 1797 Mecklenburg Co   the Trustees vs Robert Parks: judgment for £188 discharged on payment of £94 in the following installments: (1) £31.13.4 Jun. 28 next with interest and (2) £31.13.4 on Jul. 28, 1798 with interest; execution for first installment issued "to" Apr. term 1797 and returned satisfied--£31.13.4
cost of suit   £3.10.1
judgment revived by "sureperis" at Apr. term 1801 when execution issued for balance of judgment & costs--£63.13.4 and was "stayed" from Court to Court until Oct. term 1802 when the sheriff made return "therein debt" paid the Trustees & costs satisfied--£4.14.7
[total]   £103.11.4
sheriff service & coms.   £2.15.8
[total]   £106.7.0
[on back] Feb. 6, 1805 Isaac Alexander, clerk of Mecklenburg Co, certifys an execution of £106.7 against Robert Parks was returned satisfied to Oct. session 1802.

793C. Apr. 26, 1797 Ad Osborn received of Robt Parks £34.3 first installment and interest in part of judgment obtained by Trustees against him last Jan.
Jan. 30, 1802 Ad Osborn received £40 of Robert Parks by William Parks in part of judgment by the Trustees vs him in Mecklenburg Co Court; [on back] Oct. 28, 1802 Ad Osborn received £40.8.8 by Robert Parks.

793D. Jan. 30, 1805 Robert Parks (of Mecklenburg Co) to George McCulloh (of Rowan Co); power of attorney to get the money Robert Parks   paid to Adlai Osborne, agent & commissioner of trustees of University of North Carolina, agreeable to an act of Assembly. [signed] Robert Parks. Witness Ls Beard.

794. Payments to James Sprott, executor of John Taylor (of Mecklenburg Co), due to an act of relieve certain inhabitants of Mecklenburg Co & other citizens of the State:
interest on £64.1.3 from Apr. 27, 1804   £3.4
[total]   £64.1.3 principal + £3.4 interest = £67.5.3
Feb. 27, 1805 John Haywood, Public Treasurer, paid £67.5.3 to George McCulloch exq (of Rowan Co), attorney of James Sprott executor.
[no date] George McCulloch acknowledges receipt of the money. [signed] G McCulloch, attorney for James Sprott executor. Witness Ls Beard.

794B. Jan. session 1803 Mecklenburg Co   the Trustees vs John Taylor's executors: judgment for £56.13:
debt   £56.13
costs   £4.12.1
"other" costs   £0.7.6
sheriff's services   £2.8.8
[total]   £64.1.3
Feb. 5, 1805 Isaac Alexander, clerk, certifys execution issued on the above and was returned satisfied Apr. term 1804 and certifys the interest collected by the Trustees' attorney isn't stated in the records.

794C. Apr. 29, 1803 Ad Osborn received £4.2.6 from James Sprull [sic], executor; cost of suit of the Trustees vs Jno Taylor's executors; [on back] Ad Osborn received $8.25.

794D. Feb. [Jul.--lined out] 1, 1805 James Sprott, executor of John Taylor decd, (of Mecklenburg Co) to George McCulloh (of Rowan Co); power of attorney to get the money James Sprott paid to Adlai Osborne, agent & commissioner of trustees of University of North Carolina, agreeable to an act of Assembly. [signed] Jas Sprott. Witness Ls Beard.

795. Payments to Christopher Erwin, through his attorney George Smartt, (of Mecklenburg Co) due to an act of relieve certain inhabitants of Mecklenburg Co & other citizens of the State:
interest on £15.8.0 from Apr. 28, 1796 to Nov. 28, 1805   £8.16.11
[total]   £15.8 principal + £8.16.11 interest = £24.4.11

Sales of Confiscated Land

Nov. 28, 1805 John Haywood, Public Treasurer, paid £24.4.11 to George Smartt, attorney of William Lee, executor of Christopher Erwin decd.
Nov. 28, 1805 George Smartt acknowledges receipt of the money. [signed] Geo W Smartt.

795B. Apr. 28, 1796 Ad Osborn received £15.8 from Christopher Erwin the balance due for land Christopher Erwin bought in Mecklenburg Co of H E McCulloh "received without bond".

795C. Sept. 14, 1805 William Lees, executor of Christopher Erwin decd's estate, (of Mecklenburg Co) to George Smartt esq (same); power of attorney to get £15.8 from Adlai Osborne, agent & commissioner of trustees of University of North Carolina, agreeable to an act of Assembly. [signed] William Lees. Witness Joab Alexander, JP; Sept. 14, 1805 Isaac Alexander, clerk, certifys Joab Alexander is a JP.

796. Payments to Geo McCulloh, attorney of William Smith, (of Mecklenburg Co) due to an act of relieve certain inhabitants of Mecklenburg Co & other citizens of the State:
interest on £79.16 payable by installments--a third on Oct. 28, 1796 "to" Jun. 25, 1806   £15.8.5
"do" a third from Oct. 28, 1797 to Jun. 25, 1806   £13.16.6
"do on do" from Oct. 28, 1798 to Jun. 25, 1806   £12.4.7
[total]   £79.16 principal + £41.9.6 interest = £121.5.6
Jun. 1806 John Haywood, Public Treasurer, paid £121.5.6 to Geo McCulloh (of Rowan Co).
Jun. 25, 1806 George McCulloch acknowledges receipt of the money. [signed] G McCulloch, attorney for William Smith. Witness B W Goodman.

796B. Oct. 28, 1795 William Smith & John Hodge (of Mecklenburg Co) to Trustees of University of North Carolina; a bond for £190; condition: bond void if William or John pays £95 in 3 installments: (1) £31.13.4 on Oct. 28, 1796, (2) the same on Oct. 28, 1797, & (3) the same on Oct. 28, 1798 with interest beginning in one year. [signed] William Smith & John Hodge. Witness Ad Osborn & John Stinson; [on back] Will Smith's bond for 121 ac part of mortgage for McCulloh's land in Mecklenburg Co; issued to Jan. 1803; Jan. 25, 1803 credit this bond £56 "principal £79.16"; Apr. [hole in page] 1803 Ad Osborn received £79.16 principal & interest in full of this bond after deducting £15.4 [£95 - £15.4 = £79.10] per order of board of Trustees for prinl & interest "of prinl" paid H E McCulloh; £79.16 principal + (interest to Jun. 28, 1806) £41.9.6 = £121.5.6;
[no date] after deducting £15.4 from principal of this bond, balance of £79.16 was paid with £30 interest = £109.16 [signed] Ad Osborn;
principal in 3 installments of £26.12 each = £79.16; total interest £41.9.6.

796C. Jul. 24, 1805 William Smith (of Mecklenburg Co) to George McCulloh (of Rowan Co); power of attorney to get the money William Smith paid to Adlai Osborne, agent & commissioner of trustees of University of North Carolina, agreeable to an act of Assembly. [signed] Willam. Smith. Witness James Stuart.

797. Payments to Geo McCulloh, attorney of Levi Huston, attorney of William Huston (of Mecklenburg Co) due to an act of relieve certain inhabitants of Mecklenburg Co & other citizens of the State:
interest on £20.18 from Jul. 25, 1796 to Jun. 25, 1806   £12.8
[total]   £20.18 principal + £12.8 interest = £33.6
Jun. 1806 John Haywood, Public Treasurer, paid £33.6 to George McCulloh (of Rowan Co).
Jun. 25, 1806 George McCulloch acknowledges receipt of the money. [signed] G McCulloch, attorney for Levi Huston, attorney of William Huston. Witness B W Goodman.

797B. Jul. 25, 1795 William Houston (of Mecklenburg Co) to Trustees of University of North Carolina; a bond £20.18 to be paid in one year. [signed] "Wil" [page torn]. Witness S McCoy & Ad Osborn; [on back] Will Houston's bond for balance of mortgage to H E McCulloh; Jan. 25, 1797 credit "by" Levenus Huston £9.1; [no date] Ad Osborn received £20.18 principal £4.17 interest "agreeable to my report"; [also odd adding & subtracting on the sheet].

Sales of Confiscated Land

797C. Oct. 29, 1805 Levi Houston, attorney of William Houston, (of Mecklenburg Co) to George McCulloh (of Rowan Co); power of attorney to get the money Levi paid to Adlai Osborne, agent & commissioner of trustees of University of North Carolina, agreeable to an act of Assembly. [signed] Levi Huston, attorney for William Huston. Witness Ls Beard.

798. Apr. term 1797 the Trustees of University vs Jno McCreeven [or McCreaven] & Jas Osborn: judgment for £72.0 discharged on payment of £36.11 in installments: (1) £12.4 with interest, (2) £12.4 on Oct. 30 next with inerest, & (3) £12.4 on Oct. 30, 1798 with interest; execution was issued and stayed by plaintiff until Oct. term 1798 and suspended at Oct. term 1799 "sureperis" issued to revive judgment returned to Jan. term 1800 and continued until Apr. term 1801 when plaintiff recovered judgment of £36.11 with interest from Oct. 30, 1796:
judgment £36.11.0
costs   £9.3.7   [total] £45.14.7
on which execution issued on debt & costs, returned [hole in page] term 1802 cost "levd debt stayd." and execution continued until Jul. term 1803 and returned satisfied by A Osborn, attorney
sheriff's cost etc £1.12.1
"sum paid" [total] £47.6.8 exclusive of interest;
Feb. 6, 1805 Isaac Alexander, clerk of Mecklenburg Co, certifys the above is a true account of the proceedings in above suit.

799. [no date] Lewis Beard esq, attorney for the Trustees in Dist. No. 2, certified to Treasurer of Board of Trustees of University of North Carolina that Thomas Kirkpatrick paid Adlai Osborne, attorney for Trustees £41.10 on Jul. 31, 1795; see "certificates" of Lewis Beard; so Robt Williams paid George McCullock, agent of Thomas Kirkpatrick, £41.10 since the case falls within case determined in Court of Conference--Ray vs McCullock; £41.10 is the principal; interest can't be paid with a particular order from the [hole in page--"court" ?]for that purpose. [signed] Robt Williams; [on back] May 16, 1812 George McCulloh received of John Haywood, Treasurer of North Carolina, £40.16 [signed] G McCulloh, attorney for Thomas Kirkpatrick.

800. Dec. 22, 1808 Gavin Alves, Treasurer of University of North Carolina, to John Haywood, Public Treasurer; from a report to me by Adlai Osborne, former commissioner of Trustees of the University, Gavin Alves reports the case of Joseph Moore comes within the decree of the Court of Conference "passed" in Jun. 1804. On examining the books, Alves finds Moore paid £40 and interest as appears from a certificate of Mecklenburg Co clerk. [signed] Gavin Alves.

801. Receipt [or certificate] No. 50 Dec. 1804 to Jacob Fisher: allowed £61.16 "as by report of the Committee of Claims". [signed] Jo Reddick, SS, and S Cabarrus, Sp. He.

802. Dec. 31, 1804 E Holding received £40 from John Haywood, Public Treasurer, all that sum due E Holding for his services assisting in the Treasurer's Office in reguard to "the Land Business" during the "late" session of the Assembly. [signed] E Holding

803. [The following is a summary of the sheets in Treasurer & Comptroller's Records: lands, estates, boundaries, & surveys Box 7.]
803A. first folder: Confiscated Land account 1786--this folder has summaries for each Superior Court District by: James Armstrong for New Bern, Archibald Lytle for Hillsborough, Griffith John McRee for Wilmington, Hardy Murfree for Edenton, Charles Bruce for Salisbury, Nicholas Long for Halifax; there are slight differences in the two copies of some of the summaries.

803B. second folder: Confiscated property other than land 177 to 1786--these are list of sales of estates mostly in eastern North Carolina; the lists name of the buyer and amount paid but not whose property was confiscated.

Sales of Confiscated Land

803C. third folder: Confiscated Land in the hands of certain individuals 1787--this is a list of property that belonged to Archibald Hamilton and a little property that belonged to others; most of this appears to be similar to the list above in Halifax County for the sale of the property of Hamilton and others.

803D. fourth folder: Confiscated land, estate of Timothy Cleary 1785--about eleven sheets all of which are receipts to Patrick Cleary in 1785 and 1794.

804. [The following is a summary of the North Carolina Supreme Court from the loose papers in case number 727 of Robert Ray (or Rae) vs George McCulloch referred to above. See also North Carolina Reports vol. 1 p. 510-513.]
     On Feb. 6, 1767 Henry E McCulloch sold 200 ac to Rae, but didn't make a deed until Rae paid £70 due to a bond from Rae to McCulloch. Rae didn't pay the bond. On Oct. 14, 1792 Rae took a conveyance from George McCulloch, agned to "H E M", gave bond "in question" payable to George, & "took in" a bond given to "H E M". A suit was brought by George to recover the money in the last bond. Henry E McCulloch's land was confiscated. The opinion is signed by Sam Johnston, J S C "Court of Conference 1803".

     In N C Reports, the title chain is as follows: the land was sold Feb. 6, 1767 by Henry E McCulloch, by his agent, to Robert Ray for £72; the land was 200 ac in Orange Co. Ray remained on the land until his death. On Oct. 14, 1792, George McCulloch deeded the land to Robert Ray for a bond of £222.2.3 which was to be void on payments of £111.1.1 with interest "from the date". Robert died "soon after". George brought a suit in Hillsborough Superior Court since the Trustees of the University of North Carolina claimed the land. The Supreme Court decided in George McCulloch's favor.

[No. 805-812 are from Treasurer & Comptroller's Papers--Institutions, University of North Carolina 1780-1930.]
805. State of North Carolina account with James Stockart:
to cash paid by James Stockart to trustees of UNC for a tract supposed to be confiscated land referred to in his power of attorney; the treasurer of Trustees paid to NC Treasurer for use of James Stockart--principal £319.0 + interest paid at the same time £40.3.4 = £359.3.4 + interest from Mar. 23, 1800 to Mar. 23, 1800 or £193.19 = £553.2.4
Mar. 23, 1810 received £553.2.4 of John Haywood, NC Treasurer. [signed] John Stockard [sic], attorney form James Stockard. Witness Ls Beard.

Jan. 3, 1810 James Stockard (of Murray Co, TN and late of Orange Co, NC) to his son John Stockard (of Orange Co); power of attorney to recover the money James paid to the Trustees of UNC for land in Orange Co supposed to be confiscated; and the money was paid to NC Treasurer for James's use; the land has been sold to "sundry" persons and is now owned by John Stockard and Henry Albright and Archibald D Murphey. The money is to be used to discharge the land from its present "incumbrances". [signed] James Stockard. Witness Lewis Wood.

806. Dec. 3, 1810 Nicholas Holt (Orange Co) to Archibald D Murphey (same); power of attorney to get from NC Treasurer the money he paid to the Trustees of UNC for confiscated land in Orange Co; but it falls under Court of Conference decision of Ray vs McCulloh; the money was paid by the Trustees to NC Treasurer; the money is now to be paid to George McCulloh, agent for Henry E McCulloh. [signed] Nicholas Holt's mark "H". Witness T Scott.

State of North Carolina account with Nicholas Holt:
to cash received from Trustees of UNC for Nicholas Holt's use which was paid by Holt to the Trustees for confiscated land: £15.18 + interest from May 31, 1799 to Jan. 15, 1810 £10.5.6 = £26.3.6
[no date] Received £26.3.6 from John Haywood, NC Treasurer. [signed] A D Murphey.

807. Jul. 22, 1809 John Noe (Orange Co) to Archibald Murphey (same); power of attorney to get from NC Treasurer the money he paid to the Trustees of UNC for confiscated land in Orange Co but falls under Court of Conference decision of Ray vs McCulloh; the money was paid by the Trustees to NC Treasurer; the money is now to be paid to George McCulloch, agent for Henry E McCulloch. [signed] John Noe's mark " ". Witness Thos Scott.

State of North Carolina account with John Noe:

Sales of Confiscated Land

Apr. 7, 1801 to cash paid to Trustees of UNC for land bought of Wm Shepperd, their commissioner; being land formerly bought of Henry E McCulloch by bond given him by John Noe sr £45.15 + interest from Apr. 7, 1801 to Aug. 7, 1809 £22.17 = £68.12

Aug. 7, 1809 received £68.12 from John Haywood, NC Treasurer. [signed] A D Murphey; [on back] Jul. 1809 received £68.12 from A D Murphy, attorney of John Noe. [signed] Stephen Hill's mark.

808. Jun. 30, 1809 Christin Sharpe (Orange Co) to Archibald D Murphey (same); power of attorney to get from NC Treasurer the money he paid to Trustees of UNC for confiscated land in Orange Co but falls under Court of Conference decision of Ray vs McCulloh; the money was paid by Trustees to NC Treasurer; the money is now to be paid to discharge a bond dated Dec. 11, 1772 by John Noe and John Holt to Henry E McCulloh for £292 proclamation money to pay £145.17 "tested by" [security ?] Michael Holt and John Shady. [signed] Christian Sharb [german]. Witness R Wood.

State of North Carolina account with Christian Sharpe:
to amount paid by Christian Sharpe to Wm Shepperd, Commissioner of the Trustees, for confiscated land £50 + interest from Nov. 26, 1800 to Nov. 26, 1810 £30 = £80.
Jan. 30, 1811 received £80 from John Haywood, NC Treasurer. [signed] A D Murphey.

809. Sept. 30, 1809 Malachi Isely (Orange Co) to Archibald D Murphey (same); power of attorney to get form NC Treasurer the money he paid to Trustees of UNC for confiscated land in Orange Co but falls under Court of Conference decision of Ray vs McCulloh; the money was paid by the Trustees to NC Treasurer; the money is now to be paid to George McCulloh, agent for Henry E McCulloh. [signed] Milihea Iijle [or Cyle] [german]. Witness Thos Scot

State of North Carolina account with Malachai Isely:
to cash received of the Trustees of UNC for the use of Malachai Isely due to sale mentioned in wihin power of attorney £42.8.0 + interest from Nov. 24, 1800 to Nov. 28, 1810 £25.8.4 = £67.16.4.
Jan. 30, 1811 areceived £67.16.4 from John Haywood, NC Treasurer. [signed] A D Murphey, attorney for M[page torn] Isley.

810. Nov. 11, 1809 Orange Co   Malachai Hatmaker (Orange Co) to Archibald D Murphey (same); power of attorney to get from NC Treasurer the money he paid to the Trustees of UNC for confiscated land in Orange Co but falls under Court of Conference decision of Ray vs McCulloh; the money was paid by the Trustees to NC Treasurer; the money is now to be paid to George McCulloh, agent for Henry E McCulloh. [signed] Malachai Hatmaker's mark "+". Witness Walter Galbraith.

State of North Carolina account with Malachai Hatmaker:
to cash paid to Trustees of UNC for land mentioned in this power of attorney and reported by the Treasurer of Trustees to NC Treasurer   £55.0 + interest from Mar. 31, 1799 (when the money was paid to the Trustees) to Nov. 15, 1809 £34.7.6 = £89.7.6.
Nov. 15, 1809 received £89.7.6 from John Haywood, NC Treasurer. [signed] A D Murphey.

811. Jul. [hole in page], 1809 Adair Co, KY   Joseph Holmes (Adair Co, KY) to friend Edward Green (same); power of attorney to get the money he paid to Trustees of UNC for land in Orange Co on S side of Great Allemance Cr and waters thereof; the land was sold in 1774 by Henry E McCulloch to James Holmes, Samuel Homes, & Joseph Holmes; the land was confiscated due to Act of General Assembly and "compramised" by Col. William Sheppard, commissioner for the Trustees, to Joseph Holmes; the money is to be paid to George McCulloch (of Rowan Co, NC) or his attorney provided George makes to Joseph's attorney a "general warrantee" deed for the land. [signed] Joseph Holmes' mark "+". Witness Caleb H Ricketts, Jno Stapp, & Hugh Holmes.
Jul. 3, "18th year of the Commonwealth" Adair Co, KY   William Caldwell, Clerk of Adair Co Court, certifys the power of attorney was proved by C H Ricketts and J Stapp before W Caldwell. [signed] Wm Caldwell.
Jul. 3, 1809 Adair Co   William Burbridge, presiding magistrate, certifys William Caldwell is Clerk of Court. [signed] William Burbridge.

Sales of Confiscated Land

[State of] North Carolina to Joseph Holmes:
Aug. 1809 to the sum paid the University for land as per a report of the Treasurer of the University and now liable to be refunded by the State due to an Act of Assembly £292.10 + interest from May 30, 179[hole in page] to Aug. 28, 1809 £179.15 = £472.6.
[no date] received £472.6 due to power of attorney from Joseph Holmes of Kentucky for the land bought of McCulloch. [signed] Edward Green. Witness P [or G] Goodwin; [on back] recorded in Book B fol. 224   test. Ogr Waggener.

812. Mar. 23, 1809 William Roberts (Orange Co) to Gavin Alves esq (same); power of attorney to get the money he paid to Trustees of UNC for land in Orange Co sold by Henry E McCulloh to Charles Roberts and later confiscated. [signed] William Roberts. Witness A D Murphey "State of NC with William Roberts"

Apr. 11, 1799 to cash paid Trustees of the University for 200 ac in Orange Co bought for £60 from Henry E McCulloh; bond and mortgage were executed for payment per report of A D Murphey esq, attorney for the Trustees £53.0 + interest from Apr. 11, 1799 to Mar. 28, 1809 £31.13.3 = £84.13.3.
Mar. 28, 1809 paid £84.13.3 to Gavin Alves, attorney for William Roberts. [signed] John Haywood, Public Treasurer.
[no date] Galvin Alves (of Orange Co) acknowledges receipt of the money on Mar. 28. [signed] Gavin Alves, attorney for William Roberts.

813. [The following is in box CRX 76 Salisbury Dist. Criminal Action Papers--no date and 1772-1807, last folder in the box.]
Persons bound in recognizance to appear at Salisbury Superior Court on Sept. 15, 1780:
John Hardy £8,000   taking oath of allegiance to the enemy
Maj. Wm Loften and Jesse Gilbert £4,000 each   taking oath etc.
Henry Stokes £1,000   taking oath etc.
Jesse Gilbert and Stephen Hyde £500 each   taking oath etc.
Bealey Jno Lemden £2,000   taking oath etc.
Wm Lofton "security" £2,000
John McElbale £20,000   taking oath etc.
Stephen Hyde and Jesse Gilbert £10,000 each
Wm Hale £10,000   "ditto"
Charles Harbert £10,000
George Webb £20,000   "ditto"
Col. Medlock and Maj. Wm Speed £10,000 each
Chas Huckabee £5,000   "ditto"
Col. Medlock and Maj. Speed £2,500 each
James Ryall £20,000   "ditto"
John Brandon and Stephen Hyde £10,000 each
John Brooks £50,000   "ditto"
Capt. Beckner Kimble and Jesse McClenden £25,000 each
Thos Bluett £20,000   "ditto"
Wm Speed and Chas Harbert £10,000 each
Robt Pelcher £5,000   "ditto"
Stephen Hyde and Jsees Gilbert £2,500 each
Richd Yarborough £20,000   "ditto"
Maj. Speed and Maj. Loften £10,000   "ditto"
Thomas Dudley £100,000   siding the enemy
Capt. Peter ONeal and Asa Brasher £50,000 each
"taken" Jul. 27 and 28, 1780 before Wm Sharpe

Sales of Confiscated Land

[The following No. 814-817 are in box CRX 76 Salisbury Dist Court Papers.]

814. George McCullock vs Joseph and Benjamin Bell (1796):

Mar. term 1796 Salisbury Dist--plea of Joseph and Benjamin Bell: George McCullock ought no to have the action against them because on [date blank] Joseph bought from Henry Eustace McCulloch esq, then a citizen of NC, "a tract" in Montgomery Co; Joseph gave a bond [date blank] to H E McCulloch for the purchase money; on [date blank] in Montgomery Co, H E McCulloch gave a bond to Joseph Bell [money blank] to deed the land to Joseph if Joseph paid for the land; on [date blank] the Colonies (New Hampshire, Massachusetts, Rhode Island, Connecticut, New York, Pennsylvania, Delaware, Maryland, Virginia, New Jersey, North Carolina, South Carolina, & Georgia) and the King of Great Britain were at open war and "declared hostilities"; on Jul. 4, 1776 the Colonies under title of United States of America declared themselves a free and independent nation; on [date blank] the North Carolina Legislature passed a law declaring all lands, tenements, & hereditaments and movable property in the State which anyone owned on Jul. 4, 1776 who were absent from the US and were "still" absent or who aided and abetted the enemies of the US or who withdrew from the US after said date and who are still outside the US were confiscated to the use of the State unless the person at the next General Assembly Oct. 1, 1778 appeared and applied for citizenship. H E McCulloch was absent from the State on Jul. 4, 1776 and didn't appear before the Assembly and the Assembly didn't admit him as a citizen or restore his property; on Oct. [blank], 1779, the Assembly passed a law confiscating H E McCulloch's property. The plaintiff is an agent for H E McCulloch; on [date blank] he executed a title for the land; Joseph and Benjamin Bell gave an obligation to the plaintiff on which [this] suit is brought; Joseph and Benjamin Bell received George McCulloch's bond; the suit was brought about the purchase money; in 1794 the General Assembly passed a law to give H E McCulloch's confiscated property to UNC; on [date blank] Joseph and Benjamin Bell paid Adlai Osborn, attorney for UNC Trustees, [money blank] the purchase money; Osborn deeded the land to Joseph Bell; so Joseph and Benjamin Bell ask for judgment against George McCulloch. [not signed]

815. William Sanders and Charles Bruce vs Thomas Johnston:

Salisbury Dist. Equity Court Mar. term 1797--answer of Thomas Johnston and wife Frances to the complaint of William Sanders and Charles Bruce--Frances says it's true that "a tract" was seized by the Commissioners of Confiscated Property who sold it to William Sanders who sold to Frances Johnston; the land was where Charles Ledbetter decd, husband of the defendant, formerly lived; but Frances denys she knew how many acres were involved or that the land was sold, by the Commissioners to William Sanders who sold to Frances Johnston as the tract were Charles Ledbetter formerly lived, without mentioning the number of acres "as stated in the bill"; Frances says she was present when the land was sold by the Commissioners as 360 ac, and Sanders sold Frances 360 ac; she agreed to give Sanders £400 for the land--£50 "paid down" in hard money and two bonds for the remainder were executed to Sanders; she wouldn't have given so much if there had been only 300 ac; Sanders with Charles Bruce as security had a bond to Frances for £1,000 to make a deed for 360 ac "reference" to Court of Law records; Frances denys she guessed about the number of acres or told Sanders how many acres were involved; after the sale, Frances had the land surveyed, and it contained only 300 ac; so she told Sanders and asked for a title agreeable to his bond; Sanders said he would allow Frances a credit, on her bond to him, for the deficient amount; but Sanders didn't make Frances a title. Thomas Johnston says he doesn't know about the "original" bargin; after he married Frances, they frequently asked Sanders for a title. But they were told Sanders, since their marriage, got a grant for 300 ac in the name of Frances Ledbetter but didn't notify Thomas or Frances. Thomas says Sanders "frequently" said he would make allowance for the 60 ac in the bond to Frances; Thomas, at his own expense, built "a large and commodious house" on the land and improved the land "in several particulars" by establishing a fishery "of very good value" on the premises. Sanders was delighted with the improvements and then refused to make allowances for the 60 ac; Thomas and Frances put a bond "of complaints" in a suit and recovered the penalty mentioned in the bill of complaint; but they didn't intend to revoke the whole bond; "lately" Thomas had the deputy county surveyor make a very accurate survey which showed only 290.25 ac; but it omits some of the most valuable land on the "plantation" part of which is under cultivation; they believe the 290 ac are worth £1,000 "or upwards"; they ask that the complainants account for the deficiencies in the land and give them a good title. [signed] Duffy for defendants. Mar. 29, 1799 the above is true [signed] Thos Johnson and Frances Johnson's mark "+" before Max Chambers, C M Ey.

Montgomery Co May 27, 1797   due to a writ from Salisbury Dist. Superior Court: Cary Pritchard, Benm. Bell, & Edward Burton appeared before me on May 26 and swore as follows concerning the suit by Sanders & Bruce vs Thos Johnson and wife: on May 25, 1797 Pitchard, Bell, & Burton met on the improvement where Thomas and wife live; the wife bought the land from Capt. Wm Sanders; we value the property at £1,020. [signed] Isham Harris.

Sales of Confiscated Land

816. UNC Trustees vs John Newman (1795):
Salisbury Dist. Equity Court Sept. term 1795--to the Justices of said Court: the Trustees say by a law passed at Fayetteville in 1789 [the law to establish the University], the following were nominated trustees: Samuel Johnston, James Iredell, Charles Johnston, Hugh Williamson, Stephen Cabarrus, Richard Dobbs Spaight, William Blount, Benjamin Williams, John Sitgraves, Frederick Harget, Robert W Snead, Archibald Maclaine, Honorable Samuel Ashe, Robert Dickson, Benjamin Smith, Honorable Samuel Spencer, John Hay, James Hog, Henry William Harrington, William Barry Grove, Rev. Samuel McCorkle, Adlai Osborn, John Stokes, Alfred Moore, Alexander Mebane, John Hamilton, Joseph Graham, Honorable John Williams, Thomas Person, Joel Lane, Willie Jones, Benjamin Hawkins, John Haywood sr, John Macon, William Richardson Davie, Joseph Dickson, William Lenoir, Joseph McDowell, James Holland, & William Porter esqs; by a law passed in 1794 to endow the University and secure titles of certain people in Mecklenburg Co and "other" citizens who bought land from Henry Eustace McCullock prior to Jul. 4, 1779, the following land was sold: in 1767 H E McCulloch sold to John Newman (of Mecklenburg Co) 200 ac for £53; the land borders: Henry Vernon's corner white oak on waters of Sugar Cr, runs N20E 128 poles on Vernon's line to his other white oak corner, N67W 156 poles to a pine, S67W 76 poles to a white oak, S35E 84 poles to a white oak, N2W 92 poles to Moses Ferguson's and John Canon's corner, & to the beginning; the deed was recorded in Mecklenburg Co; John had a bond dated Jan. 13, 1767 to pay H E McCulloch; none of the money was paid; so the Trustees ask John to pay £53 with interest but John refused.   [not signed]

817. UNC Trustees vs James Way (1795):
[same as No. 816 above except for James Way]; in 1767 H E McCulloch sold John Way 227 ac for £60; the land borders: Henry Davis's corner ash on "the" bank of "the" creek, runs N48W 90 poles on his line to a white oak, N 84 poles to a "B O", N43E 106 poles to a white oak, S86E 118 poles to a hickory, S16E 78 poles to Thomas Harris' corner hickory, S31E 100 poles to a Spanish oak "his" other corner, S12E 42 poles crosses the creek to said Harris' and Moses [Thomas--lined out] Craig's corner white oak, & to the beginning; John Way entered a bond with McCulloch dated Jan. 15, 1767 to pay £60 with 6% interest; but the money hasn't been paid; so the Trustees bring a suit against Way. [signed] A Henderson, sol. for complainants; [on back] "a true copy" [signed] Max Chambers, C M Ey

818. [The following is in box CRX 76 Salisbury Dist. Court Papers.] a deed
Nov. 7, 1795 Adlai Osborn, Commissioner & attorney for Trustees of UNC (Iredell Co) to David Cowen (Rowan Co); for £5,000 sold (1) 12,500 ac which is tract 16 of "great" tract No. 6; granted Mar. 3, 1745 by George III to William Hoston and "afterwards" sold to William Tryon; border: SE corner of tract 15 at 2 post oaks on E side of Long Cr, runs E 250 chains, N 500 chains, W 250 chains, & S to the beginning; (2) 12,500 ac tract 17 of part said tract No. 5 granted Mar. 3, 1745 by George III to Henry Stingsby [sic]; border: on NE corner of tract No. 16, runs N 500 chains, W 250 chains, S 500 chains, E to the beginning, & joins tract 15 on S and tract 18 on W; and (3) 12,500 ac tract 19 part of said tract No. 6 granted Mar. 3, 1745 by George III to Henry Hawson; border: a gum on NE corner of tract 12, runs S 500 chains to 2 post oaks & a dogwood, E 250 chains, N 500 chains, W 250 chains, & to the beginning; the total is 37,500 ac with "revertion" of 12,500 ac "already in possession of several tenants" and held by State grants or "long actual occupancy" and dispersed among said tracts 16, 17, & 19; the latter 12,500 ac is excluded from this deed; the land escheated to the State and by Act of Assembly were granted to Trustees of UNC. [signed] Ad Osbourn. Witness A Henderson. Wit. oath Nov. 10, 1795 by Archibald Henderson esq to Spruce McCory, J S Ct.   Recorded Nov. 12, 1795 Montgomery Co Book F p. 338 J Smith P R.

[The following No. 819-825 are in CRX Box 1 Salisbury Dist Court Miscellaneous Records; Trustees of UNC vs. various people.]
819. Trustees of UNC vs James Deormond: Mar. term 1796 Salisbury Dist. Equity Court--to Mecklenburg Co sheriff--at Sept. term 1795, the Trustees complained against James Deormond, late of Mecklenbury Co; so a subpoena issued against Deormond; the Mecklenburg Co sheriff made a return this term saying Deormond is dead; so you will summon [blank] of said Deormond to appear Sept. 19 "next" at Salisbury Dist. Equity Court in Salisbury to show why [they] shouldn't be made parties to the suit and do what the Court decides.   [signed] Max Chambers, Clerk & Master of Equity Court, Mar. 17, 1796

Sales of Confiscated Land

820. Trustees of UNC vs Robert Burns: Mar. term 1796 Salisbury Dist. Equity Court--to Mecklenburg Co sheriff--at Sept. term 1795, the Trustees complained against Robert Burns, late of Mecklenburg Co; so a subpoena issued against Burns; the Mecklenburg Co sheriff made a return this term saying Burns is dead; so you will summon [blank] of said Burns to appear Sept. 19, "next" at Salisbury Dist. Equity Court in Salisbury to show why [they] shouldn't be made parties to the suit and do what the Court decides. [signed] Max Chambers, Clerk & Master of Equity Court, Mar. 17, 1796

821. Trustees of UNC vs William Beaty: [first page of the suit lost] Beaty was to pay £72.1.6 or deliver the premises to the Trustees; Beaty refused, so the Trustees foreclosed on his mortgage; the Trustees ask for Beaty's response; in [blank] 1767 Henry E McCulloh sold to William Beaty 271 ac in Mecklenburg Co; Beaty was to pay £72.1.6 with interest for the land due to a mortgage dated Jan. 16, 1767; Beaty is to answer if he paid any money; Beaty should be ordered to pay the Trustees the remaining money due including 6% interest after the Court orders him to pay. [signed] A Henderson, sol. for comps. "a true copy" [signed] Max Chambers, C M Ety; defendant's copy

822. Trustees of UNC vs Andrew Elliott: Mar. term 1796 Salisbury Dist. Equity Court--to Mecklenburg Co sheriff--at Sept. term 1795, the Trustees complained against Andrew [Alexander--lined out] Elliott, late of Mecklenburg Co; so a subpoena issued against Elliott; the Mecklenburg Co sheriff made a return this term saying Alexander Elliott [sic] is dead; so you will summon [blank] of said Elliott to appear Sept. 19, "next" at Salisbury Dist. Equity Court in Salisbury to show why [they] shouldn't be made parties to the suit and do what the Court decides. [signed] Max Chambers, Clerk & Master of Equity Court Mar. 19, 1796; [on back] notice issued to Georgia.

823. Trustees of UNC vs John Taylor: Mar. term 1796 Salisbury Dist Equity Court--to Mecklenburg Co sheriff--at Sept. term 1795, the Trustees complained against John Taylor, late of Mecklenburg Co; so a subpoena issued against Taylor; the Mecklenburg Co sheriff made a return this term saying Taylor is dead; so you will summon [blank] of said Taylor to appear Sept. 19 "next" at Salisbury Dist. Equity Court in Salisbury to show why [they] shouldn't be made parties to the suit and do what the Court decides. [signed] Max Chambers, Clerk & Master of Equity Court Mar. 19, 1796; [on back] the heirs have redeemed the mortgage.

824. Trustees of UNC vs George Ross: Sept. term 1795; the Trustees were nominated by an act of Assembly passed at Fayetteville in 1789 [see No. 816 above for names]; there was an act to endow the University passed in 1794 at Raleigh which gave the University the land Henry E McCulloch sold to citizens of Mecklenburg Co; the land was confiscated; some of the people had mortgages before Jul. 4, 1776; in 1767 H E McCulloch sold to George Ross for £25.14.6 and 6% interest 110 ac; the land is in Mecklenburg Co and borders: James Alexander's corner white oak, runs S22E 22 poles to Ezra Alexander's corner white oak, S13E 120 poles along his line to a hickory, S73W 140 poles to a white oak, N52W 90 poles to a stake in James Alexander's line, N80E 30 poles along his line to his corner, N26E 65 poles along his other line, S60E 25 poles to his "other" corner a spanish oak, & N43E to the beginning; the mortgage was recorded in Mecklenburg Co Register's Office [Book 7 p. 416]; the lease was dated Jan. 17, 1767 for £0.5; the Trustees ask the Court to summon Ross so he can say if he paid any of the money; the Trustees asked Ross to pay them, but he refused; so they foreclosed on his mortgage. [signed] A Henderson, solr. ofr comps.; [on back] No. 25; "a true copy" [signed] Max Chambers, C M Ety; defendant's copy

825. Trustees of UNC vs Walter Beaty: Sept. term 1795; the Trustees were nominated by an act of Assembly passed at Fayetteville in 1789 [see No. 816 above for names]; there was an act to endow the Universiy passed in 1794 at Raleigh which gave the University the land Henry E McCulloch sold to citizens of Mecklenbury Co; the land was confiscated; some of the people had mortgages before Jul. 4, 1776; in 1767 H E McCulloch mortgaged 240 ac to Walter Beaty for £65.2.6 and 6% interest; the land is in Mecklenburg Co and borders: a white oak on "the" side of a glade, runs S6W 36 poles to a white oak, S32W 132 poles to Spark's corner black jack, S 64 poles to his other corner white oak, S18E 136 poles to Spark's other corner black oak "just" over Campbells Cr, S66E 76 poles to a hickory, N24E 82 poles to a black oak crossing "a meander", N 57W 64 poles to a hickory, N46E 94 poles to a black oak, N 110 poles to a white oak, & crossing [blank] to the beginning; the lease was dated Jan. 16, 1767 for £0.5 and was recorded in Mecklenburg Co Register's Office [Book 7 p. 410]; Beaty didn't pay the mortgage, and he refused to pay the Trustees; so the Trustees foreclosed on his mortgage; they ask that Beaty be summoned so he can say if he paid

the mortgage.   [signed] A Henderson, solr. for complainants; [on back] No. 48; "a true copy" [signed] Max Chambers, C M Ety; defendant's copy

[The following No. 826-873 are in a book DSCR 207.314.3 Salisbury Dist. Equity Court Minutes.   The page numbers cited are from this book.   Some of the following information comes only from the Court's Docket (DSCR 207.317.2); the disposition of these cases isn't mentioned in the minutes.   All the land is in Mecklenburg Co.   Most of the original mortgages are in Mecklenburg Co's deed Book 5.]

826. Case No. 1 in Mar. 1796 Trustees of UNC vs Wm Beaty; p. 105; dismissed by complainants "alterncy of writing" & complainants pay costs.

827. Case No. 2 in Mar. 1796 Trustees of UNC vs Ebenezer Newton; p. 103, 119, & 129-134; notice to be published for 3 weeks in Georgia newspapers; on Jan. 10, 1767, Ebenezer Newton bought 190 ac for £62.14.6; the land borders: David Garrison and John McEelwer's beginning corner, runs N23W 64 poles on Garrison's line to his corner hickory, N36W 114 poles up a branch to his other corner white oak, N26E 40 poles to a white oak, N6W 134 poles to Thomas Polk's corner black oak, S73E 164 poles on his line to his corner ash on "the" creek, crosses the creek to a stake in John Allen's line, S 160 poles to Allen's line and beyond his corner stake, & to the beginning.

828. Case No. 3 in Mar. 1796 Trustees of UNC vs John Carson; p. 104; dismissed by complainants "alterncy in writing" & complainants pay costs.

829. Case No. 4 in Mar. 1796 Trustees of UNC vs John Newman; p. 104; dismissed by complainants "alterncy in writing" & complainants pay costs.

830. Case No. 5 in Mar. 1796 Trustees of UNC vs James Orr; p. 119; case dismissed; defendant assumes cost except half of the attorney's fees.

831. Case No. 6 in Mar. 1796 Trustees of UNC vs James McClure; p. 119 and 149; order to be published for 3 weeks in South Carolina and Fayetteville newspapers; no heirs found by Mecklenburg Co sheriff [final disposition of the case not indicated in minutes or docket].

832. Case No. 7 in Mar. 1796 Trustees of UNC vs John Hill; p. 104, 119, & 134-137; notice to be published in Georgia newspapers; on Jan. 30, 1767 Hill bought 190 ac for £48.18.0; the land borders: Robert Pack's beginning corner hickory, runs E 29 poles on his line to a white oak, S 100 poles to a white oak, S28W 80 poles to a hickory, N72W 64 poles to a hickory on Ezekiel Wallace's line, N21E 18 poles to his corner hickory, N45W 89 poles to a hickory, N38E 22 poles to a white oak, N31 W 88 poles to a red oak, N51W 88 poles to a red oak, N51E 138 poles to an elm, & to the beginning.

833. Case No. 8 in Mar. 1796 Trustees of UNC vs Josiah Roberts; p. 104 and 187-191; on Jan. 15, 1767 Roberts bought 163 ac for £41.14.6; the land borders: a black oak on waters of Sugar Cr, runs S1W 62 poles to a pine, S39W 70 poles to a white oak, S77W 100 poles to a stake, N31W 120 poles to a stake, N30E 80 poles to a pine, & to be beginning.

834. Case No. 9 in Mar. 1796 Trustees of UNC vs Abraham Miller; p. 104; dismissed by complainants "alterncy in writing" & complainants pay costs.

835. Case No. 10 in Mar. 1796 Trustees of UNC vs William Brown; p. 104; dismissed by complainants "alterncy in writing" & complainants pay costs.

836. Case No. 11 in Mar. 1796 Trustees of UNC vs James Johnston; p. 119, 149, & 191-194; on Jan. 14, 1767 Johnston bought 120 ac for £31.4.6; the land borders: Samuel Nelson's beginning corner hickory, runs N50E 60 poles to

Sales of Confiscated Land

Nelson's corner hickory by a branch, N8E 184 poles to a "b" jack, S75W 68 poles to a "b j", S29W 180 poles to a stake, & to the beginning.

837. Case No. 12 in Mar. 1796 Trustee of UNC vs James McCord; p. 119, 150, & 194-197; on Jan. 10, 1767 McCord bought 137 ac for £39.19.2; the land borders: a white oak on N side of a Spring Br and joins James Moore & Joseph Lee, runs S70W 100 poles to a black oak, S27E 184 poles to a black oak on Lee's line, N55E 146 poles on his line to his corner white oak, N25W 54 poles to James McCord's beginning corner black oak, & to the beginning.

838. Case No. 13 in Mar. 1796 Trustees of UNC vs James Tate; p. 119 and 197-199; on Jan. 14, 1767 Tate bought 220 ac for £59.10; the land borders: James Johnston's beginning corner hickory, N52E 60 poles, on his line to his other corner hickory, N55E 160 poles to Down's coarner black oak, S4W 90 poles [to] Down's other corner, S10W 74 poles to Down's corner "other" black oak, S25W 60 poles crossing "the" creek to a hickory in Down's line, S69W 194 poles to a black oak sapling, N57W 28 poles to a white oak, & to the beginning.

839. Case No. 14 in Mar. 1796 Trustees of UNC vs Arthur Alexander; p. 119; dismissed by complainants and complainants pay costs.

840. Case No. 15 in Mar. 1796 Trustees of UNC vs John Johnston; p. 104, 120, & 199-202; notice to be published in Knoxville, TN, Gazette; on Jan. 17, 1767 Johnston bought 227 ac for £59.3.6; the land borders Culbert Nicholson's corner small hickory, runs S27E 72 poles on his line to a stake by "the" creek, N53E 10 poles to a white oak on the bank, S31E 100 poles to a black oak, S72W 42 poles to a white oak by a branch, S23W 130 poles across a branch to a white oak, N40W 82 poles to a white oak, N 76 poles to a white oak, S79W 32 poles to a black oak, N36W 158 poles to a black oak, & to the beginning

841. Case No. 16 in Mar. 1796 Trustees of UNC vs John McClure; [on Mar. 1796 docket]; dismissed by complainants & complainants pay costs.

842. Case No. 17 in Mar. 1796 Trustees of UNC vs William Henry; p. 104, 120, 150, & 202-204; order to be published in Kentucky Gazette; on Jan. 10, 1767 Henry bought 175 ac for £45; the land borders: David Vance's corner white oak, runs S36E 82 poles to a white oak by a pond, S6W 76 poles to a white oak, S44W 92 poles to a white oak, S57W 72 poles to a hickory, N19W 136 poles to a black oak, N25E 115 poles to a hickory by a glade, & to the beginning.

843. Case No. 18 in Mar. 1796 Trustees of UNC vs Jonathan Buckalew; p. 120, 150, & 205-207; on Jan. 15, 1767 Buckalew bought 163 ac for £44.13.6; the land borders: Clark's corner white oak on waters of McCalpins Cr, runs S46E 98 poles on his line to a white oak, S75E 54 poles to a hickory, N77E 56 poles to a white oak, S33E 86 poles to a black oak, N44E 54 poles to a white oak, N45W 112 poles to a black jack, N5E 74 poles to a pine, N77W 72 poles to a white oak "crossing" the creek, & to the beginning.

844. Case No. 19 in Mar. 1796 Trustees of UNC vs David Davis; p. 120, 150, 207-210; on Jan. 21, 1767 Davis bought 242 ac for £63.17.6; the land borders: a black oak on Selyen's barony line of tract No. 3, runs N 200 poles on said line to Robert Campbell's corner white oak "in the same", N71E 110 poles to his other corner white oak, N86E 52 poles on his line to his beginning hickory, S12W 345 poles to a stake, S87W 90 poles to a stake in "the" boundary line, & along the same to the beginning.

845. Case No. 20 in Mar. 1796 Trustees of UNC vs Robert Robb; p. 120; dismissed by complainants & complainants pay costs.

846. Case No. 21 in Mar. 1796 Trustees of UNC vs William Roberts; p. 105, 120, & 138-141; order to be published in North Carolina Journal; on Jan. 20, 1767 Roberts bought 126 ac for £44; the land borders: a poplar on "the" side of a steep hill, runs N10W 50 poles to [blank], N33E 44 poles to a hickory, N60E 96 poles to a white oak, S33E 72 poles to a black jack, S55E 70 poles to a hickory, S22W 54 poles to a black jack, S36W 50 poles to a hickory, & to the beginning.

Sales of Confiscated Land

847. Case No. 22 in Mar. 1796 Trustees of UNC vs David Alexander; p. 120, 150, & 210-213; on Mar. 17, 1765 Alexander bought 155 ac for £33.13; th land borders: a black oak by "the" Great Road, runs S83W 136 poles to a black oak, S10E 48 poles to a red oak, S12W 104 poles to a black oak in "the" line of Charles Beatman Livingston's tract, S66E 48 poles along said line to a corner of the tract where Abraham Caroline lives, N57E 200 poles along that tract to a white oak another corner of the same, & to the beginning.

848. Case No. 23 in Mar. 1796 Trustees of UNC vs William Wallace; p. 105 and 121; order to be published in Knoxville, TN, Gazette; [in Sept. 1796 docket] dismissed by complainants & complainants pay costs.

849. Case No. 24 in Mar. 1796 Trustees of UNC vs Alexander Elliot; p. 151 and 213-215; on Jan. 17, 1767 Elliott bought 200 ac for £46.16; the land borders: a gum on W side of Mallards Cr, runs N50W 160 poles to a white oak, S50W 100 poles to a pine sapling and white oak, S50E 234 poles across said creek to a white oak, & to the beginning.

850. Case No. 25 in Mar. 1796 Trustees of UNC vs George Ross; p. 105; dismissed by complainants "alterncy in writing" & complainants pay costs.

851. Case No. 26 in Mar. 1796 Trustees of UNC vs William Reed; p. 121, 151, & 216; Wm and Adam Reed reply--in 1788 their father William died; they ask for abatement [no more information found].

852. Case No. 27 in Mar. 1796 Trustees of UNC vs James Campbell; p. 121, 151, & 217-219; on Mar. 20, 1765 Campbell bought 180 ac for £44; the land borders: William Wallace's corner white oak on S branch of Coddle Cr, runs N80W 62 poles to a red oak sapling, N22W 60 poles to a white oak, N8W 26 poles to a red oak, N43E 124 poles to an elm by "the" bank of a creek, & down the creek to the beginning.

853. Case No. 28 in Mar. 1796 Trustees of UNC vs John McCord; p. 121, 151, & 220-222; on Jan. 23, 1767 McCord bought 108 ac for £27; the land borders: Mary McKee's corner, runs S3W 166 poles to a black oak, S33W 64 poles to a black oak in Mr. Ree's [sic] line, N70W 60 poles to a hickory, N53W 40 poles to Kennedy's corner white oak, N19E 110 poles on David Kennedy's line to a white oak on McCord's Br, & to the beginning.

854. Case No. 29 in Mar. 1796 Trustees of UNC vs Patrick Williams; p. 121, 151, & 223-225; on Jan. 20, 1767 Williams bought 143 ac for £31; the land borders: a gum in the head of a hollow, runs S49W [or S40W] 60 poles to a white oak, S78W 70 poles across a branch to a white oak, S26W 82 poles to a stake "crossing" a branch, S20E 70 poles to a stake on "the" boundary line, E 190 poles on the same to a stake, & to the beginning.

855. Case No. 30 in Mar. 1796 Trustees of UNC vs John Bettes; p. 105, 121, & 225-227; order to be published in Kentucky Gazette; on Jan. 17, 1767 Bettes bought 130 ac for £30; the land borders: Margaret Donaldson's corner red oak, runs S71W 168 poles on her line to a gum, "by" her corner to Davis' line, S12W 60 poles on her line to his corner black oak on Kings Br, S55E 24 poles to a hickory, S20W 48 poles to a white oak, S68E 160 poles to a white oak marked for a corner & a stake, & to the beginning.

856. Case No. 31 in Mar. 1796 Trustees of UNC vs Richard Buckelew; p. 105 and 228-230; order to be published in Knoxville, TN, Gazette; on Jan. 16, 1767 Buckelew bought 465 ac for £116.5; the land borders: a black jack on a hill, runs N54E 138 poles to a black oak, N30E 122 poles to a black oak, N10E 234 poles to a black oak, N66W 80 poles to a black oak in Gribble's line, S39W 104 poles to a black oak near a spring, S1W 92 poles to a black oak, S59W 228 poles to a stake & white oak on top of a ridge, S10E 58 poles to a white oak, S22W 30 poles to a black oak, & to the beginning.

857. Case No. 32 in Mar. 1796 Trustees of UNC vs Robert Burns; p. 151 and 230-232; on Jan. 23, 1767 Burns bought 200 ac for £51.10; the land borders: a black oak on a ridge above Ezra Alexander's land, runs N10E 112 pols to a white oak including 2 springs along said line, N30E 114 poles to a hickory, N41E 112 poles to a white oak, N60W 90

poles to a pine in Flanigin's open line, S13W 60 poles to Flanigin's corner black oak, 65W [sic] 140 poles to a black oak, S13E 90 poles to a gum, S24W 120 poles to a pine, & to the beginning.

858. Case No. 33 in Mar. 1796 Trustees of UNC vs James Moore; p. 150, 122, & 142-145; order to be published in Charleston, SC, newspapers; on Jan. 10, 1767 Moore bought 145 ac for £38.7.4; the land borders: a black oak on a hill on waters of Garrisons Cr, runs N 40 poles to a black oak, N27E 140 poles to a black oak, S55E 40 poles to a black oak, S66E 66 poles to a white oak, S10W 80 poles to a black oak, E 66 poles to a white oak on Thomas Polk's line, [blank] 42W 96 poles to "his" corner hickory, & to the beginning.

859. Case No. 34 in Mar. 1796 Trustees of UNC vs David Moore; p. 122, 152, & 233-235; on Jan. 17, 1767 Moore bought 117 ac for £30.18; the land borders: a small post oak on Gov. Dobbs' boundary line, runs S63W 90 poles to a white oak, S2 W 148 poles to a hickory by a branch, S17E 100 poles to a hickory, N30E 50 poles to a post oak, N71E 22 poles to a "w o" in said Dobbs' line, & along the same to the beginning.

860. Case No. 35 in Mar. 1796 Trustees of UNC vs John Newell; p. 160, 122, & 145-149; order to be published in Augusta, GA, newspapers; on Jan. 30, 1767 Newell bought 130 ac for £33.13.8; the land borders: a white oak on "the" side of a branch, runs N8W 40 poles to a hickory, N85E 102 poles to a small hickory, S39E 78 poles to a white oak, S10W poles to a hickory, S74W 62 poles to a stake, & to the beginning.

861. Case No. 36 in Mar. 1796 Trustees of UNC vs John Taylor; p. 122; dismissed by complainants and defendant assumes cost except half of attorney's fees.

862. Case No. 37 in Mar. 1796 Trustees of UNC vs Thomas Kennedy; p. 122, 152, 235-237; on Jan. 8, 1767 Kennedy bought 243 ac for £65.13; the land borders: a hickory, runs S21E 120 poles to Barnet's corner hickory, S49E 186 poles to a white oak, N18E 110 poles to a white oak at McCords Br, N44E 52 poles to a hickory, N21E 64 poles to a black jack, N3W 78 poles to a post oak, N83W 48 poles to a red oak, & to the beginning.

863. Case No. 38 in Mar. 1796 Trustees of UNC vs James Way; p. 106; dismissed by complainants "alterncy in writing" & complainants pay costs.

864. Case No. 39 in Mar. 1796 Trustees of UNC vs John Ramsey; p. 122, 152, & 237-239; on Jan. 14, 1767 Ramsey bought 312 ac for £82.5.6; the land borders: Thomas Black's corner white oak, runs N20E 42 poles on his line to a small hickory "crossing" Four Mile Cr, N28W 170 poles to a white oak, N66W 32 poles to a hickory, S64W 48 poles to a small pine, S5W 98 poles to a black oak, S25W 107 poles to a hickory, S26E 180 poles to a white oak, N76E 40 poles to a white oak, & to the beginning.

865. Case No. 40 in Mar. 1796 Trustees of UNC vs Timothy White; p. 106, 122, & 239-241; on Mar. 25, 1767 White bought 200 ac for £20; the land borders: Holoway's corner black oak, runs S28W 50 poles to a white oak, S5E 110 poles to a hickory, S66W 100 poles to a white oak, N73W 70 poles to a hickory, N66W 80 poles to a black jack, N13E 140 poles to a Spanish oak, & to the beginning.

866. Case No. 41 in Mar. 1796 Trustees of UNC vs John Clark; p. 122; dismissed by complainants and Christopher Erwin assumes to pay cost except £5, part of attorney's fees.

867. Case No. 42 in Mar. 1796 Trustees of UNC vs Robert Brown; p. 123, 152, & 242-244; on Feb. 21, 1767 Brown bought 125 ac for £32.11; the land borders: a large black oak, runs S43W 72 poles to a white oak, S58W 106 poles to a white oak on a hill, S22E 50 poles to a black oak, S62E 165 poles to a stake, N48E 80 poles to a stake, & to the beginning.

868. Case No. 43 in Mar. 1796 Trustees of UNC vs Moses Craige; p. 106; [on Mar. 1796 docket] case dismissed by complainants and at complainant's cost.

Sales of Confiscated Land

869. Case No. 44 in Mar. 1796 Trustees of UNC vs Joseph Kennedy; p. 123, 152, & 244-246; on Jan. 9, 1767 Kennedy bought 242 ac for £65.9.4; the land borders: a white oak on a ridge of good land above his house, runs S45E 80 poles to a post oak, S5E 168 poles "crossing the" creek to a hickory, S86W 180 poles to a black oak, N26W 120 poles across the creek to a hickory, & to the beginning.

870. Case No. 45 in Mar. 1796 Trustees of UNC vs James Dormond "or Ormand"; [on Mar. 1796 docket] dismissed by complainants "alterncy in writing" & complainants pay costs.

871. Case No. 46 in Mar. 1796 Trustees of UNC vs George Allen; p. 123; dismissed by complainants and complainants pay costs.

872. Case No. 47 in Mar. 1796 Trustees of UNC vs Thomas McCall; p. 123; dismissed by complainants "alterncy in writing" & complainants pay costs.

873. Case No. 48 in Mar. 1796 Trustees of UNC vs Walter Beaty; p. 106; dismissed by complainants "alterncy in writing" & complainants pay costs.

874. [The following is a list of deeds in Mecklenburg Co from Adlai Osborne as attorney for the Trustees of UNC to various people.]
303 ac to James Osborn   Book 3 p. 341
162 ac on McCalpins Cr to John, Noble, & James Osborn   Book 15 p. 100
72 ac on McCalpins Cr to James Osborne   Book 15 p. 101
222 ac on McCalpins Cr to Frederick Shaver   Book 15 p. 101
110 ac on Sugar Cr to William Huston   Book 15 p. 102
240 ac on Kings Cr to James Flanagan   Book 15 p. 103
131 ac on Sugar Cr to Culbert Nichelson   Book 15 p. 104
[a release] to Frederick Shaver   Book 15 p. 104
[a release] to James Osborn   Book 15 p. 105
[a release] to John Osborn and Noble Osborn   Book 15 p. 105
303 ac on Four mile Cr to James Osborn   Book 15 p. 122
480 ac on McDowels Cr to Hugh Terrance   Book 15 p. 127
210 ac on McDowels Cr and Rocky R to John McK Alexander   Book 15 p. 149
347 ac on Sugar Cr to Will McCulloh   Book 15 p. 154
190 ac on McDowells Cr to Joseph Moor   Book 15 p. 181
130 ac on McCalpins Cr to John Clark   Book 15 p. 182
275 ac on Sugar Cr to John Taylor   Book 15 p. 182
410 ac on Sugar Cr to John Henry   Book 15 p. 183
226 ac on Sugar Cr to Joseph   Priest   Book 15 p. 183
94 ac on Sugar Cr to James Orr   Book 15 p. 213
1,808 ac [several tracts] to Thomas Polk's heirs   Book 15 p. 214
66 ac on McCalipins Cr to Roderic McCauley [or McAuley]   Book 15 p. 214
380 ac on Sugar Cr to John McClure   Book 15 p. 240
130 ac on McCalpins Cr to James Glass   Book 15 p. 245
269 ac on McDowels Cr to Martin Steel   Book 15 p. 246
306 ac on Four Mile Cr to John Ray   Book 15 p. 247
181 ac on McMichaels Cr to William Lees   Book 15 p. 351
63 ac on McCalpins Cr to Joseph Reed   Book 15 p. 355
375 ac on McDowels Cr to Robert Davidson   Book 16 p. 5
296 ac on Sugar Cr to James Maxwell   Book 16 p. 39
400 ac on Back Cr to John McGee   Book 16 p. 94
172 ac on McCalpins Cr to Ezekiel Black   Book 16 p. 283
210 ac on McMichaels Cr to Samuel Bigham   Book 17 p. 423
350 ac on Garr and McDowells Creeks to Matthew McClure   Book 17 p. 520

Sales of Confiscated Land

202 ac on Reedy Cr to Thomas Weir   Book 17 p. 832
182 ac on Reedy Cr to Walter Kerr   Book 18 p. 26
80 ac on McCalpins Cr to Samuel Black   Book 18 p. 72
200 ac on Four Mile Cr to Andrew Rea   Book 18 p. 103
159 ac   to Elisha Smart, trustees   Book 18 p. 275
147 ac on McMichaels Cr to Archibald Alexander   Book 19 p. 616
233 ac on McCalpins Cr to James Maxwell jr   Book 19 p. 742
212 ac on Reedy Cr to James Maxwell   Book 19 p. 743

[The following No. 875-879 are on five sheets in General Assembly Session Records Nov. 1821-Jan. 1822 Box 4, Petitions-Revolutionary War land warrants and related certificates.   This list mentions land grants primarily to UNC's Trustees for Revolutionary bound land in Tennessee; this isn't confiscated land.   A different number has been assigned to each sheet of the list.]

875.
file no. 2609 to President & Trustees assignee of John Ombry; 274 ac; warrant no. 472; location no. 2685.
file no. 2610 to President & Trustees assignee of Chaney Bush; 640 ac; warrant no. 435; location no. 2082.
file no. 2611 to President & Trustees assignee of Edwd Kelley; 640 ac; warrant no. 450; location no. 1771.
file no. 2612 to President & Trustees assignee of Ro Nicholson; 807 ac; warrant no. 631; location no. 1647.
file no. 2613 to President & Trustees assignee of Wm Walton; 1,000 ac; warrant no. 621; location no. 2513.
file no. 2614 to President & Trustees assignee of Patrick Kelly; 640 ac; warrant no. 470; location no. 1449.
file no. 2615 to President & Trustees assignee of Niser Adams; 640 ac; warrant no. 749; location no. 2248.
file no. 2616 to President & Trustees assignee of Ro Cole; 640 ac; warrant no. 564; location no. 2247.
file no. 2617 to President & Trustees assignee of Majr. Willard; 640 ac; warrant no. 560; location no. 845.
file no. 2618 to President & Trustees assignee of Collins Brown; 640 ac; warrant no. 473; location no. 1438.
file no. 2619 to President & Trustees assignee of James Yatchel; 640 ac; warrant no. 454; location no. 172.
file no. 2620 to President & Trustees assignee of Walter Wattas; 640 ac; warrant no. 453; location no. 2098.
file no. 2621 to President & Trustees assignee of Jno Brock; 640; warrant no. 447; location no. 1429.
file no. 2622 to President & Trustees assignee of Thomas Francisco; 640 ac; warrant no. 442; location no. 92.
file no. 2623 to President & Trustees assignee of Will Nowell; 640 ac; warrant no. 439; location no. 2009.
file no. 2624 to President & Trustees assignee of Oden Berebon; 640 ac; warrant no. 471; location no. 307.
file no. 2625 to President & Trustees assignee of John Conner; 640 ac; warrant no. 441; location no. 1207.
file no. 2626 to President & Trustees assignee of John Eastment; 640 ac; warrant no. 429; location no. 752.
file no. 2627 to President & Trustees assignee of John Beal; 640 ac; warrant no. 430; location no. 2587.
file no. 2628 to President & Trustees assignee of James Murphy; 640 ac warrant no. 486; location no. 752.
file no. 2629 to President & Trustees assignee of Adam Turner; 640 ac; warrant no. 477; location no. 315.
file no. 2630 to President & Trustees assignee of Edwd Lewis; 640 ac; warrant no. 459; location no. 1164.
file no. 2631 to President & Trustees assignee of Wm Flinn; 640 ac; warrant no. 463; location no. 178.
file no. 2632 to President & Trustees assignee of Joel Stokes; 640 ac; warrant no. 455; location no. 3007.
file no. 2633 to President & Trustees assignee of Jno Helbert; 640 ac; warrant no. 449; location no. 1636.
file no. 2634 to President & Trustees assignee of Wm Bridget; 640 ac; warrant no. 445; location no. 29.
file no. 2635 to President & Trustees assignee of Wm Walker; 640 ac; warrant no. 434; location no. 2805.
file no. 2636 to President & Trustees assignee of Jas Vernier; 1,494 ac; warrant no. 432; location no. 564.
file no. 2637 to President & Trustees assignee of Brutus Johnston; 1,000 ac; warrant no. 436; location no. 2259.
file no. 2638 to President & Trustees assignee of Ro Brownlop; 1,000 ac; warrant no. 444; location no. 1250.
file no. 2639 to President & Trustees assignee of Wm Dobbins; 1,000 ac; warrant no. 478; location no. 368.
file no. 2640 to President & Trustees assignee of Jas Sisk; 1,000 ac; warrant no. 425; location no. 403.

876.
file no. 2641 to President & Trustees assignee of Corn. Ruman; 1,000 ac; warrant no. 431; location no. 449
file no. 2642 to President & Trustees assignee of Jessee Parker; 1,000 ac; warrant no. 462; location no. 1996.
file no. 2643 to President & Trustees assignee of Archd Bogle; 1,000 ac; warrant no. 427; location no. 430.

Sales of Confiscated Land

file no. 2644 to President & Trustees assignee of Daney Penticost; 356 ac; warrant no. 443; location no. 1683.
file no. 2645 to President & Trustees assignee of Wm Melton; 360 ac; warrant no. 467; location no. 623.
file no. 2646 to President & Trustees assignee of Jno Sollar; 274 ac; warrant no. 428; location no. 3013.
file no. 2647 to President & Trustees assignee of Jno McKinlay; 228 ac; warrant no. 451; location no. 2323.
file no. 2648 to President & Trustees assignee of David Ivey; 754 ac; warrant no. 456; location no. 2155.
file no. 2649 to President & Trustees assignee of Benjamin Agid; 228 ac; warrant no. 464; location no. 689.
file no. 2650 to President & Trustees assignee of Jeremh Daily; 228 ac; warrant no. 466; location no. 1083.
file no. 2651 to President & Trustees assignee of Rasde. Welsh; 228 ac; warrant no. 452; location no. 2505.
file no. 2652 to President & Trustees assignee of Jessee Knight; 274 ac; warrant no. 461; location no. 2234.
file no. 2653 to President & Trustees assignee of Geo Craig; 640 ac; warrant no. 448 ac; location no. 2773.
file no. 2654 to President & Trustees assignee of Jno Jarvis; 640 ac; warrant no. 519; location no. 629.
file no. 2655 to President & Trustees assignee of Wm Grant; 640 ac; warrant no. 517; location no. 554.
file no. 2656 to President & Trustees assignee of Hubb Carter; 640 ac; warrant no. 503; location no. 677.
file no. 2657 to President & Trustees assignee of Jas King; 1,000 ac; warrant no. 502; location no. 1842.
file no. 2658 to President & Trustees assignee of Henry Sorran; 1,000 ac; warrant no. 506; location no. 1924.
file no. 2659 to President & Trustees assignee of Josh Hinton; 1,000 ac; warrant no. 528; location no. 2069.
file no. 2660 to President & Trustees assignee of Saml Slaven; 1,000 ac; warrant no. 601; location no. 1795.
file no. 2661 to President & Trustees assignee of Jno Goven; 1,000 ac; warrant no. 635; location no. 516.
file no. 2662 to President & Trustees assignee of Jno Ingram; 1,000 ac; warrant no. 628; location no. 1643.
file no. 2663 to President & Trustees assignee of Tunis Bogart; 640 ac; warrant no. 524; location no. 710.
file no. 2664 to President & Trustees assignee of Thomas Foraster; 640 ac; warrant no. 505; location no. 1604.
file no. 2665 to President & Trustees assignee of Wm Fowler; 640 ac; warrant no. 501; location no. 581.
file no. 2666 to President & Trustees assignee of Wm Bowen; 640 ac; warrant no. 513; location no. 1490.
file no. 2667 to President & Trustees assignee of John Sharpley; 640 ac; warrant no. 603; location no. 2993.
file no. 2668 to President & Trustees assignee of Geo Trader; 640 ac; warrant no. 609; location no. 2770.
file no. 2669 to President & Trustees assignee of Saml Potter; 640 ac; warrant no. 610; location no. 882.
file no. 2670 to President & Trustees assignee of Benj. Schrolfield; 640 ac; warrant no. 611; location no. 955.
file no. 2671 to President & Trustees assignee of Amos Sanderford; 640 ac; warrant no. 613; location no. 1659.

877.
file no. 2672 to President & Trustees assignee of Thos Higgins; 640 ac; warrant no. 614; location no. 88.
file no. 2673 to President & Trustees assignee of Saml Welby; 640 ac; warrant no. 615; location no. 2437.
file no. 2674 to President & Trustees assignee of Jno Harley; 640 ac; warrant no. 618; location no. 1491.
file no. 2675 to President & Trustees assignee of Isaac Young; 640 ac; warrant no. 619; location no. 1861.
file no. 2676 to President & Trustees assignee of Thos Murphley; 640 ac; warrant no. 629; location no. 2938.
file no. 2677 to President & Trustees assignee of Ro Perkins; 640 ac; warrant no. 632; location no. 1655.
file no. 2678 to President & Trustees assignee of Edwd Howell; 357 ac; warrant no. 518; location no. 2115.
file no. 2679 to President & Trustees assignee of Thomas Booker; 360 ac; warrant no. 526; location no. 2934.
file no. 2680 to President & Trustees assignee of Wm Miller; 274 ac; warrant no. 520; location no. 1711.
file no. 2681 to President & Trustees assignee of Jos McDaniel; 274 ac; warrant no. 593; location no. 1139.
file no. 2682 to President & Trustees assignee of Jno Razor; 274 ac; warrant no. 599; location no. 2214.
file no. 2683 to President & Trustees assignee of Ro Jones; 228 ac; warrant no. 530; location no. 414.
file no. 2684 to President & Trustees assignee of Stephn. Gainer; 274 ac; warrant no. 626; location no. 1008.
file no. 2685 to President & Trustees assignee of Edwd Bates; 274 ac; warrant no. 624; location no. 2696.
file no. 2686 to President & Trustees assignee of Geo Skipper; 274 ac; warrant no. 606; location no. 2445.
file no. 2687 to President & Trustees assignee of Jos Skipper; 274 ac; warrant no. 607; location no. 291.
file no. 2688 to President & Trustees assignee of Solo Campbell; 640 ac; warrant no. 617; location no. 2828.
file no. 2689 to President & Trustees assignee of Michael Watson; 274 ac; warrant no. 608; location no. 849.
file no. 2690 to President & Trustees assignee of Bamett Sturdivant; 274 ac; warrant no. 602; location no. 2554.
file no. 2691 to President & Trustees assignee of Eli Rogers; 274 ac; warrant no. 598; location no. 1798.
file no. 2692 to President & Trustees assignee of Saml Beasley; 274 ac; warrant no. 522; location no. 2353.
file no. 2693 to President & Trustees assignee of Felix Seymore; 274 ac; warrant no. 516; location no. 671.

149

Sales of Confiscated Land

file no. 2694 to President & Trustees assignee of Reubin Deale; 640 ac; warrant no. 588; location no. 2819.
file no. 2695 to President & Trustees assignee of Ephraim Baston; 640 ac; warrant no. 587; location no. 2482.
file no. 2696 to President & Trustees assignee of Francis Bird; 640 ac; warrant no. 585; location no. 1869.
file no. 2697 to President & Trustees assignee of Littleton Jones; 640 ac; warrant no. 590; location no. 2890.
file no. 2698 to President & Trustees assignee of Ralph Moore; 640 ac; warrant no. 591; location no. 303.
file no. 2699 to President & Trustees assignee of Duncan Peteason; 640 ac; warrant no. 596; location no. 104.
file no. 2700 to President & Trustees assignee of Jeremiah Smith; 640 ac; warrant no. 634; location no. 2177.
file no. 2701 to President & Trustees assignee of John Oram; 640 ac; warrant no. 622; location no. 3025.

878.
file no. 2702 to President & Trustees assignee of Nathan Jordan; 640 ac; warrant no. 616; location no. 8025.
file no. 2703 to President & Trustees assignee of Randl. Newsond; 274 ac; warrant no. 515; location no. 2935.
file no. 2704 to President & Trustees assignee of John Blount; 640 ac; warrant no. 521; location no. 954.
file no. 2705 to President & Trustees assignee of Jno Edwards; 640 ac; warrant no. 527; location no. 356.
file no. 2706 to President & Trustees assignee of Belling Lucas; 640 ac; warrant no. 509; location no. 1464.
file no. 2707 to President & Trustees assignee of John Tinker; 640 ac; warrant no. 558; location no. 2334.
file no. 2708 to President & Trustees assignee of Stephn. Cook; 640 ac; warrant no. 565; location no. 2823.
file no. 2709 to President & Trustees assignee of Thomas Boyer; 640 ac; warrant no. 562; location no. 2192.
file no. 2710 to President & Trustees assignee of Wm Cornish; 640 ac; warrant no. 561; location no. 405.
file no. 2711 to President & Trustees assignee of John Lafferty; 640 ac; warrant no. 559; location no. 1887.
file no. 2712 to President & Trustees assignee of John Churn; 640 ac; warrant no. 532; location no. 2950.
file no. 2713 to President & Trustees assignee of Jno McDonald; 640 ac; warrant no. 531; location no. 1648.
file no. 2714 to President & Trustees assignee of Henry Spells; 228 ac; warrant no. 600; location no. 1358.
file no. 2715 to President & Trustees assignee of Wm Whithead; 228 ac; warrant no. 592; location no. 2060.
file no. 2716 to Thomas Henderson assignee of Jos Burgers; 640 ac; warrant no. 514; location no. 2882.
file no. 2717 to Thomas Henderson assignee of Jos Suggins; 640 ac; warrant no. 604; location no. 2573.
file no. 2718 to Thomas Henderson assignee of Thomas Hazel; 640 ac; warrant no. 612; location no. 2680.
file no. 2719 to Thomas Henderson assignee of Benj Cannon; 1,000 ac; warrant no. 465; location no. 2738.
file no. 2720 to Thomas Henderson assignee of Thomas D Tyae; 1,000 ac; warrant no. 422; location no. 1687.
file no. 2721 to Thomas Henderson assignee of Wm Nooning; 640 ac; warrant no. 594; location no. 969.
file no. 2722 to And Dillones assignee of Fred Peck; 274 ac; warrant no. 595; location no. 2029.
file no. 2723 to Thomas Henderson assignee of Rabin Newnan; 228 ac; warrant no. 480; location no. 1316.
file no. 2724 to Thomas Searcy assignee of Rd Robert; 274 ac; warrant no. 597; location no. 2043.
file no. 2725 to And Jones assignee of Nicholas Ruark; 274 ac; warrant no. 476; location no. 2645.
file no. 2725 to And Jones assignee of Wm Gaskins; 1,000 ac; warrant no. 504; location no. 931.
file no. 2727 to Thomas Henderson assignee of Thos Johnson; 640 ac; warrant no. 627; location no. 733.
file no. 2728 to Thomas Henderson assignee of John Waters; 640 ac; warrant no. 487; location no. 447.
file no. 2729 to Thomas Henderson assignee of Henry Brown; 640 ac; warrant no. 446; location no. 1437.

879.
file no. 2146 to Lewis Stephens assignee of Brown; 228 ac; warrant no. 3063; location no. 524.
file no. 2148 to James Morgan assignee of [blank]; 274 ac; warrant no. 3272; location no. 2593.
file no. 2149 to Ephraim Rodgers assignee of [blank]; 274; warrant no. 502; location no. 2002.
file no. 2150 to William Johnson assignee of [blank]; 182 ac; warrant no. 67; location no. 1857.
file no. 2151 to Jerry Rollin assignee of Brown; 640 ac; warrant no. 155; location no. 553.
file no. 2154 to Allen Read assignee of H Williamson; 274 ac; warrant no. 10; location no. 255.
file no. 2155 to Thos Loyd assignee of L Loyd "& all"; 640 ac; warrant no. 152; location no. 2608.
file no. 2156 to William Davie assignee of [blank]; 278 ac; warrant no. 331; location no. 530.
file no. 2157 to Geo Reynolds assignee of Hall & Brown; 1,000 ac; warrant no. 384; location no. 1000.
file no. 2158 to Micajah Hicks assignee of [blank]; 228 ac; warrant no. 5268; location no. 1829.
file no. 2159 to Jno Barfield assignee of Will Wilson; 274 ac; warrant no. 4523; location no. 1736.
file no. 2160 to Josh Rials assignee of [blank]; 640 ac; warrant no. 3758; location no. 2582.

Sales of Confiscated Land

file no. 2161 to Geo Deale assignee of [blank]; 274 ac; warrant no. 3460; location no. 2752.
file no. 2162 to Thos Sharp assignee of [blank]; 250 ac; warrant no. [blank]; location no. 1738.
file no. 2163 to Hs Fredk Harper assignee of [blank]; 640 ac; warrant no. 1509; location no. 2899.
file no. 2164 to Dennis Condra assignee of Elijah Duncan; 274 ac; warrant no. 171; location no. 38 [or 338].
file no. 2165 to Hs Ab Cole assignee of Hall; 640 ac; warrant no. 284; location no. 2996.
file no. 2166 to Jas Robbins assignee of [blank]; 274 ac; warrant no. 402; location no. 1161.
file no. 2167 to Jas Clark assignee of [blank]; 274 ac; warrant no. 378; location no. 2368.
file no. 2168 to Francis Lewis assignee of [blank]; 640 ac; warrant no. 645; location no. 1028.
file no. 2169 to Stepn. Right assignee of David Dodd; 274 ac; warrant no. 764; location no. 458.
file no. 2171 to Parker Rodgers assignee of Hall; 319 ac; warrant no. 1240; location no. 296.
file no. 2172 to Josh W Kidd assignee of Gideon Akins; 1,000 ac; warrant no. 887; location no. 179.
file no. 2173 to Josh Roberts assignee of [blank]; 228 ac; warrant no. 3375; location no. 2563.
file no. 2174 to Will Deacon assignee of [blank]; 182 ac; warrant no. 1886; location no. 1098.
file no. 2182 to Bart Bowers assignee of Sols Daniel Ventines; 640 ac; warrant no. 1871; location no. 1120.
file no. 2183 to Francis McGavok assignee of [blank]; 15 ac; warrant no. 4007; location no. 1401.
file no. 2211 to Bowers McGavock & Co assignee of Frs David Short; 640 ac; warrant no. 2689; location
    no. 1935.

[The following is in DSCR 207.403.1 Salisbury Dist Court Papers.]
880. Lewis Beard, Commissioner of Confiscated Property, vs John Slane and Hugh Cuningham (1806, 1807, 1809):
880A. Sept. term 1803 Salisbury Dist. Superior Court--Ejectment: on Oct. 10, 1801 in Rowan Co, Lewis Beard, Commissioner, leased for 5 years to "John Den" "a tract" in Rowan Co; the land borders: John Davis' corner hickory saplin & post oak near "the" corner of "his" field, runs S 26 poles on his line to a black oak sapling, S60E 170 poles to a black oak, N16E 290 poles to a stake, N30W 70 poles to a black oak sapling in Israel Cox's line, S50W 80 poles along his line to a post oak, N30W 140 poles along his other line to a black oak sapling, N60W 80 poles along another of his lines to a stake & post oak, S25W 60 poles to John Davis' corner sassifras, S 160 poles on his [line], E 20 poles, S 40 poles, E 16 poles, S 46 poles, & E 14 poles to the beginning; on Oct. 10, 1801 "Richard Fin" forced "Den" off the land and continues to reside there.   [signed] E Alexander, pro. plaintiff; Nov. 17, 1803 to John Sloan: I'm told you possess or claim the within mentioned land; you will appear at Salisbury Dist. Court Mar. "next" at Salisbury to answer the charges.   [signed] "John Den".

880B. Mar. term 1806 Salisbury Dist. Court   Lewis Beard, Commr. of Confiscated Property, vs John Sloane--Ejectment: Court ordered a survey of the premises; plats are to be returned to Court; both parties agree for David Woodson sr to be the surveyor; Samuel Barclay and Morris Davis are summoned to the survey for the plaintiff and [blank] for the defendant; Rowan Co sheriff is to summon the surveyor and witnesses.   [signed] M Stokes, Clerk Sals. Superior Court.

880C. Apr. term 1807   Lewis Beard vs John Sloan: Morris Davis charges the plaintiff for attendance as witness 2 days @ 6/   £0.12 + travelling 24 miles 5/ certificate   £0.5.8 = £0.17.8.   sworn Apr. 11, 1807 before M Stokes
Mar. term 1805 Morris Davis charges the plaintiff for attendance as witness 2 days @ 10/ + travelling 24 miles 5/ certificates = £1.8.8.   sworn Apr. 11, 1807 before M Stokes
Sept. term 1806 Morris Davis charges the plaintiff for attendance as witness 1 day @ 10/   £0.10 + "certificate" 8d + travelling 24 miles 8/ = £0.18.8.   sworn Apr. 11, 1807 before M Stokes; [on back] tickets £11.15.5

880D. Lewis Beard to Thomas Carson: Oct. 1803 (1) 2 days surveying lines of Hugh Cunningham and Nicholas Michael at 20/ per day   £2.0; (2) 1 day examining John Sloan's lines @ 20/ per day   £1.0; (3) 1 day examining William Merrel's lines @ 20/ per day   £1.0; (4) making 3 plots and certificates   £1. [total] £5. Nov. 27, 1809 (Cabarrus Co) John K Carson, executor of Thomas Carson decd, swears he found the aove account against Lewis Beard, Commissioner of Confiscated Land in Thomas Carson decd's books in "his" own handwriting.   [signed] Jno K Carson before Melchor Fogleman, Cabarrus Co JP

Sales of Confiscated Land

880E. Sept. 19, 1805 at Salisbury to Rowan Co sheriff: "the" Court ordered (in a suit of "trespass quau clausum frigit" in the case of Lewis Beard, Commissioner of Confiscated Property, vs Hugh Cunningham) that a jury and surveyor view and survey the premises and make a return to the Court; so you will summon Matthew Brandon and Alexander Long as "jurors" for the plaintiff, Joseph Clark and Montfort Stokes for the defendant, & David Woodson, surveyor; return the survey to Mar. term [1805] of Court; from Montfort Stokes, Clerk. [signed] M Stokes; [on back] executed Geo Fisher, shff.

880F. Mar. term 1806 Salisbury Dist. Superior Court Lewis Beard vs Hugh Cunningham--fr qu clau frigit: the Court ordered a survey of the premises; the parties agree on David Woodson sr as surveyr; summon Lanning for the plaintiff and [blank] for the defendant to attend the survey; Rowan Co sheriff is to summon the surveyor and witnesses. "a copy of the record" [signed] M Stokes, clk Sals Sup Court.

880G. Sept. 19, 1806 at Salisbury to an Iredell Co JP--you are empowered to get a deposition from Joshua Whitehead in the case of Lewis Beard vs Hugh Cunningham; return the deposition to Court on Mar. 19 "next". [signed] M Stokes.

880H. Dec. 20, 1806 (Iredell Co) at Joshua Whitehead's house: deposition of Joshua Whitehead for the case of Lewis Beard vs Hue Connihame [sic]: Whitehead was present at William Joiles (of Rowan Co) and heard the "articles" of Hennery Uses McCullough read as follows: McCullough's articles specified "he" was to have 1,000 ac "in a manner" and no less and "square lines". [signed] Joshua Whitehead's mark "X" before H Claeett and J Keaton, both Iredell Co JP.

880I. Oct. term 1809 Rowan Co Superior Court Lewis Beard vs Hugh Cunningham: David Woodson sr charges the plaintiff (1) for 5 days attendance as surveyor on the premises @ 20/ £5; (2) 90 miles traveling to & from the land being 3 trips £1.10; (3) 3 days attendance at Apr. term 1807, 3 days attendance at Oct. 1807, 3 days attendance at Apr. 1808, 1 day at Oct. 1808, & 3 days at Apr. 1809 = 13 days £3.18; & (4) travelling 28 miles each time to & from Court = 140 miles £0.0.8. [total] £11,16.8. sworn Oct. 13, 1809 [signed] M Stokes, clk.

[The following No. 881-885 is in DSCR 207.403.1 Salisbury Dist. Court Papers; folder Confiscated Property.]
881. Samuel Bryant: Mar. term 1782 the Court considered the "forune and family" of Samuel Bryant: a wife and 8 children all daughters the youngest about 15 months old; agreeable to an Act of Assembly to set aside "so" much of the estate of anyone convicted of treason for support of the family, the Court ordered the following allotted to the family: 900 ac where the family lives, a Negro man "upwards" of 50 years old "very infirmed", 2 small Negroes (1) about 3 years old and (2) under 2 years old, about 17 head of cattle, 2 sows and shoats, 8 sheep, 4 beds and coverings with the household furniture, & a small mare and colt. "a true copy of the record" [signed] Ro Martin, C S C; [on back] due for 7 suits for debt, slander, & assault.

882. Charles Vanderver
882A. Feb. 8, 1782 received at Salisbury of Charles Vandevor sr (of Rowan Co), of Capt. John Johnston's company, David Williams--an able bodied substitute to serve 1 year in Continental Army. [signed] Elias Langham for Capt. Wm Armstrong 2nd NC Regt.

882B. Sept. [Mar.--lined out] 1790 Salisbury Dist. Superior Court to the Justices of Equity Court--complaint of Charles Vanderver against Rowan Co Commissioners of Confiscated Land: Charles was one of the unfortunate men who joined Samuel Bryan in 1780, then commander of a "party" about to join the British Army then at war with this Country; Charles thought this was the only way he could "preserve" his life; Charles stayed with Bryan about 4 months; during this time he didn't bear arms or harm anyone; on Oct. 23, 1780, Charles took the benefit of Gen. Davidson's proclamation and surrendered to Capt. Samuel Reed of NC militia; Charles complied with this proclamation; in 1782 Griffith Rutherford "pretended" to be Rowan Co Commissioner of Confiscated Property; Griffith seized all of Charles' real & personal property consisting of a "plantation", mill, & "some" slaves; Griffith hired "them" out publically for 1 year; Charles was the highest bidder for the "plantation" and mill for 505 bushels of corn; Charles gave a bond with David Crawford as security; Griffith told Charles he could have the property restored

152

if he would hire a substitute soldier for 1 year; then Charles wouldn't have to pay the rent; so Charles hired 2 substitutes for 1 year at "considerabel" expense: William Bates and David Williams; a copy of the receipt for William from Elias Langham is annexed; Charles believes both men served their full term; Griffith was notified about the substitutes; Charles' estate wasn't confiscated by any Court, law, or any means; but Griffith refused to give Charles his bond; Griffith and "others" unknown to Charles, as Rowan Co Commissioners of Confiscated Property, brought suit against Charles Vanderver and David Crawford in Rowan Co Pleas & Quarter Sessions Court for collection of the bond; the Commissioners obtained a judgment of £7117 and £5 "to" £6 costs; the judgment was levied against the land where Charles lives; this injurs Charles and is contrary to "good concience"; so Charles asks for help from the Court against Griffith and "confederates" to determine if the above statement is true.   [signed] Charles Vanderver's mark "C" before Saml Spencer and by S Macay, atto for compt; [no date] writs of injunction and subpoena to issue against Griffith Rutherford. [signed] Saml Spencer, JSCLE; bill filed Sept. 18, 1790, bond for costs given; subpoena and injunction issued; enrolled in Book 2 p. 111-115 by "J C".

882C. Aug. 9, 1792 Griffith Rutherford, "late" Rowan Co Commissioner of Confiscated Property, responds to complaint of Charles Vandever: in 1780 during the war with the King of Great Britain, Charles "attached himself" as a soldier to "a party" under Samuel Bryant's command; they were in rebellion against this State, were "associated" together to join the British troops, & did join said troops; so Charles' real & personal property was confiscated by State law; Griffith with [blank] were "regularly" appointed Rowan Co Commissioners of Confiscated Property; so they took possession of Charles' property; they rented the land and mill, as stated by Charles, for 501 [505--lined out] bushels of corn and took Charles' note with security David Crawford; Griffith doesn't know about the 2 substitutes and asks that Charles be ordered to prove the substitutes served; Griffith admits Charles surrendered in Oct. 1780 due to Gen. Davidson's proclamation; but the law [proclamation ?] said the person was suppose to serve for 1 year in the Army; Charles didn't do this; Griffith did sue in Rowan Co Court to collect the bond.   [signed] Griffith Rutherford before Max Chambers, C M Ety.

Aug. 9, 1792 answer of George Henry Beroger and Joseph Cunningham, two other Rowan Co Commissioners of Confiscated Property, to the suit of Charles Vandever: Griffith Rutherford transacted all the business before Berger and Cunningham were appointed; so they don't know about the things Charles described, but they believe Rutherford's statement.   [signed] George H Berger and Joseph Cunningham before Max Chambers, C M Ety.

883. David Woodson:
883A. Mar. 23, 1793 Salisbury Dist. Equity Court to Adlai Osborne esq (of Iredell Co); David Woodson (of Rowan Co) complains against you; so you will attend said Court Sept. 19 "next" at Salisbury to answer the charges.   [signed] Max Chambers, Clerk & Master in Equity; [on back] Mar. 28, 1793 delivered a copy of this writ to Adlai Osborn. [signed] Jno Braly, shff.

883B. Mar. term 1793 Salisbury Dist.   to Equity Court Judges--complaint of David Woodson against Adlai Osborn, Commissioner: "sometime" during the late war between Great Britain and the Colonies now United States of America, Benjamin Boothe Boot's (of Rowan Co) property was confiscated since Boot was "deemed" an enemy to "his" country; the property was put in the heads of the Commissioners of Confiscated Property; Osborn acted as one of the commissioners; about Feb. 8, 1782 Osborn rented to Woodson for 12 months a Negro woman names Lyndy [or Syndy], part of Boot's property; on the same day Woodson gave Osborn a promissory note "with" James Craige [security]; the note was for £10 payable in 1 year and £3 in 1 month; Woodson believes about a month later he paid £3 of the note; within 2 months after Feb. 8, the Negro was attached by Boot's creditors due to a suit of Maxwell Chambers esq; Woodson couldn't find, in Rowan Co Clerk's Office, the date of the attachment; there was another attachment at the same time by Hugh Boyd another creditor; this attachment was levied on a lot in Salisbury and "the balance" on a Negro in Maxwell Chambers' hands on Apr. 4, 1782; a return was made to Rowan Co Court; Maxwell Chambers did prosecute an attachment against said Lyndy, who was the only Negro woman Boot owned then that Woodson knows about; so Woodson lost the Negro to Chambers; Woodson believes tht £3 he paid is enough considering the time he owned the Negro; he believed he wouldn't have to pay the remainder; but Osborn sued Woodson for payment of the remainder in Rowan Co Court; while the suit pended, Woodson believed the Court records would help prove his case; Osborn was then and is now Clerk of Rowan Co Court; but the Court records couldn't be "conviently" produced in this case; the case was continued for "many" terms until it was tried without the records; a verdict was found against Woodson which harms him; so he appeals to this Court; Woodson asks that the Court records be produced & examined; in Mar. 1791 Woodson asked that the case be put before a "reference of men" because of the cost of appeal; the men were Lewis Beard, Mathew Locke, & John Steele esqs; Osborn asked that the case be delayed until next Rowan Co Court; Woodson applied "several" times to have "the reference" acted on; once it was put off by the absence of one of the men who was serving the public "abroad" in Congress; when the "reference" met, they didn't inform the counsel hired because Woodson's original attorney had "left the bar"; the case was set aside; a judgment was found in Salisbury "General" Court for £16.18.10 and costs against Woodson at Mar. term 1790 even though Woodson wasn't allowed to make a defense; before said Court term Osborn told Woodson the case would be decided by "the reference"; Woodson asks the Justices to consider his statement and order Rowan Co sheriff to summon Osborn to respond. [signed] "Ed A", attorney for compt.; Mar. 19, 1793 Rowan Co David Woodson swears the above is true before Spruce Macay, JCE; Salisbury Dist [no date] issue an injunction and subpoena on within complaint. [signed] Spruce Macay, JCE; filed in Office Mar. 23, 1792 [signed] Max Chambers, C M Ety.

883C. Sept. term 1793 Salisbury Dist. Equity Court David Woodson vs Adlai Osborn esq: the defendant "by protestation" doesn't acknowledge as true any of the matters in the complaint; he is advised by his "counsil" that nothing in the complaint warrants the Court's attention, and there is cause for the Court to demur; Woodson didn't say how long Lindy remained in his possession after the attachment was levied. [not signed]

883D. Sept. term 1794 Salisbury Dist Equity Court answer of Adlai Osborn: he says Woodson's statements are untrue; Osborn hired to Woodson a Negro Sindy [sic] for 12 months; she was "afterwards" attached by Maxwell Chambers esq; but Osborn says, if Woodson had "declared the manner" he held the Negro, Woodson could have kept her; Woodson didn't positively say how long he kept the Negro; Osborn accounted to the public for the full amount of Woodson's bond; Osborn denys keeping the Court records from Woodson's inspection; he blames any problems on a deputy [not named] who kept the records, although the deputy was faithful in his office; Osborn says the case was moved to county court because no action was being taken [by the reference men], and Woodson wouldn't attend unless he was notified. "sworn in open Court" [no signed by Osborn]. [signed] Max Chambers, C M Ety.

884. George McCulloch vs Thomas C Williams:
to the Judges of Salisbury Dist. Court--answer of Geoge McCulloch to T C Williams' complaint: McCulloch admits the "rule and purchase" mentioned in the complaint "perhaps" incorrectly expressed; Thomas Frohock was an agent for Henry Eustace McCulloch in North Carolina at the time of the sale; Williams bought Josiah Taylor's land and agreed, by boyd, to pay the purchase money; McCulloch doesn't know if Williams improved the land; Williams may have entered the land in the State's Land Office; the land is part of H E McCulloch's tract No. 7; McCulloch admits the Confiscation Laws dispossessed H E McCulloch of his land; from Jul. 4, 1776 to Nov. 13, 1782 there was war between the King of Great Britain and United States of America; but a treaty of peace was signed at Paris after the land sale; due to an act of Assembly on Sept. [blank],1783, it's stipulated that creditors on either side shall meet with no impediment to recover the full value in sterling money which is "contracted" as by the treaty; in the treaty Congress will "recomment" the respective State Legislatures to resolve all states, rights, & property that was confiscated that belong to British residents or the King and who haven't born arms against the US; all people can go to any port unmolested within 12 months to resolve their claims; Congress is to recommend a spirit of consideration and the people's property be restored; the teaty also stipulates no additional confiscation or prosecution of anyone; since and before the war H E McCulloch was a British subject and was creditor of Josiah Taylor's bond [date blank]; H E McCulloch didn't bear arms against the US; George McCulloch is H E McCulloch's "legitimate" attorney and agent; due to the US Constitution signed Sept. 17, 1787 (and due to the Convention of Sept. 3, 1783), it's declared that any US treaties are supreme law; due to an Act of General Assembly Sept. 3, 1783 at Tarborough and on Nov. 11, 1787, the Treaty of Paris became the law and the Courts were to be cognizant of the contents of the Treaty; as H E McCulloch's agent, George applied for settlement; he denys giving up a claim to Taylor's land, so he asked for the money; George gave Williams, on settlement, H E McCulloch's deed mentioned in the complaint, which was in Thomas Frohock's hands; Taylor hadn't paid any money, so he has no title to the land; George knows about the act of Assembly endowing UNC but doesn't believe it affects H E McCulloch's land except as it relates to the Treaty of Paris; George doesn't know about the dealings between Williams and the Trustees of UNC; Williams hasn't asked

Sales of Confiscated Land

George to secure his title against the claim of the Trustees; George asks the Court to decide the case. [signed] Evan Alexander, solicitor for defendant; Mar. 27, 1798 Salisbury Dist G McCulloch swears the above is true before Max Chambers, C M Ety; enrolled in Book 3 p. 67-74; "struck off" Sept. 1799; [There are two copies of this "answer"; the second one says "a copy" and (case) No. 56.] [This case appars on the docket but may have been discontinued due to the decision by Court of Conference in the case George McCulloch vs Robert Ray, see No. 799 above.]

885. Hudson Hughes, Joseph Chambers, & Edward Yarbrough vs Trustees of UNC:
to the Judges of Salisbury Dist. Equity Court--complaint of Hudson Hughes, Joseph Chambers, & Edward Yarbrough against the Trustees of UNC: "sometime" in Aug. 1795 Hughes and Chambers bought "a tract" from Adlai Osborn, attorney for the Trustees; the land is in Rowan Co formerly Henry Eustace McCulloch's property and sold as confiscated land due to an act of Assembly Dec. 31, 1794 which endowed UNC; on Aug. 7, 1795 Osborn deeded the land to Hughes and Chambers with Yarbrough as security for their bond of £402.7; now they're told the land was sold to William Brandon, who petitioned the Assembly because he was unable to pay; Brandon asked the State to take the land back; so the Assembly agreed and Osborn had no power to sell the land; they think it would be "dangerous" for them to pay Osborn until the title can be cleared up; but Osborn sued for payment in Rowan Co Court; so they ask the Court for relief and an injunction until the case can be decided. [signed] E Alexander, for complains.; Mar. 27, 1800 at Salisbury Hudson Hughes swears the above is true before Spruce Macay, JSCLE; filed in "the" Office Mar. 27, 1800; No. 30. [This case is mentioned in NC Reports 1 p. 436. The Supreme Court decided Brandon had returned the land to the State prior to the land being turned over to the Trustees. So the Trustees had a "good right" to sell the land, and Hughes & Chambers would have to pay the Trustees.]

[The following is in DSCR 207.928.1 Salisbury Dist. Court Miscellaneous Records 1754-1807.]
886. A list of prisoners committed to Halifax [Dist.] jail for treason from Salisbury Dist. [signed] Alex Martin Dec. 22, 1782:
Isaac Jones, Willm Henly, and Jacob Crarin [or Corarin] commd. to Hugh Tinnen Orange Co Oct. 24, 1782

[The following No. 887 and 888 are in DSCR 207.326.2 Salisbury Dist. Court Criminal Action Papers 1778-1792. The papers for 1778 and 1780 are described, but there are similar papers for every year from 1778 to 1783 and one case in 1795.]
887. Criminal Actions of treason for 1778:
887A. Archibald McCoy--treason: late of Guilford Co and a weaver; in 1777 he shouted "huzza for King George"; [on back] not a true bill [signed] Hez Alexander, foreman.

887B. Henry Daniel--examined Aug. 14, 1778: he was asked why he didn't have a pass and answered he didn't ask for one; he said he wouldn't take the oath of allegiance expecting God to protect him and "the Devil could join them before he would"; if put in the Continental Army, he would shoot the first officer that would command him; he would take the life of anyone trying to arrest him; he wouldn't be a subject of the US. sworn before James Johnston.
887C. folder for treason trials in 1778:
John Newman (of Anson Co)--he wanted to be neutral; he mentions Nathaniel Bivens
James Cheek (late of Tryon Co)--Isaac Wilcox and Saml Wilcox are witnesses for him
James Usher (of Anson Co)--John Coleman is his witness
Moses Tomlinson--a bond of £2,000 with securities John Blake and Shem Thomson for £1,000 each
  [total is] £4,000
Gilbert Blair and Nicholas Day (of Wilkes Co)--statement vs Vesey Husband; they accuse Husband of treason
Conrad Reignhart (Burke Co)--statement Jul. 29, 1778 accuses Joseph Johnson, John Orr, & Geo Dailey of treason
John Reignhart (Burke Co)--statement Jul. 29, 1778 accuses Joseph Johnson, John Perkins, Christian Reignhart,
  Honniele Warlick, & Moses Moore of treason
Joseph Cronkleton (Burke Co)--statement Jul. 23, 1778 accuses Richard Pirkins sr of treason
John Orr (Burke Co)--statement Jul. 28, 1778 says the charges by William Ward and William Piles against Orr
 are groundless
John Depoyston (Rowan Co)--indictment: he said "Huzzaw for King George"; [on back] a true bill
 [signed] Jas Macay, foreman

Sales of Confiscated Land

George Rutledge (Tryon Co)--statement Aug. 29, 1778 says Jacob Sides "God damned" Liberty money
William Piles (Burke Co)--statement Jul. 27, 1778 accused Joseph Johnson, John Orr, & Wm Ward of treason
Andrew Bolser--statement Jul. 30, 1778 says Peter Fry accused Joseph Johnson of treason

888. Criminal Actions for treason in 1780:
888A. a bond by Andrew Garron [or Garion] £40,000, Jacob Rhodes £5,000, & Valentine Beard £5,000 for A Garion to appear in Court for a charge of treason; issued Dec. 6, 1780.
    888B. Dr. John Randleman £2,000 and John Wright as security £2,000 for Randleman to appear at next Superior Court; issued Nov. 2, 1780

888C. a letter dated Nov. 13, 1779 Thomas Wade to Col. John Dunn [or Dunan] "near Salisbury": "our" Country is to be divided which renders "this" place not of great value; Charles Evans is a gentleman of South Carolina and father-in-law of Wm Holly, who brought himself into "a scrape" as a tory at Lynches Cr in the "late insurrection"; I heard "him" swear to the colonel and before two witnesses that Holly took arms and "declared" to fight for the King; "the other" was that Holly and "the others" that come with him to jail were trying to see what was the matter in the neighborhood; they found they were deceived by someone who told them the tories had taken the country; so they surrendered to Squire Thompson; Col. Lovce [or Lovee] brought them to his jail and sent them to "the" district jail; they don't appear to be convicted of high treason; so I would like to bail them or at least Holly.   [signed] Thos Wade;
[on back] if their trial was before me, I would have bailed them because I believe Newman's testimony, who was a State witness and had taken the oath to the Kings.   [signed] T Wade.

Index to Sales of Confiscated Land

Index to Sales of Confiscated Land

Index to Sales of Confiscated Land

Index to Sales of Confiscated Land

Index to Sales of Confiscated Land

Index to Sales of Confiscated Land

Index to Sales of Confiscated Land

Index to Sales of Confiscated Land

Index to Sales of Confiscated Land

Index to Sales of Confiscated Land

Index to Sales of Confiscated Land

Index to Sales of Confiscated Land

Index to Sales of Confiscated Land

170

Index to Sales of Confiscated Land

Index to Sales of Confiscated Land

Index to Sales of Confiscated Land

Index to Sales of Confiscated Land

Index to Sales of Confiscated Land

Index to Sales of Confiscated Land

629, 632, 698

Roberts, Josiah 833, 879

Roberts, William 183, 812, 846

Robertson, Abner 243F

Robertson, Isaac 592

Robertson, John 583X, 585T

Robertson, Peter 307AA

Robertson, Randolph 307E

Robeson, Mark 66, 67, 104, 105, 106B(3)

Robeson, Peter 112

Robins, William 578, 580D, 584U, 585C

Robinson, 353H, 354G

Robinson, Abner 252

Robinson, Benjm 20C

Robinson, Joseph 291C

Robinson, Thomas 578, 585D

Robinson, William 629

Rodgers, Mary 306B, 307U(2)

Rodgers, Parker 879

Rogers, Eli 877

Rogers, Ephraim 879

Rogers, Sharrick 328

Rogers, William 431, 441, 452

Roland, James 73

Rollin, Jerry 879

Romener, George 354T

Rooks, J 698

Roper, Charles 585T

Rorie, John jr 307V

Rose, Fred 453

Rose, N B 510

Rose, Wm 307P(2)

Ross, Andrew 424, 443, 453, 456

Ross, Daniel 1

Ross, George 824, 850

Ross, James 354T

Roundtree, Thos 696B

Rounsavall (Rounsebel), Benjamin 20A, 559A(2)

Rounsiford, Benemin 561B(2)

Rowell, Benjamin 307B

Rowland, Jas 696A(2)

Ruark, Nicholas 878

Rucker, Gideon (Gedian) 577, 578, 583Q, 585T

Rue, Southe 337-346

Ruffin, Joseph 243D, 243E, 246, 247

Ruman, Corn 876

Rundles, Dudley 696D

Russel, David 307C

Russel, George 583M

Russel, John 582D, 583Z, 584J, 584V, 585A

Ruth, David 772-775

Rutherford, Gen. 544

Rutherford, Griffith 20, 20D, 550, 551, 555-557, 566, 676, 882B, 882C

Rutland, Shadrach 307G(2)

Rutledge, George 887C

Ryan, Corns 696A

Ryan (Ryon), George 25, 35, 37, 38, 43, 49J, 49P-49R

Ryan, James 214, 214B, 214I, 215, 217, 218

Salter, Ed 517

Sampson, 238

Sampson, Stephen 306A, 307I

Sanderford, Amos 876

Sanders (Sandes), B 658

Sanders, John 585T

Sanders, Lemal 354T

Sanders, William 291D(7), 558, 815

Sangham, Abel 577

Sann, A 520

Sapenfield, widow 562

Sapperfield (Sappingfield), Matthias 291C(2), 567, 568

Satter, Ed 517

Saunders, Moses 1

Saunders, William 360-362, 364, 563C(4), 689

Sawyer, 147

Saxon, John 306B, 307DD(2)

Saylor, John 354T

Saylor, Lenard 354N, 354V

Scarf, Jno 696C

Scavill, 214G

Schaw, Dan 106A, 106B

Schaw, Robert 131

Schrolfield, Benj 876

Scoal, Buchanan 307C

Scoals, John 306B, 307AA

Scott, 608, 619

Scott, Nehemiah 603-608

Scott, Robert 91, 106A

Scott, T 806

Scott, Thomas 807, 809

Scrivner, James 20A, 559A

Searcy, Thomas 289, 878

Searcy, W 698

Sellenton, 200

Selwyn, 844

Sessum, Richard 248

Sessums, Solomon 243B, 248

Sewel, Henry 20B

Seymore, Felix 877

Shaddey, John 444

Shady, John 808

Shaffer, Fredk 774C

Sharb, Christian 808

Sharp, Thos 879

Sharpe, Anthony 7, 563B, 689

Sharpe, Christan 808

Sharpe, Wm 813

Sharpley, John 876

Shaver, Frederick 787, 787B, 787C, 874(2)

Shaver, Frederick sr 787C

Shaver, William 725

Shavers, Cathrine 570

Shaw, 409F

Shaw, Daniel 65, 93

Shaw, Hugh 734

Shaw, Jesse 773D

Shaw, Malcolm 50

Shaw, Robert 291A, 293, 300, 683

Shegal, John 354T

Shelton, Stephen 577, 585T

Shepherd, Col. 517

Sheppard (Shepperd), Benjamin 189D, 221, 691

Sheppard, John 221

Shepperd, 718

Shepperd, H 719, 720, 765

Shepperd, Henry 283-286, 509, 510, 792B

Shepperd (Shepard), James 585T, 625, 631

Shepperd (Shephard, Shepard), William 203, 284-286, 410, 411(3), 487, 502, 503, 508, 527, 536, 539, 577, 623-626, 707, 773B-773D, 779B, 779C, 783B, 783C, 783E, 792C, 807, 808, 811

Sherwood, Benjamin 307Y(2)

Shields, David 776

Shields, John 776D

Shields, Robert 776, 776B-776D

Shields, William 776B, 776C

Shipman, Daniel 584B, 585C

Shiteside, Tho 577

Index to Sales of Confiscated Land

Index to Sales of Confiscated Land

Index to Sales of Confiscated Land

Index to Sales of Confiscated Land

Index to Sales of Confiscated Land

Index to Sales of Confiscated Land

Index to Sales of Confiscated Land

Index to Sales of Confiscated Land

www.ingramcontent.com/pod-product-compliance
Lightning Source LLC
Chambersburg PA
CBHW051555030426
42334CB00034B/3450